Evoluation of Money, Banking and Financial Crisis

Burak DARICI & Çağatay BAŞARIR (Eds.)

Evoluation of Money, Banking and Financial Crisis

History, Theory and Policy

PETER LANG

Bibliographic Information published by the Deutsche Nationalbibliothek
The Deutsche Nationalbibliothek lists this publication in the Deutsche Nationalbibliografie; detailed bibliographic data is available online at http://dnb.d-nb.de.

Library of Congress Cataloging-in-Publication Data
A CIP catalog record for this book has been applied for at the Library of Congress.

This book project has been carried out under callforchapter.com editorial process.

Printed by CPI books GmbH, Leck

ISBN 978-3-631-81793-3 (Print)
E-ISBN 978-3-631-83545-6 (E-PDF)
E-ISBN 978-3-631-83546-3 (EPUB)
E-ISBN 978-3-631-83547-0 (MOBI)
DOI 10.3726/b17593

Peter Lang – Berlin · Bern · Bruxelles · New York · Oxford · Warszawa · Wien

This publication has been peer reviewed.

www.peterlang.com

Preface and Acknowledgments

The book entitled *Evolution of Money, Banking and Financial Crisis: Evolution, Theory, Policy* focuses primarily on the historical development of money, the change of the banking sector, and global financial crises. Money started as an exchange tool and has now become digital. Historical change in the banking system and its relationship with policymakers, global financial crises, balloons, and speculations and policies for the emergence and prevention of them are thoroughly examined in the book.

The aim of this book is to evaluate the events from different views related to the money; financial crises, causes, and prevention methods; the historical transformation of the banking sector; and the relations between the entire financial system and policymakers and their current issues.

This book covers deep researches from different perspectives upon the evolution of money by successful and expert researchers in their field. Moreover, different and rigorous analyses of all areas influenced by money were made to fill the gap of the source about the money with various dimensions.

This book contains theoretical and empirical analyses on the evolution of money, which is a new perspective that involves lots of history and brings with it various concerns. The chapters are related to the historical background of the concepts of money and cryptocurrency, banking crises, the association between finance and growth, speculation and bubble in stock markets, Islamic finance, riskiness in banking sector, stock and financial markets, exchange rate market and uncertainty, and monetary policies.

We would like to thank all the authors, contributors, and researchers who are experts in their field for their devotion, diligence, their willingness to help our readers, and their patience and support during the editorial process. We also present our endless gratitude to our families and children for being the source of our motivation.

This book has been double-blind peer reviewed.

Sincerely yours.
Editors: Burak DARICI and Çağatay BAŞARIR

Contents

List of Contributors

Ali İlhan
Dr., Tekirdağ Namık Kemal University
ailhan@nku.edu.tr

Aydanur Gacener Atış
Assoc. Prof., Ege University
aydanur.gacener@ege.edu.tr

Berna Serener
Asst. Prof., European University of Lefke
bserener@eul.edu.tr

Cem Berk
Assoc. Prof., Kırklareli University
cem.berk@klu.edu.tr

Cemil Süslü
Dr. Iskenderun Technical University
cemil.suslu@iste.edu.tr

Deniz Erer
PhD in Economics, Independent Researcher
denizerer@hotmail.com

Elif Erer
PhD in Economics, Independent Researcher
elif_erer@hotmail.com

Emre Esat Topaloğlu
Asst. Prof., Şırnak Üniversity
emresatopal@qhotmail.com

Erdal Tanas Karagöl
Prof. Dr., Ankara Yıldırım Beyazıt University,
Ankara, Turkey
erdalkaragol@hotmail.com

Eyüp Ensari Şahin
Asst. Prof., Hitit University
eyupensarisahin@hitit.edu.tr.

Hakan Altın
Assoc. Prof., Aksaray University
hakanaltin@aksaray.edu.tr

İbrahim Ethem Güney
Dr., Central Bank of the Republic of Turkey
ethem.guney@tcmb.gov.tr

İhsan Erdem Kayral
Asst. Prof., Konya Food and Agriculture University
erdem.kayral@gidatarim.edu.tr

Mehmet Barış Aslan
Asst. Prof., Bingöl University
mbaslan@bingol.edu.tr

Mehmet Selman Çolak
Asst. Economist, Central Bank of the Republic of Turkey
selman.colak@tcmb.gov.tr

Mesut Doğan
Assoc. Prof., Afyonkocatepe University
mesutdogan07@gmail.com

Metin Özdemir
Assoc. Prof., Bursa Uludağ University
mozdemir@uludag.edu.tr.

Muhammed Hasan Yılmaz
Asst. Economist, Central Bank of the Republic of Turkey
muhammed.yilmaz@tcmb.gov.tr

Muhammed Şehid Görüş
Research Assistant, Yıldırım Beyazıt University
msgorus@ybu.edu.tr

Mustafa Kevser
Asst. Prof., Bandirma Onyedi Eylul University
mkevser@bandirma.edu.tr

Nurbanu Yıldız
Master's Degree, Independent Researcher
nurbanu.koyukan@gmail.com

Önder Özgür
Research Assistant, Yıldırım Beyazıt University
oozgur@ybu.edu.tr

Pınar Karahan-Dursun
Dr., Anadolu University
pkarahan@anadolu.edu.tr

Pınar Koç Torun
Asst. Prof., Gümüşhane University
pinartorun@gumushane.edu.tr

Ramazan Ekinci
Asst. Prof., İzmir Bakırçay Üniversity
ramazan.ekinci@bakircay.edu.tr

Reşat Sakur
Asst. Prof., Şırnak Üniversity
resatsakur@hotmail.com

Sema Bayraktar
Asst. Prof., İstanbul Bilgi University
sema.bayraktar@bilgi.edu.tr

Sercan Koyunlu
Master's Degree, Independent Researcher
İstanbul Bilgi University
sercankoyunlu@hotmail.com

Serdar Yaman
Lec., Şırnak Üniversity
srdr73@gmail.com

Tuba Gülcemal
Asst. Prof., Cumhuriyet University
tgulcemal@cumhuriyet.edu.tr

Ünay Tamgaç Tezcan
Asst. Prof., TOBB University
utamgac@etu.edu.tr; unaytamgac@gmail.com.

Üzeyir Aydın
Assoc. Prof., Dokuz Eylul University
uzeyir.aydin@deu.edu.tr

Yavuz Selim Hacıhasanoğlu
Central Bank of the Republic of Turkey
Yavuz.Selim@tcmb.gov.tr

Zeki Akbakay
Asst. Prof., Bingol University
zekiakbakay@gmail.com

Ünay Tamgaç Tezcan

1 Exchange Rate Regimes and the Financial Trilemma: An Evaluation for the Post-Bretton Woods

Highlights: The choice of the exchange rate regime is one of the most argued topics in economic policy. Since the collapse of the Bretton Woods system, countries have adopted different exchange rate arrangements. In this chapter we make an evaluation of the discussions around the regime choice, and the financial trilemma. Our main focus is to provide a historic review on this discussion and how it has translated itself after the global financial crisis.More recently, the trilemma view has been brought into question after the global financial crisis. Rey (2015, 2016) argues that "whenever capital is freely mobile, the global financial cycle constrains national monetary policies regardless of the exchange rate regime." Accordingly, the classical monetary trilemma transforms into a "dilemma" or an "irreconcilable duo" where the exchange rate regime loses importance. We discuss whether the trilemma prevails and exchange rates provide effective insulating mechanisms. While the debate is still ongoing the strong standing argument is that exchange rate regime still matters. The trade-off between exchange rate stability, monetary policy autonomy, and financial integration also hold. However, with the size of global linkages the trade-offs have become harsher.

Keywords: Exchange rate regime, monetary policy autonomy, financials integration, open economy trilemma, dilemma hypothesis

Introduction

The unprecedented financial turmoil that started with the collapse of the giant Lehman Brothers in September 2008 can be regarded as a turning point in economics thinking. As the capitalist system was brought under question, the basic assumptions of fundamental economic theory, and policy making also took its toll. New questions on how the real economy and financial markets work and their interconnectedness brought in new considerations into light. The global financial crisis (GFC) has made evident the existence of global cycles.

After the crisis, a large literature evolved that analyzes the determinants of global cycles, synchronization in countries, and asset price co-movements (For a survey see Claessens and Kose 2017). One important takeout is that global financial linkages and especially global spillovers from the USA have become a dominating power in the global economy. There is a vast literature that investigates the cause and effects of these spillovers. The main driver is the capital mobility and financial connectedness. Rey (2015) points out that the "global financial cycle" created by the monetary policy in the center country, that is, the USA, affects the capital flows and credit growth in the international financial system through leverage of global banks (Cerutti, Stijn & Ratnovski, 2017).

One related question is how countries can insulate themselves from the negative effects of the global spillovers. This has brought into question how countries under different arrangements are affected by global spillovers and whether exchange rates provide effective insulating mechanisms.-In light of the recent evidence, we revisit this important concept in international finance, which is the exchange rate regime choice. Our main focus is to provide a historic review on this discussion and how the question has translated after the GFC.

The choice of the exchange rate regime is one of the most discussed subjects in economic policy making. Since the collapse of the Bretton Woods system, countries have adopted different exchange rate arrangements. While there is an extensive literature on comparison of the exchange rate regimes with respect to different performance measures, the literature fails to provide a clear cut answer. The GFC has once again shown that in the countries' quest for economic stability and growth, the exchange rate system deems to stay as an important policy issue. One argument is that with today's strong global interlinkages, monetary policies are constrained regardless of the exchange rate regime. This view has started a discussion on whether the exchange rate regime matters for monetary policy autonomy, and put the regime change into question. In this chapter, we intend to analyze the exchange rate regime choice in relation to this ongoing debate. In doing so, we will first look at how the system evolved after collapse of the Bretton Woods system, and we will discuss the changing pattern of exchange rate arrangements in the post-Bretton Woods world. One point we will pay attention to is the evolution of the financial architecture, specifically the changing pattern of "financial trilemma" among countries, and whether the traditional trilemma prevails under this new system of increased financial linkages.

The rest of the chapter is organized as follows. In this chapter, we start with a brief historic discussion on the evolution of the exchange rate system. Drawing on the experience of the countries with various exchange rate regimes since the 1980s, we summarize some of the findings around exchange rate regimes: the bipolar hypothesis in Section 3 and the exchange rate regime choice in Section 4. Then we discuss the trilemma view, and the debate that started after the GFC. Finally, the discussion is summarized, and some policy implications are presented.

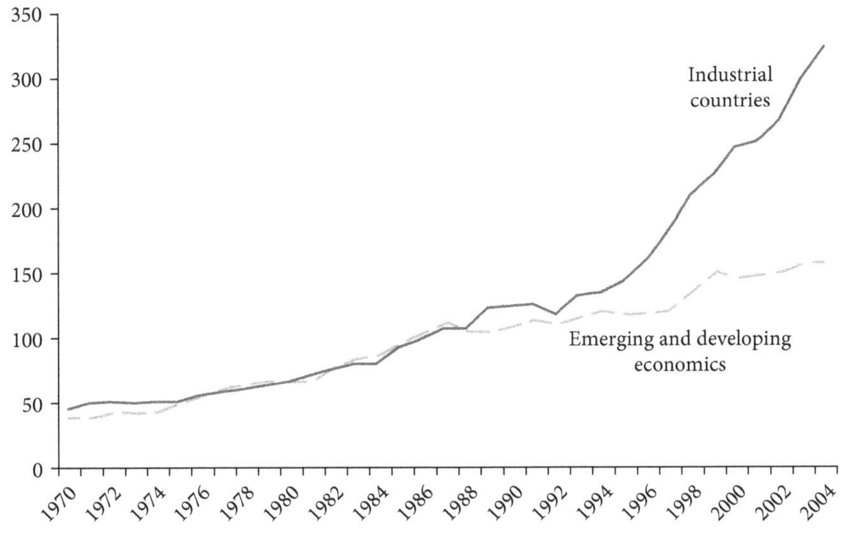

Fig. 1.1: International financial integration, 1970–2004

Notes: Ratio of sum of foreign assets and liabilities to GDP, 1970–2004. Source: Lane & Milesi-Ferretti, 2007

1 Historic Overview

After the collapse of the Bretton Woods system, from 1973 till 1994, the world entered a period of increased globalization and financial liberalization. This period is known as the "modern era of financial globalization". There has been a steady increase in financial integration with the capital account liberalizations in advanced economies in the 1980s and in emerging markets in the 1990s.

The sum of foreign assets and liabilities over GDP, plotted in Fig. 1.1, which is a measure of international financial integration, has increased by a factor of 7, from 45 % in 1970 to over 300 % in 2004 (Lane & Milesi-Ferretti, 2007). During the 1970s and 1980s, the increase was fairly gradual, but since the mid-1990s there has been an acceleration for the emerging markets/developing countries.

Whether international financial integration was, in fact, stronger in the first era of financial globalization (pre 1913 period) has been an issue of debate among economists. While some stated that the early period was more globalized (e.g., Bordo & Flandreau, 2003; Bordo & Murshid, 2006; and Quinn, 2003), some claim otherwise (Mauro et al., 2002; and Quinn & Voth, 2008). Some studies characterize the world financial integration by a U-shape with almost equal

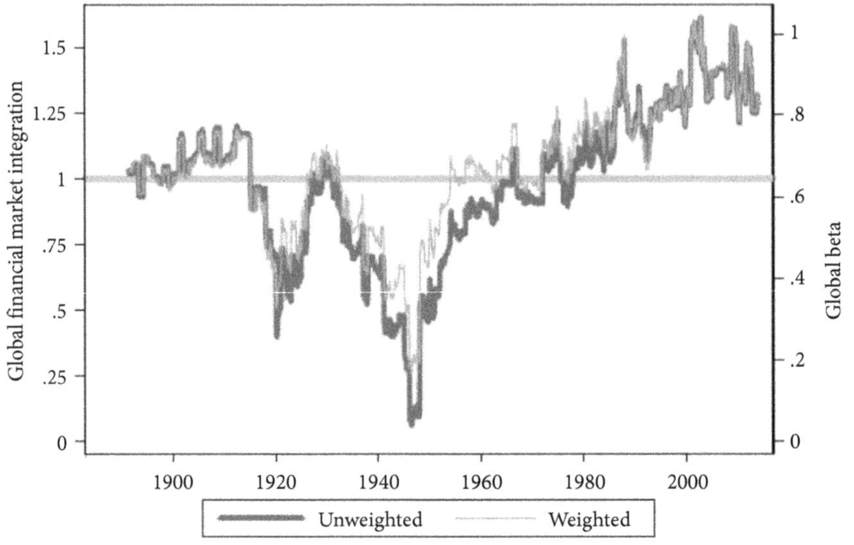

Fig. 1.2: Global financial integration, 1885–2014

Notes: Thick gray lines show the unweighted and light gray lines show the value-weighted cross-country averages of the global financial market integration measures and the corresponding conditional beta estimates. Source: Bekaert & Mehl (2019: 234)

integration before 1914 and after 1970 (Bordo & Flandreau, 2003; Obstfeld & Taylor, 2003, 2004; and Goetzmann et al., 2005). Volosovych (2011) finds support for a J-shape pattern with a trough in the 1920s.

In a recent study, Bekaert and Mehl (2019) using a sample of 17 economies accounting for two-thirds of world GDP over the sample period from 1885 to 2014 show that the pattern follows a "swoosh" shape (see Fig. 1.2).[1] There is high financial market integration in the pre-1913 period, still higher in the post-1990, and low in the interwar period. Their finding is in line with Rangvid et al. (2016) who look at equity market integration for the period 1875–2012 and find much higher financial integration in the later part of their sample relative to earlier.

1 Swoosh is the trademark logo of a famous athletic shoe and clothing manufacturer. They calculate the financial integration measure based on the excess return on the local equity index in country *i* during month *t*, expressed in dollars (which corresponds to the dollar equity return minus the 10-year US Treasury yield in monthly units).

Most emerging economies had maintained open capital accounts by the end of 1990s. The liberalization period in the emerging economies (the middle- and low-income economies) was one with frequent crises and output losses. In their struggle to fight inflation, these countries adopted fixed exchange rate regimes as a tool to import credibility in the monetary policy (Edwards, 2001). However, most of these attempted ended with a demise.[2] Starting with the tequila crisis 1994 in Mexico, many emerging economies experienced balance of payments crises accompanied by painful devaluations and output losses.[3] As both empirical and theoretical studies attempted to investigate the underlying causes and consequences of these episodes, a vast literature emerged on different types of currency crises models. (see Krugman, 1979; Flood & Garber, 1984; Obstfeld, 1986; Jeanne, 1997 for crisis literature and Kaminsky, Lizondo, Reinhart, 1998; Kaminsky, 2006 among others for crisis determinants).

2 Bipolar View

After the experience with the fragility of fixed exchange rate regimes in the 1990s, more emerging countries chose to adopt floating regimes that insulated them from the risks of speculative attacks (e.g., Indonesia, South Korea, and South Africa). The move towards exchange rate flexibility is most evident in developing Asia and Latin America. Emerging Asian economies shared this trend until 2000, at which time exchange rate stability started increasing. Some others kept operating under more rigid arrangements (e.g., Argentina and Malaysia).

In the 2000s pointing out to this divergence, several studies claimed that there has been a move towards the corner regimes of floating or pegged arrangements, known as the "bipolar view" (Eichengreen, 1994; Fischer, 2001; Summers, 2000). The declining share of the intermediate regimes in the de-jure classification supported the bipolar view (see Fig. 1.3).

The argument was that for countries well integrated into world capital markets, intermediate regimes (or soft pegs) are crisis-prone and unsustainable, also known as the "the vanishing-middle" (Eichengreen, 1994) or "hollowing-out"

---

2 The move of the European economies to the euro was not also smooth, and their way towards monetary integration was broken down by the EMS crises episodes (see Eichengreen, Rose & Wyplosz, 1995).

3 Some of the examples of the emerging market crisis episodes are: Russia in 1998; Turkey in 1994 and 2000–2001; Brazil in January 1999; Argentina 2001–2002; and the 1998 East Asian Crisis. For an analysis on fixed exchange rate regime durability in emerging economies see Tamgac (2013).

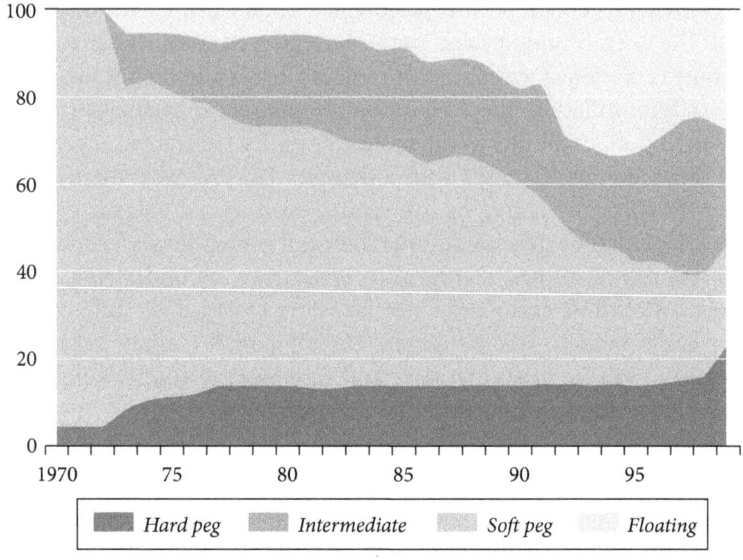

Fig. 1.3: Evolution of exchange rate regimes, 1970–2000
Source: Ghosh, Gulde, Wolf (2003) and IMF staff estimates

hypothesis (Fischer, 2001). Obstfeld and Rogoff (1995, p. 74) claim that for countries with an open capital "there is little, if any, feasible middle ground between floating rates and the adoption of a common currency."

Ghosh, Gulde, and Wolf (2003); Levy-Yeyati and Sturzenegger (2005); Bubula and Otker-Robe (2002); and Fischer (2001) are other examples that pointed out to the declining share of countries with intermediate exchange rate arrangements. However not all studies found support for the bipolar argument (e.g., Bubula & Otker-Robe, 2002). Some studies showed that the shares of the three main regimes was essentially unchanged (Rogoff et al., 2004; Dubas, Lee & Mark, 2005) or rose (Bailliu, Lafrance & Perrault, 2003) since the early 1980s.[4]

One reason for the mixed finding is related with how the exchange rate regimes were defined and specifically how the regimes are aggregated into categories. For example, Bubula and Otker-Robe (2002) and Fischer (2001) (both

4 Bailliu, Lafrance, and Perrault (2003) showed that for the 1974–1998 period intermediate regimes rose from around 20 % to around 45 %, pegs fell from around 75 % to around 40 %, and floats rose from around 5 % to around 15 %.

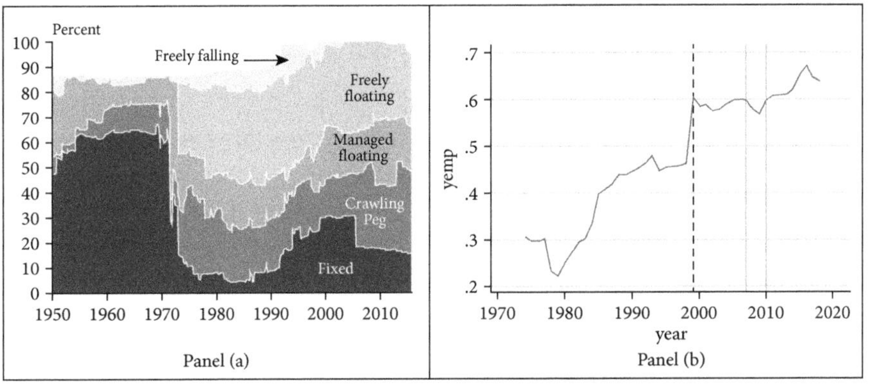

Fig. 1.4: Recent evolution of exchange rate regimes

Notes: Panel (a) shows the de facto exchange rate arrangements, coarse classification, 1946–2016: Share of world GDP in each group. Source: Ilzetzki, Reinhart and Rogoff (2019). Panel (b) shows the arithmetic mean value of the continuous de facto exchange rate regime flexibility index for 145 countries. Source: Frankel (2019)

who used the IMF de facto coding) classified the "managed floating" into the floating corner. Also because of the fear of floating, many countries that claimed to operate under floating regimes actually did not.

Nearly a decade after the famous bipolar argument, we see a continued presence of intermediate regimes such as soft pegs confirming Bubula and Ötker-Robe's (2002) argument that intermediate regimes are unlikely to disappear in the future. Also some countries flip back and forth between pegs and floats (Klein & Shambaugh, 2008).

In Figure 1.4 panel (a) shows the share of world GDP in each category of the de facto classification constructed by Ilzetzki, Reinhart, and Rogoff (2019). As can be seen, while there has been an upward trend in fixed arrangements after the 1980s, there is no validation of the bipolar hypothesis. In a recent study, Frankel (2019) constructed a continuous measure of de facto exchange rate regime classification for 145 countries in the post-Bretton Woods period from July 1974 to May 2018. The measure ranges between 0 and 1 corresponding to the hard peg and pure floating corners, and in Fig. 1.3 panel (b) shows the arithmetic mean value of the continuous ERR measure for all countries. As can be seen, there is an increasing trend towards flexible regimes, also invalidating the bipolar view. Since 2000, developing countries have converged towards managed exchange rate flexibility. Majority of the advanced economies are operating either under a floating regime or are members of the euro zone. Emerging economies have a greater diversity in exchange rate regimes, and the exchange rate regime choice is still a live policy issue.

3 Exchange Rate Regime Choice

There is a large literature on the optimal exchange rate regime choice which has extended after the collapse of the Bretton Woods system. These studies provide theoretical arguments for floating versus pegging the exchange rate. This literature examines the macroeconomic conditions that affect the regime choice and under what circumstances which exchange rate regime delivers the optimal results (e.g. Rizzo, 1998; Edwards, 1999). (For a summary on the empirical findings on the exchange rate regime choice see Rogoff et al., 20034 and von Hagen and Zhou, 2007).

One of the main supporting arguments for fixed exchange rates is the predictability they provide. Related to that is their trade enhancing function through reduced uncertainty as predicted by the optimum currency area (OCA) theories (McKinnon, 1963). On the negative side, fixed regimes fail to provide the automatic adjustment mechanism to bring the economy back to full employment when hit by a negative shock. Also they can lead to prolonged overvaluations that can hamper the economy, and are susceptible to speculative attacks.

Considering that prices are highly inflexible in the short run, flexible exchange rate regimes provide the advantage by allowing automatic adjustment of the real exchange rate when the economy is hit by an aggregate demand or supply shock (Bailliu, Lafrance, & Perrault, 2003). Also they allow the monetary policy to respond to such shocks and dampen the negative effect on the economy.

Besides the price stability advantage of fixed exchange rates, another argument is that they can act as a disciplining device in fight for inflation (Giavazzi & Giovannini, 1990). A credible fixed exchange rate replaces bad domestic monetary policy with good foreign monetary policy (see Calvo & Reinhart, 2000). However imperfect credibility of fixed exchange rates has made them subject to runs and crises, making them costly policy alternatives (see Carmignani, Colombo & Tirelli, 2005).

A closely related literature compares the performance of different exchange rate arrangements (see Moreno, 2000, 2001; Eichengreen & Leblang, 2003; Husain et al. 2005; Levy-Yeyati & Sturzenegger, 2003; Edwards & Levy-Yeyati, 2005; Gylfason, 2000). Drawing on the experience of countries with different exchange rate regimes, the main focus of this literature is whether the regime matters for macro-economic outcomes, and to evaluate regime performance on various economic measures such as inflation, output growth, trade, and insulation against domestic and foreign shocks.

While there is an extensive literature on comparison of the exchange rate regimes with respect to different performance measures, the literature fails to provide a clear-cut answer. Different studies find contrasting arguments. One reason is that the studies have different country coverage and time intervals that make it difficult to generalize the findings.[5]

Moreover, it is common that the regime in practice differs with the regime that governments claim to have in place. Many officially fixed exchange rates show considerable adjustment, referred to as the "mirage of fixed exchange rate regimes". Also countries exhibit "fear of floating" (Calvo & Reinhart, 2002), where officially floating exchange rates are heavily managed to prevent large swings in the exchange. These large differences between government declaration and the actual exchange rate behavior led to the development of de facto exchange rate regime classifications that rely on actual data.

Since countries exchange rate behavior differs with their officially declared regime, the regime classification used in the analysis becomes an important dimension when evaluating the performance of different regimes. The different findings on regime performance led to the questioning of the exchange rate classification. Therefore, this literature also gave emphasis on the difference between self-declared and actual exchange rate regimes recognized in the 1990s.[6]

Harms and Kretschmann (2009) and Petreski (2009) and recently Rao (2019) provide a survey on the relationship between exchange rate regime and economic growth. The studies point to the existence of different results, some which are due to the sample-selection bias, and the peso problem. In light of the findings, the main view is the existence of country-specific factors (such as the level of development, trade openness, financial linkages, and political factors) that make the regime choice a country-specific decision. Moreover, the outcome of the regime choice is a function of domestic and external conditions, macroeconomic fundamentals, which are also not time invariant. Such differences and the endogeneity of the regime choice make analysis on evaluation of regime performance empirically challenging. Also as Aghion et al. (2009) show growth performance of different exchange rate regimes can vary across income groups and other country-specific factors.

---

5 For an analysis of how growth performance of different exchange rate regimes can vary across income groups see Aghion, Bacchetta, Ranciere, and Rogoff (2009).

6 See Tavlas et al. (2008) for a review of the literature on de facto regimes.

In a recent empirical study Habib, Mileva and Stracca (2017) revisit the exchange rate–growth relationship for a large sample of up to 150 countries from 1970 to 2010. Using an instrumental estimation strategy to overcome the reverse causality they find a significant positive (negative) effect that reel depreciation (appreciation) has on real per capita growth over five-year average periods. However, the findings hold only for developing economies and pegs, and is not significant in advanced economies or floats. They conclude that exchange rates do matter for growth in developing economies which is in line with Rodrik (2008).

Frankel and Xie (2019) present a similar finding that the exchange rate regime choice is more important for developing countries compared to those with higher income levels. They revisit the debate about growth and regime performance using a continuous classification of exchange rate regime as estimated degree flexibility that ranges between 0 and 1 for purely fixed and the completely floating. Contrary to some previous findings, they find that growth rates are higher for more fixed de facto regimes compared to more flexible regimes.

The price stability and its contribution to trade and investment are cited as the possible causes of this finding. After converting the continuous de facto flexibility index into discrete variables using threshold pairs, they show that intermediate regimes are positively correlated with economic growth. This finding also provides evidence against the Corner Hypothesis.

In light of their findings, Frankel et al. (2019) strongly suggest that exchange rate regimes matter when it comes to the growth rate of GDP per capita. Considering that this finding holds more for developing countries it also justifies the famous saying "there is no one size fits all" (Frankel, 1999). The take out from the empirical findings on regime performance is that no exchange-rate regime is right for each country and each time. What is important is the consistency of the regime choice with the macroeconomic fundamentals (Mussa et al., 2000).

4 Trilemma View

A recent ongoing debate regarding the right exchange rate regime revolves around the classical financial trilemma argument. Below we will discuss the trilemma argument and how it stands in today's economic policy discussion after the GFC.

The classical "trilemma" argument, which is built on the Mundell-Fleming model of an open economy, is that countries cannot simultaneously have open capital mobility, exchange rate stability, and also maintain monetary policy

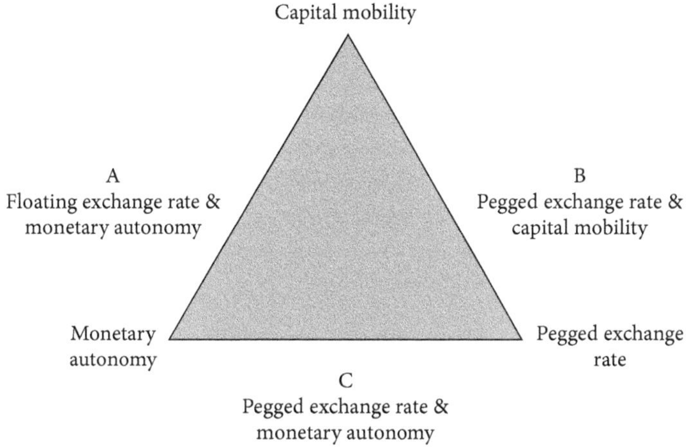

Fig. 1.5: The trilemma framework

autonomy (Mundell, 1963; Fleming, 1962).[7] They have to choose two from these three objectives of the financial architecture, which are represented by the three sides of a policy triangle (Fig. 1.5).

In that regard, monetary policy autonomy can be achieved either by having capital controls (both for fixed and floating exchange rate regimes) or adopting a flexible exchange rate regime, or both. Over the last century empirical evidence supported the existence of the trilemma trade-off (e.g., Obstfeld et al. 2005). Aizenmann, Chinn, and Ito (2010) provide recent evidence regarding the trade-offs suggested by the trilemma.

More recently, with the GFC experience, the trilemma view has been brought into question. Rey (2015, 2016) argues that "whenever capital is freely mobile, the global financial cycle constrains national monetary policies regardless of the exchange rate regime." Even under floating exchange-rate regimes "cross-border flows and leverage of global institutions transmit monetary conditions globally," and monetary policy independence is only possible with a managed capital account. Accordingly, nominal exchange rate regimes lose importance and the classical monetary trilemma transforms into a "dilemma" or an "irreconcilable duo."

7 "Trilemma" has been a term of art for logicians since the 17th century. It is described in the Oxford English Dictionary as a situation where someone faces a choice among three options, each of which comes with some inevitable problems (Mankiw, 2010).

The financial turmoil that started in September 2008 in the USA turned into a full-blown crisis affecting countries all over the globe. One important takeout is that global financial linkages and especially global spillovers from the USA have become a dominating power in the global economy. A vast literature emerged that investigates the cause and effect of these spillovers. The main cause is the capital mobility and financial connectedness. Rey (2015) points out that the "global financial cycle" created by the monetary policy in the center country, that is, the USA, affects the capital flows and credit growth in the international financial system through leverage of global banks.

> "There is a global financial cycle in capital flows, asset prices, and in credit growth. This cycle co-moves with the VIX, a measure of uncertainty and risk aversion of the markets." (2013: abstract)

The story starts with an increased capital flow surge into periphery countries triggered by increased liquidity and low interest rates in the center country. These inflows in turn increase credit, fuel asset prices, and appreciate the currency in the receiving country. As credit expands, bubbles start in consumption, equity, and housing markets. This cycle continues until the conditions in the center change, and the reversal starts (Mendoza & Terrones, 2008). In such a scenario, the periphery has no option but to follow the center. Rey's argument is that the existence of this type of global financial cycle limits the monetary power of periphery countries and diminishes the trilemma.

According to this view supported by Passari and Rey (2015), and Farhi and Werning (2014), capital controls may be the only way for non-center countries to retain monetary autonomy even when the exchange rate is flexible as they help to "lean against the wind" and smooth out capital flows. The economic policy choice in the trilemma configuration was between exchange rate regime and financial openness. The dilemma on the other hand makes the regime choice irrelevant and the policy maker is constrained to choose the right set of capital flow management strategies (capital controls and the macro-prudential regulations).

Since the financial opening both in advanced and emerging economies in the 1990s, global capital flows have been on an increasing trend until their collapse in the GFC. In Fig. 1.6 panel (b) presents the evolution of capital mobility and exchange rate stability since 1970. Since the 1990s there has been a surge in capital mobility. Concurrently, there has been an upward trend in the exchange rate stability, as the trilemma view would predict. The massive increase in gross financial flows during the pre-crisis period and the sudden reversal around the GFC is evident from panel (b) that shows the evolution of world GDP, trade, and gross capital flows since 1985.

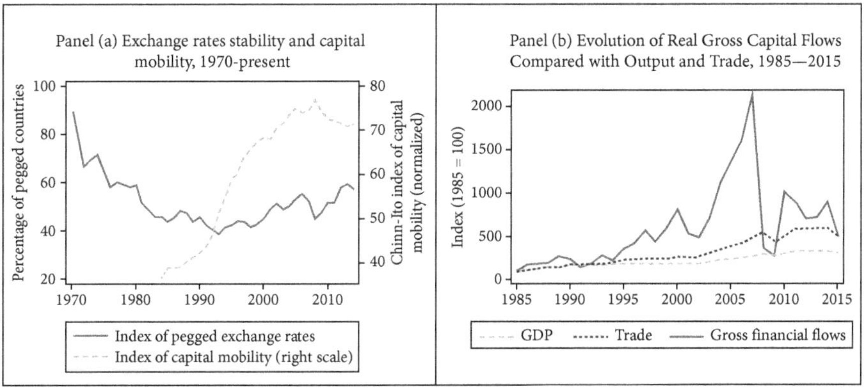

Fig. 1.6: Exchange rate stability, capital mobility, and capital flows, 1970–present

Notes: Source: Obstfeld. M. (2018). Panel (a) Data from Jorda, Schularick, and Taylor (2017) and Macrofinancial Database; Quinn, Schindler, and Toyoda (2011). Panel (b) Indices are calculated from data in real US dollars (deflated using US GDP deflator). Global trade is defined as the average of global exports and imports of goods and services. Gross global financial flows are defined as the sum of direct investment, portfolio investment, and other investments. Values are obtained by averaging inflows and outflows to account for measurement error. Data from: IMF WEO and IFS

Farhi and Werning (2014) provide a theoretical model where capital controls raise welfare even with a flexible exchange rate regime. In their New Keynesian model, controls are introduced as a "tax" over capital inflows during capital inflow surges caused by negative risk premium shocks and as "subsidies" to capital outflows when the capital flows revert. When the center country loosens its monetary policy (which tends to generate a capital flow surge into other countries), peripheral countries are compelled to follow suit by lowering their interest rates, unless they have capital control measures in place.

On the empirical side Frankel, Schmukler, and Serven (2004) in their analysis for the 1970–1999 period and Tong and Wei (2010) who study the response of equity prices during the GFC also claim that flexible exchange rate regimes are not enough to provide insulation for developing countries against global shocks. They point to the importance of capital controls rather than the nominal exchange rate arrangement.

Edwards (2012) and Obstfeld (2015), on the other hand, show that flexible exchange rate regime provides insulation against foreign shocks supporting the trilemma view.

A different view about the trilemma comes from Klein and Shambaugh (2015) who point out that governments can "round the corners" of the trilemma triangle using middle-ground policies for both capital controls and exchange rate pegs (such as softly pegged exchange rates or temporary, narrowly targeted capital controls). However, they conclude that still the simplest and most certain means for achieving some measure of monetary autonomy is to allow the exchange rate to float or to institute broad long-standing capital controls, but that middle-ground policies deserve some caution.[8] Hence they also support that the policy trilemma is still a very relevant view.

Bekaert and Mehl (2019) using their own constricted measure of de facto global financial market integration also find supporting evidence for the existence of the trilemma. They show that interest rate pass through is higher for non-floaters compared to floaters in the modern era of financial globalization confirming that flexible exchange rates give more power to the central banks to control domestic short-term interest rates despite the global financial cycles arising from US monetary policy.

In these empirical studies, usually the co-movement of policy interest rates with the center country has been used as a good proxy of monetary policy independence. One problem is that some common shocks to the center and periphery country may require the implementation of same monetary policy. Han and Wei (2018) use an innovative empirical methodology, which allows them to distinguish common monetary policy (co-movement of interest rate) as a result of policy spillovers from the central country and those that are due to common shocks. The analysis is based on the period 1990–2014 for 28 other countries, and the USA. Their findings support the argument that capital controls provide an insulation for peripheral countries both on flexible and fixed exchange rate regimes conforming the dilemma hypothesis. Also when the central country adopts loose monetary policy, the regime becomes irrelevant because peripheral countries on flexible exchange rates act like the peggers. They adopt loose monetary policies as they exhibit "fear of appreciation." When center country adopts tight monetary policy, however, peripheral countries on flexible exchange rates have monetary autonomy.

Han and Wei (2018) argue that this relationship cannot be described either by a dilemma or a trilemma, but a combination of both, what they call a "2.5-lemma" because flexible exchange rate offers asymmetric or incomplete monetary policy autonomy. The trilemma prevails (and the exchange rate regimes

8 This empirical result is close to Farhi and Werning (2012) who model the interest of some capital controls for a small open economy with a fixed exchange rate to reintroduce the interest rate differential.

become important) when the central country adopts tight monetary policy, whereas the dilemma prevails when it adopts loose monetary policies. Hence, even without capital controls, flexible exchange rate regimes provide monetary policy autonomy when central country adopts tight monetary policy and the trilemma prevails.[9]

Obstfeld (2018) compares the response of emerging economies during the GFC. He argues that those countries under flexible regimes were more successful to mitigate the effects. However, he points that there is limited power monetary policy can achieve because of financial globalization, which worsens the trade-offs of monetary policy in navigating among multiple domestic objectives. The recommendation is to use additional tools of macroeconomic and financial policy. At that point, the policy maker is constrained with a financial trilemma that differs from the monetary trilemma.

In another study Obstfeld, Ostry, and Qureshi (2019) explain the mechanism by which flexible exchange rates can provide insulation to emerging market economies and reduce the costs from global financial shocks. Using a sample of about 40 emerging market countries for the period from 1986 to 2013, they show that domestic financial variables respond differentially to global financial conditions under different exchange rate regimes. Specifically, the transmission of global financial shocks to the domestic credit, house price, banking sector leverage, and domestic output differs by the exchange rate regime. The magnitude of the cross-border transmission of the shocks is mitigated with flexible exchange rate regimes, while fixed exchange rate regimes are systematically affected more by changes in global market volatility and investor risk aversion.

The main reason is that sensitivity of cross-border capital flows (especially liability flows) to global risk aversion. Emerging economies under fixed exchange rate regimes attract more net capital flows (in percent of GDP) than intermediate and floating regimes, and they also react more when the global financial cycle turns. Under increased global risk aversion both FDI and other investment drop is larger for fixed exchange rate regimes, as compared to those with intermediate regimes or floats. The sensitivity of portfolio flows to the VXO is, however, not affected by the exchange rate regime.

Obstfeld et al. (2019) also point out to the difficulty in assessing the trilemma for advanced economies as there is a large majority belonging to the Eurozone. Another issue is that demand for euro increases with global risk aversion as it is seen as a safe haven, which differs than other emerging market countries.

9 This “2.5-lemma” pattern is also observed in Farhi and Werning (2014).

Montinel and Pedroni (2019) provide a middle ground to the debate. They point out that the trilemma still prevails; however, financial integration has altered the channels of monetary transmission. Specifically, under floating rates, monetary policy shocks have larger effects on the exchange rate. Under high capital mobility and flexible exchange rate regimes the periphery country has monetary autonomy. However, monetary autonomy is not the optimal policy because it creates high exchange rate volatility. High financial integration induces Taylor rules in periphery countries to give more weight to the exchange rate, which requires to follow the center county. In other words, financial integration creates "fear of floating" in the periphery country and to track core country policy rates. This contributes to what Rey calls the "dilemma."

> "Because this outcome reflects a monetary policy choice that is contingent on aversion to exchange rate volatility, however, it is perfectly consistent with Mundell's trilemma: periphery monetary autonomy remains feasible under high capital mobility, but when exchange rate volatility is excessively harmful, it is not optimal." Montinel & Pedroni (2019: 17)

A confirming argument is from a very recent study by Obstfeld (2020). He concludes that the trilemma still prevails; however, the policy trade-offs have become harsher due to the global financial forces. While the old trilemma was more a trade-off between output and inflation, in today's world with increased integration financial conditions have also become very important. Hence, besides macro policy shocks, financial conditions and stability concerns have become prevalent. The trilemma has changed and the debate over monetary policy autonomy has become a "monetary and financial policy autonomy." The exchange rate flexibility, however, as Obstefled writes is still important:

> "Nonetheless, even without pure floating, the "extra degree of freedom" that exchange rate flexibility offers remains essential for a wide range of countries." (2020: 26)

Conclusion

In 1971 when President Nixon abolished the connection between gold and the US dollar, the world entered a new system of monetary exchanges. A move towards flexibility started, and countries were left to choose among alternative exchange rate arrangements. After more than 40 years since the collapse of the Bretton Woods system, countries are still under a quest for the right regime choice. The policy outcomes of a regime choice still continue to be a topic of investigation.

The modern era of globalization that started in the late 1970s brought new considerations. As countries faced different challenges in their journey of liberalization and economic integration, economic theory and policy-making developed with experience.

It would not be wrong to argue that the period after 2000 marks a new period of globalization. Driven by large gross capital flows and financial linkages, a period with new and unwitnessed challenges has begun. The GFC has shown that beside the valuable past experience and knowledge, there are still and will be many unknowns through the journey in this new period. One such unknown is how countries can insulate themselves from the negative effects of this new period of globalization, and specifically, what tools can countries use to insulate themselves from the global spillovers while reaping the benefits. This has brought into question the effectiveness of different financial arrangements, and the question of the regime choice has been revived.

As Kindleberger stated, there is no way a country can insulate itself from the outside world only through exchange rate policy:

> "... it is impossible to say that the external problem can be avoided by some expedient such as allowing the exchange rate to take care of itself. Such a decision would constitute a disposition of the problem that would in no way insulate the economy from the outside world. The response of external events would merely be felt through a different sequence of economic stimuli and repercussions." (Kindleberger, 1937: 230–231)

In this chapter, we make an evaluation of the discussions around one of the main policy tools of international finance, that is, the exchange rate regime choice, and the financial trilemma. Our main focus is to provide a historic review on this discussion and how it has translated itself after the GFC.

One related question we address is whether the financial trilemma prevails and exchange rates provide effective insulating mechanisms. While the debate is still ongoing, the strong standing argument is that exchange rate regime still matters. The trade-off between exchange rate stability, monetary policy autonomy, and financial integration also hold. However, with the size of global linkages the trade-offs have become harsher.

In summary, in light of the 40 years of experience, it should be noted that there is no "one-size-fits-all" recommendation. Even though the rules of the game might be the same, as the financial system evolves, new challenges are emerging and new players are coming into play. Hence it is a dynamic game where each country has to play the game that is right for its objective.

It would not be wrong to state that time proved Kindelberg right. Forty years after the Bretton Woods and a decade after the GFC how countries can insulate themselves from external events and the role of exchange rate regime is still under debate. We conclude the discussion with a quote by Mankiw:

> "But economists should be cautious when recommending exchange-rate policy, because it is far from obvious what is best." (2010: 2)

References

Aghion, P., Bacchetta, P., Ranciere, R. & Rogoff, K. (2009) "Exchange Rate Volatility and Productivity Growth: The Role of Financial Development", Journal of Monetary Economics, 56(4): 494–513.

Aizenmann, J., Chinn, M. D. & Ito, H. (2010) "The Emerging Global Financial Architecture: Tracing and Evaluating the New Patterns of the Trilemma's Configurations", Journal of International Money and Finance, 29(4): 615–641.

Bailliu, J., Lafrance, R. & Perrault, J. F. (2003) "Does Exchange Rate Policy Matter for Growth?" International Finance, 6(3): 381–414.

Bekaert, G. & Mehl, A. (2019) "On the Global Financial Market Integration "swoosh" and the Trilemma", Journal of International Money and Finance, 94(C): 227–245.

Goetzmann, W. & Lingfeng Li, and Geert Rouwenhorst (2005) "Long-term global market correlations", Journal of Business, 78(1): 1–38.

Bordo, M. & Flandreau, M. (2003) "Core, Periphery, Exchange Rate Regimes, and Globalization, National Bureau Of Economic Research Conference Report M.D.

Bubula, A., & Otker-Robe, I. (2002) "The Evolution of Exchange Rate Regimes since 1990: Evidence from De Facto Policies", IMF Working Paper 02/155.

Calvo, G. & Reinhart, C. (2000) "Fixing for Your Life", NBER Working Paper Series No: 8006, Cambridge, MA.

Carmignani, F., Colombo, E. & Tirelli, P. (2005) "Consistency versus Credibility: How Do Countries Choose Their Exchange Rate Regime?", International Finance 0502001, University Library of Munich, Germany.

Cerutti, E., Stijn, S. & Ratnovski, L. (2017) "Global Liquidity and Cross-Border Bank Flows", Economic Policy 32(89): 81–125.

Claessens, S. & Kose, A. (2017) "Asset Prices and Macroeconomic Outcomes: A Survey", Policy Research Working Paper Series 8259, The World Bank.

Dubas, J., Lee, B. J. & Mark, N. (2005) "Effective Exchange Rate Classifications and Growth", NBER Working Paper no. 11272 (April).

Edwards, S. (1999) "The Determinants of the Choice Between Fixed and Flexible Exchange Rate Regimes". In T. Ito & A. Krueger (eds.), Changes in Exchange Rates in Rapidly Developing Countries, Chicago: University of Chicago Press, 9–28.

Edwards, S. (2001) "Exchange Rate Regimes, Capital Flows and Crisis Prevention," NBER Working Paper 8529.

Edwards, S. (2012) "The Federal Reserve, the Emerging Markets, and Capital Controls: A High-Frequency Empirical Investigation", Journal of Money, Credit and Banking, 44(s2): 151–84.

Edwards, S. & Levy-Yeyati, E. (2005) "Flexible Exchange Rates as Shock Absorbers", European Economic Review, 49(8): 2079–2105.

Eichengreen, B. (1994) "International Monetary Arrangements for the 21st Century", Washington: Brookings Institution.

Eichengreen, B. & Leblang, D. (2003) "Exchange Rates and Cohesion: Historical Perspectives and Political-Economy Considerations", Journal of Common Market Studies, 41(5): 797–822.

Eichengreen, B., Rose, A. K. & Wyplosz, C. (1995) "Speculative Attacks on Pegged Exchange Rates: An Empirical Exploration with Special Reference to the European Monetary System", Working Papers in Applied Economic Theory 95–04, Federal Reserve Bank of San Francisco.

Farhi, E. & Werning, I. (2012) "Dealing with the Trilemma: Optimal Capital Controls with Fixed Exchange Rates", NBER Working Papers 18199.

Farhi, E. & Werning, I. (2014) "Dilemma Not Trilemma? Capital Controls and Exchange Rates with Volatile Capital Flows", IMF Econ. Rev. 62(4): 569–605.

Fischer, S. (2001) "Exchange-Rate Regimes: Is the Bipolar View Correct?", Journal of Economic Perspectives, 15(2): 3–24.

Fleming, J. M. (1962) "Domestic Financial Policies Under Fixed and Under Floating Exchange Rates", Staff Papers, International Monetary Fund, 9: 369–379.

Flood, R. P. & Garber, P. M. (1984) "Collapsing Exchange-Rate Regimes: Some Linear Examples", Journal of International Economics, 17: 1–13.

Frankel, J. (1999) "No Single Currency Regime Is Right for All Countries or at All Times", Princeton Essays in International Finance No 215.

Frankel, J., Ma, X., & Xie, D. (2019) "The Impact of Exchange Rate Regimes on Economic Growth with Continuous Classification of de facto Regimes", Working Paper.

Frankel, J., Schmukler, S. & Serven, L. (2004) "Global Transmission of Interest Rates: Monetary Independence and Currency Regime", Journal of International Money and Finance, 23(5): 701–733.

Ghosh, A., Gulde, A. M. & Wolf, H. (2003) "Exchange Rate Regimes: Choices and Consequences", Cambridge, MA: MIT Press.

Giavazzi, F. & Giovannini, A. (1990) "Limiting Exchange Rate Flexibility: The European Monetary System", Journal of International Economics, 29(3–4): 385–388.

Gylfason, T. (2000) "Fix or Flex? Alternative Exchange Rate Regimes in an Era of Global Capital Mobility", North American Journal of Economics and Finance, 11(2): 173–89.

Habib, M. M., Mileva, E. & Stracca, L. (2017) "The Real Exchange Rate and Economic Growth: Revisiting the Case Using External Instruments", Journal of International Money and Finance, 73: PB: 386–398.

Han, X. & Wei, S. J. (2018) "International Transmissions of Monetary Shocks: Between a Trilemma and a Dilemma", Journal of International Economics, 110: 205–219.

Harms, P. & Kretschmann, M. (2009) "Words, Deeds and Outcomes: A Survey on the Growth Effects of Exchange Rate Regimes", Journal of Economic Surveys, 23(1): 139–164.

Husain, A. M., Mody, A. & Rogoff, K. S. (2005) "Exchange Rate Regime Durability and Performance in Developing Versus Advanced Economies", Journal of Monetary Economics, 52(1): 35–64.

Ilzetzki, E., Reinhart, C. M. & Rogoff, S. K (2019) "Exchange Arrangements Entering the Twenty-First Century: Which Anchor Will Hold?", The Quarterly Journal of Economics, 134(2): 599–646.

Jeanne, O. (1997) "Are Currency Crises Self-Fulfilling? A Test", Journal of International Economics, 43: 243–286.

Kaminsky, G. L. (2006). "Currency Crises: Are They All the Same?", Journal of International Money and Finance, 25, 503–527.

Kaminsky, G. L., Lizondo, S. & Reinhart, C. (1998). "Leading Indicators of Currency Crises", IMF Staff Papers, vol. 45, March: 1–48.

Kindleberger, C. P. (1937) "International Short-Term Capital Movements", New York: Columbia University Press.

Klein, M. W. & Shambaugh, J. C. (2015) "Rounding the Corners of the Policy Trilemma: Sources of Monetary Policy Autonomy", American Economic Journal Macroeconomics, 7(4): 33–66.

Klein, M. W. & Shambaugh, J. C. (2008) "The Dynamics of Exchange Rate Regimes: Fixes, Floats, and Flips", Journal of International Economics, 75(1): 70–92.

Krugman, P. (1979) "A Model of Balance-of-Payments Crises", Journal of Money, Credit and Banking, 11(3): 311–325.

Lane, P. R. & Milesi-Ferretti, G. M. (2007) "The External Wealth of Nations Mark II: Revised and Extended Estimates of Foreign Assets and Liabilities, 1970–2004", Journal of International Economics, 73(2): 223–250.

Levy-Yeyati, E. & Sturzenegger, F. (2003) "To Float or to Fix: Evidence on the Impact of Exchange Rate Regimes on Growth", American Economic Review, 93(4), 1173–1193.

Levy-Yeyati, E. & Sturzenegger, F. (2005) "Classifying Exchange Rate Regimes: Deeds vs. Words", European Economic Review, 49(3): 1603–1635.

Mankiw, N. G. (2010) "The Trilemma of International Finance", The New York Times, July 11, 2010.

McKinnon, I. R. (1963) "Optimum Currency Areas", The American Economic Review, 53(4): 717–725.

Mendoza, E. G. & Terrones, M. E. (2008) "An Anatomy of Credit Booms: Evidence from Macro Aggregates and Micro Data", NBER Working Papers 14049.

Montinel, P. J. & Pedroni, P. (2019) "Trilemma-Dilemma: Constraint or Choice? Some Empirical Evidence from a Structurally Identified Heterogeneous Panel VAR", Open Economies Review, 30: 1–18.

Moreno, R. (2000) "Pegging and Macroeconomic Performance in East Asia", ASEAN Economic Bulletin, 18(1): 48–63.

Moreno, R. (2001) "Pegging and Stabilization Policy in Developing Countries", Economic Review of the Federal Reserve Bank of San Francisco, 12(99): 17–29.

Mundell, R. (1963) "Capital Mobility and Stabilization Policy under Fixed and Flexible Exchange Rates", Canadian Journal of Economics, 29: 475–485.

Mussa, M, Masson, P., Swoboda, A., Jadresic, E., Mauro, P. & Berg, A. (2000) "Exchange Rate Regimes in an Increasingly Integrated World Economy", Occasional Paper 193. Washington: International Monetary Fund.

Obstfeld, M. (1986) "Rational and Self-Fulfilling Balance-of-Payments Crises", American Economic Review, 76(1): 72–81.

Obstfeld, M. (2015) "Trilemma and Tradeoffs: Living with Financial Globalization", BIS Working Paper Series No. 480. Bank for International Settlements, Basel.

Obstfeld. M. (2018) "Exchange Rates and the Global Financial Cycle" Economic Policy Challenges and Priorities a Decade after the Global Financial Crisis: Outlook for Latin America. Cartagena, Colombia.

Obstfeld, M. (2020) "Harry Johnson's "Case for Flexible Exchange Rates- 50 Years Later", NBER Working Paper 26874.

Obstfeld, M., Ostry, J. D. & Qureshi, M. S. (2019) "A Tie That Binds: Revisiting the Trilemma in Emerging Market Economies", The Review of Economics and Statistics, 101(2): 279–293.

Obstfeld, M. & Rogoff, K. (1995) "The Mirage of Fixed Exchange Rates", Journal of Economic Perspectives, 9(4): 73–96.

Obstfeld, M., Shambaugh, J. C. & Taylor, A. M. (2005) "The Trilemma in History: Tradeoffs Among Exchange Rates, Monetary Policies, and Capital Mobility", The Review of Economics and Statistics, 87(3): 423–438.

Passari, E. & Rey, H. (2015) "Financial Flows and the International Monetary System", Economic Journal, 0(584): 675–698.

Petreski, M. (2009) "Exchange-Rate Regime and Economic Growth: A Review of the Theoretical and Empirical Literature", Kiel Institute for the World Economy Discussion Paper No. 2009–31.

Rangvid, J., Santa-Clara, P. & Schmeling, M. (2016) "Capital Market Integration and Consumption Risk Sharing over the Long Run", Journal of International Economics, 103: 27–43.

Rao, G. B. (2019) "Exchange Rate Regimes and Its Impact on Growth: An Empirical Analysis of BRICS Countries", Theoretical and Applied Economics, XXVI, 2(619): 157–172.

Rey, H. (2015) "Dilemma not Trilemma: The Global Financial Cycle and Monetary Policy Independence", NBER Working Papers 21162, National Bureau of Economic Research, Inc.

Rey, H. (2016) "International Channels of Transmission of Monetary Policy and the Mundellian Trilemma", IMF Economic Review, 64(1): 6–3.

Rizzo, J. M. (1998) "The Economic Determinants of the Choice of an Exchange Rate Regime: A Probit Analysis", Economics Letters, 59(3): 283–287.

Rodrik, D. (2008) "The Real Exchange Rate and Economic Growth. Brook. Papers Econ. Activ. 39(2): 365–439.

Rogoff, S. K., Husain, A. M., Mody, A., Brooks, R. & Oomes, N. (2004) "Evolution and Performance of Exchange Rate Regimes", IMF Occasional Paper 229. IMF, Washington, DC.

Summers, L. H. (2000) "International Financial Crises: Causes, Prevention, and Cures", American Economic Review, Papers and Proceedings, 90(May): 1–16.

Tamgac, U. (2013) "Duration of Fixed Exchange Rate Regimes in Emerging Economies", Journal of International Money and Finance, 37(C): 439–467.

Tong, H. & Wei, S.-J. (2010) "The Composition Matters: Capital Inflows and Liquidity Crunch During a Global Economic Crisis", Review of Financial Studies, 24(6): 2023–2052.

Volosovych, V. (2011) "Measuring Financial Market Integration Over The Long Run: Is There A U-Shape?", Journal of International Money and Finance, 30 (7): 1535–1561.

von Hagen, J. & Zhou, J. (2007) "The choice of exchange rate regimes in developing countries: A multinomial panel analysis", Journal of International Money and Finance, 26(7): 1071–1094.

Cem Berk

2 Searching for the Roots of Cryptocurrency Throughout History: An Analysis of Bitcoin

Highlights: Barter tries to create a fair exchange of goods and services which is applied even today. Money before coin is typically a coin or object which is accepted by the community. Commodities such as cacao seed, salt, and tobacco were used as a medium of exchange. Coins are standard in weight and value which stems from Lydia and brought a rapid civilization to the World. In gold standard and silver standard the value of money was pegged to the value of the metal. Although European Monetary Union is a recent and well-known attempt for countries to accept a single currency, there were earlier attempts such as Latin Monetary Union. There are criticisms on EMU however, leading to ongoing problems such as Brexit. The end of Soviet Union and Yugoslavia are also interesting to analyze monetary consequences. This is an attempt to create a world currency which creates advantages in trade. Under bimetallic standard, money was pegged to the price of gold and silver. Paper money which is inconvertible created inflationary problems. Bretton Woods is an attempt to peg the currency into US Dollar. Currency wars still exist today, which also benefits some countries in trade. Dollarization is the use of US Dollar outside of USA. De-dollarization attempts to trade in currencies other than US Dollar. Banks are important in the use of modern money; however, the issues in money transfer created some alternatives. Digital wallets are less costly and faster when it comes to money transfer. Cryptocurrencies are also available with the help of Blockchain technology. Bitcoin as the most frequently used cryptocurrency is analyzed in this chapter to test its dynamics.

Keywords: Blockchain, digital currency, financial economics, international finance, monetary systems, payment systems

Introduction

Many systems were in practice for the exchange of goods and services in the history. Cryptocurrencies or any other modern form of payment needs to take into account these practices. All of these systems had some advantages but there were also many problems with these practices from which one can take important lessons. The goal of this work is to identify what we can take away for cryptocurrencies through the history of money.

Technology is deriving today's financial world. For example, Blockchain technology helped cryptocurrencies to appear. Actually, technology always had an effect on the money. Mining, the use of coins, and printing were all important factors that created modern forms of money.

Inflation is one of the first things to consider when a new currency is created. There has been loss of purchasing power in almost every kind of money in history. Economic depression and devaluation, which lower the value of local currency in a fixed exchange rate, are also issues to be considered with money.

Barter was first used for the exchange of goods. Some primitive forms of money were also available; and some examples are use of amber or horses for trade. After that coins were used in Lydia. At that time coins were the only kind of money.

Coins require minting process which has a cost known as seigniorage. The cost is the cost of producing coins and profit of the government. During this process, the cost of the coin can be reduced by decreasing the weight or increasing the percentage of the lower value metal. This process is called debasement.

According to the Gresham's Law, good money replaces the bad money. A debased money is not preferred against a valuable money. This might even lead to the use of an international currency instead of the local one. Another problem is the change or petty money, as the cost of it is close to the cost of silver coin, the value of which is much higher. Counterfeiting is the false money produced by someone other than the government.

Inflation could still be achieved on purpose in a silver coin system. Gold coins and bimetallism also created problems particularly due to the value of one metal with respect to the other. These problems led to the Gold Standard in 19th-century United Kingdom. Bretton Woods is a period of fixed exchange rates (Chown, 1994).

Financial experts came together at Bretton Woods in 1944 which is also the origin of International Monetary Fund (IMF) and International Bank for Reconstruction and Development (IBRD). The system brought the idea of fixed but adjustable exchange rates. The system was in practice until its collapse in 1971.

The rise of gold price was one of the reasons of the collapse. Central banks preferred to keep the reserves in gold. United States managed to control gold prices, but that resulted in decrease in US reserves. The economy was also problematic due to Vietnam war. There was a liquidity problem throughout the World. Due to fixed rates, problems with growth and unemployment could not be controlled. In 1971, Dollar's peg to the gold was terminated, and Germany and the Netherlands switched to the floating exchange rate system. In 1973, most developed countries switched to floating exchange rate which is the end of Bretton Woods system (Chown, 2003).

Printed money and the origins of banking are also discussed in this chapter. Bimetallism is the circulation of more than one metal such as gold and silver at a time. The problem with this system is that the relative value of these coins changes and their values may also vary in different countries. This creates locational arbitrage opportunity by repeatedly buying gold where it is cheap and selling it for silver where it is more expensive. Silver standard imposed a floating value of gold coins based on the value of silver. In the long run, it was ineffective to fix the value of gold coins against silver.

There has been attempts to create a world currency throughout history. Monetary unions have this target besides trade advantages. Some examples are Latin Monetary Union in the 19th century and more recently European Monetary Union (Chown, 1994).

The rest of the chapter is organized as follows. The next section focuses on the initial attempts to trade, barter, primitive money, metallic money, coins, and paper money. In Section 3, a discussion on some important monetary unions is available. In Section 4, the origins of modern banking is given. Section 5 is an analysis of dollarization and currency wars between countries. In Section 6, arguably the latest stage of money, digital money and cryptocurrencies are mentioned. Section 7 is an empirical analysis to determine the drivers of Bitcoin prices. And in conclusion, there are concluding remarks and ideas for new researches.

1 From Barter to Paper Money

Barter was the sole medium for the exchange of goods and services. The oldest transactions include parties to exchange goods and services to satisfy their needs. The later versions of the system also allow a choice between more than one good which allows preference based on their qualities. One of the most important properties for barter goods is that it should be stored easily.

Established barter markets were available in certain locations. Alternative is a gift exchange where the goods are located in a convenient spot and the other party takes the goods. They put what they consider a fair trade in exchange for the goods. However, if the goods are not considered sufficient, they are not taken, asking for a better offer from the other party.

More recently in Germany hyperinflation dates, butter was accepted as a commodity for the exchange of the goods and services. During the Second World War, cigarettes were used in Europe for barter. In Iran oil was used to obtain steel from Germany. Barter is seen in retail practice, especially in cars, real estate, watches, and computers. Barter is also used in informal or black economy.

The major drawbacks are the goods obtained from a barter could often not be consumed immediately by one party since they are more than their needs. Storing these items would cost much more when compared to a relatively costless bank account. Another is the long process of bargaining or the goods offered simply might not be of interest to the other party. The need for a standard value of exchange especially in the larger transactions created the ideas for money. As the number of commodities increase, due to large potential combinations of barters available, the system is extremely difficult to be put in practice. Money makes it clear for many people, the relative value of different goods and services in a very short time.

What we refer by money today is either printed money or coins. However, the earlier uses are referred as primitive money. It is a unit or object representing a standard value that can be used in exchange of goods and services. These objects sometimes represented other purposes as decorative appearance, political, religious, or black money. As daily lives of people constitute these values, it is not surprising to have this much of economic influence at that time. Several primitive kinds of money were used. Some examples are amber, ivory, beads, feather, nails, pigs, salt, vodka, and kettles. Cowrie, which is an ocean product, is of particular importance since it is used in many communities for a long time. As the amount of trade increased, more cowries were available. Therefore, the value of cowrie depreciated. The teeth of whales in Fiji islands, stone in the island of Yap, wampum which is beads in North America are all used as currencies. Money today is printed and guaranteed by the state in most of the developed economies.

Cattle represents animals such as pig, cows, goats, and sheep. Some economists argue that they cannot be categorized as money because they are too heavy or too valuable for a standard measure. Horses are important especially for the Kirghiz community. The issue with cattle is quantity is given priority. Old or diseased cattle are considered the same amount as the younger counterpart.

To identify what is money, its functions can be investigated. Money is a unit of exchange. Its existence is recognized by a community. It is used in the exchange of goods and services. It is used in payments and represent the amount of future payments. It shows the relative value of various goods and services. It is liquid and may be used immediately when goods and services are needed.

Metallic money was used before coins. Metals such as copper, brass, gold, and silver were used in coins. After the Second World War some European countries used aluminum coins. Historically money means silver. In China, bronze and copper cowries were made at the end of Stone Age. Iron swords and other goods from iron were also used as currency. Metals were used as money in many shapes such as rings, bracelets, or rods. In West Africa manilla made of copper or brass is used as money. Metal ingots were used in Cappadocia as money where the silver quality and weight was guaranteed by the state in 2250 BC. Large silver dumps were used in Greece; however, they were not in uniform.

The first metal coin was used in Lydia, currently located in west Turkey. Lydian coins were made of electrum. They were regular in form, standard in purity, and were backed officially by the State. These were developed in 7th century BC. They were rounded and stamped with the symbol of Lydia, the lion's head (Davies, 2002).

First paper money was invented in China. Chinese government maintained three sevenths of metals in reserve for the issued money. This is a fiat money backed by the government. Due to the war with Tatars, there were problems with money. The state printed too much money in the 12th century. The supply of money rose from 224 in 1190 to 4,949 in 1240. The money inflation resulted in loss of value of money. The 1000 cash note fell to the value equal to the note of 10 cash note (Chown, 1994).

2 Monetary Unions

A monetary union is a combination of countries whose currencies are pegged to those of others. In the extreme case, they use the same currency. In countries in the British Monetary Union (England, Northern Ireland, Scotland, and Wales), commercial banks can print money. Similarly, in the United States Monetary Union, Federal Reserve Banks can print money.

The United States Monetary Union was established following a history of rapid inflation in 1789. The US Dollar was pegged to gold and silver, therefore accepting bimetallism. A former central bank, Federal Reserve was established in 1914. Before that, States issued their own currency.

Bimetallism was in practice in France since 1803. However, the fall in the price of gold in the 1850s created an arbitrage opportunity to melt silver coins and buy gold. Therefore, the silver ratio in the coins had to be decreased. Due to the shortage of coins that made trade between neighboring countries difficult, Latin Monetary Union was established. The countries in the Union are France, Belgium, Switzerland, and Italy. They fixed the silver content of the coins to the same amount. However, due to government deficit, countries had to print their own money individually, leading to depreciation of local currency. Finally, after the First World War, the Union was terminated.

Scandinavian Monetary Union was established in 1873 by Denmark, Norway, and Sweden. The Union was also a switch from silver to gold standard for the member countries. Besides political atmosphere, trade partners namely United

Kingdom and Germany which are on the gold standard were the reason for the union. All countries accepted the new currency krona. The union was then terminated following the First World War.

It is important to note that the national monetary unions of Czechoslovakia, Soviet Union, and Yugoslavia were terminated in the 1990s. The ruble region switched to a new multiple currency zone. Following the civil wars in Yugoslavia, new countries each with a new currency emerged. Due to political and economic reasons, Czechoslovakia union members Czech Republic and Slovakia gradually accepted monetary separation.

Economic and Monetary Union (EMU) dates back to 1999 where 11 participating currencies were pegged to the single currency euro. The European Central Bank (ECB) was also established to act as the sole central bank of the region. There are, however, criticisms on EMU. Unlike conventional central banks, the ECB lacks the power to act as a lender of last resort and supervise the commercial banks in the Eurozone in a financial crisis. In addition, the Zone is not homogeneous, and therefore the decisions of the ECB might have contradictory consequences within the region (Capie & Wood, 2003).

3 The Origins of Modern Banking

Banks as described earlier are important in depositing, lending, and printing money. Printing is an issue for central banks in today's practice. Interestingly, the origin of banking dates banking to the military knights of the Solomon ("Templars"). The religious and military duties made Templars rich and they later became businessmen. They founded and operated international banking for about two centuries. They were based in Jerusalem and responsible for securing the Holy Land.

The knights had a disciplined life. They wore religious cloths and were not living with women. They were known for their fighting skills in battles. They acquired money from keeping the spoils after wars and from donations, including King Henry II. They also acquired real estate in Europe and brought the money earned through these banks to Jerusalem. They were living in castles, which is very secure for depositing money. They also transferred money overseas securely as a service. They also deposited money and gave mortgage loans in Jerusalem and Paris. They charged transaction fees for these services. They also lent to the kings such as Louis VII of France. They also had the family accounts for kings and popes. They had at most 7.000 people employed and 870 castles. Following military defeats to Mamelukes and finally losing the city of Acre in 1291 they lost power. There were also some accusations in public that they did not have ideal lifestyle and habits. King Philip of France also arrested most of the Templars and then the Templars disappeared.

After the Templars, banking activities continued in northern Italian cities such as Florence. Private family banks were founded. They offered trade finance overseas. The lending rates of banks were lower than individuals who provide lending. The Italian banks are different than Templars in many aspects. First of all, they offer service to ordinary people. They have a market-based approach as opposed to the military privileges of Templars. The word "bank" has an original meaning of a bench, just as Italian merchants sit together and lend money. The major problem for Italian banks is that the Catholic Church prohibited interest. To overcome this issue, they instead used bills of exchange where a borrower has to pay back higher amount in another currency. Bill of exchange was also a novelty for the transfer of money. Before the use of it, it took almost a month to transfer money from north to south France. In addition, one has to take into account the risk of theft when coins are used. Bills of exchange transfer took eight days and if stolen, it cannot be redeemed. The banks in Italy also helped England in conquering Wales and Scotland. In return they obtained the marketing rights of English woolen in Europe. Peruzi and Bardi Banks in Italy also got deposits from catholic churches in England. The currencies used in Europe were that of Florence and Venice. Finally, in 1343 they financed Hundred Years' War between England and France. When England defaulted, banks in Florence bankrupted. Despite these events, banks in other cities such as Genoa and Venice kept their operations. Even in Florence, the Medici family appeared in the late 14th century. These developments even led to Renaissance (Weatherford, 1997).

4 Dollarization and Currency Wars

US Dollar came with a rather unsophisticated process due to the necessity to create a national currency after independence. Before Dollar, European currencies such as British guinea were used in trade.

Before Dollar American colonies used primitive money wampum in trade. Later they set up their mint to produce Pine Tree schillings. Bills of credit was used in Massachusetts in 1690. Some of them also issued their paper money.

Colonies were important in trade. Britain exported goods to the Colonies. The Seven Years' War between France and England was particularly to obtain colonies. France lost the war, and the cost of the war also made Britain struggle. Colonies did not want to pay taxes to Britain and become independent. They created the army for $3 Million Bills of Credit. The goal was to create continental currencies. The first attempt of Bills depreciated and counterfeits of them were created. The war of independence ended in 1783. The mint was established in 1792. Federal government was responsible for the coins, and States were responsible for regulating printed money (Chown, 1994).

Dollarization is the process of the use of American Dollar outside of USA. This phenomenon is particularly available in emerging markets. In some economies interest rates are high, and there is inflation. This results in lack of respect in local currency. The value of local currency depreciates so rapidly that the people prefer to hold strong currencies such as Dollar to avoid loss of purchasing power.

Dollarization, however, comes with a cost to the emerging economy. The ability to lower local currency brings trade advantages. This encourages exports and discourages imports. Central banks have the power to print money, change the value of currency and interest rates which are crucial for the economy especially in a crisis environment. Also, ability to print brings seigniorage profit potential (Hinds, 2006).

Money makes international trade possible. When transfer of goods or services take place, money is also transferred between economic entities and nations. The circulation of money within an economy is good. This increases economic growth. Money flowing into the country is also good because these foreign investments create positive atmosphere. However, in some situations this money goes out after reaching a peak, which is again a dangerous situation. Foreign capital is today's understanding of war. When it goes out, it transfers away years of achievements obtained in an economy. This kind of investment is often called speculative capital or hot money. Central banks often play a role here by adjusting interest rates and other monetary policies to control speculative attacks (Forrest et al., 2018).

Trade of some goods such as oil and natural gas often take place in US Dollar. This means to buy certain goods; the investor has to buy US Dollar first. There are attempts to do these trades in local currencies. However, USA would not favor these attempts because people holding US Dollar and investing in US treasury bills strengthen the US economy.

5 Digital Money and Cryptocurrencies

In the era of Internet, most goods and services can be achieved online. The payment for these transactions could be costly. Likewise, when one needs to transfer money abroad, considerable costs occur. To overcome these issues, digital payment systems have been developed. These are digital wallets on internet, where one transfers money to his wallet and then makes payment to another person using the same system.

Cryptocurrency is arguably the latest evolution of the money. In 2009, someone using the nickname Satoshi Nakamoto mentioned Bitcoin in his paper. Bitcoin is a cryptocurrency using Blockchain technology. Blockchain is a ledger and it makes sure that every transaction is secure and can be seen by all peers.

Cryptocurrency is different than ordinary money in many ways. It is not a fiat currency and is not backed by any government. Unlike printing money, the number of Bitcoins that can be created is limited. It is a faster and less costly method for transfer. It is managed by cryptography, meaning certain passwords shall be used in transfer of money.

Bitcoin is produced by mining. This is a miner solving a mathematical puzzle. Each time a miner succeeds, a new block is formed, and proof of work is obtained. Miners are also rewarded with bitcoins.

Cryptocurrency is digital, it can be bought online and stored in a digital wallet. It can then be used in several online and real-life companies or it can be exchanged for another currency. Like other currencies, Bitcoin can be obtained by smaller amounts. The smaller unit for Bitcoin is Satoshi. Bitcoin is not the only cryptocurrency. There are altcoins such as Litecoin, Monero, and Ripple.

The price of the cryptocurrency is determined by the market. Since the total number of Bitcoin that can be issued is limited, changes in demand is reflected in price rapidly. Most of the Bitcoin buyers are speculators, and they do not get Bitcoin for transaction purposes. This also drives the prices up. The first transaction of Bitcoin is pizza with a cost of $25, paid as 10.000 Bitcoin. This shows the rapid increase in the price of Bitcoin.

There are also risks when buying cryptocurrency. The price of it is very volatile if it is obtained for investment purposes. The passwords can be stolen or forgotten, which means direct loss of money. The wallet can be damaged or lost. Cryptocurrency owners should be aware of these risks (Grabowski, 2019).

6 Empirical Analysis

An empirical analysis is made to check the price dynamics of Bitcoin. The goal of the research is to check the causality between Bitcoin and other variables. The variables used in the study are Grayscale Bitcoin Trust (GBTC), FTEC (Fidelity MSCI Information Technology Index), VIX (Volatility Index), S&P 500 Index, and Gold. The data is daily. The time period is between May 8, 2015 and November 15, 2019. The number of data is 1142.

According to Augmented Dickey Fuller (ADF) and Philips Perron (PP) unit root test results, the variables S&P 500 Index and Gold are stationary in level. The other variables are stationary when first differences are used. For vector auto regression 1 lag is suggested by Schwarz and Hannan-Quinn information criteria. VAR (1) model is developed. Trace and Max-eigenvalue tests indicate 4 cointegrating vectors.

The short run relationship is studied with Vector Error Correction Model. Finally, a granger causality analysis is made. According to the Granger causality results, technology and Gold Granger cause Bitcoin price. It is important to note that VIX (Volatility Index) and S&P 500 do not Granger cause the price of Bitcoin.

According to the analysis, Bitcoin is a technology-driven phenomenon. The price of Bitcoin is affected by the developments in technology. Blockchain technology is used when Bitcoin was developed. It is clear according to the analysis that the advances in technology and market prices of technology firms are correlated with the price of Bitcoin.

Gold is a precious metal whose price fluctuates according to fluctuations in other currencies. As the price of US Dollar falls, the price of gold rises. This is because gold is regarded as an alternative strong investment vehicle especially in times of struggling economy. Bitcoin likewise claims to be an alternative currency to other strong currencies. Therefore, the price of gold Granger causes the price of Bitcoin.

Conclusion

The roots of Bitcoin are embedded in the history of money. The problems of almost every kind of money is addressed in Cryptocurrencies. Although, this does not mean that Cryptocurrencies offer perfect solution.

One of the most important issues with Cryptocurrencies is that there is no official authority behind it. Sometimes for legal or tax purposes, details of the transactions such as the true holder name of the currency is required. But these cannot be learned even by official authorities.

Barter is the earliest method for obtaining goods and services. Barter is particularly efficient when there are problems in an economy such as currency depreciation and lack of liquidity. Similarly, cryptocurrency is seen as a safe haven. When there are problems with economy, public tend to switch to cryptocurrency, to avoid losses associated with currency depreciation.

In barter, there is a possibility that one gets a lower quality product than promised due to exchanging with an untrustworthy individual. Similarly, in Bitcoin, if there was no public ledger, a traitor could sabotage the system by denying the truths about a Bitcoin transaction.

In a barter transaction, you cannot typically divide one good into two to match the amount required for the transaction. Cryptocurrencies typically have smaller units. The smaller unit for Bitcoin is Satoshi.

Exchange rate is typically a problem with currencies. Especially in international trade, it is typical that people lose some money in exchanging to the currency required for purchasing the good from local currency. Especially when it is a credit card transaction, banks may not offer the best rates to the customer. Cryptocurrency solves this issue, since typically both parties use the same cryptocurrency such as Bitcoin.

Digital money systems were developed to overcome the problems with international Swift transactions. These transactions are typically costly and take time to be completed. Cryptocurrencies are also stored in digitals wallets and transfer does not require a third-party involvement such as a bank, which fastens the transfer process. In addition, the costs associated with cryptocurrency transactions are considerably lower.

Money can be debased, counterfeited, or stolen. Cryptocurrencies are standard and secure. There are no known cases where the system could be hacked by brute force. It should be noted that Bitcoin exchanges and investors should be careful with personal security.

With a typical currency, there are a lot of examples when central banks have to print too much money. This leads to inflation and loss of purchasing power. Bitcoin, however, has a deflationist tendency. This is due to the limited number of Bitcoins that can be generated under a predetermined schedule.

Monetary unions are often created to create trade advantages and claim to create a world money that is dominant in trades. Although not officially declared, Bitcoin development process and attempts to market Bitcoin shows that Bitcoin had a target to be a world currency. Due to the problems with Bitcoin mentioned in this chapter, it could not achieve this goal.

This research shows that Bitcoin is a product developed through a systematic analysis of problems occurred through the history of money and in the payment systems. Cryptocurrencies try to overcome these problems and are thus regarded as the latest evolution of money. For further research, altcoins and comparisons between cryptocurrencies could be beneficial.

References

Capie, F.H. and Wood, G.E. (2003), "Monetary Unions: Theory, History, Public Choice", Routledge.

Chown, J.F. (1994), "A History of Money from AD800", Routledge.

Chown, J. (2003), "A History of Monetary Unions", Routledge.

Davies, G. (2002), "History of Money: From Ancient Times to Present Day", University of Wales Press.

Forrest, J.Y.L., Ying, Y. and Gong Z. (2018), "Currency Wars: Offense and Defense Through Systematic Thinking", Springer.

Grabowski, M. (2019), "Cryptocurrencies: A Primer on Digital Money", Routledge Focus.

Hinds, M. (2006), "Playing Monopoly with the Devil: Dollarization and Domestic Currencies in Developing Countries", Yale University Press.

Weatherford, J. (1997), "The History of Money", Three Rivers Press.

Pınar Koç

3 Exchange Rate Pass-Through to Inflation: The Case of Turkey

Highlights: The exchange rate volatility affects to domestic price level via production costs in countries where production level depends largely on import inputs. Turkey is also one of the countries whose production level depends largely on import inputs. Thereby intermediate good import accounts for about of 76 % total import. It is expected that the exchange rate pass-through to inflation is high in Turkey. In this context, in this study, the validity and stability of the pass through effect hypothesis was analyzed in Turkey for the period 1990:01–2019:01. According to the results of the study, the pass-through effect hypothesis is valid in Turkey.

Keywords: Exchange rate, inflation, pass-through, price stability, time varying causality

Introduction

Uncertainty in the financial markets significantly affects the inflows of foreign currency and they upset global economic balances. Within this framework, the effect of exchange rate volatility on domestic prices can be defined as the exchange rate pass-through to domestic prices. The degree of pass-through effect varies from country to country, and it is higher than countries whose production is based on the use of import input. Turkey has been significantly integrated into the international markets, and it is one of the countries which has a high marginal propensity to import. The use of imported intermediate input accounts for about 76 % of total imports in Turkey. In this context, it is expected that exchange rate fluctuations increase domestic inflation when financial uncertainties are high.

Analysis of the degree pass-through effect is important to maintain price stability. Thereby, the aim of this study is to analyze the existence of the pass-through effect by using symmetric and asymmetric causality tests for the period 1990:01–2019:01. In addition to this, the time varying causality test was used to analyze the consistency of causality relationship.

This study consists of six sections. The first section is introduction section. In the second section, the pass-through effect is examined theoretically. In the third section, empirical studies analyzing the pass through effect are checked. In the other sections, the method and the results of the study are discussed.

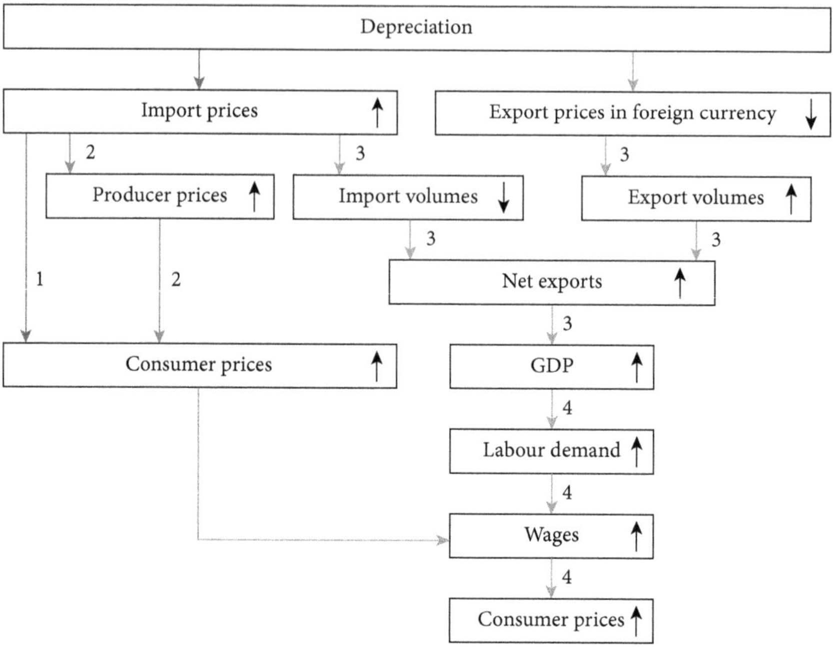

Fig. 3.1: Exchange rate pass-through to inflation
Source: ECB, 2016: 2

1 Theoretical Framework

The effect of the currency volatilities on the domestic prices is called exchange rate pass-through to inflation. The currency volatilities effect domestic prices via prices of final goods that are imported and prices of imported inputs that are used in the domestic production of goods.

The channels of direct and indirect effect are seen in Fig. 3.1. An increase in exchange rate rises import prices. An increase in import prices also reflect prices of final consumption goods. The degree of pass-through effect depends on the exporter company's pricing strategy. If prices of imported goods are determined with importer's unit of currency, an increase in the exchange rate will automatically rises prices of imported goods. Thereby, the domestic prices level also will go up. However, if prices of imported goods are determined with the local currency, currency volatilities will not increase domestic prices.

Indirect effect channels rely on production costs and real factors while the direct effect channels depend on monetary factors. Local currency depreciates when the exchange rate increases. In this case, import prices rise and export prices decrease. Net export increases. An increase in the net export increases labor demand by increasing the national income. An increase in labor demand rise production costs by rising wages. Therefore, the prices of final goods go up.

Analyzing the duration and degree of pass-through effect is important for central banks applying inflation targeting regime. In the countries where monetary policies are based on inflation targeting regime, if the actual inflation falls below targeted inflation, the nominal interest rate will be reduced by the Central Bank. In case the actual inflation exceeds the targeted inflation, the nominal interest rate will be raised to reach targeted inflation. If the degree of the pass-through effect is high, the central bank changes short-term policy interest rates. In countries where inflation targeting and floating exchange rate regime are applied together, the relationship between exchange rate and domestic prices weakens. Devaluation expectations serve as a nominal anchor in countries where fixed exchange rate regime is applied. Therefore, the exchange rate volatilities have a significant effect on inflation in these countries.

Increases in the short-term capital inflows led to economic crises in many countries applying exchange rate targeting in the 1990s. Therefore, monetary policy strategies based on inflation targeting have started to be implemented instead of exchange rate targeting in many developing and developed countries. Determining the degree of pass-through is important to minimize the differences between targeting inflation and actual inflation rate and to select optimal the interest rate in the countries implementing inflation targeting regime.

The monetary policies based on the inflation targeting regime was started to be implemented in Turkey in 2002. Central Bank of Republic of Turkey employed implicit inflation targeting regime in 2002. Open inflation targeting regime has been implemented after the necessary conditions for the transition process have been ensured. Open inflation targeting regime has been implemented in Turkey since 2006. Therefore, the analyzing pass-through effect and determining the degree of pass-through are important to ensure price stability in Turkey. Exchange rate pass-through to inflation and stability of pass-through was analyzed in Turkey for the period 1990:01–2019:01. The aim of this study is to determine the periods in which the pass-through effect emerged by using time varying symmetrical and asymmetric causality tests.

2 Literature Review

The first studies about pass-through effect were conducted in the 1980s. In the 1990s, many studies were carried about pass-through effect in the developed countries. The studies conducted by Dixit and Stiglitz (1977), Dornbusch (1987), and Krugman (1987) are based on microeconomic theory. In these studies, it was emphasized that incomplete competition conditions and the firm's pricing strategies significantly affects the degree of pass-through.

At the end of the 1990s, studies about the role of pass-through effect in ensuring monetary policy effectiveness were prepared instead of studies based on microeconomic theory because of gaining continuity exchange rate fluctuations and global trade deficits. Taylor (2000), Obstfeld and Rogoff (2000) are the studies examining pass-through effect within the framework of new macroeconomic models. Obstfeld and Rogoff (2000) emphasized that sticky prices and wages significantly affect the degree of pass-through and monetary policy effectiveness.

Obstfeld (2002) emphasized that exchange rate targeting is more effective inflation targeting because exchange rate fluctuations cannot change consumption expenditures.

Naknoi (2008) examined how nominal and cross-exchange rates affect export prices by using a stochastic dynamic general equilibrium model of comparative advantage with Money. The study concluded that productivity shocks do not change the covariance across exchange rate regimes, and the relative price of traded goods determines the real exchange rates.

Auer and Schoenle (2015) showed the effect of market structure on the pass-through effect. According to results obtained, the use of a common currency in foreign increases the pass-through effect by up to four times.

Aron et al. (2014) and Baharumshah, Sirag, and Soon (2017) deal with pass-through effect in South Africa. The results of these studies show that the pass-through effect decreases during periods of inflation targeting.

Borensztein and Queijo Von Heideken (2016) analyzed pass-through effect in South America. The study showed that the transition to free floating currency rate and increased confidence in monetary policy decrease pass-through effect.

Musti (2016), Rahadyan and Lubis (2018) examined the pass-through effect in Nigeria and Indonesia, respectively. Pass-through effect is small and slow in both countries.

Comunale and Simola (2018) explored factors determining the degree of pass-through effect. According to results obtained, global factors and financial slacks affect size of pass-through.

The study conducted by Peker and Görmüş (2008) examined the pass-through effect in Turkey for the period 1987–2007. VAR Analysis was used in the study. The results prove that exchange rates are the main determinant of inflation.

Damar (2010) dealt with pass-through effect by using VEC model for the period 1995:01–2000:06 and 2002:01–2009:12. According to the study, pass-through effect is valid in Turkey. Although there has been a significant decrease in the pass-through effect recently, exchange rate is still an important factor affecting price indicators.

Altıntaş (2014) explored pass-through effect in Turkey for the period 1994–2016. The study shows that pass through effect reduced with inflation targeting regime.

Ergin (2015) examined the pass-through effect in Turkey for the period 2005–2014. According to the results of the study, the pass-through effect hypothesis is valid in Turkey, but the effect has decreased in recent years.

Türk and Çetinkaya (2015) analyzed pass-through effect in Turkey for the period 1987–2013 by using the Granger causality test. According to the results of the study, there is a one-way causality relationship from the exchange rate to inflation.

Alptekin et al. (2016) analyzed whether the pass-through effect hypothesis is valid in Turkey by using VAR for the period 2005:01–2015:04. The pass-through effect hypothesis is valid in Turkey and it tends to decrease.

Tümtürk (2017) examined pass-through effect in Turkey for the period 1994:01–2016:09. VAR analysis was used in the study. According to the study, the effect of the exchange rates on inflation rates decreased.

Akdemir and Özçelik (2018) examined whether the pass-through effect hypothesis is valid in Turkey by using the SVAR model. The study proves that the exchange rates have effect on inflation. But, the effect of the exchange rate on inflation reduced.

Kaya (2018) analyzed the effect of the exchange rate on inflation in the period after the 2001 crisis. VAR analysis was used in the study. The results show that while crude oil import prices are more determinant on inflation in the medium term, exchange rates are more determinant in the short term.

Benk and Kösekahyaoğlu (2019) analyzed validity of the pass-through effect hypothesis in Turkey for the period 2005–2018 by using Granger causality test. The results showed that there is a two-way causality relationship from the exchange rate to CPI while there is a one-way causality relationship from exchange rate to PPI.

Yetim and Yamak (2019) analyzed whether there is a causality relationship between the exchange rate and the inflation by using asymmetric causality test developed by Hatemi-J (2012). The findings show that there is one-way causality from positive exchange rate shocks to positive CPI (Consumer Price Index) shocks.

Unlike other studies, in this study symmetric and asymmetric causality tests were used to analyze pass-through effect in Turkey. Furthermore, time varying symmetric and asymmetric causality tests were used to examine consistency of the causality relationship between variables. In this context, it was possible to examine the periods when the transition effect was seen and not.

3 Methodology and Data Set

The study was conducted for the period 1990:01–2019:01. The nominal exchange rate and CPI values were used in this study. Statistics were obtained from the OECD database. Symmetric causality test formed by Hacker and Hatemi-J (2006) and asymmetric causality test formed by Hatemi-J (2012) were used to analyze existence of pass-through effect. Time varying symmetric and asymmetric causality tests were used to analyze whether the causality relationship between variables changes over time. The hypothesis of this study is as follows:

H_0: The exchange rate has an effect on the inflation
H_1: The exchange rate has no effect on the inflation

The existence of a causal relationship between the positive exchange rate and inflation shocks means that the pass-through effect is valid.

3.1 Symmetric and Asymmetric Causality Test

Hacker and Hatemi-J (2006) emphasized that causality relationships between variables can be examined via the bootstrap method in cases where error terms do not have normal distribution by basing on causality test developed by Toda-Yamamoto (1995).

As in the causality test developed by Toda and Yamamoto, the variables do not need to be static in the same rank order to perform the causality test in the Hacker and Hatemi-J causality test. But, the maximum lag length should be determined and added to the lag length of the VAR equation.

In this context, Hacker and Hatemi-J (2006) causality test based on VAR (p + d_{max}) model is as follows:

$$y_t = \hat{v} + \widehat{A_1} y_{t-1} + \ldots + \widehat{A_p} y_{t-p} + .. + \widehat{A_{p+dmax}} y_{t-p-d} + \widehat{\varepsilon_t} \quad (1)$$

The null and the alternative hypotheses are as follows:

$$H_0: A_1 = A_2 = \ldots A_n = 0$$
$$H_1: A_1 \neq A_2 \neq \ldots A_n = 0$$

Test statistics are compared with critical values based on bootstraps to determine whether there is a causal relationship between variables. If test statistic is higher than critical value based on bootstrap the null hypothesis can be rejected. In this case, there is a causality relationship between the variables.

When the model is rearranged to test the pass-through effect, it can be expressed as follows:

$$lnCPI_t = \hat{v} + \sum_{i=1}^{k} \widehat{A_1} lnCPI_{t-i} + \sum_{J=k+1}^{dmax} \widehat{A_2} lnCPI_{t-j} + \sum_{i=1}^{k} \widehat{A_3} lnEXC_{t-i} + \sum_{J=k+1}^{dmax} \widehat{A_4} lnEXC_{t-i} \quad (2)$$

The null hypothesis is for Equation 2:

H_0: $A_1 = A_2 = A_3 = A_4 = 0$ (The exchange rate does not Granger cause the inflation). If the null hypothesis rejects, the exchange rate does Granger cause the inflation.

Hatemi-J (2012) decomposed the effect of positive and negative shocks by decomposing positive and negative components of variables and then applied the shocks to the causality test developed by Hacker and Hatemi-J (2006). The relationship between positive and negative shocks can be expressed as in Equation 3 and Equation 4.

$$lnCPI_t^+ = \hat{v} + \sum_{i=1}^{k} \widehat{A_1} lnCPI_{t-i}^+ + \sum_{J=k+1}^{dmax} \widehat{A_2} lnCPI_{t-j}^+ + \sum_{i=1}^{k} \widehat{A_3} lnEXC_{t-i}^+ + \sum_{J=k+1}^{dmax} \widehat{A_4} lnEXC_{t-j}^+ \quad (3)$$

$$lnCPI_t^- = \hat{v} + \sum_{i=1}^{k} \widehat{A_1} lnCPI_{t-i}^- + \sum_{J=k+1}^{dmax} \widehat{A_2} lnCPI_{t-j}^- + \sum_{i=1}^{k} \widehat{A_3} lnEXC_{t-i}^- + \sum_{J=k+1}^{dmax} \widehat{A_4} lnEXC_{t-j}^- \quad (4)$$

The null hypothesis in Equation 3 is as follows:

H_0: $A_1 = A_2 = A_3 = A_4 = 0$ (The positive exchange rate shocks does not Granger cause the positive inflation shocks.)

H_1: $A_1 \neq A_2 \neq A_3 \neq A_4 \neq 0$ (The positive exchange rate shocks does Granger cause the positive inflation shocks.)

The null hypothesis in Equation 4 is as follows:

H_0: $A_1 = A_2 = A_3 = A_4 = 0$ (The negative exchange rate shocks does not Granger cause the positive inflation shocks.)

H_1: $A_1 \neq A_2 \neq A_3 \neq A_4 \neq 0$ (The negative exchange rate shocks does Granger cause the negative inflation shocks.)

If test statistic is higher than critical value based on bootstrap the null hypothesis can be rejected. In this case, there is the causality relationship between the positive or negative shocks.

3.2 Time Varying Symmetric and Asymmetric Causality Tests

Causality relationships between variables can vary in time. Economic crises, policy changes, and political instabilities have given rise to change causality relationships between variables. In this context, time varying versions symmetric causality test formed by Hacker and Hatemi J (2006) and asymmetric causality test formed by Hatemi-J (2012) were used to test whether causality relationships between variables change in time, in other words consistency of the causality relationship between variables.

At first, Hatemi-J (2012) causality test is applied to the first 120 observation values. In the second stage, the first observation value is withdrawn from in the model and Hatemi-J (2012) test is applied to the first observation value to the 121_{st} observation value. In this way, the first observation value is withdrawn from in the model and the observation value following the last observation includes the model at each new stage. Hatemi- J (2012) test is applied to each new stage. This process continues until all of the observation values are used. To test the significance of these test statistics, the test statistics obtained in each observation interval are normalized with the bootstrap critical value and these values are plotted. In the graph, the values above the "1" line indicate that the basic hypothesis that symmetric or asymmetric Granger causality does not exist should be rejected.

4 Estimation Results

Series must be stationary to perform time series analyses. Kapetanios unit root test developed by Kapetanios (2005) was used to test whether the series are stationary.

Upon examining the estimation results, it is seen that values calculated for inflation and exchange rate series are smaller than the critical values. The series are not static at the level values. First differences of the series were taken to stabilize the series. The series becomes stationary when the first difference is taken.

Symmetric and asymmetric causality tests were conducted to test whether there is exchange rate pass-through to inflation. The results of symmetric causality test and asymmetric causality test estimation are presented in Tabs. 3.2 and 3.3.

Upon analyzing the estimation results, it is seen that calculated test statistics are smaller than the critical value. Therefore, there is causality from exchange rate to inflation.

Estimation results of asymmetric causality test are in Tab. 3.3. When the results are examined, it is seen that test statistics are higher than the critical

Tab. 3.1: Estimation results of Kapetonios unit root test

<table>
<tr><th>Variables</th><th>Model</th><th>t stat</th><th colspan="3">Critical values</th><th>Break Dates</th></tr>
<tr><td></td><td rowspan="6">Model A</td><td></td><td>%1</td><td>%5</td><td>%10</td><td></td></tr>
<tr><td>LNCPI</td><td>-4.348</td><td rowspan="5">-5.338</td><td rowspan="5">-4.930</td><td rowspan="5">-4.661</td><td>2002m1</td></tr>
<tr><td>LNEXC</td><td>-3.740</td><td>2001m10</td></tr>
<tr><td>Difference</td><td>t stat</td><td>Breaks</td></tr>
<tr><td>Δ LNCPI</td><td>-5.896</td><td>2001m12</td></tr>
<tr><td>Δ LNEXC</td><td>-13.419</td><td>2001m9</td></tr>
</table>

Tab. 3.2: Estimation results of symmetric causality test

Direction of Causality	Test Statistics	Critical Values		
		% 1	% 5	% 10
LNEXC→ LNCPI	19.151	11.980	6.269	4.599

Tab. 3.3: Estimation results of asymmetric causality test

Variables	Direction of Causality	Test Statistics	Critical Values		
			% 1	% 5	% 10
LNEXC→LNCPI	-→ -	4.214	12.790	6.389	4.506
	+ → +	9.669	13.026	6.568	4.583

values. Therefore, there is no causality from negative exchange rate shocks to negative inflation shocks while there is a causality from positive exchange rate shocks to positive inflation shocks.

It is thought that while there is no causality between negative shocks, the existence of causality between positive shocks can be explained by price and wage stickiness.

Time varying symmetric asymmetric causality tests were used to analyze the consistency of causality relationship inflation and exchange rate. The test statistics on the red line in Graph 3.2 and in Graph 3.3 show the periods when the pass-through effect is valid.

According to results of estimation, pass-through effect was observed during January 1990–January 1993, September 1994–October 1995, January 1997–April 1998, May 2007–August 2008, August 2010–May 2011, and September 2014–November 2016. During the period September 2014–November 2016 the pass-through effect was greater than in other periods.

According to estimation results of asymmetric causality test, in addition to periods determined by time varying symmetric causality test, pass-through

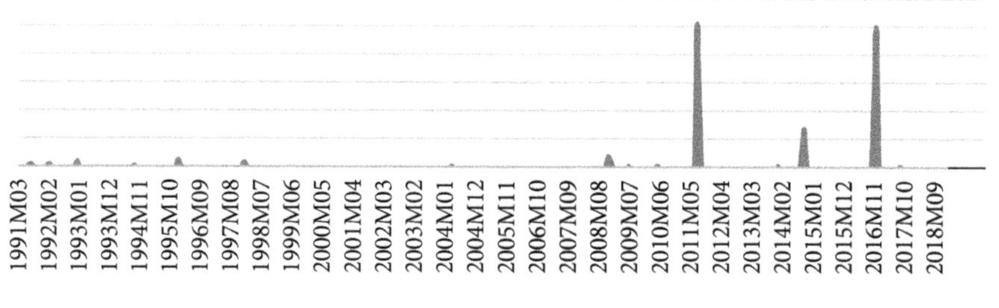

Graph 3.2: Estimation results of time varying symmetric causality test

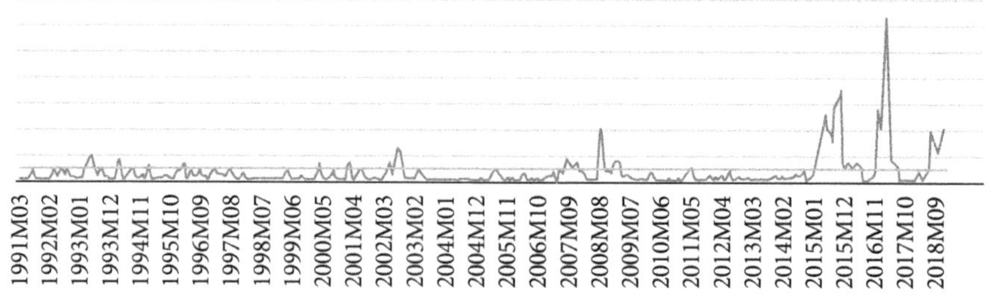

Graph 3.3: Estimation results of asymmetric causality test

effect is valid in periods January1999–February 2003 and April 2005–October 2007. In the period after January 2015, the pass-through effect is higher than other periods.

Applied monetary and fiscal policies significantly affect the degree of pass-through effect. Changing over to free floating currency rate system by adopting protection of the value of Turkish currency law and ensuring the convertibility of Turkish Lira (TL) explain the pass-through effect in the period 1991–1993. In these periods, short-term capital inflows increased rapidly as interest rate was kept higher than exchange rate changes. Therefore, TL appreciated, exports decreased while imports increased. Although it was stated that monetary policies based on monetary targeting will be implemented for the first time in 1990, the targets determined due to high current deficit and high public deficits could not be realized. The interest rate rose because the government resorted to domestic debt instead of using central bank resources to close deficit budget. In addition to this, increases in short-term capital flows caused to the growth of difference between interest rate and exchange rate. The increase in foreign exchange demand of banks that wanted to close their open positions caused the economic crisis in 1994. The inflation rates increased from 70 % to 105 % due to the crisis. Despite the implementation of the April 5th stabilization program, inflation rates declined to only 89 % in 1995.

Although Turkey's economy entered a growth trend in the period April 1995–1998, political instabilities, 1997 South Asian financial crises, and 1998 Russia Crisis caused the growth process to slow down. Because of these crises the foreign trade deficits increased. In addition to this, there was a rise in hot money outflows. It was decided that exchange rate was used as a nominal anchor by implementing an anti-inflationary stabilization policy with the standby agreement with the IMF in June 1998. Despite the November 2000 and February 2001 crises causing significant volatilities in the exchange rates and in the inflation rates, in the time varying symmetric causality test, it is seen that there is no causality between the exchange rate and the inflation rates in the period April 1998–May 2007. But, according to the results of the time varying asymmetric causality test, there is causality from positive exchange rate shocks to positive inflation shocks in the period April 1999–February 2003. The main reason of for the variability of the results is that the positive and negative shocks have the same effect in the symmetric causality test.

Periods June 2006–September 2007 are other periods in which pass-through effect is high. Exchange rate volatilities has increased due to capital outflows seen in emerging market economies since May 2006. In addition to exchange rate volatilities, increases in oil and commodity prices played an important role in feeding inflation. The causality relationship seen in August 2008 is mainly due to the global crisis.

In the period after January 2015, the pass-through effect is higher than other periods, and this effect is still continuing. Increases in exchange rates rise inflation. Uncertainties in the financial markets, the problems in military coup and election processes have caused the exchange rate and inflation spiral.

Conclusion

The exchange rates have an important effect on inflation in countries where production depends largely on imported inputs and the use of imported intermediate input accounts for about 76 % of total imports in Turkey. In this context, it is expected that the degree of the pass-through effect is high in Turkey. In this study covering the periods 1990:01–2019:01, the validity and consistency of the exchange rate pass-through to inflation in Turkey was analyzed. According to results of estimation, pass-through effect was observed in the following periods: January 1990–January 1993, September 1994–October 1995, January 1997–April 1998, May 2007–August 2008, August 2010–May 2011, and September 2014–November 2016. In the period of September 2014–November 2016, the pass-through effect is greater than in other periods.

According to estimation results of asymmetric causality test, in addition to periods determined by time varying symmetric causality test, pass-through effect is valid in periods January1999–February 2003 and April 2005–October 2007. In the period after January 2015, the pass-through effect is higher than other periods.

The results obtained in this study are consistent with studies that examined the validity of pass-through effect hypothesis. The exchange rate has an important effect on the inflation. Although this effect has recently decreased with inflation targeting regime, it strongly increased after January 2015. This finding is consistent with the results obtained by Damar (2010). Unlike other studies, in this study, it is also possible to examine the periods in which the pass-through effect is valid or not.

Monetary and fiscal policies applied, the problems in military coups and election processes have lead the exchange rate and inflation spiral by causing short-term capital outflows.

References

Akdemir, S. & Özçelik, M. (2018). Pass Through of Exchange Rates to Domestic Prices: An Application for Turkish Economy in the Period of 2003–2017. Ekonomik ve Sosyal Araştırmalar Dergisi. Cilt:14, Sayı:1, p. 35–50.

Alptekin, V., Yılmaz, K. Ç. & Taş, T. (2016). Exchange Pass Through on Prices: The Case of Turkey. Selçük Üniversitesi Sosyal Bilimler Enstitüsü Dergisi. 35, p. 1–9.

Altıntaş, H. (2014). Türkiye'de Döviz Kurunun Enflasyon Üzerine Geçiş Etkisinin Ekonometrik Analizi: 1987– 2011. Uludağ Üniversitesi İktisadi ve İdari Bilimler Fakültesi Dergisi, 33(1), 163–201.

Aron, J., Macdonald, R. & Muellbauer, J. (2014). Exchange Rate Pass Through in Developing and Emerging Markets: A Survey of Conceptual, Methodological and Policy Issues and Selected Empirical Findings. Journal of Monetary Economics. 50(1), p. 101–143.

Auer, R. & Schoenle, R. (2015). Market Structure and Exchange Rate Pass Through. Journal of International Economics. 98, p. 60–77.

Baharamshah, A. Z., Sirag, A. & Soon, S. (2017). Asymmetric Exchange Rate Pass-Through in an Emerging Market Economy: The Case of Mexico. Research in International Business and Finance. 41, p. 247–259.

Benk, H. & Köseyahyaoğlu, L. (2019). Pass Through Effect from Exchange Rate to Inflation in Turkey: A Study Over the Period 2005–2018. Uygulamalı Sosyal Bilimler ve Güzel Sanatlar Dergisi. 1(2), p. 117–133.

Borensztein, E. & Queijo Von Heideken, V. (2016). Exchange Rate Pass-Through in South America: An Overview. IDB Working Paper Series, Paner No:710.

Comunale, M. & Simola, H. (2018). The Pass Through to Consumer Prices in CIS Economies: The Role of Exchange Rates, Commodities and Other Common Factors. Research in International Business and Finance. 44, p. 186–217.

Damar, A. O. (2010). Türkiye'de Döviz Kurundan Fiyatlara Geçiş Etkisinin İncelenmesi. Uzmanlık Yeterlilik Tezi. Ankara: TCMB.

Dixit, A., & Stiglitz, J. E. (1977). Monopolistic Competition and Optimum Product Diversity. American Economic Review. 67, p. 297–308.

Dornbusch, R. (1987). Exchange Rates and Prices. American Economic Review, 77(1), p. 93–106.

ECB (2016). Exchange Rate Pass Through in Euro Area Inflation. https://www.ecb.europa.eu/pub/pdf/other/eb201607_article01.en.pdf, Erişim Tarihi: 04.04.2019.

Ergin, A. (2015). Döviz Kuru ve Enflasyon Arasındaki Geçiş Etkisi: Türkiye Örneği. Ömer Halisdemir Üniversitesi İktisadi ve İdari Bilimler Fakültesi Dergisi. 8(3), p. 13–209.

Hacker, R. S. & Hatemi-J, A. (2006). Test for Causality between Integrated Variables Using Asymptotic and Bootstrap Distributions: Theory and Application. Applied Economics. 38(13), p. 1489–1500.

Hatemi-J, A. (2012). Asymmetric Causality Tests with an Application. Empirical Economics. 43(1), p. 447–456.

Kapetanios, G. (2005). Unit Root Testing against the Alternative Hypothesis of Up to M Structural Breaks. Journal of Time Series Analysis. 26, p. 123–133.

Kaya, H. (2018). Relationship between Exchange Rate and Inflation in Turkish Economy Post-2001 Crisis: VAR Analysis of the Exchange Rate Pass-Through. Ankara Üniversitesi SBF Dergisi. 73(3), p. 841–865.

Krugman, P. (1987). Pricing to Market When the Exchange Rate Changes. In S. W. Ardnt & J.D. Richardson (Eds.), Real Financial Linkages Among Open Economies Chapter 3, (pp. 49–70). Cambridge, MA: MIT Press.

Musti, M. B. (2016). The Effect of Exchange Rate Changes on Consumer Prices in Nigeria: Evidence from VECM Model. The Economic and Finance Letters. 3, p. 30–38.

Naknoi, K. (2008). Real Exchange Rate Fluctuations, Endogenous Tradability and Exchange Rate Regimes. Journal of Monetary Economics. 55(3), p. 645–663.

Obstfeld, M. (2002). Exchange Rate and Adjustment: Perspectives from the New Open Economy Macroeconomics NBER Working Paper, Paper No: 9118.

Obstfeld, M. & Rogoff, K. (2000). The Six Major Puzzles in International Macroeconomics: Is There Common Cause? NBER Working Paper, Paper No: 7777.

Peker, O. & Görmüş, Ş. (2008). Inflationary Effects of Exchanges Rate in Turkey. Süleyman Demirel Üniversitesi İktisadi ve İdari Bilimler Fakültesi Dergisi. C.13, S.2, p. 187–202.

Rahadyan, H. & Lubis, A. (2018). Monetary Integration in the ASEAN Economic Community Challenge: The Role of the Exchange Rate on Inflation in Indonesia. International Journal of Services Technology and Management, 24 (5–6), 463–479.

Taylor, J. B. (2000). Low Inflation, Pass-Through and the Pricing Power of Firms. European Economic Review, 44, p. 1398–1408.

Toda, H. Y. & Yamamoto, T. (1995). Statistical Inferences in Vector Autoregressions with Possibly Integrated Processes. Journal of Econometrics. 66, p. 225–250.

Tümtürk, O. (2017). Exchange Rate Pass-Through into Domestic Prices and Inflation Targeting in Turkey. Yönetim ve Ekonomi. Cilt: 24, Sayı:3, p. 837–855.

Türk, E. & Çetinkaya, A. T. (2015). Döviz Kurundan Fiyatlara Geçiş Etkisinin Granger Nedesellik Testi ile İncelenmesi.Türkiye Örneği. Kırıkkale Üniversitesi Sosyal Bilimler Dergisi. 5(1), p. 27–37.

Yetim, M. & Yamak, R. (2019). Exchange Rate Pass Through in Turkey: Hatemi J Asymmetric Causality Test. Trakya Üniversitesi Sosyal Bilimler Dergisi, Cilt: 21, Sayı:1, p. 203–221.

Aydanur Gacener Atış, Deniz Erer, and Elif Erer

4 Nonlinear Exchange Rate Pass-Through to Inflation: A Comparison of Turkey and BRICS Countries

Highlights: The aim of this study is to analyze the exchange rate pass-through to inflation in view of Taylor's hypothesis by using a nonlinear time series model over the period of 1999:01–2019:12 in Turkey and BRICS countries. Due to the theoretical model of the exchange rate pass-through effect, we indicate the nonlinear dynamics of the exchange rate pass-through by estimating the Markov switching vector autoregressive (MSIAH-VAR) model. The obtained results indicate that the exchange rate pass-through to inflation is higher in unstable regimes than stable regimes in Turkey and Brazil. However, pass-through in China is significant only in an unstable regime, but in Russia it impacts a little to inflation in a stable regime. These results mean Taylor's hypothesis is valid in Turkey, Brazil, and Russia.

Keywords: Exchange rate pass-through, inflation, exchange rate, nonlinear modeling

Introduction

It is surely down to the central bank to decide over which way the monetary policy will be implemented, or rather, what kind of methods will be implemented in order to keep price stability in the economy. Thus, it is important to understand the extent of exchange rate pass-through to domestic prices in terms of assessing international spillover effects of monetary policy. As Plantin and Shin (2016) have it, exchange rate pass-through is an important factor affecting the financial risk-taking channel of monetary policy. Ball (1999) has expressed that the stance of monetary policy may be based on the degree of pass-through. So, it should be investigated how current inflation has been affected by previous changes in the exchange rate and how inflation forecasts made by the central bank will be influenced by so-called changes. For this reason, to know the degree of pass-through is vitally important to conduct appropriate monetary and exchange rate policies both in ex-post and ex-ante terms (Junttila and Korhonen, 2012).

Exchange rate pass-through to domestic prices is generally defined as the percentage change in the domestic price index due to the shocks in the exchange rate. In other words, exchange rate pass-through can be considered as the mechanism through which the price of imports in domestic currency is affected by exchange rate volatility. When the exchange rate rises, imports become more expensive. Changes in import prices arising from shocks in exchange rates lead to passing the so-called effect on the domestic price index in accordance with the share of imports in the index. Therefore, the prices of domestic goods will increase depending on the cost increases of domestic producers (Arbatlı, 2003).

The relationship between exchange rate pass-through and domestic prices may be nonlinear (Taylor, 2000; Sekine, 2006; Devereux and Yetman, 2010). Taylor (2000) discussed the effect of inflation regimes on exchange rate pass-through. According to him, it is difficult for firms to absolutely pass-through changes in the exchange rate to their export prices due to international competitive pressure in the period of low inflation regime, but it is stronger in the period of high inflation regime. Devereux and Yetman (2010) stated that a small change in the exchange rate may not affect the product prices in importing countries while a large shock in the exchange rate may cause price adjustment.

The aim of the study is to examine Taylor's hypothesis based on exchange rate pass-through to inflation by estimating nonlinear time series model over the period of 1999:01–2019:12. To this end, we applied the MSIAH-VAR model. Policymakers implementing monetary policy take into account developing an appropriate policy response to macroeconomic shocks in order to stabilize aggregate demand fluctuations. The responses of nominal or real variables to specific shocks are not always the same. Thus, appropriate policy responses should involve nonlinear dynamic responses of nominal and real macroeconomic variables. The empirical literature related to pass-through from the exchange rate to domestic prices generally has indicated the pass-through effect is higher in emerging economies than in advanced ones. However, the studies analyzing the role of asymmetry and nonlinearity on exchange rate pass-through have remained limited. In this respect, we aim to complete deficiency in the literature.

The rest of the study is designed as follows. In the second section, we exhibit the existing literature focused on exchange rate pass-through to inflation. Then, we clarify the data and econometric methodology used in the study in the third section. We exhibit empirical results from the MSIAH-VAR models in the fourth section, and conclusion in the last section.

1 Literature

The exchange rate pass-through to import prices and domestic prices has been discussed comprehensively in literature. The most prominent studies related to the effect in question are Feinberg (1986, 1989) and Woo (1984). These studies have indicated pass-through effects from exchange rate and import price changes to domestic consumer and producer prices. Feinberg (1986, 1989) examined the exchange rate pass-through to domestic producer prices in the United States and Germany and found that the pass-through effect is higher in the industries in which concentration was less and import penetration was higher. After these studies, many studies have been done on the effect in question (Dellmo, 1996; Goldberg and Knetter, 1997; Kim, 1998; Calvo and Reinhart, 2002; Hausman et al., 2006; Tica and Posedel, 2009; Jasova et al., 2016).

Goldberg and Knetter (1997) expressed that the so-called effect is less in more segmented industries. Kim (1998) found that exchange rate fluctuations have a negative effect on the producer price index in the long term in the United States. Dellmo (1996) showed the impact of import prices on the Consumer Price Index (CPI) is weak in Sweden. Calvo and Reinhart (2002) emphasized the large exchange rate pass-through effect and liability dollarization. According to Hausman et al. (2006), a high degree of the pass-through effect is one of the main reasons for concerns about exchange rate fluctuations. Jasova et al. (2016) found that the exchange rate pass-through to domestic prices in emerging countries diminished after the financial crisis because of decreasing inflation while the pass-through effect is low and stable in advanced economies.

Some studies in literature have concentrated nonlinear relationship between exchange rate pass-through and domestic producer and consumer prices (Taylor, 2000; Sekine, 2006; Al-Abri and Goodwin, 2009; Tica and Posedel, 2009; Devereux and Yetman, 2010; Nogueira Junior and Leon-Ledesma, 2010; Junttila and Korhonen, 2012; Frankel et al., 2013; Ozkan and Erden, 2015; Rincón and Rodríguez, 2016; Turner and Wood, 2017; Caselli and Roitmann, 2019). According to Taylor (2000), the exchange rate pass-through to domestic prices is less in low-inflation regime, but it is higher in the high-inflation regime. Sekine (2006) investigated exchange rate pass-through for the United States, Japan, Germany, the United Kingdom, France, and Italy using a time-varying parameter with a stochastic model. He adopted two-stage pass-through. He presented the effect of exchange rate changes to import prices in the first stage pass-through and explained the effect of import price changes to consumer prices in the second stage pass-through. From the results of the study, he found that the pass-through effect has decreased over time for all countries in both stages. Tica and Posedel (2009) analyzed the exchange rate pass-through effect using a threshold model in Croatia. From the finding of the study, they concluded that exchange rate pass-through is asymmetric and so the so-called effect is weak or statistically insignificant below threshold value while it is stronger and significant above a threshold value. Al-Abri and Goodwin (2009) examined the relationship between the nominal effective exchange rate and import prices of 16 OECD countries by using the threshold cointegration method. From the results of the study, they concluded that shocks in the nominal effective exchange rate have a greater effect on import prices, and these prices respond faster to so-called shocks than more conventional models.

Devereux and Yetman (2010) inferred from the findings of the study that a small change in the exchange rate may not affect the product prices in importing countries while a large shock in the exchange rate may cause price adjustment. Nogueira Junior and Leon-Ledesma (2010) explained the exchange rate pass-through to domestic inflation for 12 developed and emerging countries using a state-space model which allowed time variation. They showed pass-through effect tends to smooth decrease over time. However, they did not find any evidence supporting the hypothesis that lower inflation takes precedence of decreasing the degree of exchange rate pass-through. Junttila and Korhonen (2012) analyzed the exchange rate pass-through to import prices for nine OECD countries using threshold and smooth transition estimation models. They expressed that the degree of pass-through is based on the inflation regime in importing countries and that there is a positive relationship between pass-through and inflation. Frankel et al. (2013) and Ozkan and Erden (2015) indicated that the pass-through derived from exchange rate movements above a certain threshold value is higher. Rincón and Rodríguez (2016) used monthly data from Colombia for the period 2002 to 2015. The main findings show that the exchange rate pass-through is incomplete endogenous and then changes over time and it is non-linear and asymmetric in the short and long terms for the state of the economy and to exchange rate shocks. Turner and Wood (2017) investigated empirically using quarterly data for the period 1979q1–2015q1 for a sample of 17 countries. They found out a significant positive nonlinear relationship for the two largest economies (the USA and Japan). Caselli and Roitmann (2019) analyzed nonlinearities and asymmetries in the transmission of exchange rate fluctuations to prices in a panel of 27 emerging markets for the period 1990–2013. Their findings suggest that the pass-through becomes nonlinear when the exchange rate depreciates by more than 24 %.

There are various studies in relation to effect of exchange rate pass-through in Turkey (Arbatlı, 2003; Kara et al., 2007; Kara and Öğünç, 2008; Yüncüler, 2011; Kara and Öğünç, 2012; Karagöz et al., 2016). Arbatlı (2003) analyzed the extent of exchange rate pass-through to domestic prices using the Threshold VAR (TVAR) model. From the findings of the study, she concluded that the pass-through effect is lower in economic contraction. Kara et al. (2007) expressed pass-through has decreased since the floating exchange rate regime. Kara and

Öğünç (2008) investigated pass-through from imported inflation to domestic inflation using a linear VAR model. They found that pass-through to domestic prices has decreased and slowed down since inflation targeting policy. Similarly, Yüncüler (2011) estimated pass-through effect before and after inflation targeting and stated that inflation targeting leads to a decrease in the so-called effect. Kara and Öğünç (2012) analyzed the effect of the exchange rate and import prices on core consumer prices using the VAR model. From the results of the study, they concluded that the relationship between the exchange rate and consumer prices continues to decline. Also, they showed import price pass-through is as important as the exchange rate pass-through. Karagöz et al. (2016) compared Asia-Pacific, South American, and Turkish economies in terms of pass-through effect from the exchange rate to domestic prices using the Panel VAR model. From the findings of the study, they concluded that the exchange rate pass-through effect in Asia-Pacific economies is lower than in Latin American and Turkish countries.

2 Data and Methodology

In this study, we used Markov Regime Switching Vector Autoregressive (MS-VAR) model in order to examine exchange rate pass-through to domestic inflation for Turkey and BRICS (Brazil, Russia, India, China, and South Africa) during the period 1999:01–2019:12. The reason why the time period covers 1999:01–2019:12 is that the starting date of so-called variables is 1999: 01. By means of the MS-VAR model, we acquire different impulse-response functions for different economic regimes. Therefore, we show empirical evidence for the validity of the hypothesis of Taylor (2000).

MS-VAR model is an expanded version of univariate Markov regime-switching model purposed by Hamilton (1989). MS-VAR model was developed by Krolzig (1997). The underlying main idea of this model is to allow the parameters relating to the vector autoregressive model to change with regimes when the system changes occur. The MS-VAR model is based on three main conventions. The first convention is the VAR model which has a linear and time-invariant structure. The second convention is the hidden Markov chain model. Lastly, the third convention is the Markov regime-switching model (Krolzig, 1997). When the system is exposed to regime switching, the parameters of the VAR process may vary over time. However, indicating a dominated regime at time t can be invariant due to the unobserved regime variable. M indicates the number of possible regimes, which is a conditional probability density function of a time series vector, as follows:

$$p(y_t|Y_{t-1},s_t) = \begin{cases} f((y_t|Y_{t-1},\theta_1) & \text{if} \quad s_t = 1 \\ \dots & \\ f((y_t|Y_{t-1},\theta_M) & \text{if} \quad s_t = 1 \end{cases}$$

here, θ_M indicates VAR parameter vector in the regime of $m=1,\dots, M$ and Y_{t-1} are observations <<Inline_fig-01>> (Krolzig, 2000). For a given s_t regime, y_t, which is time series vector with vector autoregressive process at degree of p, is calculated as follows:

$$E(y_t|Y_{t-1},s_t) = v(s_t) + \sum_{j=1}^{p} A_j(s_t)y_{t-j}$$

In case VAR process is defined depending on an unobserved regime, the mechanism generating data have to provide assumptions regarding to the mechanism generating process. The discrete state of the regime is generated by homogenous Markov chain in the MS-VAR model.

$$\Pr\left(s_t\middle|\{s_{t-j}\}_{j=1}^{\infty},\{y_{t-j}\}_{j=1}^{\infty}\right) = \Pr(s_t|s_{t-1},p)$$

Here, p indicates the parameter vector generating regime relating to the process. MS-VAR model with M regime and degree of p are as follows:

$$y_t - \mu(s_t) = A_1(s_t)(y_{t-1} - \mu(s_{t-1})) + \dots + A_p(s_t)\left(y_{t-p} - \mu(s_{t-p})\right) + u_t$$

Here, <<Inline_Fig-02>> are parameter-varying functions defining dependent structure of parameters.

$$\mu(s_t) = \begin{cases} \mu_1 & \text{eğer } s_t = 1 \\ \dots & \\ \mu_M & \text{eğer } s_t = M \end{cases}$$

Following the studies in the literature (Goldberg and Knetter, 1997; Campa and Goldberg, 2005; Steel and King, 2004; Caselli and Roitman, 2016), we used monthly data including percentage change on the same period of the previous year of CPI, nominal effective exchange rates and output gap for Turkey and BRICS, and percentage change on the same period of the previous year of CPI for G20 countries to proxy for foreign prices. We obtain the output gap from the Industrial Production Index by using the Hodrick Prescott filter. We obtain a dataset that involves the CPI and the Industrial Production Index from the

OECD database and the nominal effective exchange rate from the Bruegel database. The variables used in this study are presented in Tab. 4.1.

Figure 4.1 indicates the cycle series from Industrial Production Index by using Hodrick Prescott filter for Turkey and BRICS countries. Figure 4.2 indicates the percentage change in the same period of the previous year of the CPI for Turkey and BRICS countries. Finally, Fig. 4.3 indicates the nominal effective exchange rate for Turkey and BRICS countries.

3 Empirical Results

Before we estimate the models related to exchange rate pass-through to domestic prices, firstly stationary of the variables is examined by Dickey-Fuller GLS (ERS) unit root test. The reason is that the analysis with nonstationary variables causes a spurious regression problem and therefore leads to a misprediction of the relationship in question. DF-GLS unit root test results for the variables are in Tab. 4.2.

According to the results of DF-GLS (ERS) unit root test with both constant and constant and trend, the variables of CPI_TR, CPI_BR, CPI_RU, CPI_IN, CPI_CN, CPI_ZA, CPI*, NEER_TR, NEER_BR, NEER_RU, NEER_IN, NEER_CN, and NEER_ZA are not stationary at %5 significance level. However, so-called variables become stationary at first differences. The variables of Outputgap_TR, Outputgap_BR, Outputgap_RU, Outputgap_IN, Outputgap_CN, and Outputgap_ZA are stationary at level. After applying the DF-GLS (ERS) unit root test for the variables in question, we investigated if the vector autoregression model has linear through LR and Davies linearity tests. The results of LR and Davies linearity tests are shown in Tab. 4.3.

According to the LR test, the models of Turkey and BRICS countries have nonlinear structures. Similarly, Davies test results indicate to reject the null hypothesis that all coefficients in the model are equal in regimes. The results of LR test to determine number of regimes show that two regimes are valid. Consequently, it can be stated that the models with two regimes are appropriate and so-called models have the coefficients across different regimes. Thus, we estimated the MSIAH-VAR model to investigate asymmetrically exchange rate pass-through to domestic prices.

The estimation results of MSIAH-VAR model with two regimes are presented in Tab. 4.4. Here, Regime 1 represents high inflation regime and Regime 2 represents low inflation regime. Table 4.5 shows regime transition probabilities from the models in questions.

Tab. 4.1: Data sources

Variables	Description	Data Source
CPI_TR	CPI for Turkey	OECD Database
CPI_BR	CPI for Brazil	OECD Database
CPI_RU	CPI for Russia	OECD Database
CPI_IN	CPI for India	OECD Database
CPI_CN	CPI for China	OECD Database
CPI_ZA	CPI for South Africa	OECD Database
CPI^*	CPI for G20 countries	OECD Database
NEER_TR	Nominal effective exchange rate for Turkey	Bruegel Database
NEER_BR	Nominal effective exchange rate for Brazil	Bruegel Database
NEER_RU	Nominal effective exchange rate for Russia	Bruegel Database
NEER_IN	Nominal effective exchange rate for India	Bruegel Database
NEER_CN	Nominal effective exchange rate for China	Bruegel Database
NEER_ZA	Nominal effective exchange rate for South Africa	Bruegel Database
Outputgap_TR	Cycle series for Turkey	OECD Database
Outputgap_BR	Cycle series for Brazil	OECD Database
Outputgap_RU	Cycle series for Russia	OECD Database
Outputgap_IN	Cycle series for India	OECD Database
Outputgap_CN	Cycle series for China	OECD Database
Outputgap_ZA	Cycle series for South Africa	OECD Database

Source: Author's own construction

As seen in Tab. 4.4, the exchange rate pass-through varies dramatically across two regimes. Accordingly, the exchange rate pass-through effect is %16 in the high inflation regime, but %5.7 in the low inflation regime in Turkey. In other words, %16 of increases in the nominal effective exchange rate is directly reflected in consumer prices in an unstable regime while it is %5.7 in the stable regime. As the effects of exchange rate pass-through in the studies for Turkish economy was found %15, the results obtained from in this study are consistent with the literature. The results of Brazil are similar to Turkey. Exchange rate pass-through to domestic consumer prices is %16 in high inflation regime and %1 in the low inflation regime. However, the exchange rate pass-through effect in China is significant (%15) in only a high inflation regime, while the exchange rate pass-through effect in Russia is very little (%3) in only a low inflation regime. The exchange rate pass-through effect to consumer prices is insignificant in both India and South Africa.

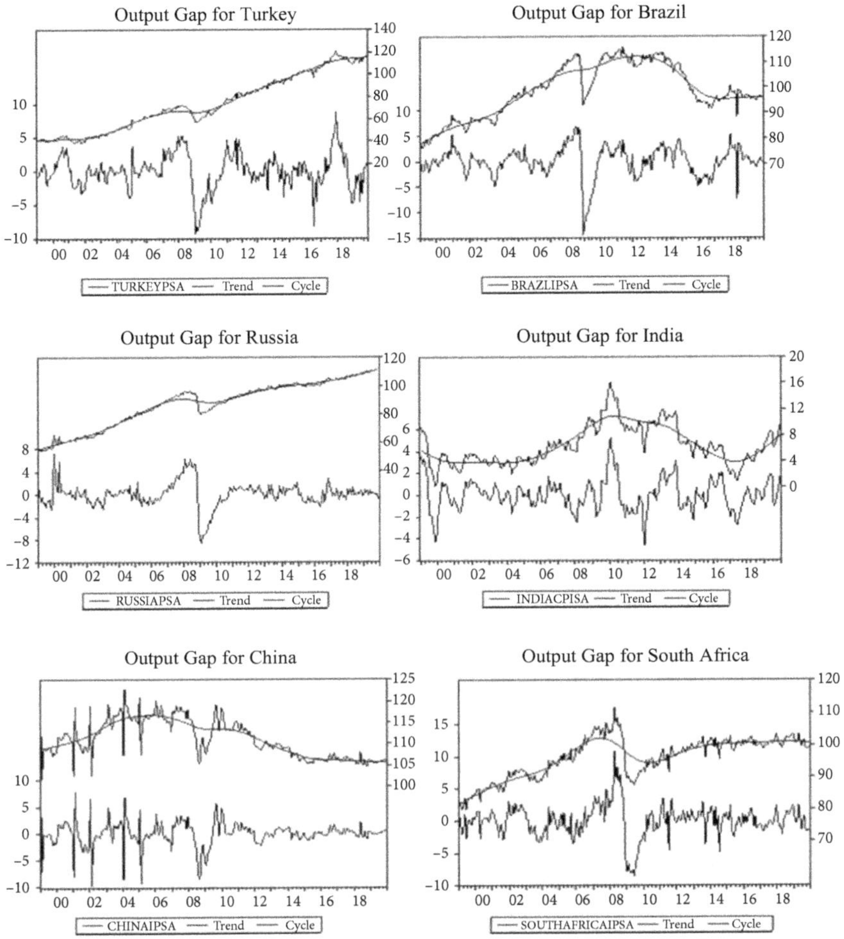

Fig. 4.1: Time series, trend, and cycle graphs of the variables for Turkey and BRICS countries

Source: Author's own calculation

Regime transition probabilities, for the involved models, are shown in Tab. 4.5. According to the MSIAH-VAR model for Turkey. Regime transition probability from Regime 1 to Regime 1 and from Regime 2 to Regime 2 are, respectively, 0.9159 and 0.9629. However, regime transition probability from Regime 1 to Regime 2 is 0.0841 and 0.0371 in other case. This result suggests that the

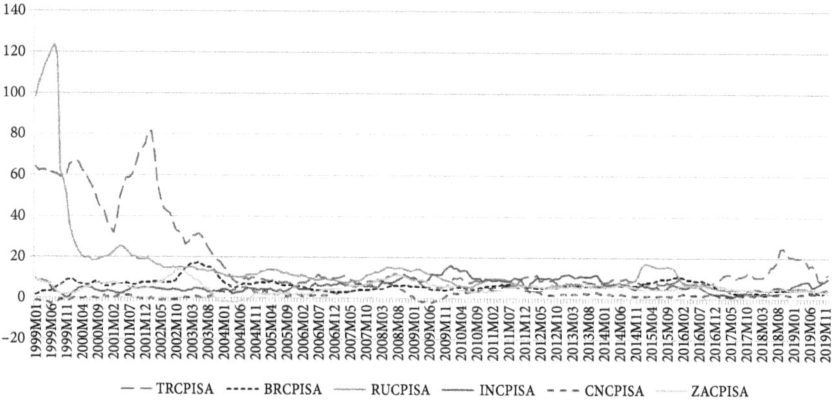

Fig. 4.2: Percentage change on the same period of the previous year of CPI for Turkey and BRICS countries

Source: Author's own calculation

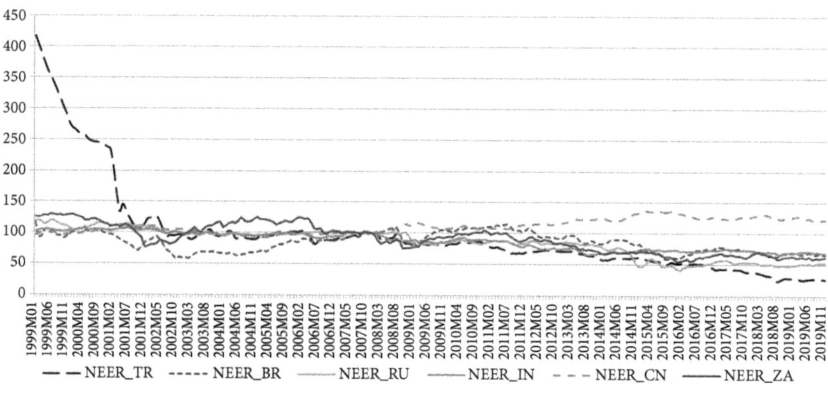

Fig. 4.3: Nominal effective exchange rate for Turkey and BRICS countries

Source: Author's own calculation

regimes are persistent in Turkey. Duration is 11.89 months in Regime 1 and 26.93 months in Regime 2 for Turkey.

As considered in the MSIAH-VAR model for Brazil, regime transition probabilities from Regime 1 to Regime 1 and from Regime 2 to Regime 2 are, respectively, 0.5254 and 0.9629. Regime transition probability from Regime 1 to Regime

Tab. 4.2: The results of DF-GLS (ERS) unit root test

Variables	Constant	Cons. Trend	Variables	Constant	Cons. Trend
CPI_TR	-0.0230 (5)	-0.8316(5)	ΔCPI_TR	-4.3206(4)***	-5.5430(4)***
CPI_BR	-1.7258 (5)	-2.6345(3)	ΔCPI_BR	-3.3421(3)***	-5.1107 (2)***
CPI_RU	-0.3570 (3)	-1.5867 (3)	ΔCPI_RU	-7.1441(7)***	-14.6779(7)***
CPI_IN	-1.6973 (4)	-2.1610 (2)	ΔCPI_IN	-2.9774(5)***	-11.4623(0)***
CPI_CN	-1.6945 (4)	-2.4172 (5)	ΔCPI_CN	-5.7422(11)***	-6.4002(11)***
CPI_ZA	-1.2276 (12)	-2.1223 (12)	ΔCPI_ZA	-3.8496(13)***	-5.5353(12)***
CPI*	-0.6598 (2)	-1.5538 (2)	ΔCPI*	-2.4703(3)***	-4.6054(3)***
NEER_TR	-0.5587 (6)	-0.7383 (6)	ΔNEER_TR	-2.1234(2)***	-4.4682(2)***
NEER_BR	-0.6962 (1)	-2.0450 (1)	ΔNEER_BR	-2.2795(0)***	-2.9363(0)***
NEER_RU	0.8683 (3)	-2.3088 (3)	ΔNEER_RU	-2.0019(8)***	-9.3027(1)***
NEER_IN	0.1919 (1)	-2.5113 (1)	ΔNEER_IN	-2.4525(4)***	-3.1595(6)***
NEER_CN	-0.1867 (5)	-2.0477 (5)	ΔNEER_CN	-2.9083(3)***	-4.4885(3)***
NEER_ZA	-0.2487 (8)	-2.0134 (8)	ΔNEER_ZA	-4.6072(7)***	-4.6019(7)***
Outputgap_TR	-3.9713 (9)***	-5.2972 (9)***			
Outputgap_BR	-4.7267 (2)***	-4.7266 (2)***			
Outputgap_ RU	-4.2381 (4)***	-4.5102(4)***			
Outputgap_IN	-5.3823(11)***	-5.2636 (11)***			
Outputgap_ CN	-2.9264 (0)***	-5.3848 (0)***			
Outputgap_ ZA	-4.3958 (1)***	-5.1443 (7)***			

Source: Author's own calculation. Hall's (1994) general-to-specific approach to lag selection has been adopted to find *k*. The initial (i.e., maximum) lag was set equal to the square root of the sample size. *** Exceeds the 5 % critical value (−1.94 for constant; −2.92 for constant and trend). * Exceeds the 1 % critical value (−2.57 for constant; −3.46 for constant and trend).

Tab. 4.3: The results of LR and Davies tests

	Turkey	**Brazil**	**Russia**	**India**	**China**	**S. Africa**
LR Test	396.70***	230.0938***	1037.1766***	122.2953***	308.1822***	167.6798***
Davies Test	0.000***	0.000***	0.000***	0.000***	0.000***	0.000***
LR Test to Determine Number of Regime						
Regimes	Turkey	Brazil	Russia	India	China	S. Africa
1 vs. 2	38.9502***	62.7301***	69.8146***	38.8239***	38.3660***	57.2269***
1 vs. 3	76.7555***	88.8635***	105.0007***	80.2908***	62.1425***	119.2824***
2 vs. 3	37.8053	26.1333	35.1859	41.4668	23.7765	62.0554

Source: Author's own calculation. ***Exceeds the 1 % critical value; 0.000 indicates probability value.

Tab. 4.4: MSIAH-VAR estimation results

High Inflation Regime (Regime 1)						
	Turkey	**Brazil**	**Russia**	**India**	**China**	**S. Africa**
Constant	-0.7455*** (0.3414)	-0.4754*** (0.2231)	-5.6430 (4.0755)	0.1206*** (0.0591)	0.0663 (0.1360)	-0.0406 (0.0835)
DCPI_1	0.6678*** (0.0968)	1.1100*** (0.1832)	0.3541 (0.2678)	0.1143** (0.0803)	-0.1831 (0.2477)	0.5223 (0.1011)
DG20CPI_1	0.4515 (1.3913)	1.085*** (0.5176)	-12.2047 (10.5747)	0.1929 (0.2345)	0.5422 (0.3979)	0.2352 (0.3177)
DNEER_1	-0.1614*** (0.0384)	-0.1681*** (0.0468)	-0.0071 (0.8185)	-0.0222 (0.0435)	-0.1513** (0.0955)	-0.0210 (0.0201)
OUTPUT_1	-0.0020 (0.1668)	-0.1484*** (0.0624)	1.0040 (1.1788)	0.0324 (0.0367)	0.1325*** (0.0316)	0.0357 (0.0236)
Standard Error	2.5109	0.676653	12.2516	0.7891	0.6777	0.7032
Low Inflation Regime (Regime 2)						
	Turkey	Brazil	Russia	India	China	S. Africa
Constant	-0.0283 (0.0725)	-0.0014 (0.0224)	-0.0383 (0.0349)	-0.3471*** (0.1160)	0.0298 (0.0345)	0.0065 (0.0265)
DCPI_1	0.1277*** (0.0624)	0.5190*** (0.0453)	0.5358*** (0.0378)	0.2532*** (0.1172)	-0.0833 (0.0600)	0.1944 (0.0668)
DG20CPI_1	0.6674*** (0.251)	0.0937 (0.0957)	-0.1379 (0.1624)	2.2707*** (0.6551)	0.1818 (0.1646)	0.4200 (0.1142)
DNEER_1	-0.0579*** (0.0295)	-0.0166*** (0.0069)	-0.0387*** (0.0178)	-0.0441 (0.0967)	0.0190 (0.0299)	-0.0455 (0.0127)
OUTPUT_1	0.0170 (0.0247)	0.0102 (0.0077)	0.0389*** (0.0156)	-0.1342*** (0.0614)	0.1026*** (0.0189)	0.0325 (0.0159)
Standard Error	0.8866	0.3231	0.4683	0.6804	0.4878	0.0325

Source: Author's own calculation. The values in parenthesis indicate standard error. _1 indicates the first lag of the variable. ** Exceeds the 5 % critical value. *** Exceeds the 1 % critical value.

2 is 0.4746 and transition probability from Regime 2 to Regime 1 is 0.0371. Duration is 2.11 months in Regime 1 and 26.97 months in Regime 2 for Brazil. For MSIAH-VAR model in Russia, regime transition probability from Regime 1 to Regime 1 is 0.6770 and from Regime 2 to Regime 2 is 0.9758. Transition probabilities from Regime 1 to Regime 2 and from Regime 2 to Regime 1 are, respectively, 0.3230 and 0.0242. Duration is 3.10 months in Regime 1 and 41.38 months in Regime 2 for Russia.

According to the MSIAH-VAR model for India, regime transition probabilities from Regime 1 to Regime 1 and from Regime 2 to Regime 2 are, respectively,

Tab. 4.5. Regime probabilities

	Regime 1	Regime 2	N of O	Probability	Duration
Turkey					
Regime 1	0.9159	0.0841	81	0.3063	11.89
Regime 2	0.0371	0.9629	169	0.6937	26.93
Brazil					
Regime 1	0.5254	0.4746	18.6	0.0725	2.11
Regime 2	0.0371	0.9629	231.4	0.9275	26.97
Russia					
Regime 1	0.6770	0.3230	19.1	0.0696	3.10
Regime 2	0.0242	0.9758	230.9	0.9304	41.38
India					
Regime 1	0.8967	0.1033	199.2	0.7986	9.68
Regime 2	0.4097	0.5903	0.8	0.2014	2.44
China					
Regime 1	0.6069	0.3931	35.9	0.1382	2.54
Regime 2	0.0630	0.9370	214.1	0.8618	15.86
S. Africa					
Regime 1	0.9389	0.0611	77	0.2790	16.37
Regime 2	0.0236	0.9764	173	0.7210	42.30

Source: Author's own calculation. *N of O*: Number of observations.

0.8967 and 0.5903. Transition probability from Regime 1 to Regime 2 is 0.1033 and 0.4097 in other case. Duration is 9.68 months in Regime 1 and 2.44 months in Regime 2 for India. For MSIAH-VAR model relating to China, regime transition probabilities from Regime 1 to Regime 1 and from Regime 2 to Regime 2 are, respectively, 0.6069 and 0.9370. Duration is 2.54 months in Regime 1 and 15.86 months in Regime 2 for China. Finally, regime transition probabilities from Regime 1 to Regime 1 and from Regime 2 to Regime 2 are, respectively, 0.9389 and 0.9764 in South Africa. Duration is 16.37 months in Regime 1 and 42.30 months in Regime 2 for South Africa. The obtained results show a low inflation regime is more persistent than a high inflation regime in Brazil, Russia, and China. In contrast to the aforementioned countries, high inflation regime is more persistent in India. However, in South Africa both regimes are persistent. Smoothed regime probabilities (Fig. 4.4) from MSIAH-VAR models for Turkey and BRICS countries are enclosed.

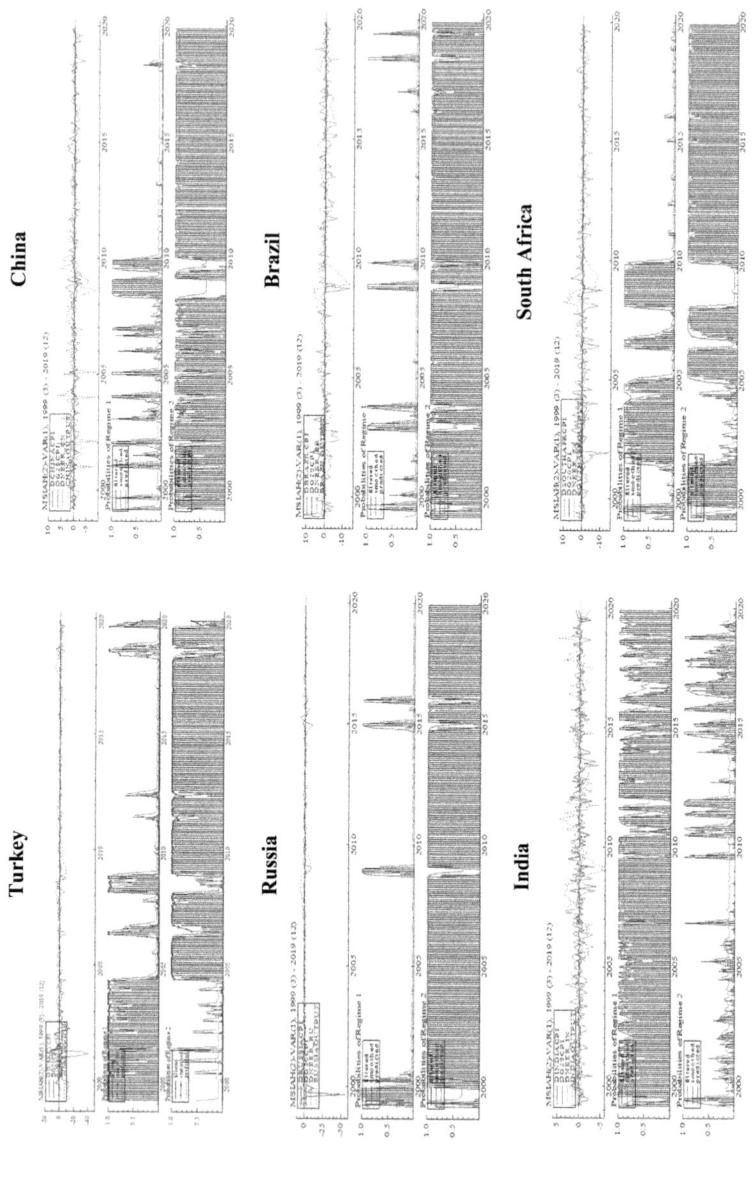

Fig. 4.4: Smoothed regime probabilities

Source: Author's own calculation

Conclusion

The exchange rate pass-through to domestic prices is significant for assessing international spillover effects of monetary policy. The degree of pass-through effects is determined by monetary policy and monetary policy instruments. Hence, analyzing of effects of pass-through is closely concerned with policy makers.

In this study, we examined the nonlinear exchange rate pass-through to domestic prices in different inflation regimes over the period of 1999:01–2019:12. In other words, we investigated whether Taylor's hypothesis stating that the degree of exchange rate pass-through to domestic prices is higher in high inflation periods is valid by using nonlinear time series models in Turkey and BRICS countries. For this purpose, we utilized from MSIAH-VAR model. From the findings of the analysis, we concluded that the degree of exchange rate pass-through to domestic inflation is about 15 % average in Turkey, Brazil, and China in unstable regime (or high inflation regime), but so-called pass-through is rather low in stable regime (or low inflation regime). In other words, Taylor's hypothesis is valid for the countries in question. This result indicates that switching to the inflation-targeting regime causes pass-through to diminish. Another result shows that in Turkey both low and high inflation regimes are persistent. A similar result is valid for South Africa. In spite of that, the low inflation regime is more persistent than a high inflation regime in Brazil, Russia, and China. The results of our study support the studies of Taylor (2000), Arbatlı (2003), and Tica and Posedel (2009).

The findings from this study are of importance to develop appropriate different policies in each economic regime, one of them is a high inflation regime and the other one is the low inflation regime. Macroeconomic variables may react differently to changes in exchange rates based on the size of the so-called shock. Thus, appropriate policy responses should involve nonlinear dynamic responses of nominal and real macroeconomic variables. Our findings may propose that policymakers implementing monetary policy should consider the degree and speed of pass-through from exchange rate shocks to inflation.

References

Al-Abri, A. and Goodwin, B. (2009). Re-examining the Exchange Rate Pass-Through into Import Prices Using Non-linear Estimation Techniques: Threshold Cointegration. *International Review of Economics and Finance*, 18(1): 142–61.

Arbatlı, E.C. (2003). Exchange Rate Pass-Through in Turkey: Looking for Asymmetries. *Central Bank Review*, 2: 85–124.

Ball, L. (1999). Policy Rules for Open Economies. In John B. Taylor (Ed.) *Monetary Policy Rules*. Chicago, IL: University of Chicago Press.

Calvo, G.A. and Reinhart, C.M. (2002). Fear of Floating. *Quarterly Journal of Economics*, 117(2): 379–08.

Campa, J. and Goldberg, L. (2005). Exchange Rate Pass-Through into Import Prices. *The Review of Economics and Statistics*, 87(4): 679–90.

Caselli, F.G. and Roitman, A. (2019). Nonlinear Exchange-Rate Pass-Through in Emerging Markets. *International Finance*, 22: 279–306.

Dellmo, H. (1996). Relationships between Swedish Producer Prices and Import Prices and the CPI. *Sveriges Riksbank Working Paper*, No:29.

Devereux, M. and Yerman, J. (2010). Price Adjustment and Exchange Rate Pass-Through. *Journal of International Money and Finance*, 29: 181–200.

Feinberg, R.M. (1986). The Interaction of Foreign Exchange and Market Power Effects on German Domestic Prices. *Journal of Industrial Economic*, 35(1): 61–70.

Feinberg, R.M. (1989). The Effects of Foreign Exchange Movements on U.S. Domestic Prices. *Review of Economics and Statistics*, 71(3): 505–11.

Frankel, J.A., Vegh, C.A. and Vuletin, G. (2013). On Graduation from Fiscal Procyclicality. *Journal of Development Economics*, 100: 32–47.

Goldberg, P.K. and Knetter, M.M. (1997). Goods Prices and Exchange Rates: What Have We Learned? *Journal of Economic Literature*, 35(3): 1243–72.

Hall, A. (1994). Testing for a Unit Root in Time Series with Pretest Data-Based Model Selection. *Journal of Business and Economic Statistics*, 12: 461–70.

Hamilton, J.D. (1989). A New Approach to the Economic Analysis of Nonstationary Time Series and the Business Cycle. *Econometrica*, 57(2): 357–84.

Hausmann, R., Panizza, U. and Rigobon, R. (2006). The Long-Run Volatility Puzzle of the Real Exchange Rate. *Journal of International Money and Finance*, 25(1): 93–124.

Jasova, M., Moessner, R. and Takats, E. (2016). Exchange Rate Pass-Through: What Has Changed Since the Crisis? *BIS Working Paper*, No:583.

Junttila, J. and Korhonen, M. (2012). The Role of Inflation Regime in the Exchange Rate Pass-Through to Import Prices. *International Review of Economics and Finance*, 24(C): 88–96.

Kara, H. and Öğünç, F. (2008). Inflation Targeting and Exchange Rate Pass Through: The Turkish Experience. *Emerging Markets Finance and Trade,* 44(6): 52–66.

Kara, H. and Öğünç, F. (2012). Döviz Kuru ve Ithalat Fiyatlarının Yurtiçi Fiyatlara Etkisi. *İktisat, İşletme ve Finans*, 317: 09–28.

Kara, A.H., Tuğer, H.K., Özlale, Ü., Tuğer, B. and Yücel, M.E. (2007). Exchange Rate Regimes and Pass-Through: Evidence from the Turkish Economy. *Contemporary Economic Policy*, 25(2): 206–25.

Karagöz, M., Demirel, B. and Bozdağ, E.G. (2016). Pass-Through Effect from Exchange Rates to the Prices in the Framework of Inflation Targeting Policy: A Comparison of Asia-Pacific, South American and Turkish Economies. *Procedia Economics and Finance*, 38: 438–45.

Kim, K.H. (1998). US Inflation and the Dollar Exchange Rate: A Vector Error Correction Model. *Applied Economics,* 30: 613–19.

Krolzig, H.M. (1997). Markov Switching Vector Autoregressions. *Modelling, Statistical Inference and Application to Business Cycle Analysis.* Berlin: Springer.

Nogueira, J.R.P. and León-Ledesma, M.A. (2010). Is Low Inflation Really Causing the Decline in Exchange Rate Pass-Through? *University of Kent Working Paper*, KDPE 1002.

Ozkan, İ. and Erden, L. (2015). Time-Varying Nature and Macroeconomic Determinants of Exchange Rate Pass-Through. *International Review of Economics and Finance,* 38:56–66.

Plantin, G. and Shin, H.S. (2016). Exchange Rates and Monetary Spillovers, *BIS Working Papers*, No: 537.

Rincón, H. and Rodríguez, N. (2016). Nonlinear Pass-Through of Exchange Rate Shocks on Inflation: A Bayesian Smooth Transition VAR Approach, *Graduate Institute of International and Development Studies Working Paper,* No:13–2016.

Sekine, T. (2006). Time Varying Exchange Rate Pass-Through: Experiences of some Industrial Countries. *BIS Working Papers*, No:2020.

Steel, D. and King, A. (2004). Exchange Rate Pass-Through: The Role of Regime Changes. *International Review of Applied Economics,* 18(3): 301–22.

Taylor, J. (2000). Low Inflation, Pass-Through and the Pricing Power of Firms. *European Economic Review*, 44(7): 1389–1408.

Tica, J. and Posedel, P. (2009). Threshold Model of the Exchange Rate Pass-Through Effect. *Eastern European Economics*, 47(6): 43–59.

Turner, P. and Wood, J. (2017). Nonlinear Exchange Rate Pass-Through in Industrial Economies. *Applied Economics*, 49(4): 397–402. Doi: 10.1080/00036846.2016.1197374.

Woo, W.T. (1984). Exchange Rates and the Prices of Nonfood, Nonfuel Products. *Brookings Papers on Economic Activity*, 2: 511–30.

Yüncüler, Ç. (2011). Pass-Through of External Factors into Price Indicators in Turkey. *Central Bank Review*, 11(2): 71–84.

Erdal Tanas Karagöl, Önder Özgür, and Muhammed Şehid Görüş

5 The Relationship Between Finance and Growth in North African Countries: Fresh Evidence from Panel Causality[1]

Highlights: In this study, we investigate the causal association between financial deepening and economic activity in five North African countries throughout 1990–2017 in panel setting. The main motivation of this study is to analyze the simultaneous relationship between financial development and economic growth. To investigate the causal linkage between financial deepening and economic growth, this study employs the panel data Toda-Yamamoto Fisher causality test, namely Emirmahmutoglu-Kose panel causality test. This test has the advantage of considering cross-sectional dependence and heterogeneity across the countries. According to the empirical findings, the full sample panel data results exhibit no causal relationship between financial deepening and economic activity. However, individual country results denote that the finance-led growth hypothesis, the unidirectional causality running from credit to GDP, is verified in Tunisia, and the growth-led finance, the unidirectional causality running from GDP to credit, is in tune in Morocco.

Keywords: Causality analysis, economic growth, financial deepening, finance-growth nexus, North Africa

Introduction

Many theorists have contributed to the literature on the relationship between financial development and economic growth. Although the studies on the finance-growth nexus have been growing rapidly, there has not yet been reached a full consensus whether financial development is a priori condition for economic growth or vice versa. In other words, disparities among economists in this issue stem from their perspective on which follows the other.

Alternative perspectives held by economists can be classified into two main strands (Ang, 2008). The first main strand of the literature can be associated with an early study of Schumpeter (1911). His study exhibits the role of financial

1 This chapter is an extended and revised version of the paper entitled "Finance-Growth Nexus in North African Countries: Panel Causality Evidence" presented at ICOAEF'19 V. International Conference on Applied Economics and Finance and Extended with Social Sciences, Kyrenia, North Cyprus, 9–11 April 2019.

intermediaries in directing the sources to the production of new technologies. The other earlier studies that assert the role of financial intermediation on reducing the financial frictions are Goldsmith (1969), Mc Kinnon (1973), and Shaw (1973). All these studies specifically argue that financial developments lower frictions in markets and increase domestic savings. Thus, the cost of funding decreases and capital accumulation rises, which in turn triggers economic activity and increases economic growth. This first strand of the literature comprises the finance-led growth hypothesis.

Conversely, the second strand of the literature refutes the argument that financial development leads to economic growth and claims that finance is an insignificant factor in economic growth (King and Levine, 1993). Defenders of this proposition are Robinson (1952) and Lucas (1988). Of them, Robinson (1952) proposes that financial development is demand-driven. When the economy expands the demand for financial services increases, which in turn triggers a well-structured financial system. In the same vein, Lucas (1988) labeled the relationship between financial development and economic growth as "overstressed."

This study investigates the causal relationship between financial development and economic activity in five North African countries (Algeria, Egypt, Morocco, Sudan, and Tunisia) throughout 1990–2017 in the panel setting. The main motivation of this study is to analyze the simultaneous relationship between financial development and economic growth. To investigate the causal linkage between financial deepening and economic growth, this study employs the panel data Toda-Yamamoto Fisher causality test, namely Emirmahmutoglu-Kose panel causality test. This test has the advantage of considering cross-sectional dependence and heterogeneity across the countries. Therefore, this test takes cross-sectional disparities among the panel countries and allows us to get the individual country results.

The remainder of the study is structured as follows. The second part of the study gives a brief overview of the existing literature. The third part introduces the data and employed methodology. The fourth part presents the empirical findings, and the fifth part discusses these empirical results. The last part concludes the study.

2 Literature Review

After the preliminary studies of the Goldsmith (1969) and King and Levine (1993), studies concentrating on the finance-growth nexus has expanded rapidly. Obviously, the increase in data availability and advancements in economic modeling accompanied by the rapid financialization of emerging economies facilitated the researches on this issue. Earlier studies concentrate on exploring the role of financial development in growth based on growth regressions, and current studies extend the literature using causality analysis and aim to shed light on the finance-growth nexus (Stolbov, 2017).

Although the literature grows rapidly in the finance-growth nexus, existing studies have not yet reached the consensus. In other words, empirical studies have been albeit with conflicting results. These disparities in the literature arise country-specific factors and the methodology has driven factors as well. This part of the study provides a summary of the existing literature.

Earlier studies of Goldsmith (1969) and King and Levine (1993) used the ordinary least squares (OLS) methodology to check whether financial development significantly affects the economic growth in large samples. They both approved that the financialization triggers the economic activity despite the variation of the level of significance across countries.

Of the earliest studies, De Gregorio and Guidotti (1995) used bank credit to the private sector as a measure of financial development and examined the relationship between long-run growth and financial depth in cross-sectional and panel data context. In the cross-sectional analysis, the study covers the data of about 100 countries over 1960–1985 while in panel data setting the period consists of 12 Latin American countries throughout 1950–1985. The cross-country sample results confirmed that financial development is positively correlated with long-run growth. Conversely, the panel data results in Latin American countries display a negative relationship between growth and financial depth.

Bloch and Tang (2003) set up an analysis to clarify the role of financial development on economic growth by both cross-country and panel data regressions in 75 countries from 1960 to 1990. Their empirical findings implied that private credit to GDP is a significant tool to explain the variation in economic growth in the cross-country setting while the significance of financial development disappears in a panel regression model. They argued that their findings express the role of country-specific factors in finance-growth nexus.

Christopoulos and Tsionas (2004) devise panel cointegration and causality tests to examine the relationship in 10 developing countries. They found that financial depth and economic growth are cointegrated. They also estimated the regression coefficients through fully modified OLS. Their findings implied that there is a long-run causality favoring the unidirectional causality running from financial depth to economic growth and no causality between these variables in the short run. Thus, the results denote that policies aiming to accelerate financial development have a delayed effect on economic activity.

Naceur and Ghazouani (2007) constructed the dynamic panel regression model to check the impact of financial development on economic growth in MENA countries covering the period from the 1980s to the beginning of the 2000s. Interestingly, their findings denoted that the banking sector development negatively affects the economic growth in these sample countries. They concluded that the unstructured banking sector impedes real economic activity. In another study, Abu-Bader and Abu-Qarn (2008) analyzed the link between financial development and economic growth in six MENA countries throughout the period 1960s to the beginning of the 2000s in time series context. They constructed the multivariate VAR model and employed the Toda-Yamamoto Granger causality test in their empirical study. They used four measures of financial development: the ratio of M2 to GDP, M2 minus currency to GDP, bank credit to the private sector over GDP, and the ratio of credit issued to the nonfinancial private sector to total domestic credit. They found evidence favoring the finance-led growth hypothesis in five out of six countries.

Odhiambo (2008) considered the finance-growth nexus in Kenya by utilizing the dynamic causality analysis. The study exhibited that the intertemporal causal relationship between finance and growth is sensitive to the measure of financial development. Besides, economic growth seems more prominent as a Granger cause of finance in Kenya. Similarly, Wolde-Rufael (2009) inserted extra variables in the analysis of finance-growth nexus in Kenya and utilized the Toda Yamamoto causality test. The study covers the period between 1966 and 2005 and incorporates the four different measures of financial development. Empirical findings provided evidence favoring the bidirectional causal relationship between the variables in three out of the four measures of financial development. Thus, they concluded that finance and growth measures are determined contemporaneously.

In their study for the Japanese economy, Chang and Huang (2010) explored the role of interest rates on the finance-growth nexus. They gathered the quarterly data over the period between 1981Q2 and 2008Q3 and constructed a battery of econometric models. Their empirical models depended on a neoclassical production function, and financial development was constituted as an input. Their study confirmed that the prevailing lower real interest rates are an important factor for isolating the role of the banking system to economic growth in the Japanese economy.

Marques, Fuinhas, and Marques (2013) examined the finance-growth nexus in Portuguese throughout the period 1993–2011. They constructed a VAR model and got empirical findings through Granger causality, variance decomposition, and impulse responses. Their findings provided evidence for the no causal relationship between bank financing and economic growth.

Considering the nonlinearities Beck, Georgiadis, and Straub (2014) investigated the relationship between financial development and economic growth in a large panel of more than 100 countries over the period between 1970 and 2011. They used the ratio of private credit to GDP as a regressor and the measure of financial development in their growth accounting model. To identify the nonlinearity, they included the square of the measure of financial development in their dynamic panel model. They found that credit expansion has a positive impact on economic growth up to a threshold level and the role of credit expansion becomes irrelevant after this certain point. They also concluded that the reason for an arising nonlinearity is the omission of factors excluded in the previous studies.

In a large sample of 101 developed and emerging countries, Ductor and Grechyna (2015) operated a dynamic panel data regression model for the period of 1970–2010. Their empirical findings denoted that the impact of financial development on economic growth is sensitive to the relative changes in the level of financial deepening and economic growth. Thus, they argued that intensive financial activities deteriorate the real economic structure.

In a recent study Stolbov (2017) analyzed the causal relationship between growth in per capita GDP and the private credit to GDP in 24 OECD countries covering the period between 1980 and 2013. They employed various novel causality tests and found that in 4 of the 24 countries the finance-led growth is in tune. Besides, they revealed that the country-specific factors are also significant in an analysis of finance-growth nexus.

More recently, Chow, Fung, and Leung (2018) used regime switching causality method to investigate the link between financial development and economic growth in Chinese provinces. They found that in developed regions the one-way causality running from financial development to economic growth is in tune which in turn verifies the finance-led growth hypothesis. Their findings also confirmed that in regions that are in early stages of their development the causality running from economic growth to financial development is likely to emerge.

The review of the overall empirical results on finance-growth nexus indicates that the causality between these variables exhibits mixed patterns and is sensitive to the country-specific factors, the time span, and the employed methodological tools. Thus, the literature calls for more empirical studies to shed light on the finance-growth nexus.

3 Data and Methodology

3.1 Data

This study investigates the causal association between financial deepening and economic activity in five North African countries (Algeria, Egypt, Morocco, Sudan, and Tunisia) throughout 1990–2017 in the panel setting.

The main motivation of this study is the simultaneous relationship between financial development and economic growth. In this sense, the study employs the ratio of domestic private credit to GDP and per capita GDP in constant 2010 US dollars. Here, the former stands as a measure of financial development and the latter represent the measure for economic growth. Both series are extracted from the World Bank World Development Indicators (WDI) database.

3.2 Methodology

To investigate the causal linkage between financial deepening and economic growth, this study employs the panel data Toda-Yamamoto Fisher causality test namely Emirmahmutoglu-Kose (EK hereafter) proposed by Emirmahmutoglu and Kose (2011).

The main advantage of this test is that it considers the cross-sectional dependence and heterogeneity across the countries. Fisher (1932) proposed the Lag-augmented (LA) vector autoregression (VAR). The EK panel causality test is an extended version of this methodology. It tests the existence of Granger causality between variables in heterogeneous mixed panels.

LA-VAR model has conventional chi-square distribution in an estimation of the VAR ($p+d_{max}$) model. Here p represents the lag order and the d_{max} shows the order of maximum integration. The EK methodology first considers the following heterogeneous panel VAR (l) model with n variables (Emirmahmutoglu and Kose, 2011):

$$z_{i,t} = \beta_i + \gamma_{i1} z_{i,t-1} + \ldots + \gamma_{il_i} z_{i,\ t-k_i} + u_{i,t}\ for\ i = 1, 2,\ \ldots,\ N,\ t = 1, 2,\ \ldots,\ T \quad (1)$$

Here i stands for the cross-sectional units, the t shows time periods, and β_i is the n dimensional vector with fixed-effects. The fixed parameter matrices, $\gamma_{i1},\ \ldots,\ \gamma_{il_i}$ vary across cross-sectional units. $u_{i,t}$'s are independent and identically distributed for all $t = 1, 2,\ \ldots,\ T$, and $E(u_{i,t}) = 0$. Also, the covariance matrices $V(u_{i,t}) = \sum u_i$ are positive definite. Lag structure, (l_i), may change across cross-sectional units.

The conventional tool to test the coefficient restrictions in VAR systems is the Wald test. The following equation represents the coefficients of the VAR system:

$$\partial_i = vec\left[\beta_i, \gamma_{i1}, \ldots \gamma_{il_i}\right] \; for \; i = 1, \; \ldots, \; N \tag{2}$$

Here, the aim is to test the $r_i$number of linear and independent coefficient restrictions. In the case of Granger non-causality, the null hypothesis is as follows:

$$H_0 = R_i\theta_i = 0 \; for \; all \; i \tag{3}$$

and the alternative is:

$$H_1 = R_i\theta_i \neq 0 \; for \; i = 1, \; \ldots, N_1; \; R_i\theta_i = 0 \; i = N_1 + 1, \ldots, \; N \tag{4}$$

Here, R_i is a matrix with rank r_i.

To test the null hypothesis of non-stationarity, this test estimates a VAR model:

$$\begin{aligned} z_{i,t} = \beta_i + \gamma_{i1} z_{i,t-1} + \ldots + \gamma_{il_i} z_{i,\,t-k_i} + \sum_{l=r_i+1}^{r_i+dmax_i} \gamma_{il} z_{i,t-1} \\ + u_{i,t} \; for \; i = 1, 2, \; \ldots, \; N, \; t = 1, 2, \; \ldots, \; T \end{aligned} \tag{5}$$

In this case, the test combines the p-values via the Fisher method:

$$EK = -2\sum_{j=1}^{G} \ln\left(p_j\right) \tag{6}$$

where p_j shows the p-value of TY causality test for the jth country. The critical values to test the null of non-stationarity are obtained via bootstrap simulations.

4 Empirical Results

The study needs to determine the integration level of the variables before executing the causality test. However, the selection of the unit root tests also depends on the presence of the cross-sectional dependence across the cross-sectional units. Thus, the study first explores the cross-sectional dependence in employed series and then determines the order of integration in the employed series.

Tab. 5.1: CD test and panel unit root test results

Variable	Breusch-Pagan LM	Pesaran Scaled LM	Bias-Corrected Scaled LM	Pesaran CD	CIPS Statistics
CREDIT	38.459***	6.363***	6.271***	1.056	-1.549
ΔCREDIT	-	-	-	-	-3.709***
GDP	264.188***	56.838***	56.745***	16.252***	-3.214***

Note: *Δ* is the first difference operator. *** denotes statistical significance at %1.

Before implementing the unit root test, this study utilizes all four cross-sectional dependence tests among countries. These are LM test of Breusch and Pagan (1980), CDLM and CD tests proposed by Pesaran (2004), and adjusted LM test of Pesaran, Ulah, and Yamagata (2008). The study carries out the cross-sectionally augmented Dickey-Fuller (CADF) test which is developed by Pesaran (2007), and gets the cross-sectionally augmented Im, Pesaran, and Shin (or CIPS) statistics. The results of cross-sectional dependence and the unit root tests are displayed in Tab. 5.1.

The results of the cross-sectional dependence tests in Tab. 5.1 imply that the null of the cross-sectional independence is rejected in all four tests for both series. Thus, these findings denote that there is a cross-sectional dependence between the cross-sectional units among the countries. Under the presence of the cross-sectional dependence, second-generation unit root tests are more appropriate to determine the integration level of the variables.

The results of the panel unit root test imply that the null of nonstationarity cannot be rejected for the GDP variable in its level form and for the CREDIT variable in its first difference. In other words, the results imply that CREDIT is integrated of I(1) and GDP is integrated of I(0). Therefore, the maximum integration order of the variables is labeled as 1.

After determining the order of integration in the series, the study proceeds to examine the direction of causality between two sets of pairs: (a) GDP→CREDIT and (b) CREDIT→GDP. To investigate the finance-growth nexus in causality framework this study employs the EK causality test. This test considers the cross-sectional dependence and heterogeneity across the countries. Table 5.2 displays the causal relationship in two sets of pairs both for a full panel of five North African countries and the individual panel members.

The panel data results denote that we fail to reject the null of non-causality in both sets of pairs. In other words, there is no significant causal relationship on

Tab. 5.2: Bootstrap panel causality test results between CREDIT and GDP

Individual/ Direction	GDP→CREDIT	CREDIT→GDP	Conclusion
	Wald statistics	Wald statistics	
Algeria	1.345	2.601	No Causality
Egypt	1.848	2.347	No Causality
Morocco	20.515***	2.333	Growth-Led Finance
Sudan	0.106	1.217	No Causality
Tunisia	1.188	14.669***	Finance-Led Growth
	Panel Fisher statistics	Panel Fisher statistics	Conclusion
Panel	25.487	24.570	No Causality

Note: *** denotes statistical significance at %1. Since there is a cross-sectional dependence in the models, we consider the 5000 bootstrap probability values.

the causality between CREDIT and GDP that seems to support the neutrality in North African countries.

However, Tab. 5.2 provides mixed results for individual countries. On the basis of the individual results between CREDIT and GDP, in two out of five series there exists a unidirectional causality between the series. Of them, our findings for Morocco denotes that the significant unidirectional causality runs from GDP to CREDIT, which in turn provides a supportive evidence growth-led finance hypothesis. On the other hand, the results exhibit the one-way causality running from CREDIT to GDP and confirm the finance-led growth hypothesis in Tunisia. In the remaining countries, the results are similar to those of the whole panel and are in favor of the non-causal relationship between CREDIT and GDP.

5 Discussion

The presence of the unidirectional causality from GDP to CREDIT in Morocco seems to suggest that economic growth is a significant indicator for the future developments in the financial sector. Our findings are not in line with the findings of Abu-Bader and Abu-Qarn (2008), whose findings provided evidence of unidirectional causal relationship running from financial development to GDP by using similar measures. Thus, our findings imply that the policies promoting economic growth will also ensure sound financial development in Morocco.

The one-way causality running from CREDIT to GDP confirms the finance-led growth hypothesis and suggests that financial development is an indicator for future economic growth. These findings are not in consensus with those of Abu-Bader and Abu-Qarn (2008). Their study exhibits no causal relationship between the similar measures of financial development and economic growth. However, our results confirm that the sound financial system in Tunisia stimulates the economic activity and induces economic growth.

Empirical findings of this study in Algeria, Egypt, and Sudan fail to find the causal relationship between CREDIT and GDP and demonstrate the lack of the link between the financial sector and the real sector. In this manner, our findings have in common with those of Naceur and Ghazouani (2007). They used a dynamic panel regression and found that there is no significant relationship between the financial system and the economic activity in MENA countries. Their reasoning is that the low institutional environment breaks up the link between the financial sector and real sector and stress the need for the sound institutional structure for the well-functioning banking system.

Conclusion

This study investigates the finance-growth nexus in five North African countries (Algeria, Egypt, Morocco, Sudan, and Tunisia) throughout 1990–2017 in the panel setting. The study uses the ratio of domestic private credit to GDP in constant 2010 US dollars as a measure of financial development and the per capita GDP in constant 2010 US dollars for a measure of economic growth.

To examine this link, the study employs a causality test proposed by Emirmahmutoglu and Kose (2011). This test has the advantage of considering the cross-sectional dependence and heterogeneity across the countries. EK panel causality test is an extended version of this methodology to test the existence of Granger causality between variables in heterogeneous mixed panels.

Empirical findings exhibit that there is no significant causal relationship between CREDIT and GDP that seems to support the neutrality in a panel of North African countries. Individual country results between CREDIT and GDP propose that in two out of five series there exists a unidirectional causality. For Morocco, significant unidirectional causality runs from GDP to CREDIT, which in turn provides a supportive evidence growth-led finance hypothesis. On the other hand, the results exhibit the one-way causality running from CREDIT to GDP and confirm the finance-led growth hypothesis in Tunisia. In the remaining countries, the results are similar to those of the whole panel and are in favor of the non-causal relationship between CREDIT and GDP.

As a conclusion, this study exhibits mixed results in addressing the finance-growth nexus in North African countries. Further studies might concentrate on the detailed analysis of the country-specific factors influencing the way of causal linkage between two sets of pairs by employing the alternative econometric techniques.

References

Abu-Bader, S., and Abu-Qarn, A. S. (2008) "Financial Development and Economic Growth: Empirical Evidence from Six MENA Countries". Review of Development Economics, 12(4): 803–817.

Ang, J. B. (2008) "A Survey of Recent Developments in the Literature of Finance and Growth". Journal of economic Surveys, 22(3): 536–576.

Beck, R., Georgiadis, G., and Straub, R. (2014) "The Finance and Growth Nexus Revisited. Economics Letters, 124(3): 382–385.

Bloch, H., and Tang, S. H. K. (2003) "The Role of Financial Development in Economic Growth". Progress in Development Studies, 3(3): 243–251.

Breusch, T., and Pagan, A. (1980) "The Lagrange Multiplier Test and Its Applications to Model Specification in Econometrics". The Review of Economic Studies, 47(1): 239–253.

Chang, S. H., and Huang, L. C. (2010) "The Nexus of Finance and GDP Growth in Japan: Do Real Interest Rates Matter?". Japan and the World Economy, 22(4): 235–242.

Chow, W. W., Fung, M. K., and Leung, M. K. (2018) "Finance-Growth Nexus in China from an Endogenous Switching Perspective". The Journal of International Trade & Economic Development, 27(4): 443–462.

Christopoulos, D. K., and Tsionas, E. G. (2004) "Financial Development and Economic Growth: Evidence from Panel Unit Root and Cointegration Tests". Journal of Development Economics, 73(1): 55–74.

De Gregorio, J., and Guidotti, P. E. (1995) "Financial Development and Economic Growth". World Development, 23(3): 433–448.

Ductor, L., and Grechyna, D. (2015) "Financial Development, Real Sector, and Economic Growth". International Review of Economics & Finance, 37: 393–405.

Emirmahmutoglu, F., and Kose, N. (2011) "Testing for Granger Causality in Heterogeneous Mixed Panels". Economic Modelling, 28(3): 870–876.

Fisher, R. A. (1932) "Statistical Methods for Research Workers", 4th Edition. Edinburgh: Oliver and Boyd.

Goldsmith, R. W. (1969) "Financial Structure and Development". New Haven: Yale University Press.

King, R. G., and Levine, R. (1993) "Finance and Growth: Schumpeter Might Be Right". The Quarterly Journal of Economics, 108(3): 717–737.

Lucas, R. E., Jr (1988) "On the Mechanics of Economic Development". Journal of Monetary Economics, 22: 3–42.

Marques, L. M., Fuinhas, J. A., and Marques, A. C. (2013) "Does the Stock Market Cause Economic Growth? Portuguese Evidence of Economic Regime Change". Economic Modelling, 32: 316–324.

McKinnon, R. I. (1973) "Money and Capital in Economic Development", Washington, DC: Brookings Institution.

Naceur, S. B., and Ghazouani, S. (2007) "Stock Markets, Banks, and Economic Growth: Empirical Evidence from the MENA Region". Research in International Business and Finance, 21(2): 297–315.

Odhiambo, N. M. (2008) "Financial Development in Kenya: A Dynamic Test of the Finance-Led Growth Hypothesis". Economic Issues, 13(2): 21–36.

Pesaran, M. (2004) "General Diagnostic Tests for Cross Section Dependence in Panels". Cesifo Working Paper Series 1229. Cesifo Group Munich.

Pesaran, M. (2007) "A Simple Panel Unit Root Test in the Presence of Cross-Section Dependence". Journal of Applied Econometrics, 22(2): 265–312.

Pesaran, M. H., Ullah, A., & Yamagata, T. (2008) "A Bias-Adjusted LM Test of Error Cross-Section Independence". The Econometrics Journal, 11: 105–127.

Robinson, J. (1952) "The Rate of Interest and Other Essays". London: Macmillan.

Schumpeter, J. A. (1911) "The Theory of Economic Development". Oxford: Oxford University Press.

Shaw, E. S. (1973) "Financial Deepening in Economic Development". New York: Oxford University Press.

Stolbov, M. (2017) "Causality between Credit Depth and Economic Growth: Evidence from 24 OECD Countries". Empirical Economics, 53(2): 493–524.

Wolde-Rufael, Y. (2009) "Re-examining the Financial Development and Economic Growth Nexus in Kenya". Economic Modelling, 26(6): 1140–1146.

Section 2 Financial Systems, Stock Markets, and Financial Crisis

Yavuz Selim Hacıhasanoğlu and Mehmet Selman Çolak*

6 Exchange Rate Uncertainty and Dollarization in Turkey

Highlights: Dollarization in developing countries has been discussed extensively. While a high level of dollarization deteriorates the monetary policy transmission mechanism, it also affects financial stability and price stability negatively. Foreign currency debt of corporates in emerging markets, which has reached record levels in the last decade, is considered as an important financial risk factor. Especially in times of local currency depreciation, it is difficult for firms to pay their foreign currency debts and firms go into bankruptcy. Since foreign currency loans are an important risk factor, it is important to understand the relationship of these loans with foreign currency deposits and to determine how the relationship has changed in different periods. This allows countries to develop different macro-prudential policies in different periods. In this study, the relationship between deposit and loan dollarization of Turkey for the period 2005–2019 is examined in a time-varying framework. Findings show that deposit dollarization feeds credit dollarization more in periods when exchange rate uncertainty increases. It is considered that the conversion of deposits to loans has increased as banks' use of foreign currency funds is limited during periods of uncertainty.

Keywords: Credit dollarization, deposit dollarization, foreign currency borrowing, exchange rate uncertainty, time-varying multivariate causality

Introduction

Credit and deposit dollarization, which is frequently discussed in developing countries, deteriorates the monetary policy transmission mechanism (Acosta-Ormaechea and Coble, 2011; Ozsoz and Rengifo , 2016), financial stability (Pomerleano, 1998; Cowan et al., 2005; Acharya et al. 2015; Barajas and others, 2016; Alfaro et al., 2017), and price stability (Honohan & Shi, 2002; Fendoğlu et al., 2019). In the literature, credit dollarization is explained by three factors: deposit dollarization, banks' foreign currency (FX) debts from foreign banks, and exporter firms requesting FX loans to benefit from the cost advantage. While the first two factors show the supply channel of the banks, the third factor refers to the demand channel of the firms.

---

* The views expressed in this paper belong to authors and do not reflect the official views and opinions of the Central Bank of the Republic of Turkey or its staff.

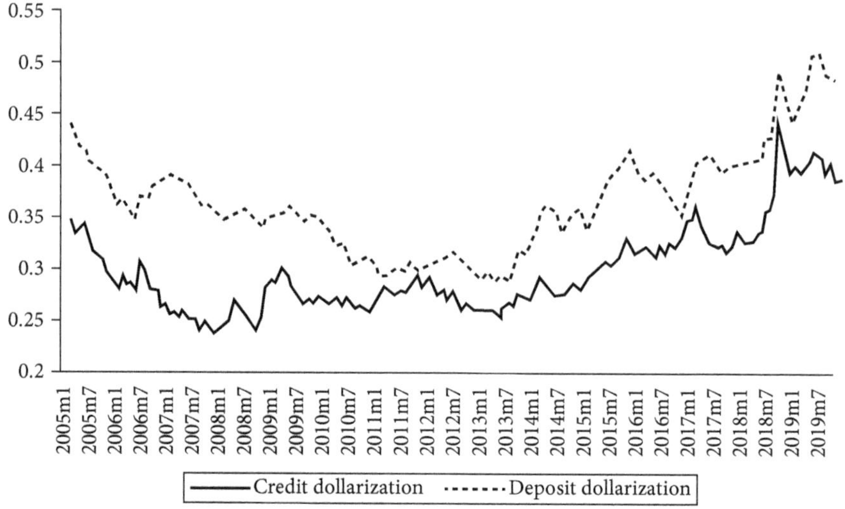

Fig. 6.1: Credit and deposit dollarization
Source: BRSA

Because of the liquidity generated as a result of expansionary monetary policies of developed countries after the global financial crisis, dollarization in developing countries has increased significantly. The record level of FX debt in the last decade in developing countries is considered as an important financial risk factor in developing countries (IMF, 2015; Feyen et al., 2017). As shown in Fig. 6.1, dollarization in Turkey has also began to increase after the global financial crisis, which has increased to 39 percent in credit dollarization and 48 percent in deposit dollarization as of October 2019. Higher share of FX debt in Turkey compared to other emerging countries makes the Turkish case interesting to examine the relationship between the credit and deposit dollarization (Fendoğlu et al., 2019).

Due to the restriction of foreign currency denominated debt of households in 2009, households does not have currency risk in Turkey. On the other hand, as of October 2019, the total FX open position of real sector firms, which is around USD 176 billion (CBRT), is considered as an important risk factor. Currency mismatches in the firms' balance sheets may lead to exchange rate risk and problems throughout the financial system if their financial hedge against FX debt are insufficient. Especially in times when the local currency depreciates, it is difficult for the real sector companies to pay their FX debts and the companies go into bankruptcy. The bankruptcy of firms can affect other firms with which they have a commercial relationship and the banks with which they have a credit relationship, creating a systemic risk (Kiyotaki & Moore, 2002; Tucker & Li, 2014; Barajas et al., 2016; Bocola & Lorenzoni, 2018; Kara, Hacıhasanoğlu and Ünalmış, 2019).

As FX loans are an important risk factor, it is important to understand the relationship between FX loans and FX deposits and to determine how this relationship has changed in different periods. This will enable to implement different macro-prudential policies in different periods.

Using Turkish data, Alp and Yalçın (2015) find that FX revenues of firms affect credit dollarization while Özsöz et al. (2015) suggest that the supply channel is important in credit dollarization. In this study, time-varying relationship between deposit and credit dollarization over time is examined using the methodology in Rossi and Wang (2019) for the period 2005–2019. Since the traditional Granger causality methodology does not show the dynamics of the relationship between the variables over time, it does not allow to follow the changes in the relationship when the exchange rate volatility is high or low. The results suggest that during the periods of higher exchange rate volatility, deposit dollarization feeds credit dollarization while this mechanism has weakened in periods when the exchange rate volatility has decreased. During periods of high uncertainty, it is considered that the conversion of FX deposits to FX loans increased with the decrease of banks' foreign funding. This situation shows that it is appropriate to develop policies aiming to deter FX deposits in times of high exchange rate volatility to reduce dollarization. While the data and methodology are explained in the second part of the study, the findings are summarized in the third part. The fourth part includes the results.

1 Data and Methodology

Publicly available banking data[1] from the Banking Regulation and Supervision Agency (BRSA) website is used in the study. The data includes monthly banking sector balance sheet items for the period January 2005–May 2019. By making use of TL-FX separation in balance sheet data, "FX Loan/Total Loan" and "FX Deposit/Total Deposit" rates are calculated for each month. Aside from FX deposits, non-core liabilities (such as FX issuances, syndication, and securitization), which are important FX sources of banks, are not included in the analysis.

1 https://www.bddk.org.tr/BultenAylik.

Variable	Obs	Mean	Std. Dev.	Min	Max
Credit Dollarization (FX Credit / Total Credit)	173	0.294457	0.040593	0.235394	0.441816
Deposit Dollarization (FX Deposit / Total Deposit)	173	0.361077	0.047798	0.28595	0.509618
Exchange Rate (Basket, % Change)	173	10.58129	15.26606	-15.7238	82.18372
Public Dept/GDP	173	36.8301	7.268887	27.90975	55.1336
Capital Inflow/GDP	173	3.234091	2.155855	-0.45974	7.51198
GDP Growth	173	5.505484	3.939337	-6.94929	11.89397
Inflation	173	9.333489	3.451134	3.986039	25.24032
CDS	173	231.0554	79.41228	119.161	535.759

Tab. 6.1: Summary statistics

Some other macroeconomic variables such as exchange rate, public debt, capital flows, GDP, inflation, and CDS, which may be important in credit dollarization, are also controlled in the model. Macro variables are obtained from publicly available CBRT Electronic Data Delivery System (EDDS) and Turkey Statistical Institute (TurkStat) databases. In addition, the currency volatility series implied by one-year TL/USD buying options is used as an indicator of exchange rate volatility. Implied exchange rate volatility is obtained from Bloomberg. Summary statistics for the variables are given in Tab. 6.1.[2]

We analyze how credit and deposit dollarization changed over time using the Granger causality methodology in the paper by Rossi and Wang (2019). This methodology is more powerful than the traditional Granger causality test when the series have instabilities. Figure 6.1 clearly demonstrates the instability in credit and deposit dollarization. Rossi and Wang (2019) methodology allow the VAR model to be estimated with time-varying coefficients.

$$y_t = \beta_{1,y,t} y_{t-1} + \beta_{2,x,t} x_{t-1} + \ldots \beta_{m,y,t} y_{t-m} + \beta_{m,x,t} x_{t-m} + \varepsilon_t \qquad (1)$$

where $\beta_{j,y,t}, j = 1, \ldots m$ and $\beta_{j,x,t}, j = 1, \ldots m$ are time-varying coefficients, $[y_t, y_{t-1}, x_{t-1}, \ldots, x_{t-m}]'$ are variables in the model, and ε_t is heteroskedastic and serially correlated error term.

The VAR model consists of eight endogenous variables: "FX Loan/Total Loan," "FX Deposit/Total Deposit," basket exchange rate, "Public Debt/GDP," "Capital Flows/GDP," GDP growth, inflation, and CDS. The Wald statistics obtained after estimating the model show the time-varying Granger causality relationship

2 Quarterly GDP data which is obtained from TURKSTAT has been converted into monthly series with the interpolation method developed by Fernandez (1981).

	1 Lag		
Zero Hypothesis (H0)	**Chi2**	**P-Value**	**Decision**
Deposit Dollarization does not Granger-cause Credit Dollarization	0.4848	0.486	Do not Reject

Tab. 6.2: Granger causality for the whole period

between credit and deposit dollarization and the level of significance of the relationship.

1.1. Analysis

In the study, using the Schwarz information criterion, the number of lags to be used in the model is determined as 1. In addition, 0.15 is chosen for the trimming parameter in accordance with the Rossi and Wang (2019) methodology. This value is applied as a standard in the structural break literature, excluding possible structural break periods.

Table 6.2 shows the results of the traditional Granger causality test for the VAR model, which assumes that the model parameters are constant. The results show that considering the entire sample period, there is no Granger causality from deposit dollarization to credit dollarization.

Figure 6.2, which shows the change in exchange rate volatility over time, indicates that the volatility is high in the periods of 2008, 2011–2012, and 2018–2019. In Fig. 6.3, which is drawn by calculating Equation (1) in accordance with the paper of Rossi and Wang (2019), Wald statistics showing the Granger causality between credit-deposit dollarization is given as a time series. The figure shows that causality often exists at a 5 percent significance level. In addition, it shows that causality is high during periods of high exchange rate volatility. In other words, in times of stress periods with high exchange rate volatility, an increased causality is observed from deposit dollarization to credit dollarization. Exchange rate volatility was high during 2008–2009 in the global financial crisis and 2011–2012 in the European debt crisis. Depositors in these periods increased their foreign currency deposit with the increasing uncertainties, falling consumer confidence, and the expectation of an increase in the exchange rate. In these periods, banks extended the excess foreign currencies they obtained to companies as foreign currency loans. This situation caused causality from deposit to credit in dollarization. The causality relationship is stronger in 2011–2012 than in the previous global crisis period. This situation can be explained by

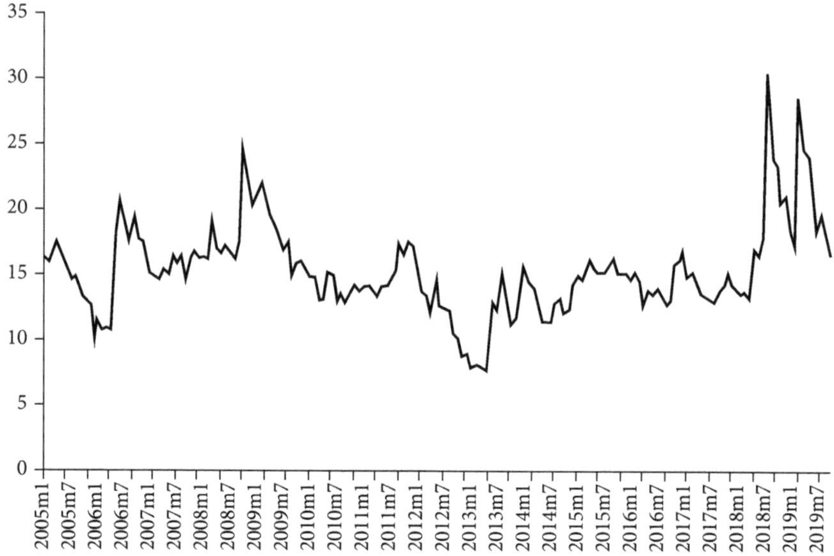

Fig. 6.2: FX volatility
Source: Authors' calculations

the fact that the economic activity was at a better level than the global crisis in 2011–2012, and the demand side also supported FX loans. In other words, banks have more appetite to make foreign currency loans available to firms, which strengthened causality.

Choosing the trimming parameter as 0.15 causes loss of the values at the beginning and end of the observation period. We can repeat the Rossi and Wang (2019) methodology to increase both the number of observations and test whether we can see the exchange rate volatility (Fig. 6.2) seen in 2018 in the Wald statistic value. The result is presented in Fig. 6.4. Granger causality, which is realized from deposit dollarization to credit dollarization as expected, rises similar to previous high exchange rate volatility periods. This indicates that during periods of high volatility in exchange rates, deposit dollarization feeds credit dollarization, so policymakers should take measures to reduce deposit dollarization to prevent credit dollarization during high volatility periods.

In order to test the robustness of the results, we determine the lagged values in the model in accordance with the procedure in Toda and Yamamoto's (1995) paper. Figure 6.5 shows the results. As seen in the figure, a high level of Granger

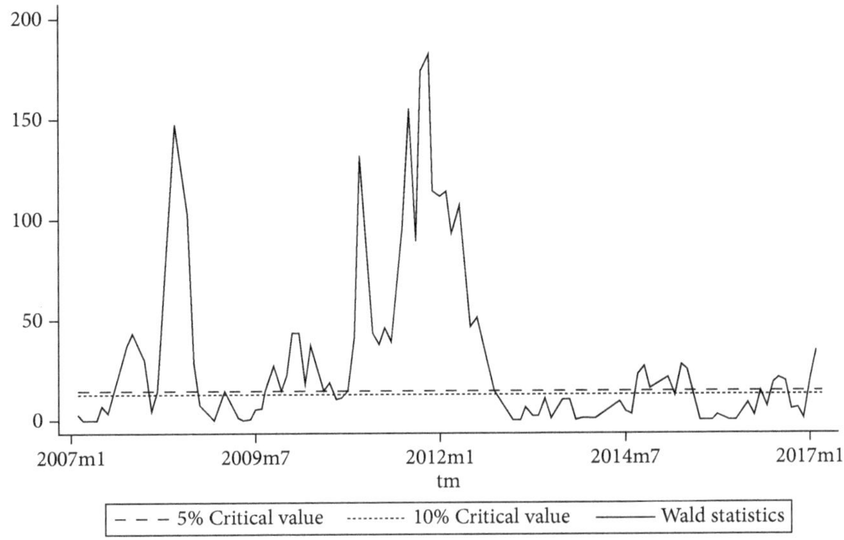

Fig. 6.3: Time-varying Granger causality

Notes: VAR(1) under SIC, trimming %15

H_0: Deposit dollarization does not Granger-causes credit dollarization

causality from deposit to credit dollarization during high exchange rate volatility periods does not change with the choice of different lag values.

Conclusion

This study analyzes the time-varying Granger causality between deposit and credit dollarization in Turkey from January 2005 to May 2019 using Rossi and Wang (2019) methodology. The results show that the causality is not valid for all time and that it changes over time and is stronger especially in periods where exchange rate volatility is high. The results do not change when choosing alternative lag values, and whether structural break periods are taken into account.

This indicates that policies to deter deposit dollarization may be more effective in periods when exchange rate volatility is high in order to reduce credit dollarization. While such measures support financial stability by reducing dollarization, it will also contribute to price stability by balancing the price increases caused by the high foreign currency indebted sectors, as shown in Fendoğlu et al. (2019).

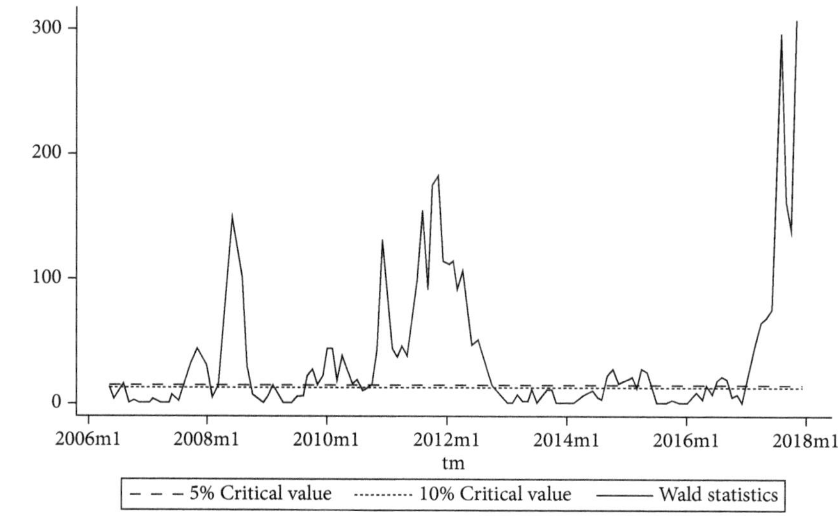

Fig. 6.4: Time-varying Granger causality

Notes: VAR(1) under SIC

H_0: Deposit dollarization does not Granger-causes credit dollarization

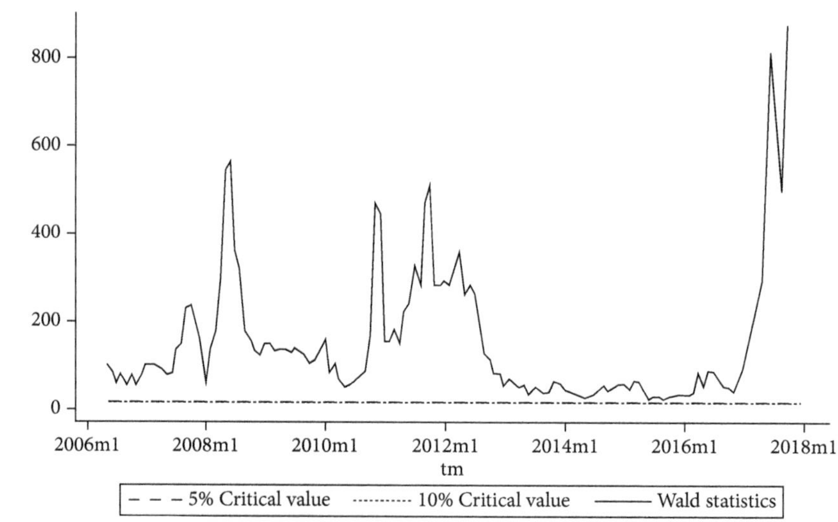

Fig. 6.5: Time-varying Granger causality

Notes: VAR(2) under SIC, Todo-Yamamoto procedure

H_0: Deposit dollarization does not Granger-causes credit dollarization

References

Acharya, V., S. Cecchetti, J. de Gregorio, Ş. Kalemli-Özcan, P. Lane, and U. Panizza (2015). "Corporate Debt in Emerging Economies: A Threat to Financial Stability," Committee on International Policy Reform, Brookings Institutions and CIGI.

Acosta-Ormaechea, Santiago, and David Coble (2011). "The Monetary Transmission in Dollarized and Non-Dollarized Economies; The Cases of Chile, New Zealand, Peru and Uruguay," IMF Working Papers 11/87, International Monetary Fund.

Alfaro, L., G. Asis, A. Chari, and U. Panizza (2017). Lessons Unlearned? Corporate Debt in Emerging Markets. Working Paper (October).

Alp, Bengü, ve C. Yalçın (2015). Türkiye'de Şirketlerin Borç Dolarizasyonu ve Büyüme Performansı. Ç. Tebliği, TCMB 15/01.

Barajas, Adolfo, Sergio Restrepo, Roberto Steiner, Juan Camilo Medellín, ve César Pabón (2016). Balance Sheet Effects in Colombian Non-financial Firms.

Bocola, L. ve G. Lorenzoni (2018). Financial Crises, Dollarization, and Lending of Last Resort in Open Economies. NBER Working Paper Series, No. 23984.

Cowan, K., E. Hansen, and L. O. Herrera (2005). Currency Mismatches, Balance Sheet Effects and Hedging in Chilean Non-financial Corporations. IADB Working Paper no. 521. Washington, DC: Inter-American Development Bank.

Fendoğlu, S., M. S. Çolak, ve Y. S. Hacıhasanoğlu (2019). "Foreign Currency Debt and the Exchange Rate Pass-Through," Working Papers 1924, Research and Monetary Policy Department, Central Bank of the Republic of Turkey.

Fernandez, R. B. (1981). A Methodological Note on the Estimation of Time Series. The Review of Economics and Statistics, 63(3), 471–476.

Feyen, E., N. Fiess, I. Huertas, and L. Lambert (2017). Which Emerging Markets and Developing Countries Face Corporate Sector Vulnerabilities. World Bank Policy Research Working Paper No. 8198.

Honohan, Patrick & Anging Shi (2002). "Deposit Dollarization and the Financial Sector in Emerging Economies," Policy Research Working Paper Series 2748, The World Bank.

IMF (2015). Chapter 3- Corporate Debt in Emerging Markets – A Concern? Global Financial Stability Report (October, 2015)- Vulnerabilities, Legacies, and Policy Challenges.

Kara, A., Y. S. Hacıhasanoğlu, ve D. Ünalmış (2019). Financial Contagion and the Role of Firm Characteristics, Finance Research Letters, 101389.

Kiyotaki, N. ve J. Moore (2002). Balance-sheet Contagion. American Economic Review, 92(2), 46–50.

Ozsoz, Emre, and Erick W. Rengifo (2016). Understanding Dollarization: Causes and Impact of Partial Dollarization on Developing and Emerging Markets. Berlin, De Gruyter Oldenbourg.

Pomerleano, M. (1998). The East Asian Crisis and Corporate Finances: The Untold Microeconomic Story. Emerging Markets Quarterly, Winter, 14–27.

Rossi, B., and Y. Wang (2019). VAR-Based Granger-Causality Test in the Presence of Instabilities. The Stata Journal, 19(4), 883–899.

Toda, H. Y. and T. Yamamoto (1995). Statistical Inferences in Vector Autoregressions with Possibly Integrated Processes. Journal of Econometrics, 66, 225–250.

Tucker, D. ve D. Li (2014). Risks and Spillovers. Background Study for IMF 2014 Triennial Surveillance Review (Washington DC).

Berna Serener

7 Banking, Currency and Fiscal Crisis

Highlights: The aim of this chapter is to analyze banking, currency, and fiscal crisis. Historically, banking crises were merely bank panics. Following the deregulation and liberalization of financial markets, banking crises began to emerge. Fiscal crises occur when fiscal authorities are unable to meet their principal and interest payments. Currency crises, on the other hand, are caused by the depreciation of a currency as a result of a speculative attack. Today, all three types of crisis are interconnected, meaning that twin and triple crises are common. This chapter analyzes several factors affecting banking crises. Not all currency crises are the same. Currency crises are analyzed using first-, second-, and third-generation models. Noneconomic factors affecting currency crises are discussed. The effects of the choice of currency regime on currency crises are examined. The options for monetary authorities facing currency crises are elaborated. Finally, the events that led to the Asian and Eurozone crises are reviewed.

Keywords: Currency crises, banking crises, fiscal crises, models, boom-bust cycle

Introduction

In the Bretton Woods era, no banking crises occurred. However, during the 1980s after deregulations, as the competition intensified, the financial instability of the banking system increased (Keeley, 1990). In order to maximize profits, banks began to take excessive risks. Consequently, the 1990s were marked by crises around the world.

Bank crises were just panics prior to the development of deposit insurance. Depositors were concerned that they would not be able to withdraw their money from the banks, which resulted in a run on the bank. When the lender of last resort did not intervene, banking panics would reduce the money supply in the economy (Bernanke, 1983). Faced with liquidity problems, banks would sell assets excessively. Banking panics would then spread throughout the system as the banks were interconnected, ultimately resulting in the collapse of the banking system. Bank panics would become bank crises as a result of deposit insurance that was put into place. The costly process of bailing out the banks became a burden for the governments and fiscal deficits often developed as a result. Furthermore, banks chose to take more risks as a result of government guarantees. Moral hazard and fiscal imbalances were two negative results of governments guaranteeing banks' liabilities.

Currency crises occur as a result of speculative attacks on fixed exchange system. Fiscal crises are the result of governments not being able to make their principal and interest payments. In the globalized world, banking, fiscal, and currency crises are interconnected. Situations where two crises occur simultaneously are called twin crises, whereas the occurrence of three crises is defined as triple crises. Eichengreen, Rose, and Wypolsz (2003) argued that economies, particularly those in emerging markets, can face three crises at the same time due to original sin. Original sin refers to the situation where both the private sector and the public sector hold liabilities denominated in foreign currencies. Following a currency crisis, the domestic currency depreciates, and the fiscal deficit increases as a result of short-term foreign currency denominated liabilities. Thus, the currency crisis turns into a fiscal crisis. Bank bail outs can increase fiscal imbalances during periods of banking crisis. Banking crises thus spillover into debt crises.

1 Banking Crises

Banking crises were just panics and manias during the 1970s (Kauko, 2014). During the 1980s, researchers started to analyze banking by using econometric models. One of the predictors of a banking crisis is the boom-bust cycle. Loans grow excessively before a crisis, whereas the prices of real estate, commodities, and financial securities skyrocket. Stock market bubbles are also common before a crisis. When the economy is booming, domestic funds become insufficient to finance the increased demand for loans. Thus, banks borrow from abroad to give loans domestically. Foreign debt increases and the public purchases imported goods. Capital inflow bonanzas that are larger than normal capital inflows trigger above average credit expansion (Demirgüç-Kunt and Detragiache 1998, 2005). Capital inflows are followed by appreciation of the exchange rate regime. An increase in net foreign debt accompanied with a fixed exchange regime increases the likelihood of a crisis (Peria and Domaç, 2003). Eventually, as the bubble bursts, the cycle ends. Prices decrease, the currency collapses, and a banking crisis occurs. The boom-bust cycle will be repeated.

According to Demirgüç-Kunt and Detragiache (1998), crises should have the distinctive trait of at least one of the following features. First, ratio of non-performing loans to total assets should exceed 10 %. Second, a minimum of 2 % of GDP should be spent on operations to rescue failing institutions. Third, the crisis should cause a large number of banks to be nationalized. Fourth, a significantly high number of bank runs should occur.

Although a number of different factors can contribute to a banking crisis, only the main ones will be discussed in this section. As stated by Duttagopta and Cashin (2001), vulnerabilities, which are weaknesses in the banking sector, combined with triggers, which are adverse economic shocks, cause banking crises in emerging markets. They identified macroeconomic instability, low profitability, and high foreign exchange rate risk as vulnerabilities. Triggers, on the other hand, include the ratio of export prices to import prices, high currency depreciation, and large dollarization of bank liabilities.

Excessive lending or the growth of credit stock is experienced just before a crisis erupts. Many researchers have attempted to identify how long it takes for a credit expansion to develop into a banking crisis. Jorda, Schularick, and Taylor (2011) observed that growth in credit as a percentage of GDP continues for four years before the crisis starts. Demirgüç-Kunt and Detragiache (2000), on the other hand, noticed a two-year lag between a banking crisis and economic growth. Bordo and Meissner (2012) concluded that a period of five years was needed for the growth in excessive lending to cure a banking crisis. The presence of a deposit guarantee scheme protecting small investors decreases the likelihood of a crisis (Davis and Karim, 2008). Demirgüç-Kunt and Detragiache (2002) did not observe such an effect of a deposit insurance scheme on banking crises in their research.

Another important fact that can contribute to a banking crisis is whether the current account is in deficit or surplus (Davis, Mack and Phoa, 2016). The demand for credit growth by the private sector precedes a banking crisis. If a country is running a current account deficit, it means that credit is financed by borrowing internationally. An increase in private sector credit growth coupled with a current account surplus means that credit growth is caused by domestic savings. Whenever foreign borrowing is financing a credit boom, the probability of a banking crisis increases.

Minsky (1977) was the first researcher to emphasize the function of asset price bubbles in banking crises. Real estate lending may give the impression it is relatively less risky as it is not fully collateralized. However, asset price bubbles in the real estate markets of Sweden (Kokko, 1999) and USA (Connor, Flavin and O'Kelly, 2012) have been observed. According to Barrell, Davis, Karim, and Liadze (2010), a surge in housing prices starts three years prior to the onset of a banking crisis. Singh (2011) observed that a banking crisis occurred within two and an half years after an increase in stock market prices in India.

Governments offer implicit guarantees to too-big-to-fail banks because the failure of these banks would have negative repercussions for the whole economy. In an economy with an atomistic banking system, banks facing intense competition may choose to accept more risks than necessary in order to maximize profits (Keeley, 1990). Atomistic banking systems are more prone to banking crises than concentrated banking systems (Aizenman and Pasricha, 2012). The liberalization of banking systems increases the likelihood of a banking crisis because it makes it easier for funds to flow from abroad and for banks to take on excessive risks (Demirgüç-Kunt and Detragiache, 1998).

2 Currency Crises

2.1 Theories

Currency crises occur when a speculative attack causes investor to sell large amounts of domestic currency (Terra, 2015). As currency crises are not all the same, they are explained using three different models. According to the first generation of models, currency crises occur due to lack of alignment between the government's fiscal policy and exchange rates (Terra, 2015). The credit policy of the government and the fixed exchange rate regime should be consistent. It is widely believed that panic, irrational behavior, or uncertainty cause speculative attacks. However, first-generation models argue that a speculative attack occurs when a government uses a fixed exchange rate regime and an expansionist credit policy at the same time. The money supply increases as a result of the credit expansion policy. Governments are forced to sell international reserves. When the international reserves are exhausted, the government leaves the fixed exchange rate regime. Speculators assume that the currency will depreciate and will demand more foreign currency. They will attack the currency by selling domestic currency and buying foreign currency. As a result, the international reserves of the country will decrease. If the government wants to prevent the currency from depreciating, it needs to sell international reserves to supply the foreign currency demanded.

The second-generation models were developed during the 1990s during the European Monetary System (EMU) crisis (Terra, 2015). The countries involved in this crisis were developed and therefore had sufficient international reserves to defend their currencies. Moreover, their economic policies were consistent. Obstfeld (1986) explained the second-generation models. First, Obstfeld (1986) argued that abandoning the fixed exchange rate regime is political. Second, the cost of defending an exchange rate is important. These models are called self-fulfilling currency crisis models as expectations are important. If speculators believe that the currency will depreciate, they will attack the currency and the exchange rate will depreciate. The government will decide whether or not to defend the exchange rate depending on the cost. The higher the expectation of depreciation, the more expensive it will be to maintain the fixed exchange rate and the higher the probability that the fixed exchange rate regime will be abandoned. If expectations are high enough, the crisis will become a self-fulfilling prophecy.

The third-generation models were developed during the Asian crisis in the late 1990s and use the boom-bust cycle. The third-generation models use heterogeneous approach and pay attention to weaknesses due to moral hazard, vulnerabilities of balance sheets, and private information. These models can be divided into two groups (Terra, 2015). The first group of models emphasizes the weaknesses in the balance sheets of banks and firms. Illiquidity of the banking system causes financial fragility and thus banking and currency crises are related. Second, when the assets of firms and banks are denominated in local currencies but the liabilities are denominated in foreign currency, these firms experience a mismatch of assets and liabilities, which increases the risk of a currency crisis when the currency depreciates.

The fourth-generation models are the newest models. These models argue that institutional factors cause currency crises. Weak institutions worsen problems by not allocating resources properly in times of high risk and uncertainty. According to these models, political problems, capital account openness, central bank independence, stock market development, bank supervision, depositor safety, legal regimes, and shareholder rights give rise to institutional weaknesses (Shimpalee and Breuer, 2006).

2.2 Noneconomic Factors Affecting Currency Crises

Economic factors are not the only ones that determine the occurrence of a currency crisis. Political conditions and institutional factors should also be taken into consideration when evaluating the likelihood of such a crisis. Institutional features connected to fiscal, financial, price, and macroeconomic stability prevent currency crises. According to Block (2003), left-wing governments are more prone to currency crises. The currencies of strong governments who hold the majority of seats in the legislature have less possibility of being attacked by speculators. Democracy decreases the likelihood of a currency crisis.

Institutions impact currency crises in two different ways (Li and Inclan, 2001). Good institutions positively affect the health of the overall economy. Institutions that cause bad economic fundamentals will increase the risk of a currency crisis. Institutions send signals to participants in the market about future economic growth prospects, which in turn influences the expectations of people in the market. Institutions that contribute to bad economic fundamentals attract speculative capital inflows, raise uncertainty in the market, and increase the probability of a crisis. Shimpalee and Breuer (2006) examined 30 countries for the period between 1984 and 2002 and concluded that corruption, a de facto exchange regime, government instability, and weak legislation raise the likelihood of a currency crisis.

Currency crises are contagious because of financial linkages. In their investigation of 41 emerging markets, Caramazza, Ricci, and Salgado (2004) found that crises in Mexico, Asia, and Russia spread from one economy to another through linkages. Four linkages through which crises spread have been identified. The first factor is common shocks. Changes in interest rates or appreciation/depreciation of a currency in a country can affect other economies. The second factor is trade linkages. In the increasingly globalized world, countries are integrated through trade. A change in the value of a currency in one country can negatively affect another country's trade through exports and imports. The third factor is the financial linkages. Countries form linkages with each other by investing and lending. Financial vulnerabilities increase in times of crises through such linkages. When a crisis breaks out in a particular country, investors will look for ways to liquidate their portfolios. Similarly, if a country is highly indebted to another country that is experiencing a crisis, investors' risk perception of the creditor country's assets will increase. Eventually, capital may flow out of the creditor country. The fourth factor is the changes in investors' opinions. An economy experiencing weak fundamentals becomes more vulnerable when other countries suffer. Investors may become more risk averse, they may be afraid of speculative attacks, or their expectations may change unexpectedly.

2.3 The Choice of a Currency Regime

Countries have the option of choosing pegged (fixed), intermediate, or floating regimes. It is important to choose the right regime as macroeconomic performance depends on the appropriateness of the regime (Reinhart and Rogoff, 2004). Frankel (1999) stated that "the choice of exchange rate arrangement should depend on the particular circumstances facing the country." Optimum Currency Area (OCA) theory states that the choice of exchange rate regime should depend on "trade links, openness, size and the characteristics of the shocks the economy is subject to" (Aşıcı, 2011). Economic and political features should be in line with the exchange rate regime. Fixed exchange rates are used to fight inflationary expectation. However, according to the impossible trinity hypothesis, preserving macroeconomic stability with an independent monetary policy, freedom of international capital mobility, and maintaining a fixed exchange rate regime is impossible (Obstfeld, Shambaugh and Taylor, 2005). Using data from 183 countries, Aşıcı (2011) found evidence supporting the impossible trinity hypothesis. Thus, the relationship between capital account openness and the tendency to use a fixed exchange rate regime is negative. Aşıcı (2011) also found a positive relationship between trade concentration and the tendency to peg a currency. The author also found support for the sustainability hypothesis. Politically strong governments find it easier to peg a currency compared to weak governments. More specifically, for weak governments with large deficits, maintaining a fixed exchange rate regime is more difficult.

Faced with the option of choosing different currency regimes, it is imperative that countries choose the right one. However, researchers have reported conflicting results on the effect of different currency regimes on currency crises. Fischer (2001) argued that in order to prevent speculative attacks on local currencies, monetary authorities should adopt fixed exchange rates (hard pegs). Hard pegs can increase the trustworthiness of currencies because governments show dedication to abandon an independent monetary policy. Furthermore, governments using fixed exchange rates show higher transparency. Esaka (2011) found support for the assertion that compared to other regimes, hard pegs decrease the probability of currency crises. By adopting a fixed exchange regime, monetary authorities explicitly commit to one regime. Thus, speculators find it easier to target fixed regimes since the target is known. However, it is harder to attack a flexible exchange regime. Esaka (2011) claimed that fixed regimes attract capital inflows from international investors since there is no exchange rate risk. Therefore, fixed regimes are more liable to currency crises. Radelet and Sachs (1998) argued that if the fixed regime is coupled with a liberalized capital account, the likelihood of a currency crisis is increased.

Exchange regimes whose central banks show explicit commitments by law are called de jure exchange regimes. De jure exchange rate regimes only exist on paper. De facto exchange rates, on the other hand, are the true exchange rates a country uses in practice. Fear of announcing a peg is caused by the fact that countries are reluctant to declare that they use a fixed exchange regime in order not to attract speculators (Levy-Yeyati and Sturzenegger (2005). Faced with the fear of fixing, countries often adopt fixed exchange rate systems but publicly announce they have floating exchange rate regimes. Ghosh, Golde, and Wolf (2003) used de jure exchange rate regimes and claimed that floating regimes have a higher probability of crises. Reinhart and Rogoff (2004), on the other hand, used de facto exchange regimes for the period of 1970 to 2000 and argued that the likelihood of a currency crisis is higher for managed floating regimes. Using de facto classification, Levy-Yeyati and Sturzenegger (2005) found that the probability of a currency crisis is higher for pegged regimes. However, they found no evidence of a relationship between pegged regimes and currency crises when using their own classification of exchange rate regimes.

Some countries use consistent pegs. For these countries, the exchange rate regime they announce and the one they use are the same. Countries using consistent pegs face a lower risk of currency crisis (Esaka, 2014). These countries are perceived as more credible by market participants as they are committed to sustaining a fixed exchange rate regime.

2.4 Monetary Policy Response to Currency Crises

The response of a monetary policy in order to defend a domestic currency after a currency crisis was examined by Eijffinger and Karataş (2012). The authors argued that from 1986 to 2009, the use of a tight monetary policy was successful for both advanced and emerging economies. However, the monetary policy was not effective in either advanced or emerging economies during recent crises. In general, increasing interest rates results in the stabilization of exchange rates for advanced economies. For emerging economies, monetary policy should consider economic fragilities in order to fight currency crises.

Central banks face several options once a currency crisis starts. Erler, Bauer, and Herz (2015) analyzed different scenarios involving monetary intervention. If a central bank decides to intervene, the result can be either successful or unsuccessful. The central bank needs to evaluate the costs of both intervening and not intervening. In the first scenario, a currency depreciates suddenly and the central bank does not intervene. In the second scenario where the currency is successfully defended, the central bank will experience the best economic performance. In the third scenario, the central bank is not successful at defending its currency. In this instance, further depreciation of the currency is inevitable and the losses will be undesirable and intense.

3. Fiscal Crises

The aim of fiscal policy is to keep the public revenues and expenditures in balance to prevent a crisis. Debt crises are more damaging than banking and currency crises (Furceri and Zdzienicka, 2012). Moreover, fiscal crises are contagious as they spread because correlations of financial assets returns among different international markets increase. Second, the spillover effects of a fiscal crisis can be experienced as countries are connected through trading and investing.

During an economic downturn, fiscal crises inflate the contraction of economic growth (Medas, Poghosyan, Farah-Yacoob and Gerling, 2018). When the gap between public revenues and expenditures enlarges, unemployment and inflation increase. In the literature, sovereign debt crises and fiscal crises are used interchangeably. Studies on fiscal crises mostly concentrate on defaulting on, rejecting to pay, and restructuring debt. However, sovereign debt crises are not the only cause of fiscal crises. Fiscal crises can occur because of governments defaulting on domestic public debt, exogenous shocks, and skyrocketing inflation (Reinhart and Rogoff, 2009). Depreciation of the exchange rate, increases in the cost borrowing, and slowing down of the economy can also give rise to fiscal crises. Moreover, exogenous shocks prompted by banking crises can initiate banking crises. Dias (2017) argued that the rate at which countries react to the crisis, the effects of the crisis, and the problems countries face during crisis are not the same across different European countries.

Countries encounter distress when expenditures and revenues are imbalanced. If a government is not capable of paying the principle and the interest on its debt, debt crises are inevitable. The higher the debt, the higher is the probability of default. Roch and Uhlig (2018) claimed that debt crises have self-fulfilling characteristics. When market participants are afraid of defaulting, the risk premium of sovereign debt goes up and the likelihood of a sovereign default increases.

Some countries facing imbalances do not default as they are rescued by the IMF. It is clear that debt crises are not costless. During the European crises, GDP fell and unemployment increased, ultimately causing the countries to fall into recession (Dias, 2017). Using a group of emerging countries, Tavares (2019) concluded that unemployment increased by 15 % during the crisis. According to Rose (2005), after the fiscal crisis, trading of goods and services decreased by 8 %. In a research conducted on 154 countries for the period of 1970 to 2008, it was found that output decreased by 10 % after the debt crisis (Furceri and Zdzienicka, 2012).

A fiscal crisis affects a country's aggregate demand and its ability to access international capital markets. According to Arteta and Hale (2008), 25 % of emerging countries, especially those in Latin America, raise capital from external sources. Both during and after sovereign debt crises, domestic firms find it hard to access international markets to obtain foreign credit. According to Tomz and Wright (2005), more than 50 % of countries who default are unable to access capital markets for more than twelve years. Aggregate demand, on the other hand, decreases for two reasons. First, a country that asks for assistance from the IMF is often encouraged to follow tight monetary and fiscal policies. A fiscal crisis due to an exogenous shock also decreases aggregate demand (Arteta and Hale, 2008). Facing a fall in aggregate demand, firms encounter a decrease in profits and choose to reduce production and do not take on further debt.

The impact of fiscal policy on consumption depends on the amount of public debt (Sutherland, 1997). When the levels of debt are reasonable, consumers believe that they will not be alive to pay taxes in the future to finance the debt. Therefore, consumers will continue spending. However, when the level of debt is extremely high, consumers believe that they will be forced to pay extra taxes and this results in a decrease in consumer consumption.

The Asian Crisis and Eurozone Crisis

The Asian crisis that occurred in 1998–1992 was a twin currency and debt crisis. Unlike developed countries, the Asian tigers lacked the ability to borrow in their own currencies. Economic growth was financed through borrowing in dollars at relatively low international interest rates. Liabilities denominated in foreign currencies, which is known as the "original sin," government guarantees, and depreciation of currencies caused this crisis (Eichengreen and Hausmann, 2005). Original sin increases the probability that a banking crisis will occur during a currency crisis. Faced with a currency crisis, countries need more tax revenues and export earnings to pay off foreign debt. Banks in these countries give out risky loans. Banks in the Four Tigers did not see the need to hedge their liabilities as the governments not only guaranteed domestic debt but also foreign debt (Burnside, Eichenbaum, and Rebelo 2004). Lending increased and capital flew from abroad creating a market boom. Faced with an economic boom, banks gave out more loans while investing in short-term international securities. The increase in consumption and the growing current account deficit were the results of the booming economy. Devaluation occurred as the speculators believed that currencies were overvalued. Banks became insolvent as they were holding foreign currency denominated loans.

Following the fiscal crises of 2007–2009, the Eurozone crisis started in 2010. These crises were the twin crises of banking and fiscal crises. In 2009, the Greek government defaulted on its debt. Sovereign default of the Greek government led to banking crises across Europe because different countries held each other's debt. Diversification of portfolios was often achieved through holding the sovereign debt of other European countries. Foreign debt is often used as collateral to boost lending. When a member state defaults, bank portfolios of other member states become weaker.

Conclusion

All economies go through the boom-bust cycle. In the increasingly globalized world, economies are linked through the trading of goods and investing in capital markets. Crises are contagious in a globalized, liberalized world. It is inevitable that countries will face one of the currency, fiscal or banking crises. It is imperative for countries to take the necessary precautions when their economies are booming. For instance, foreign currency denominated liabilities should be limited. Hedging instruments should be used to protect against the risks. Banks should pay attention to maturity mismatches of assets and liabilities. Finally, monetary authorities should show a keen interest in the problem of moral hazard in the banking industry.

References

Aizenman, J., and Pasricha, G. K. (2012) "Determinants of Financial Stress and Recovery During the Great Recession", International Journal of Finance and Economics, 17(4): 347–372.

Arteta, C., and Hale, G. (2008) "Sovereign Debt Crises and Credit to the Private Sector", Journal of International Economics, 74(1): 53–69.

Aşıcı, A. A. (2011) "Exchange Rate Regime Choice and Currency Crises", Economic Systems, 35(3): 419–436.

Barrell, R., Davis, E. P., Karim, D., and Liadze, I. (2010) "Bank Regulation, Property Prices and Early Warning Systems for Banking Crises in OECD Countries", Journal of Banking and Finance, 34(9): 2255–2264.

Bernanke, B. S. (1983) "Non-monetary Effects of the Financial Crisis in the Propagation of the Great Depression", American Economic Review,73(1): 257–276.

Block, S. A. (2003) "Political Conditions and Currency Crises in Emerging Markets", Emerging Markets Review, 4(3): 287–309.

Bordo, M. D., and Meissner, C. M. (2012) "Does Inequality Lead to a Financial Crisis?", Journal of International Money and Finance", 31(8): 2147–2161.

Burnside, C., Eichenbaum, M., and Rebelo, S. (2004) "Government Guarantees and Self-fulfilling Speculative Attacks", Journal of Economic Theory, 119(1): 31–63.

Caramazza, F., Ricci, L., and Salgado, R. (2004) "International Financial Contagion in Currency Crises", Journal of International Money and Finance, 23(1): 51–70.

Connor, G., Flavin, T., and O'Kelly, B. (2012) "The US and Irish Credit Crises: Their Distinctive Differences and Common Features. Journal of International Money and Finance, 31(1): 60–79.

Davis, E. P., and Karim, D. (2008) "Comparing Early Warning Systems for Banking Crises", Journal of Financial Stability, 4(2): 89–120.

Davis, J. S., Mack, A., Phoa, W., and Vandenabeele, A. (2016) "Credit Booms, Banking Crises, and the Current Account. Journal of International Money and Finance", 60I: 360–377.

Demirgüç-Kunt, A., and Detragiache, E. (1998) The Determinants of Banking Crises in Developing and Developed Countries, IMF Staff Paper, 45, 81–109.

Demirgüç-Kunt, A., and Detragiache, E. (2000) "Monitoring Banking Sector Fragility: A Multivariate Logit Approach", The World Bank Economic Review, 14(2): 287–307.

Demirgüç-Kunt, A., and Detragiache, E. (2002) "Does Deposit Insurance Increase Banking System Stability? An Empirical Investigation", Journal of Monetary Economics, 49(7): 1373–1406.

Demirgüç-Kunt, A., and Detragiache, E. (2005) "Cross-country Empirical Studies of Systemic Bank Distress: A Survey", National Institute Economic Review, 192(1): 68–83.

Dias, J. (2017). "Unemployment and Sovereign Debt Crisis in the Eurozone: A k-means-r Analysis", Physica A: Statistical Mechanics and Its Applications, 482(15): 108–117.

Duttagupta, R., and Cashin, P. (2011) "Anatomy of Banking Crises in Developing and Emerging Market Countries", Journal of International Money and Finance, 30(2): 354–376.

Eichengreen, B., Rose, A.K., and Wypolsz, C. (2003) "Contagious Currency Crises", Eichengreen (Ed.), Capital Flows and Crises, MIT Press, Cambridge, MA, 155–185.

Eijffinger, S. C., and Karataş, B. (2012) "Currency Crises and Monetary Policy: A Study on Advanced and Emerging Economies", Journal of International Money and Finance, 31(5): 948–974.

Erler, A., Bauer, C., and Herz, B. (2015) "To Intervene, or Not to Intervene: Monetary Policy and the Costs of Currency Crises", Journal of International Money and Finance, 51: 432–456.

Esaka, T. (2011) "Do Hard Pegs Avoid Currency Crises? An Evaluation Using Matching Estimators", Economics Letters, 113(1): 35–38.

Esaka, T. (2014) "Are Consistent Pegs Really More Prone to Currency Crises?", Journal of International Money and Finance, 44I: 136–163.

Fischer, S. (2001) "Exchange Rate Regimes: Is the Bipolar View Correct?", Journal of Economic Perspectives, 15(2): 3–24.

Frankel, J. A. (1999) "No Single Currency Regime Is Right for All Countries or at All Times" (No. w7338), National Bureau of Economic Research.

Furceri, D., and Zdzienicka, A. (2012) "How Costly Are Debt Crises?", Journal of International Money and Finance, 31(4): 726–742.

Ghosh, A., Gulde, A. M., and Wolf, H. (2003) Exchange Rate Regimes: Choices and Consequences. MIT Press, MA.

Jordà, Ò., Schularick, M., and Taylor, A. M. (2011) "Financial Crises, Credit booms, and External Imbalances: 140 Years of Lessons", IMF Economic Review, 59(2): 340–378.

Kauko, K. (2014) "How to Foresee Banking Crises? A Survey of the Empirical Literature", Economic Systems, 38(3): 289–308.

Keeley, M. C. (1990) "Deposit Insurance, Risk, and Market Power in Banking", The American EconomicReview, 80(5): 1183–1200.

Kokko, A. (1999) "Asienkrisen: Ma˚ nga Likheter Med Den Svenska Krisen", (The Asian crisis, many similarities with the Swedishcrisis), Ekonomisk Debatt, 27(2): 81–92.

Levy-Yeyati, E., and Sturzenegger, F. (2005) "Classifying Exchange Rate Regimes: Deeds vs. Words. European Economic Review", 49(6): 1603–1635.

Li, Q., and Inclan, M. (2001, September) "Fundamentals, Expectations, Institutions, and Currency crisis", In Prepared for Presentation at the Annual Meeting of the American Political Science Association (Vol. 20).

Medas, P., Poghosyan, T., Xu, Y., Farah-Yacoub, J., and Gerling, K. (2018) "Fiscal Crises", Journal of International Money and Finance, 88: 191–207.

Minsky, H. P. (1977) "The Financial Instability Hypothesis: An Interpretation of Keynes and an alternative to "Standard" Theory", Challenge, 20(1): 20–27.

Obstfeld, M. (1986) "Speculative Attack and the External Constraint in a Maximizing Model of the Balance of Payments", Canadian Journal of Economics, 29: 1–20.

Obstfeld, M., Shambaugh, J. C., and Taylor, A. M. (2005) "The Trilemma in History: Tradeoffs Among Exchange Rates, Monetary Policies, and Capital Mobility", Review of Economics and Statistics, 87(3): 423–438.

Peria, M., and Domaç, I. (2003) "Banking Crises and Exchange Rate Regimes: Is There a Link?", Journal of International Economics, 61(1): 41–72.

Radelet, S., Sachs, J. D., Cooper, R. N., &Bosworth, B. P. (1998) "The East Asian Financial Crisis: Diagnosis, Remedies, Prospects. Brookings Papers on Economic Activity, 1998(1): 1–90.

Reinhart, C. M. and Rogoff, K. S. (2004) "The Modern History of Exchange Rate Arrangements: A Reinterpretation", The Quarterly Journal of Economics, 119(1): 1–48.

Reinhart, C. M., and Rogoff, K. S. (2009). This Time Is Different: Eight Centuries of Financial Folly. Princeton University Press.New Jersey.

Roch, F., and Uhlig, H. (2018) "The Dynamics of Sovereign Debt Crises and Bailouts", Journal of International Economics, 114I: 1–13.

Rose, A. K. (2005) "One Reason Countries Pay Their Debts: Renegotiation and International Trade", Journal of Development Economics, 77(1): 189–206.

Shimpalee, P. L., and Breuer, J. B. (2006) "Currency Crises and Institutions", Journal of International Money and Finance, 25(1): 125–145.

Singh, T. R. (2011) "An Ordered Probit Model of an Early Warning System for Predicting Financial Crisis in India", IFC Bulletin, 25: 185–201.

Sutherland, A. (1997) "Fiscal Crises and Aggregate Demand: Can High Public Debt Reverse the Effects of Fiscal Policy?", Journal of Public Economics, 65(2): 147–162.

Tavares, T. (2019) "Labor Market Distortions Under Sovereign Debt Default Crises", Journal of Economic Dynamics and Control, 108: 103749.

Terra, C. (2015) "Principles of International Finance and Open Economy Macroeconomics", 1st Edition, Elsevier Science Press, San Diago, United States.

Tomz, M., and Wright, M. L. (2005) "Sovereign Debt, Defaults and Bailouts" Paper presented at the NBER IFM SI 2005.

Tuba Gülcemal

8 Financial Systems Importance, Differences, and Convergence

Highlights: The financial sector only encompasses the supply of financial services while the financial system includes both supply and demand and the way in which supply and demand are matched. The money and capital markets make possible the exchange of current income for future income and the transformation of savings into investment so that production, employment, and income can grow, and living standards can improve. The importance of financial markets and financial intermediaries differs across countries. The financial sector performs two important functions like reducing information and transaction costs and facilitating the trading, diversification, and management of risk. What are the differences in financial systems and how do these affect macroeconomic outcomes? This chapter discusses these and other positive and negative aspects of bank-based and market-based systems.

Key words: Financial systems, bank-based systems, market-based systems

Introduction

Financial systems have been accepted as an important area of public policy and academic research. The existence of a strong financial system is important for a stable economy. The quality of a country's financial system is important. Since it is the responsibility of policy makers to develop and improve financial systems, they are concerned about it. Almost all components of the action plan of the financial sector in the European Union have been implemented recently. International organizations such as the World Bank and the IMF have made great efforts and spent money to help the improvement the financial systems of countries that have some impact on them. Many questions come to mind such as what the financial systems matter mean and why they are important, what financial systems mean exactly, and what determines their quality. Are there any generalized standards for the evaluation of the financial systems, who and what are financial systems important for, and what can policy makers do to improve the financial system? This section tries to explain these issues.

Among other things, the frequency and severity of financial crises after the collapse of Bretton Woods fixed exchange rate regime system increased attention in financial systems. In many countries, the wave of liberalization of national financial systems in the 1970s and 1980s continued with a wave of readjustment in the latter decades. It is difficult to evaluate the economic, social, and political consequences of these developments on an overall scale (Schmidt and Hryckiewicz,2006).

The financial system determines the amount and cost of funds available for the payment of thousands of goods and services that we buy on daily basis. Everything that happens in the financial system has a strong impact on the health of the global economy. When funds have higher cost and less accessibility, spending on goods and services also decreases. As a result, the growth of the economy slows down and unemployment rate increases since business firms stop the production and layoffs increase. In contrast, when the cost of funds declines and loanable funds become more readily available, spending in the economy often increases, more jobs are created, and the economy's growth accelerates (Rose and Marquis, 2006).

1 Economic Functions Performed by the Global Financial System

The Global Financial System has basic economic functions that create a need for money and capital markets like savings, wealth, liquidity, credit, payments, risk protection, and policy functions. We can group these functions of the financial systems into two main functions: (1) reducing information and transaction costs and (2) facilitating the trading, diversification, and management of risk to explain why the financial sector may stimulate capital formation and technological innovation, two of the driving forces of economic growth.

1.1. Reducing Information Asymmetry and Transaction Costs

The financial system helps overcome an information asymmetry between borrowers and lenders. The information asymmetry problem occurs ex post when borrowers, but not investors, can observe actual behavior. Once a loan has been granted, there is a risk that the borrower will engage in activities that are undesirable from the perspective of the lender (moral hazard). Financial markets and intermediaries also mitigate the information acquisition and enforcement costs of monitoring borrowers. Financial intermediaries may reduce the costs of acquiring and processing information and thereby improve resource allocation. Without intermediaries, each investor would face the large fixed cost associated with evaluating investment projects. Also, financial markets may reduce information costs.

The financial system reduces the time and money spent in carrying out financial transactions. Financial intermediaries can reduce transaction costs as they have developed expertise and can take advantage of economies of scale and scope. If present trends continue, electronic means of payment, including *computer terminals in homes, offices, and stores* and *digital cash* (accessed by an encoded plastic card), will eventually replace checks and other pieces of paper as the principal means of paying in the future. Indeed, electronic means of payment are growing rapidly today, while checks and other paper-based means of payment are declining in volume.

1.2. Trading, Diversification, and Management of Risk

The second main service the financial sector provides is facilitating the trading, diversification, and management of risk. Financial systems may mitigate the risks associated with individual investment projects by providing opportunities for trading and diversifying risk which – in the end – may affect long-run economic growth. In general, high-return projects tend to be riskier than low-return projects. Thus, financial systems that make it easier for people to diversify risk by offering a broad range of high-risk (like equity) and low-risk (like government bonds) investment opportunities tend to induce a portfolio shift towards projects with higher expected returns (Haan, Oosterloo and Schoenmaker, 2009: 9). Liquidity is created by financial intermediaries as well as financial markets. For instance, a bank transforms short-term liquid deposits into long-term illiquid loans, therefore making it possible for households to withdraw deposits without interrupting industrial production. Similarly, stock markets reduce liquidity risks by allowing stock holders to trade their shares, while firms still have access to long-term capital.

The financial system permits individuals and institutions to engage in both *risk sharing* and *risk reduction*. Risk sharing occurs when an individual or institution transfers risk exposure to someone willing to accept that risk (an insurance company) while risk reduction usually takes place when we diversify our wealth across a wide variety of different assets so that our overall losses are likely to be more limited.

Risk can be mitigated if the intermediation system is well capitalized, because capital acts as a buffer. Given the low levels of private capital in emerging economies, historically, the government has created capital for intermediaries by keeping the rates intermediaries pay investors low. This has become infeasible as deregulation and competition has given investors more choice. Consequently, the task of averting the collapse of the system of intermediation in the face of severe macroeconomic volatility has shifted directly to the government. Governments have had to absorb risk by promising the intermediation system capital, implicitly or explicitly, in case the system is in danger (Rajan and Zingales, 2001: 478).

Financial services use digital transformation like other sectors. This digital transformation can generate cyber risks, such as cyber attacks, IT risks linked to, for example, outdated systems. If these risks were to materialize simultaneously in different institutions, this could have systemic consequences.

2. Financial Systems, Development, and Growth

From Goldsmith (1969) to the present, a growing body of empirical analyses involving firm-level studies, industry-level studies, individual country-studies, and broad cross-country comparisons demonstrate a strong positive link between the functioning of the financial system and long-run economic growth. Theory and evidence make it difficult to conclude that the financial system merely and automatically responds to industrialization and economic activity or that financial development is an inconsequential addendum to the process of economic growth (Levine, 1997). Levine's other studies (Demirgüç-Kunt and Levine, 2001; Levine, 2005) address the endogeneity problems inherent in finance and growth regressions use a number of different econometric techniques on datasets ranging from microlevel firm data to international comparative studies. These studies and many others also (Papaioannou and Gregorios, 2008) report evidence that financial development causes economic growth.

Technological improvements, lower transaction costs, and financial arrangements affect financial systems. Monetary and fiscal policies affect the taxation of financial intermediaries and the provision of financial services. Legal systems affect financial systems and political changes and national institutions critically influence financial development. That means nonfinancial developments also affect financial systems. Furthermore, economic growth itself alters the willingness of savers and investors to pay the costs associated with participating in the financial system. As stated in the work of Papaioannou and Gregorios (2008) the evidence based on cross-country and cross-sectional regressions faces various problems in providing causality between financial development and economic growth. First, it is almost impossible to account for all possible factors that may foster growth. Second, the effect of financial development may be heterogeneous across countries. Third, there can be reverse causation: financial development can be both the cause and the consequence of economic growth. As a result, the indicators of financial development as generally used in these studies (such as private domestic credit to GDP and market capitalization as a share of GDP) lack a sound theoretical basis.

3. Differences Between National Financial Systems

There are not adequate theories of why different financial structures emerge or why financial structures change. All financial systems combine bank-based and market-based intermediation. Differences in legal tradition (La Porta et al. 1997 and Levine, 1997) and differences in national resource endowments that produce different political and institutional structures might be incorporated into future models of financial development. Furthermore, economists need to develop an analytical basis for making comparisons of financial structures and need models that elucidate the conditions, if any, under which different financial structures are better at mitigating information and transaction costs (Levine, 1997).

Banks and markets are similarly important for economic growth (Levine, 2004). However, the literature published after the great financial crisis of 2008 generally has a preference for market-based systems. This is because a financial crisis or a housing market crisis is economically more severe in bank-based than in market-based financial structures. Banks overextend and misallocate credit in financial upturns and ration credit in financial downturns more than markets (Langfield Pagano, 2015).

The real economic benefits of bank-based financial structures therefore depend on the stability of the financial system. But this stability can be upset by systemic risk. Systemic risk may be defined as a disruption to the flow of financial services that is (i) caused by an impairment of all or parts of the financial system and (ii) has the potential to have serious negative consequences for the real economy. Banks can generate systemic risk for a number of reasons. First, they are highly leveraged. When asset values are rising – leveraged institutions can extract higher returns on their equity. However, when asset values are falling – these institutions may be required to raise capital or shrink their balance sheet in order to meet regulatory requirements. In a system of leveraged banks, fire sales amplify downturns. Also, when higher bank leverage induces stronger creditor discipline, systemic risk rises on account of contagious bank runs prompted by creditors liquidating their claims (Acharya and Thakor, 2016). Second, the large asset-liability mismatches of banks make them vulnerable to liquidity and interest rate shocks, and in the extreme to bank runs. This contributes to systemic risk. Third, banks trade with each other through many markets, intermediaries, and systems. This creates long intermediation chains, adds complexity, and leads banks to be highly interconnected. Interconnectedness is a key driver of systemic importance. Due to settlement, liquidity, and funding risk, this interconnectedness can propagate losses through the financial system, as losses for one bank may cause losses for another (Bats and Houben, 2017: 2–3). Market-based financing is less likely to contribute to systemic risk. Market-based financing is less leveraged, has more asset-liability matching, and more direct financing from savers to investors, implying less financial system interconnectedness.

Bats and Houben's paper (2017) assessed the merits of bank-based versus market-based financing by exploring the relationship between financial structure and systemic risk by a fixed effects regression model for 22 OECD countries over 16 years. One of the remarkable results is that banks are found not to generate systemic risk when bank-based financing is limited. The findings indicate that the financial structure of the United States is close to optimal in terms of systemic risk. Other countries can increase their resilience to systemic risk by reducing the share of bank-based financing and increasing that of market-based debt and especially market-based stock financing. The design of financial sector and fiscal policies can take this into account. Moreover, adjustments in regulatory requirements change the inherent contribution of different financial structures to systemic risk.

The size of financial markets and the importance of bank and non-bank financial intermediaries (such as mutual funds, private pension funds, and insurance companies) differ substantially across countries as illustrated by Tab. 8.1.

Comparing the current market cap-to-GNI ratio (also known as Buffett Indicator) of a country to its historical average can be used to estimate the current valuation and expected returns of a nation's stock market. *Gross National Income* (GNI) can be used instead of GDP due to its closer relationship with stock market returns.

A key question is how these differences in financial systems affect macroeconomic outcomes. For instance, do bank-based financial systems (like that of Germany) lead to higher rates of economic growth than market-based systems (like that of the UK). The post-war high growth rates of Germany and Japan – where banks are dominant in the financial system – was often considered as "evidence" that bank-based systems outperform market-based systems. However, more detailed empirical work, using microlevel data, has frequently failed to identify the superiority of bank-based systems. Also, the much better growth performance of Anglo-American countries during the 1990s raised skepticism about the acclaimed advantages of bank-based systems.

As seen in Tabs. 8.1 and 8.2 total domestic stock market capitalization as a ratio to GDP/GNI during 2013–2019 is %112–%126 per cent in the United Kingdom, while in Italy stock market capitalization amounted to %35,3 per cent.

German bank credit was 78 per cent of GDP, while in India this ratio was around only 50.04 per cent.

Tab. 8.1: Total domestic market cap to GNI ratio

Nation	2019	2018	2017	2016	2015	2014	2013
United States	172.47 %	144.40 %	160.15 %	144.20 %	136.22 %	147.82 %	140.63 %
Canada	139.54 %	115.98 %	139.73 %	133.97 %	111.77 %	124.77 %	120.34 %
India	75.06 %	76.89 %	87.85 %	70.24 %	70.66 %	78.46 %	62.15 %
Japan	117.94 %	105.48 %	122.09 %	104.54 %	115.41 %	103.42 %	95.93 %
South Korea	96.68 %	89.15 %	108.25 %	92.12 %	90.93 %	89.07 %	90.50 %
China	82.96 %	62.02 %	87.13 %	89.55 %	95.94 %	77.71 %	59.28 %
Germany	53.15 %	44.99 %	56.16 %	51.00 %	51.92 %	48.17 %	48.75 %
Italy	35.35 %	30.39 %	36.13 %	31.17 %	35.31 %	29.00 %	27.87 %
United Kingdom	112.83 %	102.02 %	119.71 %	115.42 %	114.51 %	117.47 %	126.14 %
Russia	44.70 %	38.30 %	41.16 %	45.18 %	39.99 %	33.64 %	39.78 %

Source: http://siblisresearch.com/data/market-cap-to-gdp-ratios/

Tab. 8.2: Domestic bank credit to private sector (%of GDP)

Nation	2018	2017	2016	2015	2014	2013
United States	52.05	52.5	52.35	51.04	49.81	49.3622083
India	50.04	48.77	49.19	51.86	51.88	52.38
Japan	107.48	106.48	104.10	102.02	103.54	104.13
South Korea	150.33	144.79	142.95	140.07	138.35	134.90
China	161.13	157.01	157.5	153.2	140.7	134.31
Germany	78.2	77.67	77.31	78.01	79.3	82.09
Italy	75.97	79.9	84.5	87.19	88.4	90.7
United Kingdom	134.46	133.6	131.9	130.7	135.54	149.4
Russia	51.2	52.0	52.86	55.92	54.80	47.92
Greece	89.0	99.06	107.37	112.2	116.19	118.10

Source: https://data.worldbank.org/indicator/FD.AST.PRVT.GD.ZS?end=2018&locations=GB-AT-US-IN-JP-CA-CN-DE-IT-RU-KR&name_desc=true&start=2012&view=chart

What are the theoretical reasons explaining differences in the growth performance of countries with bank-based or market-based systems? As Levine (2005) pointed out, the case for a bank-based system refers to the role of markets in providing financial functions. Atomistic markets face a free-rider problem: When an investor acquires information about an investment project and behaves accordingly, he reveals this information to all investors, thereby dissuading other investors from devoting resources towards acquiring information. So, investors do not have strong incentives to properly acquire information as they cannot keep the benefits of this information. Consequently, innovative projects that foster growth may not be identified. Banks, however, may keep the information they acquire, often by having long-run relationships with firms, and use it in a profitable way. Since banks can make investments without revealing their decisions immediately in public markets, they have the right incentives to do research on investment projects. Furthermore, banks with close ties to firms may be more effective than atomistic markets at exerting pressure on firms to repay their loans. Often firms obtain a variety of financial services from their bank and also maintain checking accounts with it, thereby increasing the bank's information about the borrower. Proponents of market-based financial systems claim that markets provide a richer set of instruments to manage risks. While bank-based systems may provide inexpensive, basic risk-management services for standardized situations, market-based systems provide greater flexibility to tailor make products (Haan, Oosterloo and Schoenmaker, 2009).

While there is considerable evidence that financial development is good for economic growth, there is no clear evidence that one kind of financial system is better for growth than another. For instance, Levine (2002) finds that the quality of the financial services produced by the entire financial system (intermediaries and markets) matters for economic growth. However, various recent studies suggest that differences in financial systems may influence the type of activity in which a country specializes. Banks may be effective at eliminating duplication of information gathering and processing but may not be effective gatherers and processors of information in new, uncertain situations involving innovative products and processes, in which case securities markets work better.

In practice, financial systems are always a mixture of financial markets and financial intermediaries. A well-functioning financial system requires particular government actions. Government regulation is needed to protect property rights and to enforce contracts. Government regulation is needed to encourage proper information provision so that providers of funds can take better decisions on how to allocate their money. Government should arrange for regulation and supervision of financial institutions in order to ensure their soundness. Finally, governments are responsible for competition policy to ensure competition.

Gambacorta et al. (2014) suggest that banks and markets differ considerably in their moderating effects on business cycle fluctuations. Banks are more likely to supply loans during a "normal" downturn, thus smoothing the impact of the recession. But their shock-absorbing capacity is impaired when the downturn is associated with a financial crisis. In this case, recessions in countries with

Tab. 8.3: Bank-based and market-based financial systems

	Bank-based	Market-based
Low-uncertainty investment	+	-
Economic growth	+	+
Consumption smoothing	-	+
High-uncertainty investment	-	+
Investment smoothing	+	-

Source: Haan, Oosterloo, and Schoenmaker, 2009

bank-oriented systems are three times more severe than in those with a market-oriented financial structure.

Some authors argue that financial markets and financial intermediaries may provide complementary growth-enhancing financial services to the economy. Stock markets may complement banks by spurring competition for corporate control and by offering alternative services. The financial system is a set of contracts that is defined and made more or less effective by legal rights and enforcement mechanisms. Legal system differences are key in explaining international differences in financial structure. Additionally, differences in financial systems also affect macroeconomic outcomes and it is not clear which financial system is better for growth than another. Financial systems characterised by a greater degree of relationship-based lending are able to smooth business investment more effectively in the face of changes in the business cycle. Tab. 8.3 summarises these factors.

4. Financial Stability

Financial stability expresses the strength and stable functioning of financial markets, institutions, and payment systems. Financial stability is about building a financial system that can function in good times and bad and can absorb all the good and bad things that happen in the economy at any moment; it is not about preventing failure or stopping people or businesses from making or losing money. It is just helping to create conditions where the system keeps working effectively even with such events (https://www.federalreserve.gov/faqs/what-is-financial-stability.htm). The true value of financial stability is best illustrated in its absence, in periods of financial instability. During these periods, banks are reluctant to finance profitable projects, asset prices deviate excessively from their intrinsic values, and payments may not arrive on time. Major instability can lead to bank runs, hyperinflation, or a stock market crash. It can severely shake confidence in the financial and economic system. It will also prevent the effective functioning of monetary policy.

Banks working with high liquidity or capital adequacy, which is one of the measures taken for the soundness of the financial system open to external shocks, reduces the risk of the banks but on the other hand it prevents the efficient distribution of financial resources. This situation creates a dilemma between financial soundness and efficiency. Some of the public policies implemented for the purpose of ensuring and maintaining financial stability are effective in the short term (such as deposit insurance application, central bank being the lender of last resort), but may not be effective in the long term (such as decreased market discipline and moral risk).

Financial stability is closely related to systemic risk. Systemic risk is defined as the risk that an event will trigger a loss of economic value or confidence in and increases uncertainty about a substantial portion of the financial system that is serious enough to quite probably have significant adverse effects on the real economy.

Financial stability, in addition to facilitating access to macroeconomic targets, is regarded as the power of financial system in maintaining, distribution, and management of financial risk. Even if unexpected developments or shocks occur, the financial system affects the overall performance of the economy. A financial stability targeting role involves analyses of potential threats to financial stability, assessment of the present situation and the outlook ahead, and policy actions based on the risk assessment. Available instruments to financial stability targeting central banks are monetary policy; lender of last resort policy; and financial instruments like financial stability reports, speeches, and meetings with market participants. Regulation is, of course, an important instrument to provide financial stability, and by cooperating with the regulatory authority, the central bank can influence the regulation of the financial system, the regulation of financial institutions, markets, and infrastructure (Bårdsen, Lindquist and Tsomocos, 2006: 3).

Financial instability indicators are volatility in financial asset prices, deterioration in the national and international functioning of financial markets and institutions, and deviation of spending from the production performance of the economy (Yücememiş, 2019: 255). Since excessive fluctuations in interest rates will also cause financial instability, the stable course of interest rates is important.

While examining the factors that threaten financial stability, it is seen that there are actually two complementary approaches. The first approach focuses on risk factors that originate and develop within the financial system and contagion. Central banks typically monitor systemically important financial institutions, securities markets, and payments systems in order to detect trends in credit, liquidity, and market risks that may increase financial fragility and weaken the stability of the financial system Common exposures across financial institutions, either direct counterparty exposures or via third parties, are typically also scrutinized, since common exposures are channels of contagion, which may cause problems at a single financial institution to spread and give rise to systemic problems. The second approach focuses on risks that originate and develop outside the financial system, reflecting that the fragility of the financial system depends on macroeconomic conditions (Bårdsen, Lindquist and Tsomocos, 2006: 4). A series of structural economic trends deserve particular attention on the grounds that they may ultimately also have an impact on financial stability. In addition to a number of risks related to concrete political processes, developments in the digitization of the economy, climate change, and related policies, as well as specific risks related to money laundering or terrorist financing, deserve due attention (Financial Stability Report, 2019).

A common measure of stability at the level of individual institutions is the z-score. It explicitly compares buffers (capitalization and returns) with risk (volatility of returns) to measure a bank's solvency risk. The z-score is defined as $z \equiv (k+\mu)/\sigma$, where k is equity capital as percent of assets, μ is return as percent of assets, and σ is standard deviation of return on assets as a proxy for return volatility. The popularity of the z-score stems from the fact that it has a clear (negative) relationship to the probability of a financial institution's insolvency, that is, the probability that the value of its assets becomes lower than the value of its debt. A higher z-score therefore implies a lower probability of insolvency. Papers that used the z-score for analysis bank stability include Boyd and Runkle (1993); Beck, Demirgüç-Kunt, and Levine (2007); Detragiache, Tressel and Gupta (2008); Laeven and Levine (2009); and Čihák and Hesse (2010). Also, the z-score looks at each financial institution separately, potentially overlooking the risk that a default in one financial institution may cause loss to other financial institutions in the system. An advantage of the z-score is that it can be also used for institutions for which more sophisticated and market-based data are not available. Also, the z-scores allow comparing the risk of default in different groups of institutions, which may differ in their ownership or objectives, but face the risk of insolvency.

Tab. 8.4 summarizes the endogenous and exogenous potential sources of risk to financial stability.

Tab. 8.4: Potential sources of risk to financial stability

Endogenous	Exogenous
Institutions-based:	Macroeconomic disturbances:
Financial risks	Economic-environment risk
Operational risk	Policy imbalances
Information technology weaknesses	
Legal/integrity risk	
Reputation risk	
Business strategy risk	
Capital adequacy risk	
Market-based:	
Counterparty risk	
Asset-price misalignment	
Run on markets	
Credit	
Liquidity	
Infrastructure-based:	
Clearance, payment, and settlement-system risk	
	Event risk:
Infrastructure fragilities	Natural disaster
Regulatory	Political events
Legal	Large business failure
Supervisory	

Source: Schinassy, 2006, Houben et al. 2004

Conclusion

Financial systems reduce information and transaction cost and lower the cost of channeling funds needed for new investment and innovation. Another main function of financial systems is trading, diversification, and management of risk. Financial systems influence economic growth in the long run by offering investment opportunities and diversifying risk for individual investment projects. High-return projects are generally riskier than low-return projects. In that way, financial systems make it easier for people to diversify risk by offering a broad range of high-risk and low-risk investment chances tend to induce a portfolio shift towards projects with higher expected returns. All cross-country, case-study, and industry- and firm-level analyses suggest that the functioning of financial systems is vitally linked to economic growth. Countries with larger banks and more active stock markets grow faster even after controlling for many other factors underlying economic growth. Furthermore, the financial system creates the possibility for savers to hold liquid assets – like equity, bonds, or demand deposits that they can sell quickly and easily if they seek access to their savings, simultaneously transforming these liquid financial instruments into long-term capital investments.

Decomposing countries by the efficiency of national legal systems in supporting financial transactions is more useful than decomposing countries according to bank-based or market-based financial systems.

References

Acharya, V. and Thakor A. (2016). The dark side of liquidity creation: Leverage and systemic risk. Journal of Financial Intermediation, 28, 4–21. https://doi.org/10.1016/j.jfi.2016.08.004

Bårdsen, Gunnar, Lindquist, Kjersti-Gro and Tsomocos, Dimitrios P. (2006). Evaluation of Macroeconomic Models for Financial Stability Analysis, Working Paper, No.1, ISBN 82-7553-345-7, Norges Bank, Oslo, http://hdl.handle.net/11250/2498358

Bats, Joost and Houben, Aerdt (2017). Bank-Based versus Market-Based Financing: Implications for Systemic Risk. (DNB Working Paper; No. 577). Amsterdam: De Nederlandsche Bank NV. https://pure.uva.nl/ws/files/21141582/Bank_based_versus.pdfttf

Beck, T., Demirgüç-Kunt, A. & Levine, R.(2007). Finance, inequality and the poor. J Econ Growth. 12, 27–49. https://doi.org/10.1007/s10887-007-9010-6

Boyd, John H. and Runkle, David E. (1993), Size and performance of banking firms: Testing the predictions of theory, Journal of Monetary Economics, 31, (1), 47–67.

Čihák, M. and Hesse, H. (2010), "Islamic banks and financial stability: an empirical analysis", Journal of Financial Services Research, Vol. 38 No. 2–3, pp. 95–113. DOI: 10.1007/s10693-010-0089-0

Demirgüç-Kunt, A. and Levine, R. (2001). Financial structure and economic growth: Perspectives and lessons. In A. Demirguc-Kunt and R. Levine (Eds.), Financial structure and economic growth: a crosscountry comparison of banks, markets, and development, 3–14.Cambridge, MA: The MIT Press.

Detragiache, E., Tressel, T. and Gupta, P. (2008). Foreign Banks in Poor Countries: Theory and Evidence. The Journal of Finance, 63: 2123–2160. doi:10.1111/j.15406261.2008.01392.x

Federal Reserve Bank (2020). https://www.federalreserve.gov/faqs/what-is-financial-stability.htm

Financial Stability Report (2019). National Bank of Belgium https://www.nbb.be/en/articles/financial-stability-report-2019

Gambacorta, Leonardo, Yang, Jing and Tsatsaronis, Kostas (2014). Financial Structure and Growth. BIS Quarterly Review, 21–35. https://www.bis.org/publ/qtrpdf/r_qt1403e.pdf

Haan, Jakob de, Oosterloo, Sander and Schoenmaker, Dirk (2009). European Financial Markets and Institutions. Cambridge University Press. ISBN-13 978-0-511-50686 4.

Houben, Aerdt, Kakes, Jan and Schinasi, Garry (2004). Toward a Framework for Safeguarding Financial Stability. IMF Working Paper, WP/04/101

Langfield, Sam and Pagano, Marco (2015). Bank Bias in Europe: Effects on Systemic Risk and Growth. ECB Working Paper 1797. https://www.ecb.europa.eu/pub/pdf/scpwps/ecbwp1797.en.pdf

La Porta, Rafael, Florencio Lopez-De-Silanes, Shleifer A.and Vishny, R. (1997). Legal Determinants of External Finance. The Journal of Finance, 52(3), 1131–1150. doi:10.2307/2329518

Laeven, Luc and Levine, R. (2009). Bank governance, regulation and risk taking. Journal of Financial Economics, 93(2), 259-275, ISSN 0304-405X, https://doi.org/10.1016/j.jfineco.2008.09.003.

Levine, Ross (1997). Financial Development and Economic Growth: Views and Agenda. Journal of Economic Literature, 35(2), 688–726.

Levine, Ross (2002). Bank-Based or Market-Based Financial Systems: Which Is Better? Journal of Financial Intermediation, 11(4), 398–428. https://doi.org/10.1006/jfin.2002.0341

Levine, Ross (2004). Finance and Growth: Theory and Evidence NBER Working Paper No. w10766. SSRN: https://ssrn.com/abstract=592145

Levine, R. (2005). Finance and Growth: Theory and Evidence, in: Philippe Aghion and Stefan Durlauf, eds, Handbook of Economic Growth, Amsterdam.

Papaioannou, Elias and Gregorios S. (2008). Democratisation and Growth. The Economic Journal,118(532), 1520–1551, http://dx.doi.org/10.1111/j.1468-0297.2008.02189.x

Rajan, Raghuram G. and Zingales, Luigi (2001). Financial Systems, Industrial Structure, and Growth Source: Oxford Review of Economic Policy, Vol. 17, No. 4, Finance, Law, and Economic Growth, pp. 467–482, Published by: Oxford University Press Stable http://www.jstor.org/stable/23606715

Rose, Peter and Marquis, Milton (2006). Money and Capital Markets: Financial Institutions and Instruments in a Global Market Place, 9/e, ISBN: 0072957395 http://highered.mheducation.com/sites/0072957395/information_center_view0/table_of_contents.html

Schinassy, J. (2006). Safeguarding Financial Stability. Washington: International Monetary Fund. https://www.imf.org/External/Pubs/NFT/2005/SFS/eng/sfs.pdf

Schmidt, Reinhard H. (1999): Differences between Financial Systems in Europe: Consequences for EMU, Working Paper Series: Finance & Accounting, No.35, JohannWolfgang Goethe Universität Frankfurt am Main, Fachbereich Wirtschaftswissenschaften, Frankfurt a.M., http://citeseerx.ist.psu.edu/viewdoc/download?doi=10.1.1.477.611&rep=rep1&type=pdf

Schmidt, Reinhard H. and Hryckiewicz, Aneta (2006). Financial Systems-Importance, Differences and Convergence, IMFS Working Paper Series, No. 4, Goethe University Frankfurt, Institute for Monetary and Financial Stability (IMFS), Frankfurt a. M., https://www.econstor.eu/handle/10419/97758

World Bank Data (2020) https://data.worldbank.org/indicator/FD.AST.PRVT.GD.ZS?end=2018&locations=GB-AT-US-IN-JP-CA-CN-DE-IT-RU-KR&name_desc=true&start=2012&view=chart

Yücememiş, Başak Tanınmış (2019). Finansal Piyasalar Para ve Bankacılık (Ed. Başak Tanınmış Yücememiş ve Levent Çinko). Nobel Yayıncılık.

Eyyüp Ensari Şahin

9 Financial Speculation and Bubble: An Empirical Investigation of Bubble in the Turkish Stock Market

Highlights: Rapid transformation in technology and science supports Thomas Khun's paradigm shift foresight. Especially developments in the financial markets affect the government, political authority, and eventually individual investors. One of the important developments resulting these effects is speculation. According to the definition by Kaldor (1960 and 1976), speculation is not the benefit provided from the use of an asset, but the highness of the return to be obtained as a result of resale in the next period. In the first part of the study, the history of financial speculations will be explained comparatively with the help of significant financial speculations experienced, crisis-speculation, and manipulation concepts. In the second part of the study, major financial speculations will be examined in the light of the studies in the literature. In the third and last part of the study, with reference to the tulip mania which occurred in the Netherlands and known as the biggest wave of speculation influencing the whole world, South Sea Bubble, Mississippi Bubble, US Stock and Real Estate Bubble, Japan Real Estate Bubble, Swedish Real Estate Bubble, Internet Bubble, and Mortgage Crisis, the existence of speculative bubble price formation is tested using the Generalized Supremum Augmented Dickey–Fuller (GSADF) test using the daily closing prices (2006–2019) of the Istanbul Stock Exchange Istanbul 100 (XU100). In conclusion, balloon price formation was seen in weekly closing prices of XU100 Index.

Keywords: Speculation, financial bubble, GSADF

Introduction

The volume of capital moving around the world has reached large amounts. In the 1980s, after the market liberalization and the integration of technology into the business world were accepted by all parties, capital markets started to develop rapidly and find application in the whole world. In the 1980s, after the liberalization of the market and acceptation of the integration of technology into the business world by all parts, capital markets started to develop rapidly and find implementation areas in the whole world. Capital markets are an important part of the financial system, together with financial institutions of the financial system. Capital markets can be defined as institutions that provide fund exchanges by bringing the savers and the ones who are in need for capital and the structures consisting of institutions that regulate and supervise these institutions. Capital markets are markets that enable various long-term transactions. However, fund size created as a result of the short-term capital movements in these markets revealed negative results especially for fragile and developing economies as a result of the ability to make a rapid entry and exit. National finance markets have rapidly integrated as a result of the spread of capital to cross-border areas with the idea of making higher profits at lower risk and financial liberalization.

The concept of speculation revealed itself exactly at this point; and when the papers and articles related to finance literature or other subjects are examined, it is emphasized that leading to major crises globally Tulip Mania, 1929 Great Crash, and other crises were caused as a result of speculations (Aytekin, 2018: 200). With the idea that there is a direct relationship between the liberalization of the financial movements and crisis, a capital outflow was observed before the crisis. Considering the historical process of financial speculations, we see the bubble in the tulip prices affecting the whole of Europe, especially the Netherlands that is known as the "tulip mania" in the literature. Rising prices in this period put investors in expectation of more price increases. Excess demand resulting from these expectations causes asset prices to increase further (İskenderoğlu and Akdağ, 2019: 1086). This process starting with the tulip mania has come up to today following the South Sea bubble, which tried to trade in a monopolistic structure and emphasizes the activities of South Sea Company founded in 1711 by George Caswall and John Blunt, Mississippi Bubble in 1720 due to speculative movements to companies founded by John Law in France, US stock market and real estate bubble, and the 1929 great depression and balloon price formations causing the 2008 global crisis. Speculation and bubble price is the common subject of many studies in the literature (Santoni, 1987: 17). Balloon formations in the price of a financial asset or a good are usually caused by speculative transactions. Brunnermeier (2009) defined the concept of bubble in financial assets as sudden price increases and the collapses immediately after (2009: 3). Kindleberger (1996) defined the concept of bubble as an upward price movement for a long time and subsequently a sudden fall. Garber (1990) described the concept as any false business enterprise with a high level of speculation. With reference to this definition, bubble price formation must occur as a result of any speculative event (Oran, 2011: 151–161). The broadest and most descriptive of these definitions is made in the book *A History of Financial Crisis* by Charles Kindleberger and Robert Z. Aliber (2011) within five stages. These stages are displacement, boom, euphoria, crisis, and revulsion.

The aim of the study is to test whether there is a bubble formation at closing prices in XU100. In this context, in the first part of the study, the history of financial speculations will be reviewed comparatively with the help of important financial speculations, crisis-speculation, and manipulation concepts. In the second part of the study, big financial speculations and studies conducted in different regions will be examined in the light of the studies in the literature. The study will be completed with application and results section.

1 Literature Review

In this part of the study, the relevant literature will be examined in detail. Aytekin (2018) examined the historical development of the speculation phenomenon and its role in the capital markets, and presented a theoretical conclusion that speculations may be the cause of crises. Based on literature examples that speculations can trigger crises, it is concluded that the speculative and short-term movements of financial capital initially contributed to the capital markets positively, but country economies encounter with a rapid collapse with the outflow of capital. The theoretical proposal of the study supports the five stages of the financial balloons defined by Charles Kindleberger and Robert Z. Aliber (2011).

In his study titled "The History of Speculations," Mazgit (2007) explained that the desire to become rich in a fast and easy way could cause investors to get frustrated after a certain period of time based on the great speculations in history and the accompanying crises. Mazgit emphasized that the occasions happened not only in financial markets but also with different commercial goods, and especially mentioned about the subject of conscious investment and knowledge-based investment.

Blanchard (1979) concluded that speculative bubbles follow market collapse and are consistent with the theory of rational expectations. It was emphasized that it is very difficult to detect the presence of rational bubbles with a general evaluation. Later, many studies have been conducted in the literature with the use of statistical methods, and the existence of speculative bubbles has been investigated using different variables. West (1987), Horvath and Watson (1995), Campbell and Shiller (1987), and Zhou et al. (2003) investigated the existence of speculative bubbles with cointegration test in their study. Roterman and Wilfing (2014) and Narayan and Narayan (2013) in their study, by referring to Phillips et al. (2012) who conducted the initial work, found statistically significant relationship between trade volumes in financial markets, financial asset volatility, and financial asset bubble. Scheinkman and Xiong (2003) concluded that Tobin's tax can significantly reduce speculative trade when transaction costs are low, but have a limited impact on the size or price volatility of the bubble.

Blanchard and Watson (1982) tested the rationality of price bubbles to determine whether or not they were valid in the financial market. In the study, they concluded that the presence of bubble can be statistically measured by running and tail tests. Çağlı and Mandacı (2017) aimed to detect the presence of speculative bubbles by using dividend yield ratio calculated for BIST indices.

Consequently, empirical evidence was obtained for the presence of rational speculative bubbles. They also found that the exchange rate, real sector confidence index, and industrial production index have significant marginal effects on the number of speculative bubbles. Akkaya (2018) used the logistic regression and cointegration tests in the study determining the bubbles and the variables that affect the formation of bubbles. Results of logistic regression and Granger causality test show that there is a relationship between the stock portfolio of nonresidents and bubbles in Borsa İstanbul Return Index.

In the study of Çıtak (2019), the presence of speculative balloons on BIST index closing prices were determined, and some macroeconomic variables affecting balloon formation were stated with the Logit Model. In the study, it was aimed to determine the presence of speculative bubble in BIST XU 100 Index closing prices. In this context, a Generalized Supremum Augmented Dickey–Fuller (GSADF) unit root test developed by Phillips et al. (2013) was used. The GSADF test was developed to complete the weaknesses of the SADF test. While the SADF test can calculate a single bubble period in prices, the GSADF test has been used by many researchers in the literature to detect multiple bubbles (LeRoy and Porter, 1981; Gürkaynak, 2005; Shiller (2003); Campbell and Shiller, 1987; Parvar and Waters, 2010; Teletar and Binay (2002); Santoni, 1987; Bozoklu and Zeren, 2013; Rotermann and Wilfling (2014); Yanık and Aytürk, 2011).

2 Econometric Model and Data

In the study, BIST XU100 Index weekly closing prices between the years 2000 and 2019 were used. The data of the study were achieved from the Data Stream database. In the study, a SADF-based test that could test speculative prices was proposed following the study of Phillips et al. (2012). However, in the study of Phillips et al. (2015), it was stated that the SADF test has a limited ability to detect the presence of multiple bubbles, and the GSADF test, which is more successful in detecting multiple bubbles, has been proposed. GSADF uses the standard regression equation shown in Equation 1:

$$y_t = m + \lambda y_{t-1} + \sum_{i=1}^{p} p_{r,r2}^{j} \Delta y_{t-i} + \varepsilon_t, \varepsilon_t \sim iid(0, \sigma 2), t = 1, \ldots, T \quad (1)$$

Here $y_{t,}$ shows the time series process (it shows the weekly closing prices in the study) p, p is the maximum lag length included in the procedure, Δ is the difference operator, and r_1 and r_2 show the window size of the total data[1]. Null hypothesis states that there is price bubble in SADF and GSADF unit root tests H_0: λ =1'e and alternative hypothesis states that there is no price bubble in unit root H_1: λ >1. Model shown in Equation 1 is estimated repeatedly using subsets of sample data, which is increased by one observation at each pass in iterative regression (Philips et al. 2015: 1080–1085). In the study, generalized equals (Sup) ADF (GSADF) unit root test developed by Phillips et al. (2012) was used in order to determine the speculative bubbles and their periods of occurrence. This test was created by repeated testing of the ADF (Augmented Dickey–Fuller) test equation (Phillips et al. 2012: 10).

Critical values are obtained by Monte Carlo simulation in GSADF test. The rejection of the null hypothesis indicates the presence of bubbles. GSADF equation is defined as follows:

$$GSADF_{r0} = sup_{r2\, \in [r0,1]} SADF_{r2}\ (r_0) \quad (2)$$

After detection of the presence of bubbles, backward SADF (BSADF) statistics series are used to determine the periods of the formed bubbles.

2.1 Empirical Results

The results of the analysis carried out in the study where the balloon price formation on the Borsa XU100 daily closing prices was investigated is given in this part of the study. Descriptive statistics, unit root test results, and GSADF test results of the variables used in the study are given.

When Graph 9.1 is analyzed, the closing prices of XU100 have been found as 43.290 as of the years used in the analysis (2006–2019). When the closing prices are ranked from the smallest value to the highest degree, the median value was found as 43.053. Skewness showing deviation from normal distribution was found to be 0.177. The skewness coefficient being close to zero can be interpreted as the data shows normal distribution. Kurtosis value shows that the data are

1 Window size is 2 % of the number of observations.

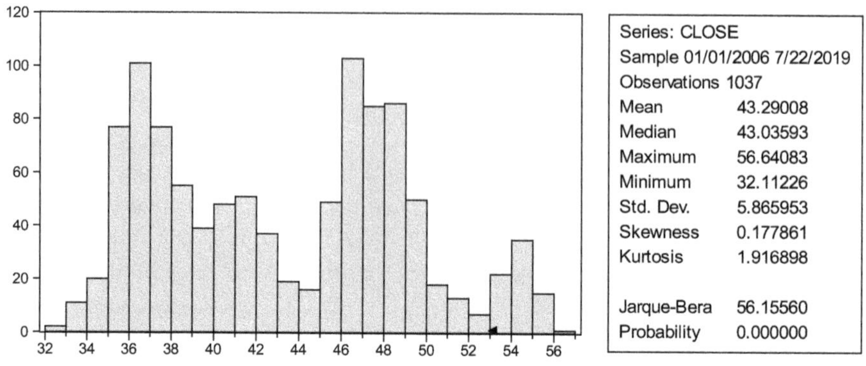

Graph 9.1: Descriptive statistics results

Tab. 9.1. ADF and Philips–Perron unit root test results

Variable	Test	Level Value		First Difference	
XU100	ADF	-0.348135	0.9151	-33.72122	0.0000
	PP	-0.324073	0.9188	-33.69226	0.0000

Tab. 9.2. XU100 Index GSADF test results

				Critical Value		
	Observation	**P value**	**T statistic**	**%99**	**%95**	**%90**
XU100	1038	0,000	5.82178	2.01945	1.03391	1.35003
Window size is 2 % of the number of observations.						

skewed to the right. In summary, a symmetric distribution cannot be obtained by joining the histogram graph points. For this purpose, ADF and Philips–Perron unit root test was performed in order to make the data stationary. The test results are given in Tab. 9.1.

Table 9.1 shows the ADF and Phillips–Perron unit root test results of the variable used in the study. In the study, it was concluded that the XU100 Index data are stationary at the first differences. In the study, the existence of speculative bubble price formation in the prices of the XU100 Index is examined by GSADF tests. Results for GSADF tests are shown in Tab. 9.2.

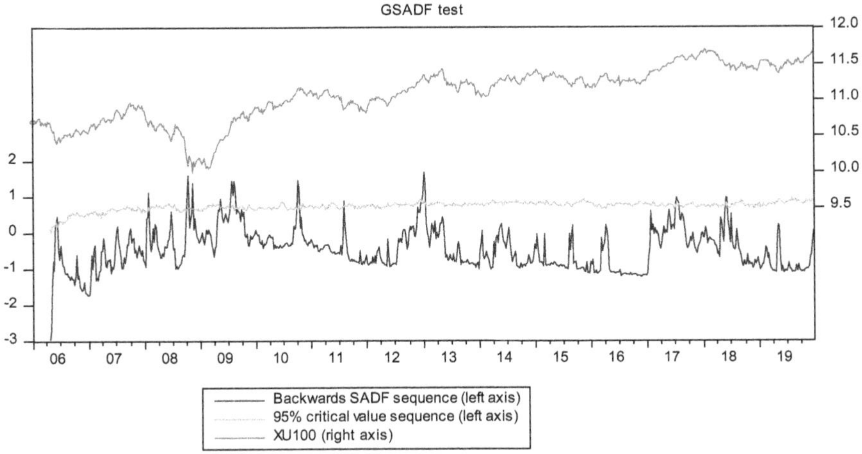

Fig. 9.1: XU100 Index BSADF pattern. Monte Carlo simulation is calculated as 1038 observation value X 1000 iteration X 16 window size

Tab. 9.3. Dates of XU100 Index bubble price

Date	Date
21.05.2006	09.12.2010
20.01.2008	07.08.2011
10.05.2008	30.12.2012
19.10.2008	16.07.2017
21.10.2008	23.07.2017
10.05.2009	03.06.2018
19.07.2009	10.01.2019
07.09.2009	15.02.2019
26.09.2010	27.03.2019

When the GSADF test results are examined, the estimated test statistic for the XU100 Index closing prices has higher results than the critical values of the statistics. The existence of a speculative bubble formation is determined for the periods analyzed by rejecting the H_0 hypothesis. After the presence of the bubbles are detected, in the second stage, the periods of the bubbles are determined.

Balloon price formations are shown in Fig. 9.1, where especially in 2008 and 2009 sudden increases in prices can be clearly seen. Table 9.3 shows the days of the price of the balloons.

Table 9.3 shows the days of occurrence of bubble price formation as a result of GSADF test statistics. It can be concluded that investors invested in stocks to turn the crisis into an opportunity, especially during and after the effects of the 2007 mortgage crisis, and thereby a bubble occurred in prices. In the analysis period, it is observed that the increase in prices in the XU100 Index as a result of speculative movements formed the bubble price, whereas the bubble prices are not continuous.

Conclusion

Financial markets managed to attract investments to a large extent as a result of the financial liberalization. Especially the stock markets that bring public companies with fund requirements and investors with excess funds provide an environment for both foreign portfolio investments and investments of domestic residents together with the crisis. Price changes in financial markets are the areas that investors are continuously involved in, and the change usually takes place depending on supply and demand. This is one of the factors causing the change in the general situation of prices. Investors act rationally about the investment instrument they demand and behave in accordance with the information announced to the public.

The term "efficient markets" was first used in 1965 by Eugene Fama, winner of the 2013 Nobel Prize in Economics, in the study "The Behavior of Stock Market Prices" (Rossi, 2015: 286; Delcey, 2019: 5). Fama defines the efficient market as "a market where many rational investors who want to maximize their profits to the highest level are actively competing, the future price of each stock is tried to be estimated and all important current information can be obtained by almost all market participants" (Kulalı, 2016; Yakut and Gemici, 2017). The result of the study shows that the bubble price formations estimated in the XU100 Index correspond to the crisis period and important events for our country. According to the studies in the literature, BIST gives an effective market view in a weak form (Kıyılar, 1997; Telatar and Binay 2002; Ertaş and Özkan, 2018). In other words, publicly announced information can have a significant impact on prices. The study conducted by Akkaya (2018) that concludes the nonresidents statistically related to stock prices supports the findings of the bubble price formation in our study. It can be said that especially during the crisis periods, foreign investors invested in the stock markets of the developing countries in order to get higher returns in the crisis, which also causes the formation of bubbles in prices.

In summary, in the study in which the 2006–2019 BIST XU100 Index daily closing prices were used, it was concluded that the market, which is effective in a weak form, caused the formation of bubble prices as a result of the information reflected to the public and investors' interest in periods of crisis.

References

Akkaya, M. (2018). "Borsa İstanbul Hissesenedi Getirilerinde Balon Oluşumu Üzerine bir Uygulama". Cumhuriyet Üniversitesi İktisadi ve İdari Bilimler Dergisi, 19(1), 188–200.

Aytekin, G. K. (2018). "Uluslararası Sermaye Hareketleri Kapsamında Sıcak Para Akımlarının Ekonomik Etkileri ve Spekülasyon". Uluslararası Beşeri Bilimler ve Eğitim Dergisi, 4(7), 184–207.

Blanchard, O. J. (1979). "Speculative bubbles, crashes and rational expectations". Economics Letters, 3(4), 387–389.

Blanchard, O. J., and Watson, M. W. (1982). "Bubbles, rational expectations and financial markets in P. WACHTEL (ed.). Crises in the Economic and Financial Structure, Lexington: Lexington Books,

Bozoklu, Ş., and Zeren, F. (2013). "Türkiye Hisse Senedi Piyasasinda Rasyonel Köpükler: Sakli Eş Bütünleşme Yaklaşimi". Finansal Araştırmalar ve Çalışmalar Dergisi, 5(9), 17–31.

Brunnermeier, M. K. (2009). "Deciphering the liquidity and credit crunch 2007–2008". Journal of Economic Perspectives, 23(1), 77–100.

Çağli, E. Ç., and Mandaci, P. E. (2017). "Borsa İstanbul'da Rasyonel Balon Varlığı: Sektör Endeksleri Üzerine Bir Analiz". Finans Politik & Ekonomik Yorumlar, 54(629), 63–76.

Campbell, J., and Shiller, R. (1987). "Cointegration and Tests of Present Value Models". Journal of Political Economy, 95(5), 1062–88.

Çıtak, F. (2019). "Türkiye Hisse Senedi Piyasasında Spekülatif Balon Varlığının Ampirik İncelenmesi" Uluslararası Ekonomi ve Yenilik Dergisi, 5(2), 247–262.

Delcey, T. (2019). "Samuelson vs Fama on the Efficient Market Hypothesis: The Point of View of Expertise". Economia. History, Methodology, Philosophy, (9–1), 37–58.

Ertaş, F. C., and Özkan, O. (2018). "Piyasa Etkinliği Açısından Adaptif Piyasa Hipotezi'nin Test Edilmesi: Türkiye ve ABD Hisse Senedi Piyasaları Örneği". Finans Politik & Ekonomik Yorumlar, 55(642), 23.

Garber, P. M. (1990). "Famous First Bubbles". Journal of Economic Perspectives, 4(2), 35–54.

Gürkaynak, R. S., Sack, B., and Swanson, E. (2005). "The Sensitivity of Long-Term Interest Rates to Economic News: Evidence and Implications for Macroeconomic Models". American Economic Review, 95(1), 425–436.

Horvath, M., and Watson, M. W. (1995). "Testing for Cointegration When Some of the Cointegrating Vectors Are Prespecified". Econometric Theory, 11(5), 984–1014.

Iskenderoglu, O., and Akdag, S. (2019). "Türkiye'de Reel Konut Fiyatlarında Balonların Varlığı Üzerine Uygulamalı Bir Analiz". Business and Economics Research Journal, 10(5), 1085–1093.

Jahan-Parvar, M. R., and Waters, G. A. (2010). "Equity Price Bubbles in the Middle Eastern and North African Financial Markets". Emerging Markets Review, 11(1), 39–48.

Kaldor, N. (1960). [1939]. "Speculation and Economic Stability. Essays on Economic Stability and Growth". Review of Economic Studies, 7, 1–27.

Kaldor, N. (1976). "Speculation and Economic Stability". In The Economics of Futures Trading (pp. 111–123). Palgrave Macmillan, London.

Kindleberger, C. P. (1996). "World Economic Primacy: 1500–1990". Oxford University Press on Demand. Third Edition, London.

Kindleberger, C., and Aliber, R. Z. (2011). "Manias, Panics and Crashes: A History of Financial Crises". Palgrave Macmillan. Sixth Edition, London.

Kıyılar, M. (1997). "Etkin Pazar Kuramı ve Etkin Pazar Kuraminin İMKB'de Test Edilmesi". Ankara: CMB Publication.

Kulali, İ. (2016). "A Conflict between the Efficient Market Hypothesis and Behavioral Finance". International Journal of Finance & Banking Studies, 5(2), 46.

LeRoy, S. F., and Porter, R. D. (1981). "The Present-Value Relation: Tests Based on Implied Variance Bounds. Econometrica": Journal of the Econometric Society, 49(3), 555–574.

Mazgit, İ. (2007). "Sermaye Piyasalarında Spekülasyon: Tarihin Tekerrürü". Finans Politik & Ekonomik Yorumlar, (10), 9.

Narayan, P. K., and Narayan, S. (2013). "The Short-Run Relationship between the Financial System and Economic Growth: New Evidence from Regional Panels". International Review of Financial Analysis, 29, 70–78.

Oran, A. (2011). "Balonlari Daha iyi Tanimaya Çalişmak: Balon Tanimlari, Modelleri ve Lale Çilginliği Örneği". Dokuz Eylül Üniversitesi İktisadi İdari Bilimler Fakültesi Dergisi, 26(1), 151–161.

Parvar, M. R. J., and Waters, G. A. (2010). "Equity Price Bubbles in the Middle Eastern and North African Financial Markets". Emerging Markets Review, 11(1), 39–48.

Phillip, S., Peter, C. B., Shi, Shuping, and Yu, Jun (2015)., "Testing for Multiple Bubbles: Historical Episodes of Exuberance and Collapse in the S&P 500". International Economic Review, 56(4), 1043–78.

Phillips, P., Shi, S., and Yu, J. (2012). "Testing for Multiple Bubbles". Accessed Date: https://papers.ssrn.com/sol3/papers.cfm?abstract_id=1981976

Rossi, M. (2015). "The Efficient Market Hypothesis and Calendar Anomalies: A Literature Review". International Journal of Managerial and Financial Accounting, 7(3–4), 285–296.

Rotermann, B., and Wilfling, B. (2014). "Periodically Collapsing Evans Bubbles and Stock-Price Volatility". Economics Letters, 123(3), 383–386.

Santoni, G. J. (1987). "The Great Bull Markets 1924–29 and 1982–87: Speculative Bubbles or Economic Fundamentals?". Federal Reserve Bank of St. Louis Review, 69(9), 16–29.

Scheinkman, J. A., and Xiong, W. (2003). "Overconfidence and Speculative Bubbles". Journal of Political Economy, 111(6), 1183–1220.

Shiller, R. J. (2003). "From Efficient Markets Theory to Behavioral Finance". Journal of Economic Perspectives, 17(1), 83–104.

Telatar, E., and Binay, H. S. (2002). "İMKB Endeksinin PARCH Modellemesi". Akdeniz İİBF Dergisi, 3, 114–121.

West, K. D. (1987). "A Specification Test for Speculative Bubbles". The Quarterly Journal of Economics, 102(3), 553–580.

Yakut, E., and Gemici, E. (2017). "LR, C5. 0, CART, DVM Yöntemlerini Kullanarak Hisse Senedi Getiri Sınıflandırma Tahmini Yapılması ve Kullanılan Yöntemlerin Karşılaştırılması": Türkiye'de BIST'de Bir Uygulama. Ege Akademik Bakis, 17(4), 461–479.

Yanık, S., and Aytürk, Y. (2011). "Rational Speculative Bubbles in Istanbul Stock Exchange". Muhasebe ve Finansman Dergisi, (51), 175–190.

Zhou, Y., and Zhong, P. (2003). Suppression of Large Intraluminal Bubble Expansion in Shock Wave Lithotripsy without Compromising Stone Commination": Refinement of Reflector Geometry. The Journal of the Acoustical Society of America, 113(1), 586–597.

Mustafa Kevser and Mesut Doğan

10 Islamic Finance in the Framework of Financial Crisis and the Evaluation of Islamic Finance

Highlights: The aim of this study is to evaluate the methods used in Islamic finance and Islamic banking, and to examine the situation of Islamic finance and the state of Islamic banking under the crises, and whether Islamic finance and Islamic banking are effective tools against financial crises in a theoretical framework. In this study, the way Islamic finance and Islamic banking work, and the situation of Islamic finance and Islamic banking with the crises are discussed by a literature review, and then a detailed evaluation is presented.

Keywords: Islamic finance, Islamic banking, financial crisis

Introduction

Economic developments in the 1970s increased the volatility of oil prices, interest rates, and exchange rates and also caused the financial instruments to fluctuate and become more risky. After the 1980s, many countries relinquished the import substitution policies and started the integration process with the world and opened to international markets; therefore, countries have become closer to each other economically, and other countries started to be affected by the important economic developments experienced by a country. With the impacts of globalization, the increase in the interaction between the countries has become more significant particularly in times of crisis, and the effects of the financial difficulties experienced by great economies on the countries with which they had economic relations were more obviously observed. Lately, the global financial crisis in 2008 accelerated the countries' search for hedging and aversion of risks.

The global financial crisis in 2008 caused the number of transactions in the United States credit markets to decrease and a significant depreciation of the stock markets. In this period, foreign capital flows and bank borrowings decreased significantly, and many enterprises faced financial difficulties. These developments in the United States, which has the largest economy in the world, eventuated in negative influences on international financial markets (Dönmez, 2009). Researches show that unregulated and unsecured use of financial leveraged products is an important factor of the 2008 global financial crisis (Hussien et al., 2019).

The use of sources imprecisely and unsecured in this way has made it difficult to access the funds needed in the current economic structure, causing the welfare and development of countries to be unsustainable (Çanakçı, 2014).

Following the 2008 global financial crisis, asset-based structure that promotes social justice and interest-free principle of Islamic finance and Islamic banking products have attracted more attention from investors and academics. Thereby, participation banking specific to Turkey and Islamic banking globally have been evaluated as an option to protect from the crisis and make investment in real assets.

The "Islamic" features of Islamic finance and the financial instruments offered by Islamic banking, in other words their formation under Islamic law, did not constitute an impediment to their participation in conventional markets. The sum of Islamic asset volumes in the top twenty countries that featured in the world has exceeded approximately 1 trillion each year since the last five years. As well as Muslim countries such as United Arab Emirates, Indonesia, Qatar, Kuwait, Malaysia, Sudan, Saudi Arabia and Turkey also the countries such as Britain, Switzerland and Thailand open their economies and financial sectors to the use of Islamic financial instruments (Karasu, 2016).

1 Importance of Islamic Finance

The Islamic economy came to life with the existence of the religion of Islam and gained a corporate identity after the migration of the Prophet Mohammad (S.A.V) to Medina in 622. Islamic finance is a financial system that operates according to Islamic rules and principles (Shanmugam and Zahari, 2009). In other words, it constitutes the basis that the financial activities and transactions carried out within the framework of Islamic finance should comply with Islamic law.

As a result of observing the harmony of Islamic finance in theory and practice, the opinion that Islamic finance is a new opportunity for world economies and societies has started to gain importance. The idea that it is more reliable compared to the modern financial system, which is based on interest even in the most difficult times as a matter of its nature, is approved by investors and academics.

Islamic finance and Islamic banking have an important function in terms of including the idle funds of individuals with interest sensitivity to the economy. Islamic finance is of great importance in terms of financing opportunities provided to individuals or businesses that have difficulty to access the financial opportunities due to interest sensitivity, or with regard to individuals or businesses with concerns that their investments will include interest income.

Islamic banks, within the framework of their structures and principles, make a sufficient analysis of the credit risk of the fundraiser individuals, and prevent the debt levels from exceeding the real economic size level. Accordingly, Islamic finance and Islamic banking are more controlled than conventional banks in terms of credit management and risk monitoring. This situation is of great importance for the economy in general. Within the framework of these properties of Islamic finance and Islamic banking, the 2008 global financial crisis demonstrates that Islamic banks contribute to the equilibrium of the market, discipline the markets, and are a type of banking that does not trigger crises (Özsoy, 2012).

2 Funding Methods of Islamic Finance

The basis of all financial crises, especially the 2008 financial crisis originating from the United States, is the instability of the financial sector and its reflection on the real sector (Diaw, 2015: 94–95). The fact that banks expanded their credit volumes with high risk appetite but that the loan growth was carried out in an unsoundly structure within an uncontrolled framework before the global financial crisis is observed as an important indicator that conventional banks reflect their unstable structures to the real sector. Under this circumstance, as stated by Krugman (2009), there is a need to rethink the issues causing financial failure. From this point of view, Islamic finance and Islamic banking funding methods provide asset-backed financing to the real sector and introduce a different perspective than the unstable structure that conventional banks reflect to the real sector.

The financing of the real sector is provided by seven different methods in Islamic banking: mudarabah (labor-capital partnership), musharaka (profit-loss partnership), murabahah (cost+profit margin sale), Ijatah (lease financing), benevolent loan (interest-free loan), salam (forward purchase), and tekaful (insurance). The most commonly used method of financing is the murabahah in Turkey for the supply of the raw materials needed by business or merchandise supply of commercial enterprises. Other methods are also applied in practice.

- **Mudarabah:** In muradabah contracts, one of the parties presents the capital and the other presents its labor, knowledge, and experience. In this method, the contracts are made mainly between the savers and the Islamic bank. In the contract between the parties, the owner of the participation account opened at the Islamic bank is called the investor, and the Islamic bank is called as the mudarip. In this context, the mudarabah is a funding method established between the Islamic bank and the credit customer of the bank within the scope of the labor and capital partnership (Ersan, 2007). In the mudaraba method, the profit is shared between the investor and the mudarib, while the cost and loss only belong to the investor. In the Mudarabah method, capital is given to the bank, not the debt, by the savings owner. The bank is obliged to make continuous calculations in order to use its capital in interest-free areas and to ensure that the distribution of profit/loss is fair. Besides, it is not certain that profit will be made at the end of the maturity, and loss can be observed as a result of the partnership.

- **Musharaka:** In Islamic law, musharaka is defined as capital partnership. In the musharaka method, two or more real or legal persons provide a certain amount of capital together in order to undertake an enterprise. In the musharaka method, both labor and capital are presented together actively. In this aspect, the musharaka method differs from the mudarabah method, that there is a passive investor. In the musharaka contracts made between the Islamic bank and the customer, the Islamic bank assumes the obligation to provide some of the capital demanded by the customer. However, the customer provides the remaining part of the capital according to its own financial structure and the features of the project. Besides, the customer undertakes the responsibility of the enterprise's supervision and monitoring activities within the scope of its own expertise and professional competence. Responsibilities remaining on the customer ensures that the customer gets more shares from the profit as a result of the enterprise (Alkış, 2018: 128).
- **Murabahah:** Murabahah is one of the funding methods which is commonly used by Islamic banks in the Islamic financial system. In the Murabahah method, there are three parties: the buyer, the seller, and the Islamic bank. During the Murabahah transaction, the Islamic bank buys the commodity to be funded from the seller at the demand of its customer. The Islamic bank, which purchases commodity from the supplier on behalf of its customer, becomes a seller at the next stage and sells the commodity in its own property to its customer for the account. The main components to be found in the contract between the parties during the operation of the Murabahah method are: (1) The Islamic bank must have the property of the commodity before any contract between the customer and the seller is formed, and (2) commodity that belongs to the Islamic bank must be sold to the customer before consumption. In this context, the Islamic bank sells its own commercial goods to its customers on a timely basis, and gains a forward sales profit from this

sale. The gained profit of the Islamic bank is based on trade and differs from interest.

- **Ijatah (lease financing):** It is a contract signed between the leaseholder who pays a certain charge in order to be able to use a specified property in a certain term and the owner of the property, and the leaseholder has the right of use the property (Kara, 2019). In the contract, the Islamic bank is the leaser and the customer is the lessor. In the Ijatah method, the customer determines the features of the machinery and equipment that is needed to be rent. The Islamic bank purchases the machine or equipment from the vendor and rents it to its customer. The customer of the Islamic bank starts to pay the rent regularly for the machinery or equipment according to the agreement made with the Islamic bank. When the contract expires, the customer purchases the machinery and equipment that is hired from the bank for a low price. In general, such a process can be defined as a form of leasing, ending with purchasing. The Islamic bank gains a rental income as a result of this contract, and this income differs from the interest returns.
- **Benevolent loan**: Benevolent loan is a nonrefundable loan process and must be made in order to gain spiritual rewards (Özdemir, 2012). In the karz transactions, the borrower only pays back the amount or quantity received. For benevolent loan, gold, silver, money circulating in the market, and goods that are consumed and can be measured as kilogram are used for the contracts. Currently, Islamic banks provide funds by benevolent loans to reliable and highly credible customers who have problems with their cash flows and solve the financial problems of these customers this way. Benevolent loan operations serve the cooperation, justice, and human base purposes of the Islamic finance and Islamic banking. Although karz transactions have social and economic advantages that spread across the society, it is not possible to find application area at a large-scale in today's economic structure and market conditions. Islamic banks cannot supply credit continuously without charge. In this context, the karz transactions are exceptional applications for Islamic banks and are implemented with a few days' maturity.
- **Salam:** Salam is the cash sale of the goods that it has not yet produced to be delivered at a later date by a legal or natural person with cash need. A farmer who has a cash shortage can sell the tea to the factory before the harvest time, so the cash problem can be eliminated. The agreement made between the parties for this transaction is an example of salam. The products whose production process is not completed yet can be sold with salam contracts. When the contract expires, if the seller does not have the products at that time, the same products must be supplied and delivered from the market. Therefore,

salam contracts impose responsibilities to the seller in terms of quality, quantity, and maturity (Aktepe, 2013: 50–51).

- **Tekaful:** Tekaful is an insurance system that operates in accordance with the Islamic procedures and principles. The purpose of the tekaful system is to minimize losses against the risks by bringing the individuals in a certain risk group together and compensate for the losses by eliminating the negative effects on the social life of individuals. Nonprofit insurance holders gather together in the tekaful system, and it is based on the principle of undertaking the risk to others account. Interest, high risk, uncertain or unclear issues in the contract, and investment areas that are not appropriate in Islam are not included in the tekaful insurance system. In this respect, tekaful insurance system is a type of insurance where the risk is distributed among the participants and interest-free areas are invested in. Directing the excess funds in interest-free areas indicates that investments are made in the real sector and are not made in speculative areas. Therefore, tekaful insurance transactions and applications differ from the conventional insurance system, where only commercial factors are based on, and areas containing interest, gambling, and suspicion are not excluded.

It is observed that the funding methods of Islamic banks mentioned above have the ability to eliminate the basic dynamics causing financial crises. The tools such as sloppy loans given within the framework of the excess liquidity and securitization that caused the 2008 financial crisis cannot find a place in the Islamic banking system, and at the same time lack of transparency is eliminated because the methods of funding are carried out within the framework of the principle of joining profit and loss together with a partnership.

3 Status and Development of Islamic Finance in the Framework of Financial Crisis

It was previously stated that Islamic Finance and Islamic banks operating within the framework of Islamic finance are separated from conventional banks by fund raising and funding methods. Due to differences in fund raising and funding methods, the ways and levels of banks operating with Islamic procedures and principles and conventional banks differ when affected by macroeconomic variables, global economic conjuncture, and financial crises.

The 2008 global financial crisis, which is generally defined as the biggest financial crisis after the Great Depression of 1929 and having devastating effects all over the world by academics and the business world, caused the economists and investors to reevaluate the financial institutions. Especially during the 2008 financial crisis, the performances and relatively stable structures of Islamic financial institutions have increased the demand for financial products with Islamic procedures and principles by investors who want to diversify their investments not only in the Middle East and Muslim countries but also all over the world (Zarrouk, El Ghak and Al Haija; 2017: 2).

Islamic banks operate on risk-sharing basis and are separated from conventional banks in this framework. Islamic banks operating based on *Shariah* do not comply with the interest rate transactions of their participants (Siddiqi, 2006; Basov and Bhatti, 2016); and in this framework, the fact that Islamic banking meets the funding demands arising from the real business transactions of corporations by targeting the financing of the real sector prevents the problem of investment in speculative fields and goods in products, which are the main factors of the financial crises. However, conventional banks focusing on debt financing, investing in speculative products called toxic products, and carrying out high leveraged transactions are considered as the main elements of the crises. In this context, Stout (2011) stated that the main reason of the 2008 financial crisis is the excessive risks taken by the US banks within the framework of derivative products, and Ahmed (2010) indicated that speculative transactions together with interest and usury are the main causes of the financial crisis.

There are many reasons for financial crises, and many factors are effective in crises created by traditional financial markets and conventional banks. Financial crises in general are having serious economic problems as a result of substantial increase in loans that are not repaid to the banking sector with the high volatility of the goods and services markets and financial markets.

Especially with the phenomenon of globalization, the acceleration in capital movements brought the lack of supervision and regulation in traditional financial markets and conventional banks, financial institutions that desire to increase their market share tended to use risky products, and the budgets of financial institutions and countries deteriorated within the framework of currency wars. This approach, presented by traditional financial markets and conventional banks within the framework of capitalist system, has prepared a suitable ground for financial crises.

Yazıcı (2016) stated that demand is created without supply in the economy and emphasized the interaction of the volatile structure caused by interest with inflation. In addition, while the differences in the maturity and liquidity characteristics of the resources and placements of conventional banks cause short position problem, the loans are distributed sloppily as a result of the excess of liquidity created for the purpose of reducing interest, and uncontrolled securitization is carried out for the continuation of the interest rate decrease (Yazıcı, 2016: 65–67). Chapra (2011) explained the risky and improvident loan management of conventional banks with three factors:

1) Insufficient discipline as there is no profit-loss sharing between lenders and borrowers,
2) Increased use of derivative instruments, especially credit swaps, and
3) "Too big to fail" approaches of the big banks.

Accordingly, Kayed and Hassan (2011) drew attention to the insufficiency of the regulatory institutions and high credit appetite because of the high return expectations on the basis of the 2008 financial crises. In contrast, Islamic finance and Islamic banking focus on social welfare, in discordance with profit maximization (Asutay, 2007). According to Islamic economists, being based on justice with approaches such as reducing income inequality and implementing the principle of social welfare is one of the most important points that distinguish Islamic finance and Islamic banks from others. Above and beyond the technical approaches of finance, Islamic banking operates within the framework of socio-economic objectives such as equal income distribution (Usmani, 2009). Within the scope of Islamic banking theory, Siddique and Iqbal (2014) pointed the two main objectives of Islamic banking:

1) Removal of equity financing and fixed income debt financing and
2) Maintaining the fair distribution of resources and welfare

In this scope, Islamic finance and Islamic banks focus on the financing of the real sector rather than speculative fields. Islamic banks focusing on real sector financing means that there is a tangible asset in exchange for the extended loans. This situation increases the asset quality of the financial markets and the banking sector, especially in times of crisis, for the reason that the loans supplied by Islamic banks are based on assets that provides a more reliable environment for both borrowers and lenders. Indeed, Hasan and Dridi (2010) indicated that Islamic banks play an important role in maintaining economic and financial stability during the financial crisis periods. El-Gamal (2006) also stated that Islamic finance operates more equitable and sustainable practices compared to conventional banks.

This asset-based structure of Islamic finance and Islamic banking that is free from speculative products has attracted attention as an alternative finance model, especially in the 2008 financial crisis period. The role of variable interest rates that trigger the crisis provided sufficient ground for Islamic economists to offer Islamic finance and Islamic banking as a way to protect them from financial turbulences (Uddin et al., 2017: 401).

4 Literature on Islamic Finance and Financial Crisis

After the financial crises in the world, especially the 2008 global financial crisis, the rapid rise in Islamic finance and Islamic banking has drawn concern by academicians and industry experts. The main questions here are, "What is the situation of Islamic finance and Islamic banking against the financial crises? Can Islamic finance and Islamic banking be effective in order to deal with financial crises?" Many researches have been done on the subject.

According to some researchers, Islamic banking procedures and principles such as risk sharing, transactions based on real asset, financing of the real sector, and ethical approach protect Islamic banks from the effects of the crisis (Chowdhury et. Al., 2016, Hasan and Dridi, 2010; Ahmad, 2010, Siddiqi, 2006).

Hasan and Dridi (2010) analyzed 120 Islamic and conventional banks in the period of 2007–2010 data operating in Bahrain research (including offshore), Jordan, Kuwait, Malaysia, Qatar, Saudi Arabia, Turkey, and the United Arab Emirates. According to the results of the research, Islamic banks had a better performance than conventional banks during the 2008 global financial crisis. Islamic banks have presented a more stable structure, especially with better credit and asset growth.

On the other hand, there are studies showing that Islamic banking is not very effective when dealing with financial crises (Hussein et al., 2019; Uddin et al., 2017; Chapra, 2011; Saddy, 2009, Venardos, 2009). Researches that determine that Islamic banking is not effective against financial crises address two main problems. The first of these problems is that Islamic banks underperform their potential due to poor risk management. In addition, it is referred that Islamic banks are departing away from operating within the framework of basic Islamic principles, and consequently they cannot be protected from the devastating effects of financial crises. The second problem pointed out for Islamic banks is about asset quality. Even though Islamic banks are protected from the first stage of financial crises, they will be affected by the second stage of financial crises due to asset-based loan placements. Because financial crises will have a negative impact on the real sector in the long run, as the business cycle causes a decline in asset prices, the asset quality of Islamic banks will also be negatively affected (El Said and Ziemba, 2009).

Both principal factors and factors related to financial structure are at the basis of studies that Islamic banking is more resistant to financial crises and less affected by financial crises. Due to the fact that the interest is forbidden by the religion of Islam, it is not possible to demand or pay interest on the rented money, and in this context, and proposing a principal on an asset-based financing model (El Gamal, 2006: 3) define the principal and Shariah dimension of Islamic banking. Within this scope, Islamic finance aims to prevent speculative transactions and at the same time eliminate entropy caused by interest. Because interest rate rise for conventional banks also means that entropy in financial ecosystem is in an increasing trend (El Diwany, 2011: 27–33).

Islamic banking prioritizes justice when it is compared with the conventional banking system. In this context, the fundamental motivation of Islamic banking is to serve with humanitarian context and openness and to operate within the framework of moral values. This principle in the attitude results in Islamic banks financing only the activities that contribute to economic growth directly and activities which have high feasibility. In principle, an Islamic bank does not provide funding for investments having an uncertain future or extremely risky projects, and Islamic banks do not operate in the sectors of gambling, speculative transactions, and alcoholic beverages within the context of Shariah. Islamic banks also minimize asymmetric information and moral hazard problems at the same time as a result of the principles mentioned (Hussien, et al., 2019).

Due to the mentioned reasons, it has been determined in many studies that Islamic banks had a successful performance during periods of financial crisis. Rajhi (2013), Mobarek, and Kalonov (2014) stated that the financial stability of Islamic banks is better than conventional banks in the Middle East, Africa, and Asia. Miniaoui and Gohou (2013) and Parashar and Venkatesh (2010) stated that Islamic banks are not affected by the global financial crises in broad terms as a result of their high capital and cash reserves.

Chapra (2008) stated that if the funders and entrepreneurs share the risk that is the basis of Islamic finance and Islamic banking, the financial system will also meet a serious discipline. In such a case, funders will have to estimate the risks more carefully, and the entrepreneur will make more effort for efficient use of funds and a bilateral control mechanism will develop. In such a case, funders will have to estimate the risks more carefully, and the entrepreneur will strive for more efficient use of funds and a bilateral control mechanism will develop. In this context, starting with Chapra's (2008) statement, it will be possible to control uncontrolled credit growth, which is one of the main factors of financial crises, in this way and to preclude one of the main factors of financial crises. Similar to the work of Chapra (2008), Siddiqi (2008) also stated that the profit/loss sharing model would be appropriate for a system integrating risk management and value creation. Fund-seekers and funders will be very careful in their choices in such

Tab. 10.1. Comparison of Islamic banking versus conventional banking

Islamic Banking	Conventional Banking
Profit/loss sharing basis, financing of the real sector	Financing of speculative and toxic products
Stable structure in credit and asset growth	Volatility in credit and asset growth
Prioritizing of justice and moral values	Profit-focused banking approach
Credit process management with high sense of control	Unregulated credit processes
Minimization of moral hazard and adverse selection problems	High moral hazard and adverse selection problems
Higher profitability	Lower profitability

Source: Derived by the author.

a structure for the reason that they will share profit and loss, and those who use funds will pay particular attention to bank choices. Al-Suwailem (2010) indicated that interest is the main cause of financial crises, and stated that it causes financial and economic instability. The study revealed that interest creates a debt inflation compared to real products by creating a distinction between the real economy and the financial sector.

Yazıcı (2016) compared Islamic banks with conventional banks, and stated that in conventional banks, where interest is used as the primary instrument, interest affects input costs, thereby causing cost inflation, increasing demand without production, thereby increasing future prices. Yazıcı (2016) stated that the Islamic banking system, in which the borrowers and lenders share the risk, which means the partnership to profit and loss approach, is more effective in order to create a balanced economic structure than the traditional system with interest rate that disrupts the effective functioning of financial markets with its inflationary effects.

We comparatively present the findings obtained within the scope of our study in the framework of the 2008 global financial crisis in Tab. 10.1.

In this context, the studies investigating the situation of Islamic finance and Islamic banking against financial crises and seeking answers to the question of whether it can play an effective role in order to prevent financial crises present the difference of Islamic finance from conventional banks with its principal dimensions and funding methods. This difference distinguishes the position of Islamic finance and Islamic banking against the financial crises and the role of Islamic finance in coping with crises from conventional banks.

Conclusion and Recommendations

Islamic finance and Islamic banking supply the financing of the real sector by performing asset-based transactions. Islamic banks eliminate uncertainty in financial markets with their financing methods. In addition, they prevent speculative, highly leveraged, and excessively risky transactions, which are the fundamental causes of financial crises.

One of the basic principles of Islamic finance and Islamic banking is the share of profit and loss, in other words, risk sharing. The financial system is to be open and transparent as a requirement of the Islamic banking's risk sharing-based activities. Openness and transparency allow lenders to analyze the risk carefully, thereby make high market discipline possible. Markets working with high discipline enables a healthy loan portfolio and allows repayment of loans on time. The repayment of loans on time provides the continuity of healthy loan portfolio and high asset quality.

Islamic banking has started to rise rapidly with the 2007–2008 global financial crisis and attracted the attention of investors. Islamic banking, offering different products and services to investors who want to diversify the investments and also distribute the risk, has a less risky structure than conventional banks because it provides real-sector financing directly. Besides that, conventional banks cause cost and demand inflation and impact financial markets and macroeconomic structure in a negative way. Islamic banks, as for that, suggest a balanced economic structure and a fair distribution of income.

There are many studies proposing that Islamic banks show better performance in times of financial crisis. Product diversification, economies of scale, and stronger respectability have impact on this better performance of Islamic banks. The fact that Islamic banks use a more realistic approach in the areas of product pricing and collateralization, in comparison to conventional banks, is one of the effective factors about their performance especially in the 2008 global financial crisis. The 2008 global financial crisis has shown that the consequences should be very devastating if confidence in financial markets is lost. Islamic finance and Islamic banks are completely based on trust in this framework, avoiding speculation and ensuring their customers in order to make rational investments. Within this scope, Islamic banking presents a more stable and healthy financial structure when it is compared to conventional banks.

It is not a realistic approach to expect Islamic banks to replace conventional banks in a short time. Islamic banking is still at the beginning phase of its life and has a very little share in the international financial system. In this scope, the Islamic finance and Islamic banking system is not strong enough in order to solve the problems from the conventional banking system and ensure the proper functioning of the financial system. Asset-based structure of Islamic finance and Islamic banking and risk-sharing basis can play an effective role in ensuring stability and fighting financial crises, but this depends on increasing its share in the financial system. Steps taken by public authorities in order to increase the share of Islamic banking in the financial system will make contribution to the transparent, controllable structure of financial markets, and in addition, it will maintain diversification for investors looking for alternative investment areas and investment instruments.

References

Ahmed, A. (2010) "Global Financial Crisis: An Islamic Finance Perspective", International Journal of Islamic and Middle Eastern Finance and Management, 3(4): 306–320.

Aktepe, İ. E. (2013) "Sorularla Katılım Bankacılığı", İstanbul, TKBB Yayınları.

Alkış, A. (2018) "İslam Hukukunda Katılım Bankacılığı Fon Toplama ve Kullandırma Yöntemleri", Al-Farabi Uluslararası Sosyal Bilimler Dergisi, 2(3): 120–133.

Al-Suwailem, S. (2010) "Al Azmaat Al Maaliyaah Fii Daw İ Al İkhtisad Al Islami", Jaami'ah Imaam Muhammad İbn Saud Al Islamiyah.

Asutay, M. (2007) "Conceptualisation of the Second Best Solution in Overcoming the Social Failure of Islamic Banking and Finance: Examining the Overpowering of Homoislamicus by Homoeconomicus", IIUM Journal of Economics and Management, 15(2): 167–195.

Basov, S. and Bhatti, M. I. (2016) "Islamic Finance in the Light of Modern Economic Theory", First Edition, Basingstoke: Palgrave Macmillan.

Çanakçı, M. (2014) "Çok Kutuplu Dünyada İslami Finans Piyasalarının Gelişimi ve Sukuk İhraçları", Türkiye İslam İktisadı Dergisi, 1(2): 43–58.

Chapra, M. U. (2008) "Discussion Forum on the Financial Crisis: Comments from Islamic Perspective", IIUM Journal of Economics and Management, 16(2): 111–138.

Chapra, M. U. (2011) "The Global Financial Crisis: Some Suggestions for Reform of the Global Financial Architecture in the Light of Islamic Finance", Thunderbird International Business Review, 53(5): 565–579.

Chowdhury, M. A. F., Shoyeb, M., Akbar, C. ve Islam, M. N. (2016) "Risk Sharing Paradigm of Islamic Banks: Case of Bangladesh", Advances İn Islamic Finance, Marketing and Management: An Asian Perspective, Emerald Group Publishing Limited, 103–130.

Diaw, A. (2015) "The Global Financial Crisis and Islamic Finance: A Review of Selected Literature", Journal of Islamic Accounting and Business Research, 6(1): 94–106.

Dönmez, P. A. (2009) "Küresel Kriz ve Ülkeler Tarafından Alınan Önlemler Kronolojisi", Bankacılar Dergisi, (68), 85–101.

El Diwany, T. (2011) "Faiz Sorunu" Mehmet Saraç (eds), İz Yayıncılık, İstanbul.

El-Gamal, M. A. (2006). Islamic Finance: Law, Economics and Practise. New York. NY: Cambridge University Press.

El-Said, A., and Ziemba, R. (2009) "Stress-Testing Islamic Finance", Available at: https://moneymaven.io/economonitor/us/stress-testing-islamic-finance-_hiyPBazrkmm_URz00JApA (accessed 20 December 2019).

Ersan, Ö. (2007) "Katılım Bankalarının Finansal Etkinliği ve Mevduat Bankaları ile Rekabet Edebilirliği", Yayımlanmamış Doktora Tezi, Afyonkarahisar Kocatepe Üniversitesi, Sosyal Bilimler Enstitüsü.

Hasan, M., and Dridi, J. (2010) "The Effects of the Global Crisis on Islamic and Conventional Banks: A Comparative Study", IMF Working Papers, 10(201): 1–46.

Hussien, M. E., Alam, Md. M., Murad, Md. W., and Wahid, A. N. M. (2019) "The Performance of Islamic Banks during the 2008 Global Financial Crisis", Journal of Islamic Accounting and Business Research, 10(3): 407–420.

Kara, B. Ş. (2019) "Türkiye Ve Dünyada Gölge Bankacılık Uygulamaları, 2008 Küresel Finansal Krizdeki Rolü, İslami Bankacılık İle İlişkisi", Yayımlanmamış Yüksek Lisans Tezi, Marmara Üniversitesi Bankacılık ve Sigortacılık Enstitüsü Bankacılık Anabilim Dalı, İstanbul.

Karasu, O. (2016) "2008 Küresel Finans Krizi Sonrasında İslami Finans Araçlarının Analizi", İstanbul Ticaret Üniversitesi, Sosyal Bilimler Enstitüsü İktisat Anabilim Dalı, İstanbul.

Kayed, R., and Hassan, M. (2011) "The Global Financial Crisis and Islamic Finance", Thunderbird International Business Review, 53(5): 551–564.

Krugman, P. (2009) "How Did Economist Get It Wrong?" New York Times, 2 September.

Miniaoui, H., and Gohou, G. (2013) "Did Islamic Banking Perform Better during the Financial Crisis? Evidence from the UAE", Journal of Islamic Economics, Banking and Finance, 9(2): 115–130.

Mobarek, A., and Kalonov, A. (2014) "Comparative Performance Analysis between Conventional and Islamic Banks: Empirical Evidence from OIC Countries", Applied Economics, 46(3): 253–270.

Özdemir, A. (2012). Karz Akdinin Mahiyeti ve Faizli İşlemleri Önleme Fonksiyonu. Çukurova Üniversitesi İlahiyat Fakültesi Dergisi, 12(1), 125–145.

Özsoy, M. (2012) "Katılım Bankacılığına Giriş", İstanbul: Winomy Yayınları.

Parashar, S. P. and Venkatesh, J. (2010) "How Did Islamic Banks Do during Global Financial Crisis?", Banks and Bank Systems, 5(4): 54–62.

Rajhi, W. (2013) "Islamic Banks and Financial Stability: A Comparative Empirical Analysis between MENA and Southeast Asian Countries", Région et Développement, 37: 149–177.

Saddy, F. (2009) "Risky business", Islamic Banking & Finance, *7(3): 23.*

Shanmugam, B., and Zahari, Z. R. (2009) "A Primer on Islamic Finance. Research Foundation of Cfa Institute", Bala Shanmugam Monash University.

Siddiqi, M. N. (2006) "Banking without İnterest", First Edition. Lahor: The Islamic Foundation.

Siddiqi, M. N. (2008) "Discussion Forum on the Financial Crisis: Comments from Islamic Perspective", IIUM Journal of Economics and Management, 16(2): 111–138.

Siddique, M. Z., and Iqbal, M. (2014) "A Framework for Evaluating Islamic Banking from "Within", Islamic Studies, 53(1), 1–2: 5–36.

Stout, L. (2011) "Derivatives and Legal Origin of the 2008 Credit Crisis", Harvard Business Law Review, 1: 1–38.

Uddin, A., Chowdhury, M. A. F., and Islam, Md. N. (2017) "Resiliency between Islamic and Conventional Banks in Bangladesh: Dynamic GMM and Quantile Regression Approaches", International Journal of Islamic and Middle Eastern Finance and Management, 10(3): 400–418.

Usmani, M. T. (2009) "Interest Free Banking (URDU)", Karachi: Idarah Ma'rafatul Quran (Quranic Studies Publishers).

Venardos, A. M. (2009) "Current Issues in Islamic Banking and Finance. Resilience and Stability in the Present System", Singapore: World Scientific Publishing.

Yazıcı, R. (2016) "Finansal Krizlerin Önlenmesinde Katılım Bankacılığı Sisteminin Rolü Üzerine Bir Değerlendirme", Sakarya İktisat Dergisi, 5(1): 59–82.

Zarrouk, H., Ghak, T. E., and Haija, E. A. A. (2017) "Financial Development, Islamic Finance and Economic Growth: Evidence of the UAE", Journal of Islamic Accounting and Business Research, 8(1): 2–22.

S. Nurbanu Yıldız and Üzeyir Aydın

11 Analysis of Reserve Option Mechanism Applied for Providing Financial Stability

Highlights: The reserve option mechanism, which is thought to work as an automatic stabilizer in the money, foreign exchange, and financial markets, also enables the Central Bank to intervene in the exchange rate volatility in the domestic markets and the producer and consumer price indexes through exchange rate transparency. In this context, the aim of the study is to analyze the effects of the reserve option mechanism on foreign exchange reserve changes, inflation uncertainty, inflation rate, and interest rate between October 2011 to December 2018 using vector autoregression models. According to the results, the change in the CBRT's foreign currency reserves responds positively while the inflation uncertainty, the inflation rate, and the interest rate respond negatively to a standard error shock in the reserve option mechanism. The effect of these responses extends about two months.

Key Words: Reserve options mechanism, financial stability, VAR model, tools of monetary policy

Introduction

Besides various aims and objectives, the primary objective of the Central Bank is to achieve price stability. As monetary targeting and exchange rate targeting strategies can be used or like in Turkey inflation targeting regime is implemented to achieve this objective. However, new policy compositions are formed in order to control the monetary expansion after the global 2008 banking crisis. In this sense, price stability objective of the Central Bank as well as the financial stability objective is questioned and policies have been developed for this purpose. Because, while price stability is aimed by controlling money supply, volatilities of the other economic variables caused economic instability. Until mid-2010, new policy tools are used in order to eliminate the effects of the global crisis on the economy, strengthen financial structure, and maintain stability completely. For this purpose, the Central Bank has developed reserve option mechanism (ROM) in the role of automatic balancer to limit the negative effects of extreme volatility on macroeconomic and financial stability and transfer the under-the-mattress gold to the economic system besides the policy tools such as interest rate corridor, required reserves, and liquidity management.

ROM is the mechanism that enables the banks to hold some part of the required ratio as foreign exchange (US dollar or euro) or gold determined by the

Central Bank while they meet the obligation of required reserves in TL. Reserve option coefficient (ROK) is the coefficient that shows how much of the Central Bank's required reserves are held in gold or foreign currency.

ROM, which is a new policy tool developed by the Central Bank, enables the control and management of foreign exchange liquidity, currency volatilities, and capital movements. The amount of ROM to be used is found by multiplying the coefficients for the percentage tranches, which are expressed as the reserve ratio coefficient, determined by the Central Bank. Banks prefer to keep most of the required reserves for TL liabilities in foreign currencies during periods of intense capital inflows due to low foreign exchange resource costs. On the contrary, in the periods of capital outflows, they prefer to keep the required ratios in TL since the cost of foreign exchange resources increases. Banks are based on the resource cost for the liabilities they have to keep in the CBRT.

The CBRT tries to manage the liquidity in the market by affecting the funding costs of banks changing the interest rate corridor, reserve requirements, and ROM ratios. Thus, it aims to affect the exchange rate increase, depreciation or appreciation of TL, liquidity supply and demand due to the capital movements. At this point, whether the CBRT is successful or not is very important both in terms of price and financial stability. In this context, whether the ROM, which is thought to work as an automatic balancer in money, foreign exchange, and financial markets, allows the Central Bank to influence the exchange rate volatilities in domestic markets and the producer and consumer price indices via exchange rate transience constitutes the main problematic of this study.

In this context, the objective of this study is to analyze the effect of ROM on change of foreign exchange reserves of CBRT, inflation, and benchmark interest rate. In other words, it is to test the success of ROM.

Within the framework, firstly literature survey is reviewed. Then method and the data set to be used in the analyses are defined. Lastly, empirical findings are analyzed, and the study is concluded with the policy propositions derived from the analyses.

1 Literature Review

Although there are many studies about the subject, the following part reviews the Turkish literature shortly.

Küçüksaraç (2012) concluded that an optimal application of ROM and ROK by CBRT enables to increase the gross foreign exchange reserves and control the credit growth of banks and can affect the short run interest rates by changing ROK in the study.

According to Alper et al. (2012), Rom is a useful tool for macroeconomic and financial stability goals and more effective in terms of limiting the negative effects of capital inflows on exchange rate and foreign currency loans than similar tools, but ROM needs to be tested for various shocks in time.

Oduncu et al. (2013) investigated the effect of the ROM on foreign exchange volatility using a GARCH model. It was concluded that ROM has a decreasing effect on exchange rate volatility.

Demirhan (2013) emphasized interest rate corridor and ROM as important tools used by CBRT in order to maintain financial stability. It is stated that these tools are effective on capital inflows and the tools are used to decrease the instability of capital flows by CBRT.

Alkın (2015) searched the new consensus model and tested the causality and cointegration relationship between real interest rate flattening variable, inflation gap, output gap, and exchange rate and concluded that CBRT raises the interest rates if actual interest rate is higher than expected inflation rate and also CBRT considers the past values of interest rates while making interest rate decisions, and moreover attracts attention to interest rates about financial stability.

Ergin and Aydın (2017) referred the construction and context of ROM mentioning the role of monetary policy in maintaining the financial stability. It is stated that ROM maintains a more powerful and resistant financial structure in a possible crisis, strengthens foreign exchange reserves and limits the volatility of exchange rates, and plays an active role on the mechanism transferring savings to investments.

Kantar (2017) investigated the effects of ROM on exchange rate volatility. In the study, it is found that the ROM decreases exchange rate volatility and is effective on negative shocks.

Tezer (2019) found that the ROM developed by CBRT is useful for foreign exchange reserve position but inefficient in affecting the fragilities and controlling power on exchange rates and interest rates because of the negativities of macroeconomic structure.

To summarize, when we consider the literature as a whole, studies show that ROM benefits the banks, decreases the exchange rate volatility, strengthens the foreign exchange reserves, and contributes to financial stability. It is possible to come across findings in the opposite direction in the least.

2 Aim, Hypothesis, and Methodology

The objective of this study is to analyze the effect of ROM on exchange of foreign exchange reserves, inflation uncertainty, inflation rate, and benchmark interest rate. Within the scope of the aim of the study, the following hypotheses are formed:

Hypothesis 1: The response of the CBRT foreign exchange reserve to a shock in the ROM is positive.
Hypothesis 2: The response of CPI inflation uncertainty and PPI inflation rate to a shock in ROM is negative.
Hypothesis 3: The response of the two-year bond interest rate to a shock in the ROM is negative.
Hypothesis 4: ROM is effective policy design in both short and long term.

The vector autoregression (VAR) model was used in the study for the testing of hypotheses. The VAR model is multivariate dynamic time series analysis. The VAR model is used to model the dynamic behavior of economic and financial time series and is an extended version of the univariate autoregressive model. The lagged VAR model of p can be expressed as follows (Engle,1982; Tse and Tsui, 2002; Engle and Sheppard, 2001; Tsay, 2011; Gujarati, 2004):

$$y_t = \mu + \Gamma_1 y_{t-1} + \ldots + \Gamma_p y_{t-p} + \varepsilon_t \quad (1)$$

ε_t defines the zero mean and $E\left[\varepsilon_t {\varepsilon_t}'\right] = \Omega$ covariance matrix error term. In other terms, error terms are white noise. Γ_i is the coefficient matrix with (nxn) dimension. This equation system can be written as a VAR model as follows:

$$\Gamma(L)\, y_t = \mu + \varepsilon_t \quad (2)$$

Here, (L)defines the polynomial matrix of lag operator. VAR model with 2 lags can be written as the following form:

$$\begin{pmatrix} y_{1t} \\ y_{2t} \end{pmatrix} = \begin{pmatrix} c_1 \\ c_2 \end{pmatrix} + \begin{pmatrix} \pi_{11}^1 & \pi_{12}^1 \\ \pi_{21}^1 & \pi_{22}^1 \end{pmatrix} \begin{pmatrix} y_{1t-1} \\ y_{2t-1} \end{pmatrix} + \begin{pmatrix} \pi_{11}^2 & \pi_{12}^2 \\ \pi_{21}^2 & \pi_{22}^2 \end{pmatrix} \begin{pmatrix} y_{1t-2} \\ y_{2t-2} \end{pmatrix} + \begin{pmatrix} \varepsilon_{1t} \\ \varepsilon_{2t} \end{pmatrix} \quad (3)$$

or

$$y_{1t} = c_1 + \pi_{11}^1 y_{1t-1} + \pi_{12}^1 y_{1t-2} + \pi_{11}^2 y_{1t-2} + \pi_{12}^2 y_{2t-2} + \varepsilon_{1t}$$

$$y_{2t} = c_1 + \pi_{21}^1 y_{1t-1} + \pi_{22}^1 y_{1t-2} + \pi_{21}^2 y_{1t-2} + \pi_{22}^2 y_{2t-2} + \varepsilon_{2t} \quad (4)$$

In the VAR model, instead of coefficient interpretation, remarks based on impulse-response functions are made. Impulse-response functions show the response of the other variable against one standard error shock of a variable.

Tab. 11.1: Variables used in analysis

Variables	Definitions	Source
ROM	Ratio of Turkish Lira required reserves ROM $ROM = \frac{Amount\ of\ Foreign\ Currency\ Held\ for\ Turkish\ Lira\ Required\ Reserves\ within\ ROM}{Gross\ Foreign\ Exchange\ Reserve\ of\ CBRT}$	TCMB EVDS
Inflation CPI	CPI-based inflation uncertainty	TCMB EVDS
Inflation PPI	PPI-based inflation uncertainty	TCMB EVDS
Stock_ Reserves	Change in foreign exchange reserve CBRT gross reserves	TCMB EVDS
Bond Interest Rate	2-year benchmark bond interest rate	TCMB EVDS

Source: Edited by authors

2.1 Data Sets and Variables

In order to test the above hypothesis, variables to be used in the analysis and definitions of these variables are given in Tab. 11.1.

The variables used in the analysis are in the monthly frequency for the period October 2011 to December 2018. All variables are seasonally adjusted using the moving averages method. At the same time, the logarithm of all variables is taken.

Data subject to analysis must contain after 2011 period because the reserve option mechanism carried out by the CBRT to minimize the disruptive effects of excessive fluctuations in capital movements on financial and economic stability has been used since October 2011. This situation constitutes an important constraint in the study. Nevertheless, when the literature is analyzed, studies analyzing data with similar monthly and quarterly frequency with autoregressive conditional variance models are also seen (Çapar, 2010; Erdem, 2017).

When the graphs of the variables are analyzed, it is seen that the volatility increases after mid-2018 when the change in foreign exchanges are high (Fig. 11.1). The benchmark interest rate has entered an upward trend albeit slowly, and this rise took place in the form of a rapid climb again in mid-2018. While inflation uncertainty follows a horizontal trend between 2011 and 2017, after 2017 it entered into an increasing trend and became unstable. It is observed

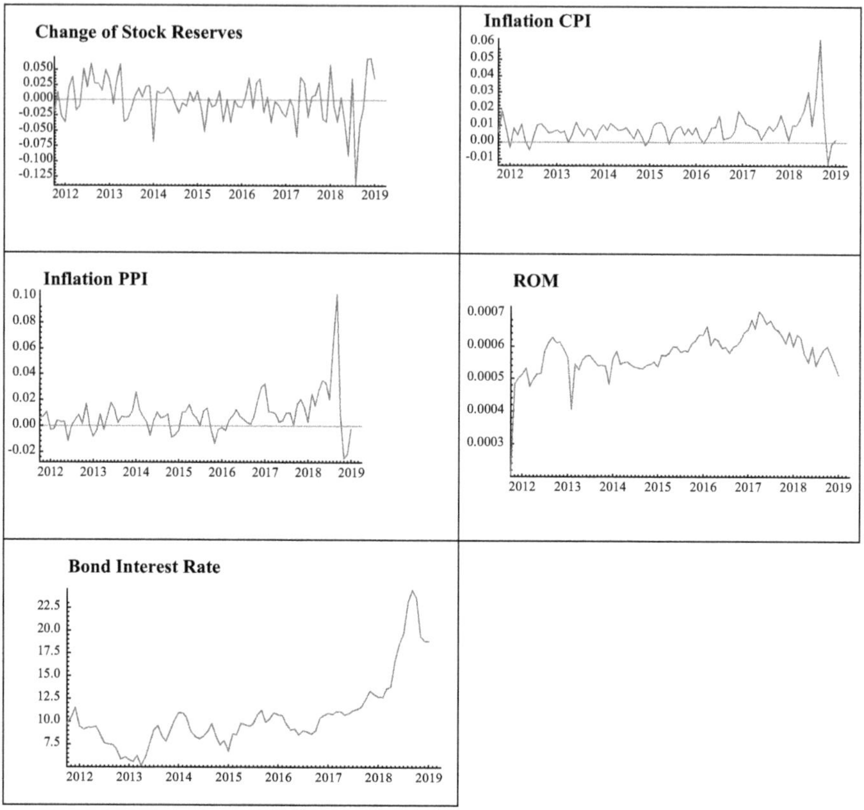

Fig. 11.1: Graphs of variables
Source: Edited by authors

that volatility has increased in all variables since mid-2018 due to fluctuations in exchange rates.

3 Empirical Findings

Firstly, stationaries of variables were investigated. Afterwards, a VAR model was used to test the hypotheses created depending on the purpose.

3.1 Stationarity Analysis of Series

Augmented Dickey-Fuller (ADF), Phillips-Perron (PP), and KPSS unit root tests were used to examine the stationarity of variables. Results of the unit root tests

Tab. 11.2: ADF, Phillips-Perron, and KPSS unit root test results

	ADF		**Phillips-Perron**		**KPSS**	
Variables	**With Constant**	**Constant and Trends**	**With Constant**	**Constant and Trends**	**With Constant**	**Constant and Trends**
ROM	-3.1902(1)**	-2.9729(1)	-6.6763(5)***	-6.9923(5)***	0.7734(6)***	0.1373(5)*
Inflation_CPI	-4.1646(3)***	-4.7495(3)***	-5.9437(3)***	-6.0079(5)***	0.4443(3)*	0.0813(1)
Inflation_PPI	-1.5157(8)	-2.2917(9)	-4.7250(7)***	-4.6441(9)***	0.5229(3)**	0.1273(0)*
Stock_ Reserves	-8.2213(0)***	-8.4898(0)***	-8.3098(4)***	-8.4876(4)***	0.3079(4)	0.0508(3)
Bond Interest Rate	-0.6324(0)	-2.8015(1)	-0.7832(1)	-2.4445(2)	0.7926(7)***	0.1652(6)**
ΔBond Interest Rate	-8.0173(0)***	-8.1262(0)***	-8.0006(3)***	-8.0597(5)***	0.1568(2)	0.0392(4)
Critical Values	%1 -3.50	%1 -4.06	%1 -3.50	%1 -4.06	%1 0.73	%1 0.21
	%5 -2.89	%5 -3.46	%5 -2.89	%5 -3.46	%5 0.46	%5 0.14
	%10 -2.58	%10 -3.15	%10 -2.58	%10 -3.15	%10 0.34	%10 0.11

Note: ***,**, and * show significance at 1 %, 5 %, and 10 % significance levels, respectively. Values in parentheses show lag lengths. Δ indicates that the first difference of the variable is taken

Source: Derived by Authors

for variables are given in Tab 11.2. When fixed term unit root test results are examined, it is seen ROM, Inflation_cpi, and change in foreign exchange reserves are stationary at level at 10 % significance. But however, inflation_ppi is stationary at first difference. According to Phillips-Perron unit root test results, ROM, inflation_ppi, inflation_cpi, and reserve_currency variables are stationary at level. According to KPSS unit root tests, reserve_currency variable is stationary at level; ROM, inflation_ppi, inflation_cpi, and interest rate variables are stationary at first difference.

When the unit root test results with constant and with trend in Tab. 11.2 are investigated, it is stated that inflation_ppi and reserve currency are stationary at level and ROM and inflation_cpi are stationary at first difference due to ADF unit root test. According to Phillips-Perron unit root test results, ROM, inflation_cpi, inflation_ppi, and reserve currency are stationary al level. When we consider KPSS test results, inflation_ppi and reserve currency are stationary at level and ROM, inflation_cpi, and bond_interest variables are stationary at first difference. For the reason that ADF, Phillips-Perron, and KPSS unit root tests have different results and due to the political and geopolitical and financial shocks of the period under consideration, stationarity of variables is also examined with Zivot-Andrews test.

Tab. 11.3: Results of Zivot-Andrews unit root test

Variables	With Constant	Break Date	With Trends	Break Date	Constant and Trends	Break Date
ROM	-3.8558(1)	2017M11	-4.4294(1)**	2017M8	-4.9087(1)*	2016M12
Inflation_CPI	-5.3124(3)**	2017M11	-5.3633(3)***	2016M9	-5.4533(3)**	2016M2
Inflation_PPI	-6.9235(1)***	2017M10	-6.7993(1)***	2016M12	-6.8882(1)***	2015M10
Stock_Reserves	-8.8136(0)***	2013M5	-8.5434(0)***	2017M12	-9.1058(0)***	2013M5
Bond Interest Rate	-33.4667(1)	2017M10	-3.5484(1)	2017M5	-3.7200(1)	2016M3
Δ Bond Interest Rate	-8.4414(0)***	2013M5	-8.2270(0)***	2013M7	-8.4804(0)***	2014M2
Critical Values	%1 -5.34 %5 -4.93 %10 -4.58		%1 -4.80 %5 -4.42 %10 -4.11		%1 -5.57 %5 -5.08 %10 -4.82	

Source: Derived by authors

Note: ***,**, and * show significance at 1 %, 5 %, and 10 % significance levels, respectively. Values in parentheses show lag lengths. Δ indicates that the first difference of the variable is taken

Zivot-Andrews unit root test results are shown in Tab. 11.3. According to the constant term unit root test, inflation_ppi, inflation_cpi, and reserve_currency are stationary at level; however, it can be stated that the ROM variable is stationary at first difference. According to trend unit root test, ROM, inflation_cpi, and reserve_currency variables are stationary at the level; and the bond_interest rate variable is stationary at first difference. Finally, according to the test results with constant term and with trend, it is seen that ROM, inflation_ppi, inflation_cpi, and reserve_currency are stationary at level.

3.2 Impact Analysis of ROM with VAR Model

VAR model is used in the study to determine the effect of ROM on change of foreign exchange reserves, inflation uncertainty, and benchmark interest rate. The VAR model allows to examine the dynamic relationship between stationary series of different degrees. All series are included in the analysis at their stationary values.

The VAR model, which emerges as a result of Sims' (1980) elimination of the internal and external variable separation, reveals the effect of the shocks that occur in the variables through the impulse-response functions. For the VAR model, firstly it is necessary to determine the appropriate lag length.

According to the information criteria in Tab. 11.4, appropriate lag lengths are seen as lag 1, lag 3, and lag 12.

Tab. 11.4: Lag length determination of VAR model

Lag Length	LogL	LR	FPE	AIC	SC	HQ
0	1321.397	NA	1.03e-20	-34.66834	-34.54567	-34.61931
1	1385.895	120.5100	2.88e-21	-35.94461	-35.33126*	-35.69948*
2	1402.407	29.11297	2.86e-21	-35.95808	-34.85405	-35.51685
3	1419.462	28.27509*	2.80e-21*	-35.98584	-34.39112	-35.34851
4	1431.900	19.31277	3.13e-21	-35.89212	-33.80673	-35.05869
5	1442.428	15.23788	3.72e-21	-35.74812	-33.17204	-34.71859
6	1454.162	15.74779	4.34e-21	-35.63585	-32.56909	-34.41022
7	1464.724	13.06284	5.33e-21	-35.49273	-31.93529	-34.07100
8	1476.154	12.93469	6.54e-21	-35.37248	-31.32436	-33.75466
9	1500.695	25.18608	5.85e-21	-35.59722	-31.05843	-33.78330
10	1523.403	20.91550	5.70e-21	-35.77376	-30.74428	-33.76373
11	1548.394	20.38741	5.49e-21	-36.01036	-30.49021	-33.80424
12	1570.423	15.65198	6.08e-21	-36.16901	-30.15817	-33.76679

LR: Iterative Modified LR Test Statistics (5 % Significant Level)

FPE: Final Prediction Error

AIC: Akaike Information Criteria

SC: Schwarz Information Criteria

HQ: Hannan-Quinn Information Criteria

Source: Derived by authors

However, when autocorrelation and variance difference test results are examined, the optimal lag length is determined as 3. Table 11.5 shows the LM autocorrelation test result of VAR model with 3 lags. Accordingly, the null hypothesis, which states that there is no autocorrelation between error terms, cannot be rejected. Therefore, there is no autocorrelation problem in the model.

White variance test results related to VAR models with 3 lags are given at Tab. 11.6.

According to the results in Tab. 11.6, the null hypothesis, which states that the variances for the errors are equal, cannot be rejected. Therefore, there is no heteroscedasticity problem in the model.

On the other hand, the validity of the tests applied for coefficient estimators depends on the normal distribution of the error terms. For this, the Normality (Jarque-Bera) test, which is one of the diagnostic tests, is performed. H_0 cannot be rejected, (JB = 0.345> X2α, sd = 5.99), errors terms have normal distribution.

Tab. 11.5: Results of the serial autocorrelation test

Lag Length	LM-Stat	Prob.
1	27.56711	0.0356
2	13.80127	0.6135
3	15.01216	0.5237
4	22.77656	0.1198

Source: Derived by authors

Tab. 11.6: Results of the White test

Dependent Variable	R-Square	F(48,33)	Prob.	Ki-Square(48)	Prob.
Res1*res1	0.812715	2.983373	0.0007	66.64262	0.0386
res2*res2	0.890438	5.587461	0.0000	73.01588	0.0115
res3*res3	0.757263	2.144787	0.0115	62.09559	0.0831
res4*res4	0.626219	1.151811	0.3382	51.34993	0.3438
res2*res1	0.705819	1.649498	0.0662	57.87717	0.1555
res3*res1	0.742789	1.985402	0.0202	60.90869	0.1000
res3*res2	0.830073	3.358346	0.0002	68.06596	0.0299
res4*res1	0.640114	1.222830	0.2739	52.48939	0.3042
res4*res2	0.765426	2.243340	0.0082	62.76490	0.0747
res4*res3	0.790910	2.600556	0.0024	64.85461	0.0528
Ki-square	df	Prob.			
515.2352	480	0.1288			

Source: Derived by authors

In order for the created VAR model to be stable, the AR reverse roots must be inside the unit circle. Accordingly, the unit circle for the AR reverse roots of the 3 lagged VAR model is shown in Fig. 11.2. Therefore, it can be stated that the characteristic inverse roots of the AR are inside the unit circle, in other words, the model is stable.

Impulse-response functions are derived from the VAR model in order to analyze the impact of one standard error shock in the ROM on the variables included in the analysis. Impulse-response functions are given in Fig. 11.3.

According to the impulse-response functions, the change in the CBRT's foreign currency reserves reacts positively for two months against one standard

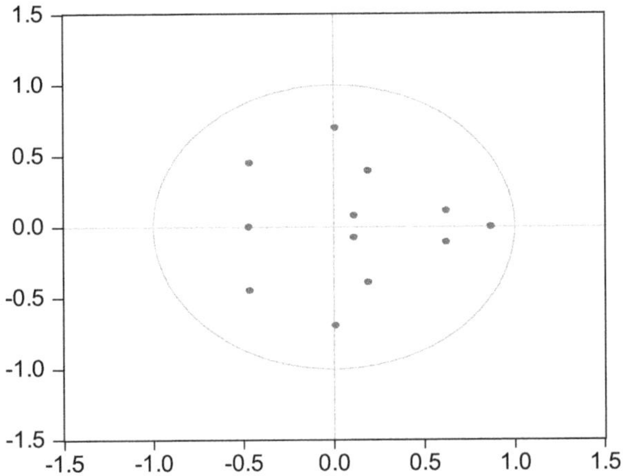

Fig. 11.2: Unit circle to AR characteristic inverse roots
Source: Derived by authors

error shock that occurs in the ROM. The response of the PPI inflation uncertainty and the CPI inflation rate against one standard error shock in the ROM is similar, giving a low negative response for two months, and then this reaction becomes meaningless. Similarly, the response of the two-year bond interest rate against an increase in ROM is negative in the second month, and then this reaction becomes meaningless. When these results are evaluated together, the hypothesis 1/2/3 created based on the purpose cannot be rejected. Therefore, a shock occurred in ROM; the response of CBRT's foreign exchange reserves, CPI, PPI, and two-year bond interest rates of change are in line with the hypotheses and suitable for economic expectations.

Table 11.7 shows the variance decomposition tables regarding the change in the CBRT's foreign exchange reserve, the PPI inflation uncertainty, and the CPI inflation rate. The variance decomposition table shows how many percentage of the changes in the variable are caused by itself or caused by the other variables. Accordingly, 68.37 % of the change in foreign exchange reserves in the second month is originated from itself, 4.91 % from PPI inflation uncertainty, 9.56 % from CPI inflation rate, 8.72 % from ROM, and 8.41 % from two-year bond interest rate. In the third month, 64.87 % of the change in foreign exchange reserves originates from itself, 4.68 % from the uncertainty of the PPI inflation, 9.16 % from the CPI inflation rate, 9.59 % from the ROM, and 11.67 % from the 2-year bond interest rate. In the twelfth month, 63.82 % of the change in foreign

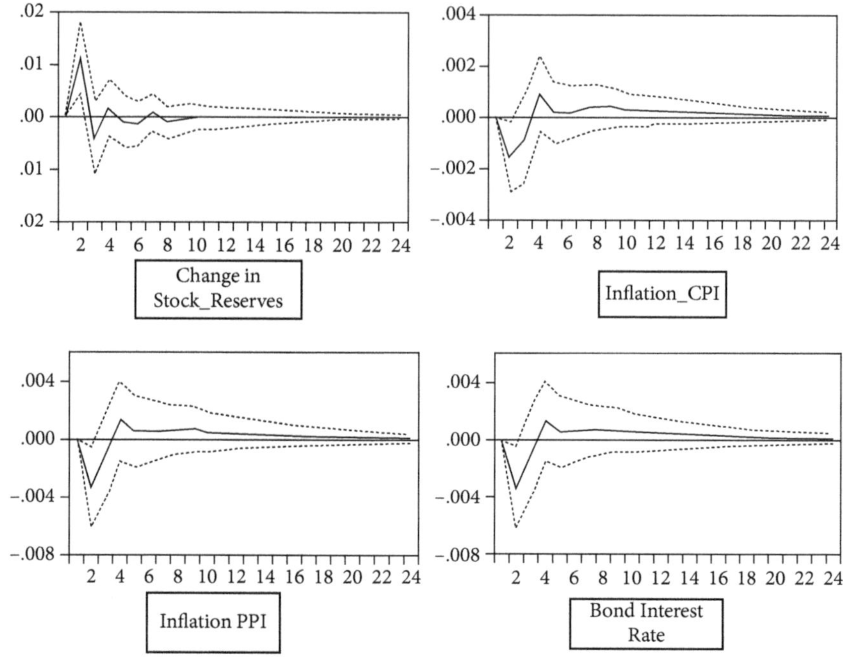

Fig. 11.3: ROM impulse-response function
Source: Derived by authors

exchange reserves originated from itself, 6.66 % from PPI inflation uncertainty, 8.93 % from CPI inflation rate, 9.33 % from ROM, and 11.23 % from 2-year bond interest rate.

When the variance decomposition table of the PPI inflation uncertainty is examined, 56.22 % of the changes in the PPI inflation uncertainty in the second month are from itself, 15.85 % from the change in foreign exchange reserves, 23.95 % from the CPI inflation rate, 2.69 % from ROM, and 1.27 % is due to 2-year bond interest rate. In the third month, 50.43 % of the changes in the CPI inflation uncertainty stem from itself, 14.37 % from the change in foreign exchange reserves, 28.62 % from the CPI inflation rate, 2.45 % from the ROM, and 4.11 % from the 2-year bond interest rate. In the twelfth month, 48.21 % of the changes in the PPI inflation uncertainty stem from itself, 16.92 % of the change in foreign exchange reserves, 27.18 % of the CPI inflation rate, 3.15 % of the ROM, and 4.52 % of the 2-year bond interest rate.

Tab. 11.7: Variance decomposition results

Variance Decomposition Results of Change in Stock Reserves						
Period	**Std. Error**	**Stock Reserves**	**Inflation CPI**	**Inflation PPI**	**ROM**	**Bond Interest Rate**
1	0.028622	100.0000	0.000000	0.000000	0.000000	0.000000
2	0.034875	68.37753	4.912633	9.565261	8.724846	8.419727
3	0.036324	64.87976	4.685248	9.168171	9.593100	11.67372
4	0.037546	64.36362	6.677446	8.827916	9.124871	11.00615
5	0.037656	64.23633	6.652941	8.820027	9.142660	11.14804
6	0.037742	64.08110	6.624958	8.838865	9.223145	11.23193
7	0.037769	64.00092	6.653622	8.833654	9.293516	11.21829
8	0.037814	63.86083	6.664483	8.905491	9.343690	11.22550
9	0.037826	63.82807	6.668564	8.938272	9.337906	11.22719
10	0.037829	63.82421	6.667642	8.937055	9.338026	11.23307
11	0.037830	63.82304	6.668838	8.937060	9.338717	11.23234
12	0.037831	63.82034	6.669746	8.938520	9.338581	11.23281
Variance Decomposition Results of Change in CPI Inflation						
Period	Std. Error	Stock Reserves	Inflation CPI	Inflation PPI	ROM	Bond Interest Rate
1	0.005935	10.18306	89.81694	0.000000	0.000000	0.000000
2	0.008539	15.85055	56.22523	23.95620	2.691343	1.276679
3	0.009038	14.37133	50.43601	28.62555	2.451497	4.115612
4	0.009205	15.79490	49.15430	27.81431	3.138924	4.097570
5	0.009311	16.99118	48.68420	27.19023	3.107179	4.027212
6	0.009377	16.85415	48.35531	27.36590	3.065023	4.359615
7	0.009411	16.93310	48.27535	27.17175	3.090094	4.529703
8	0.009425	16.93061	48.25189	27.18070	3.113291	4.523511
9	0.009429	16.92595	48.22532	27.18593	3.142166	4.520634
10	0.009429	16.93153	48.21865	27.18289	3.142616	4.524321
11	0.009431	16.92670	48.22026	27.17692	3.148977	4.527148
12	0.009433	16.92114	48.21024	27.18582	3.157385	4.525410
Variance Decomposition Results of Change in PPI Inflation						
Period	Std. Error	Stock Reserves	Inflation CPI	Inflation PPI	ROM	Bond Interest Rate
1	0.011903	11.84260	43.67737	44.48003	0.000000	0.000000
2	0.016558	14.64691	29.55212	47.68933	3.184269	4.927373

(continued on next page)

Tab. 11.7: Continued

Variance Decomposition Results of Change in Stock Reserves						
3	0.017478	13.78115	26.62022	48.18120	2.859729	8.557700
4	0.017848	15.19262	25.97969	46.59365	3.224742	9.009304
5	0.017930	15.74937	25.93097	46.17950	3.195631	8.944522
6	0.017971	15.70598	25.86425	46.15611	3.237766	9.035893
7	0.017999	15.71943	25.95482	46.01566	3.264300	9.045789
8	0.018020	15.70976	25.94494	46.01369	3.307242	9.024369
9	0.018025	15.70927	25.93341	46.01599	3.321520	9.019806
10	0.018027	15.71133	25.93008	46.01001	3.328259	9.020321
11	0.018030	15.70641	25.93762	45.99969	3.338562	9.017718
12	0.018032	15.70229	25.93492	45.99860	3.348410	9.015780
Variance Decomposition Results of Change in Bond Interest Rate						
Period	Std. Error	Stock Reserves	Inflation CPI	Inflation PPI	ROM	Bond Interest Rate
1	3.10E-05	12.56991	0.766570	6.205841	0.000942	80.45673
2	3.61E-05	17.35440	0.776602	7.667050	6.358419	67.84353
3	4.16E-05	16.57707	3.078148	7.592435	7.491585	65.26077
4	4.64E-05	16.76331	4.177105	7.415331	7.316012	64.32824
5	4.94E-05	16.63273	4.143894	7.511357	7.571693	64.14032
6	5.21E-05	16.57947	4.209225	7.483146	7.722663	64.00549
7	5.36E-05	16.60901	4.208524	7.484034	7.718478	63.97995
8	5.49E-05	16.57828	4.289777	7.575403	7.705701	63.85084
9	5.57E-05	16.59368	4.284407	7.565746	7.696417	63.85975
10	5.64E-05	16.59815	4.287522	7.565043	7.697878	63.85141
11	5.68E-05	16.59701	4.287184	7.567242	7.704352	63.84421
12	5.72E-05	16.59709	4.287081	7.567688	7.704209	63.84393
Source: Derived by authors						

When the variance decomposition table regarding the CPI inflation rate is analyzed, 47.68 % of the changes in the CPI inflation rate in the second month are from itself, 14.64 % from the change in foreign currency reserves, 29.55 % from the uncertainties of PPI inflation, 3.18 % from ROM, and 4.92 % from 2-year bond interest rate. In the third month, 48.18 % of the changes in the CPI inflation rate stemmed from itself, 13.78 % from the change in foreign exchange reserves, 26.62 % from the PPI inflation uncertainty, 2.85 % from ROM, and

8.55 % from the 2-year bond interest rate. At the twelfth month, 45.99 % of the changes in the CPI inflation rate were due to itself, 15.70 % from the change in foreign exchange reserves, 25.93 % from the uncertainty of the PPI inflation, 3.34 % from the ROM, and 9.01 % from the 2-year bond interest rate.

Finally, when the variance decomposition table for the 2-year bond interest rate is analyzed, in the second month, 67.84 % of the changes in the 2-year bond interest rate are from itself, 17.35 % from the change in foreign exchange reserves, 0.77 % from the PPI inflation uncertainty, 7.66 % from the CPI inflation rate, and 6.35 % from the ROM. In the third month, 65.26 % of the changes in the 2-year bond interest rate arise from itself, 16.57 % from the change in foreign exchange reserves, 3.07 % from PPI inflation uncertainty, 7.59 % from CPI inflation rate, and 7.70 % from ROM.

Conclusions

Central banks in many developed and developing countries have made arrangements in policy practices in order to eliminate the negative effects of the global crisis on their economies. The CBRT also made innovations in the monetary policies implemented after the postcrisis period. Within the framework of the inflation targeting regime, a new policy has been developed using a combination of interest corridor, reserve requirements, liquidity management, and the ROM. In this study, the success of the reserve option mechanism has been analyzed.

With the analyses, Hypothesis 1 (the response of the CBRT foreign exchange reserve to a shock in the ROM is positive), Hypothesis 2 (the response of CPI inflation uncertainty and PPI inflation rate to a shock in ROM is negative), Hypothesis 3 (the response of the two-year bond interest rate to a shock in the ROM is negative), and Hypothesis 4 (ROM is effective policy design in both short and long term) are tested for validity. According to the analysis results obtained, the change in the CBRT's foreign exchange reserves is positive against one standard error shock in the ROM, whereas the PPI inflation uncertainty, the CPI inflation rate, and the 2-year bond interest rate reacted negatively. It was concluded that the effects of these reactions lasted approximately two months. In this case, it can be stated that the first three of the hypotheses tested are valid.

Therefore, if the ROM is used by the CBRT as an intervention tool for the economy, the intervention effects are seen in a period of two months; we can say that intervention effects became meaningless after two months. According to this result, ROM is a short-term intervention tool and loses its effect in the long run. Accordingly, Hypothesis 4, which claims that ROM is an effective policy design in both short and long term, cannot be confirmed.

According to these results, it is necessary to make alternative policy tool designs that will sustain the affect of the ROM in the long term, which is an important market intervention tool against a shock in the short term. With this in mind, instead of policies that take into account only static political and economic developments, it would be appropriate to follow dynamic policies that prioritize all developments on a global scale and consider their impact, financial spread, and meeting among countries. For this, it is necessary to investigate the determinants of financial stress and analyze the spatial effects that reveal financial and commercial commitment between countries. For this reason, policy makers need to monitor international uncertainty and other countries' financial health indicators and researches as well as local macroeconomic and monetary variables.

References

Alkın, H. (2015). Yeni Uzlaşı Modelinin Eleştirisi, Post Keynesyen Enflasyon Hedeflemesi Modelleri Ve Para Politikası Kuralları, Akdeniz Üniversitesi. Sosyal Bilimler Enstitüsü Yayınlanmış Yüksek Lisans Tezi, Antalya.

Alper, K., Kara, H., ve Yörükoğlu, M. (2012). "Rezerv Opsiyonu Mekanizması", *TCMB Ekonomi notları*, sayı:2012–28,2012.

Çapar, U. (2010). *Enflasyon hedeflemesinin Enflasyon ve Output Volatilitesi Üzerindeki Etkisi.* (Yayınlanmış Yüksek Lisans Tezi). Niğde: Pamukkale Üniversitesi İktisat Anabilim Dalı.

Demirhan, B. (2013). Türkiye'de Yeni Yaklaşım Çerçevesinde Para Politikalarının Finansal İstikrarı Sağlama Yönünde Uygulanması. Afyon Kocatepe Üniversitesi, *İİBF Dergisi.*C.XV, S. II. Ss.22–23.

Engle, R. F. (1982). Autoregressive Conditional Heteroskedasticity with Estimates of the Variance of U.K. Inflation. *Econometrica*, 50, pp. 987–1008.

Engle, R. F., ve Sheppard K. (2001). Theoretical and Empirical Properties of Dynamic Conditional Correlation Multivariate GARCH, NBER Working Series.

Erdem, H. F. (2017). Gıda Enflasyonunun Enflasyon Belirsizliği Üzerine Etkisi. *Karadeniz Teknik Üniversitesi Sosyal Bilimler Enstitüsü Sosyal Bilimler Dergisi.* Cilt 7(14).

Ergin, A., ve Aydın, H. İ. (2017). Finansal İstikrarı Sağlamaya Yönelik Bir Araç: Rezerv Opsiyon Mekanizması. *Batman Üniversitesi Yaşam Bilimleri Dergisi.* Cilt 7, Sayı 1/1: 11–12.

Gujarati, (2004). Basic Econometrics (4th ed.). Lewiston, NY, USA: The McGraw-Hill Companies.

Kantar, L. (2017). *Rezerv Opsiyon Mekanizması Ve Döviz Kuru Volatilitesi: Türkiye Üzerine Bir Uygulama.* (Yayınlanmış Doktora Tezi). İstanbul: İstanbul Üniversitesi Sosyal Bilimler Enstitüsü.

Küçüksaraç, D., ve Özel Ö. (2012). Rezerv Opsiyonu Mekanizması ve Optimal Rezerv Opsiyonu Katsayılarının Hesaplanması. *TCMB Çalışma Tebliği* No:12/32:5, pp. 27–28.

Oduncu, A., Ermişoğlu, E., ve Akçelik, Y. (2013). Merkez Bankasının Yeni Enstrümanı Rezerv Opsiyonu Mekanizması ve Kur Oynaklığı. *Bankacılar Dergisi*, Sayı 86:43.

Sims, Christopher A. (1980). "MacroeconomicsandReality." *Econometrica.* January, 48:1, pp. 1–48.

Tezer, H. (2019). "Merkez Bankasının Rezerv Opsiyon Mekanizması (Rom) Uygulamaları, Para ve Döviz Kuru Karşısında Etkinliği", *International Social Sciences Studies Journal*, 5(29): p. 402.

Tsay, R. (2011). Analysis of Financial Time Series (2nd ed.). New York: John Wiley and Sons.

Tse, Y. K., ve Tsui, A. K. C. (2002). A Multivariate GARCH Model with Time-Varying Correlations, *Journal of Business and Economic Statistics*, 20, pp. 351–362.

Mehmet Barış Aslan

12 An Econometric Analysis of the Current Account Deficit-External Debt Relationship: The Case of Turkey

Highlights: In the global world of the 1980s, when neoliberal economic policies came to life, the current account deficit problem is an important part of the causes of the economic crises faced, especially in developing countries. Turkey is one of the countries in question. Since the same period, increased foreign debts and current account deficit financing with these debts, this problem has become more important for Turkey. The aim of the study, based on this, is to investigate the relationship between the current account deficit and external debt in Turkey using annual data from 1980 to 2018 using the time-series econometric method. The results of the study, in which Engle Granger cointegration and Granger causality tests were conducted, revealed that there is a long-run cointegration and bidirectional causality between two variables.

Keywords: External debt, current account deficit, Granger causality test, Engle Granger cointegration

Introduction

The current account balance of a country that is included in a balance of payments consists of the current account balance, foreign trade, services, net investment income, and current transfer balance. Current account deficit is the negative difference between the amount of foreign currency entering the country and the amount of foreign currency leaving the country whether the current account deficit is based on international commodity trade or service accounts such as international commodity trade, transportation, tourism, and insurance and transfer accounts. Since the current account deficit causes an adverse effect on the macroeconomic balance of a country, it also plays an important role in these countries having a fragile structure against economic crises. Therefore, the governments of the countries finance these deficits primarily from their own reserves and then using with external debts.

External debts, which should be included in extraordinary financing methods according to the classical economics, are a financing method that should be channeled into long-term investment expenditures by economy management. However, this rule, which can be valid for developed countries, may become a different requirement for some countries considering their economic conditions. In other words, underdeveloped or developing countries having insufficient domestic savings can use this type of borrowing to finance both chronic current account deficits and current expenses. This situation causes many studies on the relationship between external borrowing and current account deficit, especially in underdeveloped and developing countries, which are facing current account deficit problems.

In this context, when the studies conducted outside of Turkey is examined, while in some countries results indicate that the foreign debts are the cause of the current account deficit (Aristovnik, 2006: 13, Kwalingana and Nkuna, 2009), in some other countries, opposite results are obtained that the current account deficit is the reason for the increase in foreign debts (Hasan, 1999: 435–470, Hervey and Merkel, 2000: 2–13, Kemal, 2001: 263–281, Edo, 2002: 221–236, Jurciç et al., 2012: 265–290). Also, some study results show that there is a bidirectional causality relationship between both variables (Chete, 2001, 219–238, Jawaid and Raza, 2012: 357–366, Mehta and Kayumi, 2014: 54–65), and according to few study results, no causality relationship was found between these two variables (Loganathan et al., 2010: 130).

When studies conducted in Turkey are analyzed, most of the results are similar with the results observed outside Turkey. In other words, while the results of the majority studies show that the current account deficit has a statistically significant effect on the foreign debt stock (Karagöz, K., 2007: 109, Koyuncu, F. T. and Tekeli, S., 2010: 123–130, Peker, O. and Bölükbaş, M., 2013: 296, Üzümcü, A. and Kırpık, N., 2015: 597–618, Yıldız, F., 2019: 3416–3438), some studies revealed that foreign debt has an effect on the current account deficit (Çakır and Sözen, 2016: 30–31). Some other studies introduced that there is a bidirectional causal relationship between both variables (Çeştepe et al., 2014: 100–108, Bal, 2017: 18–19).

One of the countries experiencing chronic deficit problem is Turkey. In Turkey, inflation targeting strategies are implemented having the primary objective of ensuring price stability since 2002. Expansionary monetary policies implemented by the developed countries in order to overcome the crisis have led to a rapid increase in the volume of loans in the developing countries such as Turkey. This increase in credit volume, which led to an increase in domestic demand, has started to increase in the current account deficit together with the weak foreign demand. Against this situation, which started to create a financial imbalance, the CBRT has set a new monetary policy framework that includes financial stability as well as price stability by the end of 2010. In this context, new monetary policy instruments have been used in addition to interest rates

Tab. 12.1: External debt and current account in Turkey in years (million dollar)

Years	Total External Debt Stock	External Debt/GDP %	Government Sector/Total %	Private Sector/Total %	Current Account	Current Account/ GDP %
2003	144,179	45,9	0,66	0,34	-7,554	-2,4
2004	161,154	40	0,6	0,4	-14,198	-3,5
2005	170,775	34,2	0,5	0,5	-20,980	-4,2
2006	208,002	38	0,42	0,58	-31,168	-5,6
2007	249,925	36,9	0,36	0,64	-36,949	-5,5
2008	280,832	36,2	0,33	0,67	-39,425	-5,2
2009	268,873	41,6	0,36	0,64	-11,358	-1,8
2010	291,782	37,8	0,35	0,65	-44,616	-5,8
2011	305,416	36,7	0,34	0,66	-74,402	-8,9
2012	342,29	39,3	0,33	0,67	-47,963	-5,5
2013	392,809	41,3	0,32	0,68	-63,642	-6,7
2014	405,883	43,4	0,30	0,70	-43,610	-4,7
2015	400,292	46,4	0,29	0,71	-32,145	-3,7
2016	409,729	47,5	0,30	0,70	-33,139	-3,8
2017	455,545	53,5	0,3	0,7	-47,347	-5,6
2018	444,878	56,7	0,33	0,67	-27,032	-3,5

Source: Derived from the data of T. C. Ministry of Treasury and Finance and World Bank.

in order to limit the volume of loans in particular and to reduce the current account deficit, to prevent TL from moving independent from its economic context (Doğan and Akbakay, 2016: 148–149). Although the current account deficit shows a falling tendency after 2011, its share in GDP is still high. When Tab. 12.1 is examined in 2003, the current account balance deficit is approximately -7.6 billion dollar in Turkey, and by the year 2011 it is raised to approximately 74.4 billion dollars, which is an increase of approximately tenfold. These deficits, which followed a fluctuating path, decreased to approximately -63.6 billion dollars in 2013, -33.1 billion dollars in 2016, and approximately -27 billion dollars in 2018.

When the total external debt of Turkey is examined, it is seen that the amount approximately increased by a threefold from 2003 to 2008. The most important reason of this increase results from the rise in private sector external borrowings between the same periods. Private sector external borrowing, which constituted about 34 % of the total foreign debt stock in 2003, presents approximately 67 % of total external debt by 2018. The share of public sector external borrowings to the total external debt fell from 66 % to 30 % between the same periods approximately.

Some international standards have been developed in order to indicate that a country has a medium or high debt stock. One of these standards is developed by the World Bank and IMF. According to these standards, if the ratio of a country's total debts to GDP is between 30 % and 50 %, it indicates that the country has a middle debt stock. However, if this ratio is over 50 %, it means that the country has a high level of debt stock (Ersoy, 2013: 103). Based on this standard, it is easy to see what debt structure Turkey has as can be seen in Tab. 12.1. Both the base year is 2018 or the previous year, these percentages are 56.7 % and 53.5 % and compared to the mentioned standard, it is demonstrated that debtor country's high level of Turkey is highly indebted.

Considering the ratio of current account balance data between 2003 and 2018 to GDP data calculated between the same periods, it can be said that it followed an uneven course but has a rising trend. It is observed that the highest increase (-8.9 %) occurred in 2011, and it is noteworthy that the lowest increase (-1.8 %) coincided with the 2008 crisis period. When the foreign debt/GDP data between the same periods are examined, it can be said that it follows a likewise course with the current account balance data. The highest increase in external debt (56.3 %) is observed in 2018, while the lowest increase (34.2 %) is in 2005.

1 Econometric Application

1.1 Data Set and Methodology

In the study, the relationship between these variables is tested by time-series econometric method in the period between 1980 and 2018 using the current account deficit and foreign debt data for Turkey. All of the data was obtained from the electronic database of the T.C. Ministry of Treasury and Finance, World Bank, and Central Bank Electronic Database (EVDS) and included in the analysis in dollar terms.

Unit root tests carried out in order to avoid the spurious regression problem in the study have great importance in terms of the reliability of the results obtained from the study. From this point of, in the study, stationary analyses of the series were performed first. Stationary analyzes were carried out using Augmented Dickey-Fuller (ADF) and Phillips Perron (PP) tests. Unlike the Dickey-Fuller (DF) test, ADF Test is defined as the unit root test applied to the new model created by adding the lags of the dependent variable to solve the autocorrelation problem that may occur in the right side of the new equation in the model (Uğurlu, E., 2009: 1–17). In the stationary analysis of the variables, firstly ADF unit root test was performed using the following models. Unit root analyses are tested for all three models with no trend and constant terms, with constant, and with trend and constant terms.

Model with no trend and no constant:

$$\Delta Y_t = \partial \mathrm{Y}_{t-i} + \sum_{i=1}^{s} \varnothing_i \Delta \mathrm{Y}_{t-i} + \mu_t \tag{1}$$

Model with constant:

$$\Delta Y_t = \propto_0 \partial \mathrm{Y}_{t-i} + \sum_{i=1}^{s} \varnothing_i \Delta \mathrm{Y}_{t-i} + \mu_t \tag{2}$$

Model with trend and constant:

$$\Delta Y_t = \alpha_0 + \beta_1 \mathrm{t} + \partial \mathrm{Y}_{t-i} + \sum_{i=1}^{s} \varnothing_i \Delta \mathrm{Y}_{t-i} + \mu_t \tag{3}$$

The first equation shows the model with the constant term and no trend (1), the second equation shows the model only with constant term (2), and the third equation shows the model with constant and trend (3) (Yıldız, A., and Aksoy, E. E., 2014: 7). A unit root test is performed in which the null hypothesis states that the data is not stationary and the alternative hypothesis states that the data is stationary. The results evaluated within the absolute value are compared with the critical values of MacKinnon. If the values obtained are lower than the MacKinnon table values, the zero hypothesis cannot be rejected and the series are considered to be non-stationary. Otherwise, it is decided that the series are stationary (Çetin, M., 2012: 219).

ADF test can cause some problems in terms of moving average factors. This test includes constant variance and independent error terms. On the other hand, Philips (1987) and Philips and Perron (1988) tests, which move in the opposite direction, contain error terms that are related to each other and have heteroscedastic variance (Kızılkaya, Sofuoğlu ve Çoban, 2015: 255–269). Thereby, given all these factors, Philips-Perron (PP) unit root test was carried out together with the ADF unit root test for all variables used in the study in order to obtain reliable results regarding the stationary tests of the variables.

In the next step of the study, Engle Granger cointegration test was applied to determine the long-run cointegration relationship of the series. The precondition of this test developed by Engle Granger (1987) as a two-stage estimator is that the nonstationary series in level values must become stationary when the first differences are taken (Karış, Ç., and Ayla, D., 2018: 255–271). If this precondition is not met, or in other words, if the series do not become stationary when the first differences are taken, then the spurious model of regression may be faced in the predicted model. One of the most important indicators of the spurious regression problem is that the calculated R^2 value of the model is higher than the Durbin-Watson statistical value. However, if the residuals of the model are stationary, it is assumed that there will be no long-run spurious regression, and there is a cointegration relationship between the series.

In the first step of the test, the parameters of the integrative vector were estimated by the Least Squares (OLS) Regression Method and the following equations adapted to the study.

$$CAD_t = \alpha_0 + a_1 FOD_t + \varepsilon_{1t} \tag{4}$$

$$FOD_t = \beta_0 + \beta_1 CAD_t + \varepsilon_{2t} \tag{5}$$

CAD and *FOD* values in the equation refer to the current account deficit of Turkey and total debt series, and the ε_{1t} and ε_{2t} d values refer to the error terms of Equation 4 and Equation 5, respectively.

In the second step of the test, the ADF unit root test was applied to the residues obtained from the regression, and the stationarity test was carried out using the following equations.

$$\Delta\varepsilon_{i,t} = \partial\varepsilon_{i,t-1} + \sum_{i=0}^{n} \delta_i \Delta\varepsilon_{i,t-1} + \varepsilon_{i,t} \quad (i = 3, 4) \tag{6}$$

In the Engle Granger (1987) test based on regression residues, the $\varepsilon_{i,t}$ series are not based on observational data. For the reason that it is a predictive data set derived from the regression equation given above, stability determination of the calculated unit root statistics values is made by comparing with the table critical values developed by Engle and Yoo (1987), not with MacKinnon critical values. As a result of the test, the residuals are stationary at the level values, so that there is a long-run cointegration relationship between the variables (Yılancı, 2009: 208).

The Error Correction Model (ECM), which is estimated at the next stage, is an analysis model in which a lagged value of the error term series is added to the regression model to test the causality relationship between the variables in the cointegration relationship. ECM is estimated using the following regression equations that are adapted to the study.

$$CAD_t = \alpha_0 + \sum_{i=0}^{k} \beta_i \Delta CAD_{t-i} + \sum_{j=1}^{l} \forall \Delta FOD_{t-j} + \varnothing ECM_{1t-1} + u_{1t} \quad (7)$$

$$FOD_t = \varphi_0 + \sum_{i=0}^{k} \omega_i \Delta FOD_{t-i} + \sum_{j=1}^{l} \gamma \Delta CAD_{t-j} + \sigma ECM_{2t-1} + u_{2t} \quad (8)$$

Models 7 and 8 define the short-run relationship between the CAD and FOD variables. In other words, these models show the short-run and immediate effects of the FOD (CAD) variable on the CAD (FOD) variable. The error term coefficients of $\varnothing$ and σ are symbols that show the degree to which the imbalances in both models have stabilized in the short run. These coefficients are expected to be negative and statistically significant according to the economic expectations (Gujarati, D., 2012: 242).

In the last part of the study, Granger causality test was applied to determine the long-term causality relationship between the variables. The prior condition for this test is the determination of the optimal lag length obtained within the scope of alternative information criteria, as well as the series used in the analysis having a stationary structure. The lag length is based on the determination of the lag length that does not cause diagnostic problems in the residues of vector error correction with the use of the Vector Autoregressive Model (VAR) (Işık, N. vd., 2017: 90). Due to the use of annual data in the study, the maximum lag length was determined as 5 in the determination of the optimal lag length.

According to Granger (1969), the definition of causality is based entirely on the predictability of some series. If any series contains useful information in past terms in the prediction of the other, and if this information is not included in the other series used in the prediction, this series is said to be the cause of the other. According to Granger (1969), who stated that the time line plays an important role in the definitions of the causality, a fully deterministic series, that is, the path that can be predicted from its own path, cannot be said to have causal effects other than its past (Granger, C. W. J., 1969: 430). Granger causality model estimates with two variables adapted to study are applied through the following formulas.

$$\Delta CAD_t = \sum_{i=0}^{m} \rho_i CAD_{t-i} + \sum_{j=1}^{m} \omega_i FOD_{t-j} + u_{1t} \tag{9}$$

$$\Delta FOD_t = \sum_{i=0}^{m} \vartheta_i FOD_{t-i} + \sum_{j=1}^{m} \tau_i CAD_{t-j} + u_{2t} \tag{10}$$

u_{1t} and u_{2t} in the equations show error terms. The terms ρ, ω, ϑ, and τ symbolize the lag coefficients, while m indicates the lag length. With this test, the zero hypothesis established with the assumption that the "Current Account Balance (CAD) variable is not the Granger cause of the External Debts (FOD) variable" is tested against the alternative hypothesis established as the "Current Account Balance (CAD) variable is the Granger cause of the Foreign Debts (FOD) variable." If the probability value is statistically lower than the 5 % significance level, then the null hypothesis is rejected. This result also means the acceptance of the alternative hypothesis established as "Current Account Balance (CAD) variable is the Granger cause of the Foreign Debts (FOD) variable" (Tekin, B. and Yener, E., 2018: 543).

1.2 Empirical Findings

In this study, the stationarity of the series was tested with ADF and Philips-Perron (PP) unit root analysis applied to both variables. Optimal lag length of the ADF test was selected based on Schwarz information criterion, and PP test bandwidth was selected based on Newey-West bandwidth automatically. Results of the analysis are shown in Tab. 12.2.

Both unit root test results indicate that variables containing unit root in their level values become stationary when the first differences are taken. This result also demonstrates that the prior condition for the applicability of Engle Granger cointegration and Granger causality analysis was realized.

After determining that the series have a stationary structure, Engle Granger cointegration test was performed. The results of the two-step cointegration analysis applied using the Least Squares Method (OLS) and ADF unit root analysis are given in Tab. 12.3.

The application, which consists of two steps, was made by converting and analyzing both variables into dependent variables. In the model, firstly, the obtained Durbin-Watson statistical value and R^2 values were compared, and it was seen that Durbin-Watson statistical values were greater than R2 values. This

Tab. 12.2: Unit root tests

Variables	**ADF (1(0))**			**PP (0))**		
	Intercept	**Intercept/ Trend**	**None**	**Intercept**	**Intercept/ Trend**	**None**
CAD	-1,85	-3,14	-1,28	-1,63	-3,10	-0,96
FOD	0,27	-1,94	1,87	0,27	-1,96	1,82
Variables	ADF (1(1))			PP (1))		
	Intercept	Intercept/ Trend	None	Intercept	Intercept/ Trend	None
CAD	-7,82***	-7,69***	-7,88***	-8,34***	-8,18***	-8,30***
FOD	-5,72***	-5,79***	-5,09***	-5,72***	-5,79***	-5.11***
Significance e Level	Critical Values			Critical Values		
	Intercept	Intercept/ Trend	None	Intercept	Intercept/ Trend	None
%1	-3,62	-4,23	-2,63	-3,62	-4,23	-2,63
%5	-2,94	-3,54	-1,95	-2,94	-3,54	-1,95
%10	-2,61	-3,20	-1,61	-2,61	-3,20	-1,61

Note: (***) indicates 1 % significance level.

Tab. 12.3: Test results of the two-step cointegration (OLS method)

Engle Granger Cointegration Results (1. Step)				
Equations	$CAD_t = \alpha_0 + a_1 FOD_t + \varepsilon_{1t}$		$FOD_t = \beta_0 + \beta_1 CAD_t + \varepsilon_{2t}$	
Coefficient (Independent Variables)	0,11***		7,45***	
Probability Value	(0,00)		(0,00)	
Coefficient (Constant Term)	-4,80**		6,56***	
Probability Value	(0,02)		(0,00)	
Engle Granger Cointegration Results (2. Step)				
Error Term ADF Test Statistic	With Intercept/Trends No Intercept/Trend		With Intercept/Trend No intercept/Trend	
	-4,39***	-4,42***	-4.69***	-3.53**
Engel Granger Critical Values	(-4,37) (%1)	(-4,37) (%1)	(-4,37) (%1)	(-3,28) (%5)
R^2	0,83		0,83	
Probability	0.00		0,00	
Durbin-Watson sta.	1,42		1,11	

Note: *** %1 and ** %5 define the significance levels.

Tab. 12.4: Error correction model

Equations	Equation 1		Equation 2	
Independent Variables	**Coefficient**	**t- Statistic**	**Coefficient**	**t- Statistic**
C	-2,23**	-1,97*	9,54***	2,82
FOD	0,30***	8,27	-	-
CAD	-	-	2,11***	7,14
DUMMY VAR.	-3,60	-0,88	5,80	0,28
ECM	-0,76***	-5,66	-0,17***	-2,81
R^2	0,7518		0,5996	
Adjusted R^2	0,7299		0,5758	
Durbin-Watson Stat	1,4720		1,4008	
Probability	0,0000		0,0000	
Autocorrelation	4,72 (0,09)		3,41 (0,18)	
Normality	2,16 (0,34)		3,49 (0,17)	
Heteroscedasticity	4,21 (0,24)		6,89 (0,08)	
Ramsey Test	0,04 (0,85)		0,02 (0,97)	

Note: *** %1, **, %5, and * %10 are the significance levels.

result showed that there was no spurious regression problem in both models. The coefficient of the model from which the CAD variable was taken as dependent variable was statistically significant at the level of 1 %. The coefficient of the model in which the FOD variable was taken as the dependent variable was also statistically significant at the level of 1 %. These results showed that there is a long-run relationship between external debts held by Turkey and current account deficit data for Turkey.

In the second step of the test, when the values obtained from the ADF unit root test applied to the residues of both models are compared with the critical values of Engle and Yoo (1987) (with constant, with constant-trend, and without constant and trend), the statistical values of all tests are higher than Engle and Yoo (1987) critical values at 1 % and 5 % significance levels and the residues of the model were stationary in the level values (I (0)). This result also indicates that the variables in the model have a long-run cointegration relationship.

After determination of the long-term cointegration relationship between the variables of the model, two different error correction models were established by adding one period-lagged value of the residues of each model. The results of two different models, where each variable is included as the dependent variable, are shown in Tab. 12.4.

The results show that, in the short run, a 1 % increase in total external debt causes approximately 0.30 % increase in the current account deficit; a 1 % increase in the current account deficit causes 2.11 % increase in the total foreign debt in Turkey. The calculated Error Term Coefficients (ECM) were negative in both models and statistically significant at 1 % significance level. This shows that there is a long-term relationship between the variables of the models. In addition, this result shows that the deviations in the short run will adjust by 77 % in the model in which FOD is included as an independent variable and 17 % in the model where CAD is taken as an independent variable.

When the diagnostic test results of the model are examined, it is observed that Durbin-Watson statistical values are higher than R^2 values, and there was no spurious regression problem in the model. When all other diagnostic test statistics results are examined, the statistical significance values are higher than 0.05 %; and it is understood that there is no serial correlation, normality, heteroscedasticity, and modeling error in the models, and therefore both models show a reliable view.

Cusum and CusumQ tests, which are applied for the determination of structural changes in models, showed that there are structural breaks in both models. Considering the periodic intervals of the structural breaks, the dummy variables were included in both models, and therefore it was observed that the residues of the model remained within the limits and the parameters displayed a stable view. The condition before and after the artificial variable included in the model is given below with the graphics of Cusum and Cusum of Squares.

The Engle Granger cointegration test analyzed the presence of a long-term relationship between the CAD and FOD variables used in the study. However, this cointegration test does not give any results regarding the direction of the long-term relationship. The direction of the relationship is determined with the Granger causality test (Ata, A.Y. and Yücel, F.(2003): 105). The optimum lag length to be used in this test should be determined before using the Granger causality test. The identification of the optimum lag length is made with a test based on the VAR model for determining the minimum values of different information criteria. Due to the annual use of the data used in the study, the maximum number of lags is determined as 5, and the results of the analysis to determine the optimum lag length are shown in Tab. 12.5.

The results showed that the minimum values in all information criteria occurred in the 4th lag. Granger causality test results, in which the optimum lag length is determined as 4 (Four), are given in Tab. 12.6.

According to the analysis results, the null hypothesis stating that the "current account balance (CAD) variable is not the Granger cause of the external debts

Model 1 (Independent Variable=FOD)

(Cusum Test before dummy variable)

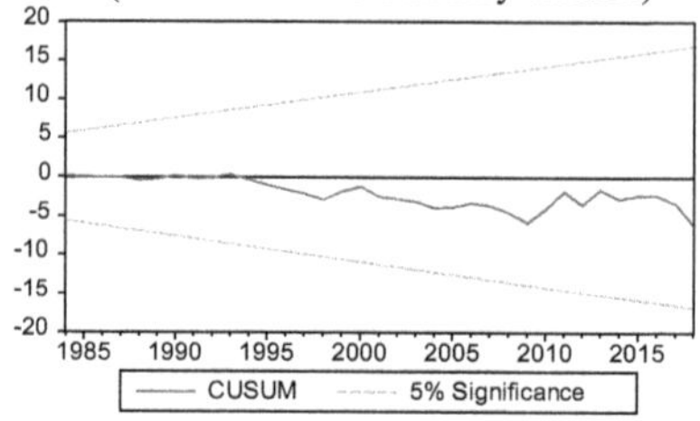

(Cusum Q Test after dummy variable)

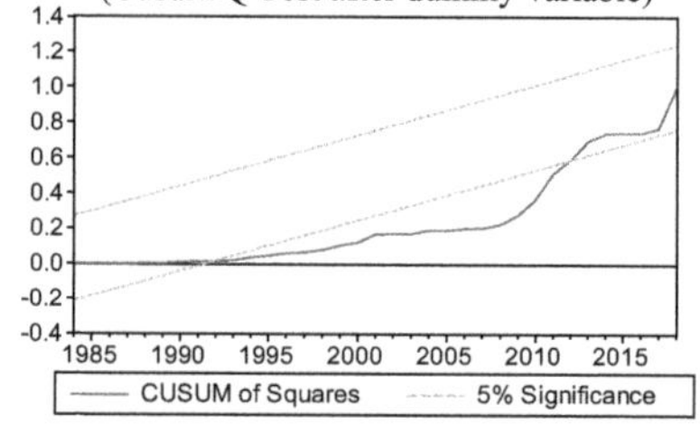

Model 1 (Independent variable=FOD)

(Cusum Test before dummy variable)

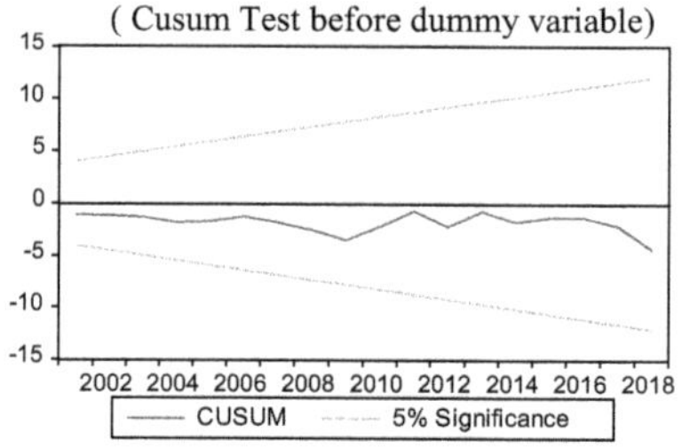

(Cusum Q Test after dummy variable)

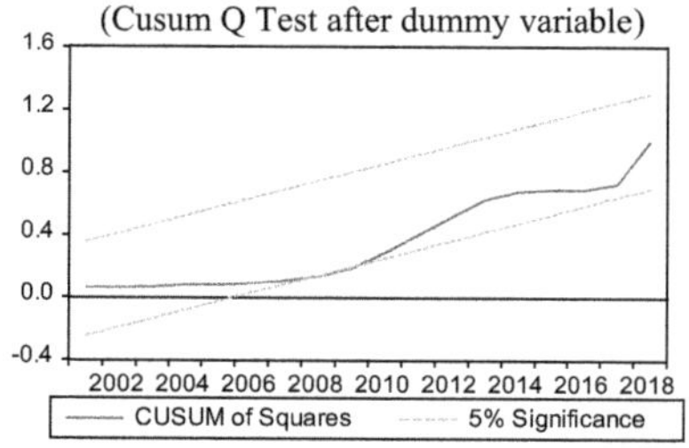

Model 2 (Independent variable =CAD)

(Cusum Test before dummy variable)

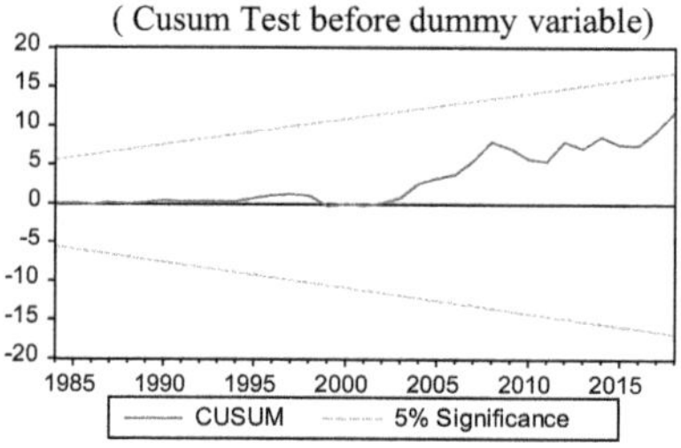

(Cusum Q Test after dummy variable)

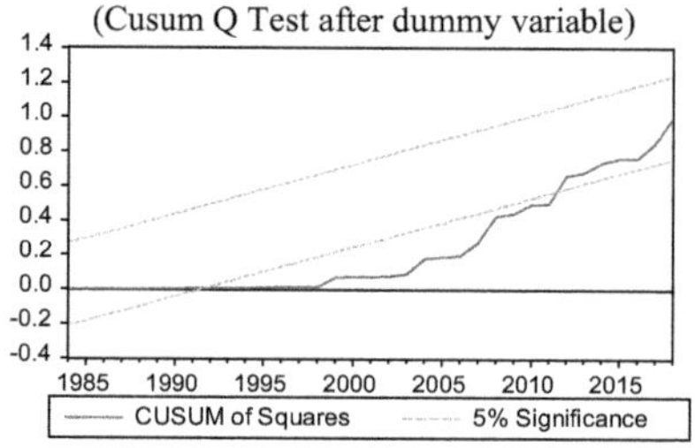

Model 2 (Independent variable =CAD)

(Cusum Test before dummy variable)

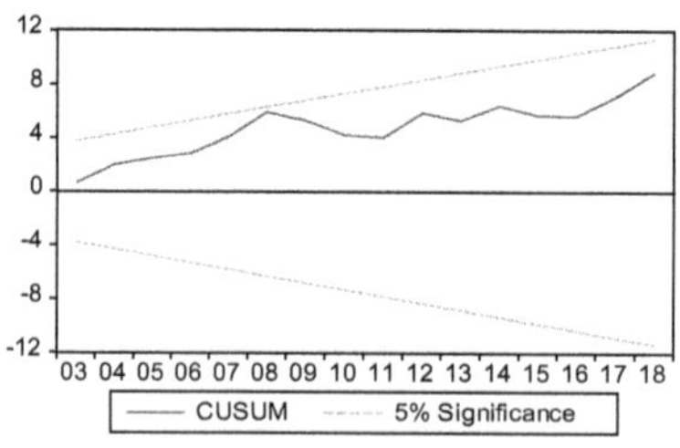

(Cusum Q Test after dummy variable)

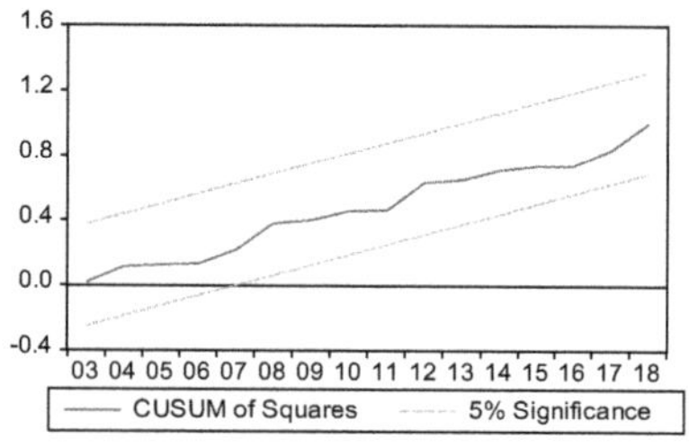

Graph 12.1: Cusum and Cusum of Squares

Source: Derived by the author

Tab. 12.5: Determination of the optimum lag length

Lag	LogL	LR	FPE	AIC	SC	HQ
0	-1804.018	NA	2.26e+42	103.2010	103.2899	103.2317
1	-1734.020	127.9978	5.21e+40	99.42969	99.69632	99.52173
2	-1728.066	10.20650	4.68e+40	99.31804	99.76243	99.47144
3	-1724.842	5.158286	4.92e+40	99.36239	99.98453	99.57715
4	-1712.524	18.30132*	3.10e+40*	98.88706*	99.68696*	99.16319*

* shows the optimum lag length.

Tab. 12.6: Results of the Granger causality test

Null Hypothesis	F-Statistic Value	Probability Value	Result
External debts are not the cause of current account deficit.	6.94639	0.0006	Rejection of the null hypothesis Acceptation of the alternative hypothesis
Current account deficit is not the cause of the external debts	4.29185	0.0085	Rejection of the null hypothesis Acceptation of the alternative hypothesis

(FOD) variable" and the "External Debts (FOD) variable is not the Granger cause of the current account balance (CAD) variable" are both rejected. Probability value is statistically lower than 5 % significance level; and for this reason, the alternative hypotheses stating that "current account balance (CAD) variable is the Granger cause of the external debts (FOD) variable" and the "External Debts (FOD) variable is the Granger cause of the current account balance (CAD) variable" are accepted. In other words, it is observed that there is a bidirectional and long-term causality relationship from the CAD to the FOD and from the FOD to the CAD.

Conclusion

External borrowing strategies can lead to some crises that disrupt macroeconomic stability as they can play an important role in a country's economic development. The differentiation of these effects is in line with the types of expenditures in which external borrowings are channeled. External debts that are directed to short- and long-term investments can have a positive effect on macroeconomic development. If the foreign debts are directed to current and transfer expenditures by the public sector or if they are directed to consumption loans especially by the financial sector may increase the total foreign demand, thereby creating a negative impact on the current account balance, which may cause some financial and commercial crises.

Some of the results obtained from study consisting the data between the years 1980 and 2018 shows that debts used by Turkey have a positive impact on the balance of payment both in the short and the long term. Consequently, this type of debt provided by Turkey that has a positive effect on total foreign demand and shows that a significant part of these debts is channeled to low efficient expenditures that increase foreign demand rather than long- and short-term investment expenditures. Some other findings show that the current account deficit increases the external borrowing in Turkey, so that a vicious circle is observed for Turkish economy in fact. It is considered that one of the main factors causing this situation is expansionary monetary policies applied by the economies of developed countries. Together with the developing countries, these types of policies that increase the hot money inflow to Turkey create pressure on aggregate demand rather than real investments and therefore have caused the existing deficits become a chronic problem continuing until today.

Results obtained from the study that aim to determine the relationship between current account deficits and external debts show the need for a number of deep-rooted, realistic, and solution-oriented revisions. The realization of such revisions is directly proportionate to the increase of capital resources. For the supply of capital accumulation in Turkey, the external leakage of payments especially in the energy, pharmaceutical, medical, and middle- and top-level technological products should be reduced to the minimum level. In this context, the continuity of the quest for energy resources that has started in Turkey is of great importance in the framework of the access to that capital accumulation. In addition, almost half of the external borrowings obtained by the private sector are used as loans for consumption by the financial institutions. It is thought that if this sort of are directed to short- and long-term investments rather than consumption, some of the revenues obtained can be used in the payment of external debts and the rest of them may again be canalized to investments.

References

Aristovnik, A. (2006). The Determinants and Excessiveness of Current Account Deficits in Eastern Europe and the Former Soviet Union, The William Davidson Institute Working Paper, No. (827): 13.

Ata, A. Y. and Yücel, F. (2003). Eş-Bütünleşme ve Nedensellik Testleri Altında İkiz Açıklar Hipotezi: Türkiye Uygulaması, Çukurova Üniversitesi Sosyal Bilimler Enstitüsü Dergisi, Vol.12, No.12, pp.97–110.

Bal, O. (2017). Kalkınmakta olan ülkelerin diş borç, cari açık sorunu: Türkiye örneği, Uluslararası Hakemli Ekonomi Yönetimi Araştırmaları Dergisi, No.14, pp.18–19.

Çakır, A. S. B. and Sözen, İ. (2016). Türkiye'de Cari İşlemler Dengesini Etkileyen Finansal Değişkenlerin VAR Analizi, Akademik Hassasiyetler, Vol.3, No.5, pp.19–42.

Çeştepe, H., Ursavaş, U. and Güdenoğlu, E. (2014). Türkiye'de Cari Açık ve Dış Borç Arasındaki Nedensellik İlişkisinin Analizi, Karadeniz Ve Balkan Ekonomik Ve Politik Araştırmalar Sempozyu, 3–5 September, Zonguldak, Turkey.

Çetin, M. (2012). Sabit Sermaye Yatırımları ve Ekonomik Büyüme: Ampirik Bir Analiz, Eskişehir Osmangazi Üniversitesi İ.İ.B.F Dergisi, Vol.7, No.1, pp.211–230.

Chete, L. N. (2001). Explaining Current Account Behavior in Nigeria, The Nigerian Journal of Economic and Social Studies, No. 43, pp.219–238.

Doğan, B. B. and Akbakay, Z. (2016). Türkiye'de Enflasyon Hedeflemesi Stratejisinin Uygulanması, Dicle Üniversitesi Sosyal Bilimler Enstitüsü Dergisi, Vol.8, No.17, pp.136–155.

Edo, S. (2002). The External Debt Problem in Africa: A Comparative Study of Nigeria and Morocco, African Development Review, Vol.14, No.2, pp.221–236.

Engle, R. F. and Yoo, B. S. (1987). Forecasting and Testing in Co-integrated Systems, Journal of Econometrics, No.35, pp.143–159.

Ersoy, H. (2013). Küresel Kriz: Dış Borçlar ve Cari Açık Perspektifinden Türkiye Analizi, Maliye Finans Yazıları, Vol.27, No.100, p.103.

Granger, C. W. J. (1969). Investigating Causal Relations by Econometric Models and Cross-spectral Methods, Econometrica, Vol.37, No.3, pp.424–438.

Gujarati, D. (2012). Econometrics by Example, MacMillan Education UK, Chapter 14, p.242.

Hasan, P. (1999). Pakistan's Debt Problem: Its Changing Nature and Growing Gravity, The Pakistan Development Review, Vol.38, No.4, pp.435–470.

Hervey, J. L. and Merkel, L. S. (2000). A Record Current Account Deficit: Causes and Implications, Economic Perspectives, Federal Reserve Bank of Chicago, No.4, pp.2–13.

Işık, N., Yılmaz, S. S. and Kılınç, E. C. (2017). The Relationship between Current Account Balance and Types of Credits: An Application on Selected OECD Countries, Çankırı Karatekin Üniversitesi İktisadi ve İdari Bilimler Fakültesi Dergisi, Vol.7, No.2, pp.105–126.

Jawaid, S. T. and Raza, S. A. (2012). Dynamics of Current Account Deficit: A Lesson from Pakistan, Transition Studies Review, Vol.19, No.3, pp.357–366.

Jurciç, L., Josiç, H. and Josiç, M. (2012). Empiric Analysis of External Debt in Croatia: VAR Model Approach, Economic Review, Vol.63, No.5–6, pp.265–290.

Karagöz, K. (2007). Türkiye'de Dış Borçlanmanın Nedenleri Ekonometrik Bir Değerlendirme, Sayıştay Dergisi, No.66–67, pp.99–110.

Karış, Ç. and Ayla, D. (2018). Türkiye'de Doğrudan Yabancı Yatırımlar ve Ticari Dışa Açıklık İlişkisinin Ekonometrik Analizi, Bingöl Üniversitesi Sosyal Bilimler Enstitüsü Dergisi, Vol.8, No.16, pp.255–271.

Kemal, A. R. (2001). Debt Accumulation and Its Implications for Growth and Poverty, Pakistan Development Review, Vol.40, No.4, pp.263–281.

Kwalingana, S. and Nkuna, O. (2009). The Determinants of Current Account Imbalances in Malawi, Munich Personal RePEc Archive (MPRA), Paper No. 14694.

Koyuncu, F. T. and Tekeli, S. (2010). 1990 Sonrası Dönemde Türkiye'de Dış Borç Stoku Üzerinde Etkili Olan Ekonomik Faktörlerin Analizi, Ekonomi Bilimleri Dergisi, Vol.2, No.1, pp.123–130.

Loganathan, N., Sukemi, M. N. and Sanusi, N. A. (2010). External Debt and Macroeconomics Performance in Malaysia: Sustainable or Not?, Global Economy and Financial Journal, Vol.3, No.2, pp.122–132.

Mehta, B. M. and Kayumi, H. F. (2014). Effects of India's Current Account Deficits on External Debts and Foreign Exchange Rates, IOSR Journal of Economics and Finance, Vol.1, No.7, pp.54–65.

Peker, O. and Bölükbaş, M. (2013). Türkiye'de Dış Borçlanmanın Belirleyicileri: Ekonometrik Bir Analiz, Atatürk Üniversitesi İktisadi ve İdari Bilimler Fakültesi Dergisi, Vol.27, No.2, pp.289–302.

Kızılkaya, O., Sofuoğlu, E. and Çoban, O. (2015). Ekonomik Büyüme, Enerji Tüketimi ve Çevre Kirliliği Analizi: Türkiye Örneği, Kırıkkale Üniversitesi Sosyal Bilimler Dergisi, Vol.6, No.2, pp.255–269.

Tekin, B. and Yener, E. (2018). BRICS ve G7 Ülkeleri ile Türkiye'de Hisse Senetleri Piyasaları ve Ekonomik Büyüme Arasındaki Nedensellik ve Eş Bütünleşme İlişkilerinin Karşılaştırmalı Analizi, Ankara Hacı Bayram Veli Üniversitesi İktisadi ve İdari Bilimler Fakültesi Dergisi, Vol.20, No.3, p.543.

Uğurlu, E. (2009). Durağanlık ve Birim Kök Sınamaları, İstanbul Aydın Üniversitesi Ekonomi ve Finans Bölümü (Ders Notları), pp.1–17.

Üzümcü, A. and Kırpık, N. (2015). Türkiye Ekonomisinde 1980–2014 Döneminde Cari İşlemler Bilançosu Açıkları ve Dış Borçlanma İlişkisinin Analizi", 1st International Caucasus-Central Asia Foreign Trade And Logistics Congress, 1–3 October, Kars, Turkey.

Yılancı, V. (2009). Fisher Hipotezinin Türkiye İçin Sınanması: Doğrusal Olmayan Eş Bütünleşme Analizi, Atatürk Üniversitesi İktisadi ve İdari Bilimler Dergisi, Vol.23, No.4, p.208.

Yıldız, F. (2019). Türkiye Ekonomisinde Dış Borç, Ekonomik Büyüme ve Cari İşlemler Dengesi İlişkisinin Analizi, Manas Sosyal Araştırmalar Dergisi, Vol.8, No.4, pp.3416–3438.

Yıldız, A. and Aksoy, E. E. (2014). Morgan Stanley Gelişmekte Olan Borsa Endeksi ile BIST Endeksi Arasındaki Eş Bütünleşme İlişkisinin Analiz Edilmesi, Atatürk Üniversitesi İktisadi ve İdari Bilimler Dergisi, Vol.28. No.1, pp.1–23

Zeki Akbakay

13 Impact of Financial Development on Current Deficit in Turkey: ARDL Bound Test Analysis

Highlights: Current account imbalances, which constitute an important part of global imbalances, are among the causes of the fragility of the Turkish economy. The current account deficit problem, which emerged as a reflection of the economic policies, external factors, and structural characteristics of the economy, has been on the upward trend especially since the early 2000s. The aim of this study is to demonstrate the impact of financial development on the current account deficit in Turkey. In the study using annual data from 1980–2018, domestic credit provided to the private sector is included in the analysis as independent variable. According to the results of the ARDL analysis used in the study, it was observed that domestic credit to the private sector had a strong impact on the increase in the current account deficit in the short run, and only this effect weakened in the long run.

Keywords: Current deficit, financial development, exchange rate, ARDL

Introduction

One of the four fundamental accounts of the balance of payments is current account which is an income and expenditure account showing the consequences of a country's economic relationships with the other countries of the world. Current account represents the difference between the amount of foreign currency entering and leaving the country depending on the goods and services movements among countries. If the difference is negative or if the amount of foreign currency entering in the country is less than the foreign currency leaving out in the context of goods and services trade, it is defined as current account deficit. If the natural resource insufficiencies of the country like energy lack is left aside, some structural factors such as index of openness, composition of foreign trade goods, and saving-investment level besides monetary and fiscal policies are determinants of current account deficit.

Current account deficit (I-S=CA) is the difference between domestic savings (S) and domestic investments (I). In a country, if the aggregate domestic savings is less than aggregate domestic investments, a current account deficit equaling to the difference occurs which can only be financed by foreign savings. Thereby if there is a current account deficit in an economy, it indicates that the domestic investment depends on foreign savings. One of the financial factors on the domestic savings and investments is credits. According to the monetarist approach explaining the relationship between financial development and current account deficit, an increase in money supply affects current account deficits by changing saving and investment behaviors. In this context, an increase in credits causes domestic demand increase more than income together with consumption and investment expenditure, so the current account deficit is increased especially in developing countries.

Another approach explaining why the capital flows from developing countries to developed countries links the current account deficit to the difference of financial development among countries. This approach states that the financial system of the developing countries supports savings and dissuades investments or supports that developing countries are willing to give current account surplus in order to reach high-quality financial assets in the developed countries (Gruber and Kamin, 2009: 668).

In which direction is the effect of financial development on current account deficit is not clear theoretically. Financial development can increase the level of savings if it can increase the consumption and investment expenditures due to the loosening constraints on borrowings (Devadas and Loayza, 2018:2; Ya-Qiongand Rui, 2013: 2934). Chinn and Ito (2007) state that positive effect of financial development on investments is clear due to the transaction costs, capital costs, and decreasing investment risk besides reducing the level of asymmetric information but this condition may not be valid for savings. Inasmuch, deeper financial markets stimulate savings according to traditional approach, and a contrary approach states that developed financial markets lead to lower saving rates because of decreasing precautionary savings (Chinn and Ito, 2007: 549–550).

Whether the effect is positive or negative can change depending on the country-specific features like development level of the country, level of openness, and marginal propensity to saving. Within the framework of monetary transmission mechanism, decreasing interest rates due to the increase in money supply raise consumption and investment savings. Relatively increasing investment rates to savings causes the current account deficit to rise consequently. On the other side, devaluation of the domestic currency together with the falling interest rates can lead to a decrease in imports and an increase in exports. Accordingly, if a monetary expansion caused an increase or a decrease in current account deficit depends on which effect is more effective (Alper and Oransay, 2015: 76).

Growth of credit volume is the most important determinant of financial instability. Credit growth having a character of predicting financial crisis is also one of the leading variables determining the current account deficit. According to Jorda et al. (2011) the relationship between credit growth and current account deficit becoming the same side of the medallion gradually has become more powerful, thereby this relationship between these two variables has increased the risk of financial crisis (Jorda et al., 2011: 343).

Current account deficit points a financial instability for national economies, and thus it is a leading topic of public debates; and in this context, this topic is followed by the politicians intently and solution-oriented politics are developed. In order to achieve successful politics targeting macroeconomic and financial stability, it is very important to understand the relationship between current account deficit and credit growth. Inasmuch as an indicator of the financial development, the distortionary effect of excessive credit expansion on macroeconomic and financial stability should be discussed, although increasing the credit access opportunity of economic actors has a central role for economic development (Ekinci et al., 2019: 1–3).

Mendoza and Torrenes (2012) state that banking crisis, currency crisis, and sudden stops are often followed by a credit extension period. However, financial and economic fluctuations are not simultaneous since financial instabilities can continue in stable macroeconomic environments, and for this reason they cannot be noticed easily. When we look at the global economic crisis, debt crisis in Latin America in the 1980s, in Mexico in 1944, and global financial crisis in 2008–2009 all broke out in a stable macroeconomic environment. In one aspect, these crisis have improved that how much financial stability is needed for macroeconomic stability. In this context, central banks accepted new policy approaches focusing on financial stability together with the price stability. Concordantly, number of studies underlining financial factors and current account deficit have risen together with the financial crisis.

However, there are many studies stating that current account deficit can be a sign of macroeconomic problem or a financial crisis only after an equivalent value according to the economic structures and development levels of the country. According to Edwars (2005), it is not sustainable if the current account deficit exceeds GDP by 6 %. Similarly, Mussa (2005) says that it is not possible to maintain a current account deficit reaching 5 % of GDP in the long run. Although a current account deficit of 4–6 % of the GDP is a sign of danger for macroeconomic stability in the literature, it is quite important how this account is financed and how the compound of the account is. The main problem here is especially financing the current account deficit with short run capital flows or currency reserves. In this context, according to Milesi-Ferretti and Razin, stating that 5 % equivalent value is not enough informative about the sustainability of current account deficit, structural factors such as currency policies of the countries, maturity, and component of foreign debts and level of openness should be considered (Milesi-Ferretti and Razin, 1996).

Gosh and Ramakrishnan (2006) emphasize that the factors as "good" or "bad" without analyzing the factors of current account deficit. In this sense, whether the current account deficit for a certain period reflecting the fundamental economic trends is desired by a country depends on the reasons of the deficit.

High and chronic current account deficit is one of the most discussed economic problems in Turkey. In the import substitution development strategy period of the 1980s and afterwards export-oriented development strategy failed to solve the problem. After 2002, Turkey has current account deficit continuously and has exceeded the threshold ratio of 4–6 % that is stated in the literature. According to the 2019 IMF report, Turkey is listed as one of the countries with high level of current account deficit (Cebeddu et al., 2019). Between 1974 and 2002 periods, although there was a saving surplus in the private sector in Turkey on average, current account deficit was seen due to relatively high budget deficits (Aydın and Beşballı, 2018: 10). After the 2000s, it is seen that the main determinant of the current account deficit is saving-investment gap, not the budget deficit. IMF data shows that the difference between domestic savings and domestic investment diverges gradually. In 2002, ratio of domestic savings to GDP is 21.6 % and the ratio of investments to GDP is about 21.2 %. Beginning from 2003, the difference between savings and investments increases in the favor of investments and in 2011, when the amount of current account deficit is at a peak, the ratio was 8.8 % of GDP and in 2018 it was 2.5 % of GDP (Cebeddu et al., 2019). Government savings increased in this period due to the fiscal discipline, and private savings decreased due to the increasing consumption expensed as a result of a decrease in interest rates and increase in credit value. However, current account deficit increased according to the low levels of aggregate saving levels because the fall of private investments is bigger than the rise of government savings (World Bank, 2011).

After 2001, domestic demand increased with the rise of credit volume depending upon the recovery of Turkish economy and loose monetary policies of developed countries applied within the crisis recovery strategies. The weakness of foreign demand and appreciation of Turkish Lira worsened the current account balance problem together with the powerful domestic demand. Under these circumstances, Central Bank of Turkey started to implement a new monetary policy aiming to decrease the domestic investments and consumer demands resulting from credit expansion and connected macrofinancial risks. However, credit is still a variable which contributes current account deficit (IMF, 2018: 14).

The aim of this study is to determine whether the financial development has any effect on current account deficit in Turkey. In this purpose, firstly some studies in the literature will be referred in the following sections. After the data and method of the study are introduced, an econometric application is implemented and the results are analyzed. In the conclusion section, a general evaluation is made.

1 Literature

When the empirical literature is examined, one of the fundamental determiners of the current account deficit is credits to the private sector. Loosening the contractions on borrowing in the process of financial sector deregulation has a negative effect on current account deficit by decreasing the private sector savings in the first phase (Terrrones and Carderelli, 2005: 99). Even if there is an equilibrium in current account in the global crisis period, current account deficit is again seen in many countries in the recovery period (Chinn, 2017: 1). Expansionary monetary policies within the context of recovery policies applied by the developed countries after 2008 global crises also made easy access to credit in the developing countries. Studies examining the effect of financial development on macroeconomic and financial stability have risen for the reason that increasing credit volume rises financial risks at the same time. Some of these studies investigate the relationship between credit expansion and current account deficit. Especially prior to the last crisis, a strong relationship is revealed between credits and current account deficit statistically so private sector credits are added to IMF's EBA (The External Balance Assessment) methodology used for the external equilibrium analysis representing a variable for financial factors. In this context, according to one of the latest works of Cubeddu et al. (2019), a 10 % increase in the share of credits to GDP ratio caused 1 % rise in the current account deficit to GDP ratio. Similarly, Phillips et al. (2013) using EBA methodology of IMF show that a 10 % increase in credits to GDP ratio raises the current account deficit to GDP ratio by 0.3 %. Ekinci et al. (2015) revealed in this study including 49 developed and developing countries that credit expansion affects current account balance negatively, and this effect is more powerful in the developing countries. In this context, according to the authors, the effects of credit expansion on current account deficit is more disruptive in the early phases of financial development.

Mendoza and Terrones (2012) investigated the relationship between credit booms and demand between 1960 and 2010 both for developed and developing countries. Results of the study show that expansion of credits rise current account deficit via domestic demand.

In the study of Atoyan (2013) about European developing economies and developed economies, excess demand in the periods when low unemployment rate, high credit expansion, and capital flows are observed together before crisis times effects current account deficit negatively. It is stated in the study that raising investments are more effective than decreasing savings in increasing the current account deficit for European economies, so the real determinant of current account deficit in European countries is decreasing savings. In other words, current account deficit is about the increase in investments in emerging European countries, and it is about increasing consumptions in developed European countries.

In the study consisting of 94 developed and developing countries, Cheung et al. (2013) emphasize rather significant and negative relationship between financial development represented by the ration of private sector credits to GDP and current account deficit. According to the authors, the reason of this changes according to country conditions. One of the possible reasons is the concept called "saving glut" of Bernanke (2005), which explains the current account imbalances with difference levels of financial development of countries. Accordingly, capital flows to countries with developed financial markets from emerging markets cause current account deficits. Another possible reason is that in some countries current account deficit is seen because developed institutions and financial markets lower the need of precautionary savings. Starting from the empirical findings of Chinn and Ito (2005, 2008) proposing that the effect of financial development on investment is bigger than the effect on savings, an argument stating that saving levels in countries with more developed financial markets is not always true. According to the authors, this argument is valid only in countries with developed judicial system and open financial markets. But situations are different for less developed and developing countries. In these countries, an increase in financial development level caused higher levels of savings. In this context, the reason of current account surplus in Asian economies with insufficient level of financial development is not the domestic savings but the lack of sufficient investment levels. According to these results, the type of relationship between financial development and current account balance depends on the properties of the countries. Thereby authors emphasize that effects of the financial development should be evaluated carefully. Similar to these results, the findings of the study by Gruber and Kamin (2009) support inefficiently the hypothesis that the differences of financial developments explain the current account surplus of developing countries or the current account deficit of USA.

Alper and Oransay (2015) investigated the relationship between current account deficit and financial development in OECD countries and found that financial development decreased the current account deficit, but current account deficit has no effect on financial development.

According to the results of the study by Brissimis et al. (2010) for Greek, rising credit volume resulting from the financial liberalization of the 1990s and monetary integration in 2001 decreased the private savings and has a significant role in current account deficit. From most of the studies about Turkey, it is concluded that financial development causes increases in current account deficits. Göçer et al. (2013), Atış and Saygılı (2014), and Akçayır and Albeni (2016) found cointegration between credit volume and increase in credit volume rises the current account deficit.

2 Data and Model

The effect of financial development on current account deficit in Turkey is investigated using the data between the 1980 and 2018 period in the study. For this purpose, share of current account deficit to GDP is used as dependent variable, domestic credits to private sector is used as independent variable, and real effective exchange rate index is used as the control variable. Rising of real effective exchange rate index shows the real appreciation of TL, and decreasing of real effective exchange rate index shows the real depreciation of TL. All of the data is taken from FRED database.

After 2013 IMF uses the ratio of domestic credits private sector to GDP ratio because this variable reflects the effect of financial development on current account deficit having some advantages like in many empirical studies, and one of the advantages is long-term time series can be achieved easily for all the countries (IMF, 2013), and another is the results can be compared to literature, owing to widespread use (Ekinci et al., 2015: 1810).

The relationship between current account deficit and financial development is estimated using the following model:

$$\mathrm{CA_t} = \alpha_0 + \alpha_1 \mathrm{KREDI_t} + \alpha_2 \mathrm{RER} + \varepsilon_t \tag{1}$$

In this model: CA is current account deficit/GDP, KREDI is domestic credits to private sector/GDP, RER is real effective exchange rate, $\propto_0$ is the constant, $\propto_1$ and $\propto_2$ are the elasticity coefficients of independent variables, and ε_t is the error term.

3 Methodology and Empirical Findings

3.1 Unit Root Analysis

The reality of the relationship between the variables in time series regression analysis depends on the stationarity of series. Thus, spurious regression problem can be seen in a model if nonstationary series are used in the model for the reason that this type of series cause spurious regression problems. For this reason, stationarity of the series is important in time series analysis. In this context, series are tested with stationarity test firstly. In order to determine the stationarity of the series Augmented Dickey-Fuller and Phillips-Perron tests, widely used in the literature, are applied.

ARDL bound testing approach can be applied regardless of the series being level stationary I(0), stationary at level one I(1), or stationary at different levels (I(0) and I(1)). In this context, ARDL bound testing approach removes the constraints about the level of stationarity of series, and diagnostic tests are not needed. This is a very important advantage of ARDL bound testing approach. Second advantage of this approach is giving confidential results even with small number of observations by contrast with Engle-Granger and Johansen cointegration tests (Narayan & Narayan, 2004: 102).

As per the results of ADF and PP unit root tests presented in Tab. 13.1, CA variable is stationary at level I(0) and the KREDİ and RER variables have unit root and become stationary when first differences are taken I(0). For the reason that the variables are stationary at different levels and the number of observations is

Tab. 13.1: ADF and PP unit tests results

Variable	I(0)			I(1)		
	Constant	Constant/ Trend	Constant/No Trend	Constant	Constant/ Trend	Constant/ No Trend
CA	-3,11**	-4,21*	-0,64	-7,40*	-7,31*	-7,51*
KREDI	1,20	-0,52	2,91	-4,07*	--4,46*	-3,76*
RER	-1,52	-2,00	-0,66	-7,10*	-6,97*	-7,18*
Phillips-Perron Test						
CA	-3,28*	-4,35*	-1,96*	-10,55*	-10,68*	-10,72*
KREDI	0,78	-0,68	2,34	-4,02*	-4,46*	-3,67*
RER	-1,59	-2,10	-0,66	-7,04*	-6,93*	-7,11*

Note: * 1 % and ** 5 % indicate significance levels. The ADF test was automatically selected based on a maximum of 9 lag lengths and SIC information criteria.

Tab. 13.2: Bound test

F Statistics	Number of Variable (k)	Critical Value: (%1) Significance Value	
		Upper Limit	Lover Limit
11,36*	2	5,15	6,36

Note: 1 % indicates the level of significance.

small, Engle-Granger and Johansen cointegration tests are not available. Under these conditions, ARDL bound testing approach can be used.

3.2 ARDL Cointegration Test

By using ARDL bound testing approach developed by Pesaran et al. (2001), cointegration of variables at level can be tested. Cointegration relationship of variables is estimated using below equation by bound testing which is based on ordinary least squares (OLS), and unrestricted error correction model m is the lag length of the model.

$$\begin{aligned} {}'CA_t = \alpha_0 + \sum_{i=1}^{m} \alpha_{1i}{}'CA_{t-i} + \sum_{i=0}^{m} \alpha_{2i}{}'KREDI_{t-i} + \sum_{i=0}^{m} \alpha_{3i}{}'RER_{t-i} \\ + \alpha_4 CA_{t-1} + \alpha_5 KREDI_{t-1} + \alpha_6{}'RER_{t-i} \quad + \mu_t \end{aligned} \tag{2}$$

Results of cointegration analysis made by using ARDL bound testing is given in Tab. 13.2. F statistic value and critical value derived from Pesaran et al. (2001: 300) show the bounds.

F statistic (11.36) is greater than the maximum value of these critical values (6.36) at 1 % significance level indicating a long-run relationship between the variables. In this context, a spurious regression problem is not possible for an analysis using the level values of the model (Yapraklı, 2010: 153).

3.3 ARDL Model Estimation

After determining a cointegration relationship between the variables, model estimations should be made. At this point, model estimations are implemented by ARDL (p, q) method. ARDL model whose maximum length lag is determined by Schwarz information criteria (SIC) is defined as follows:

Tab. 13.3: Model ARDL (2, 1, 0) test results (CAC dependent variable)

Variable	Coefficient	t-Statistics
CAC (-1)	0,058	0,463
CAC(-2)	-0,240***	-1,192
KREDI	0,283*	3,247
KREDI(-1)	-0,234**	-2,688
RER	0,093*	4,263
C	-5,821*	-3,935
R^2	0.77	
Adjusted R2	0.74	
Prob.	0,000	

Note: *, **, *** %1, %5, and %10 show the level of significance, respectively.

$$CA_t = \alpha_0 + \sum_{i=1}^{p} \alpha_{1i} CA_{t-i} + \sum_{i=0}^{q1} \alpha_{2i} KREDI_{t-i} + \sum_{i=0}^{q2} \alpha_{3i} RER_{t-i} + \mu_t \quad (3)$$

In this equation, $\propto_0$ is the constant, $\propto_1$ and $\propto_2$ are coefficients, p is the lag length of dependent variable, q_1 and q_2 are the lag lengths of independent variables, and μ is the error term. Results of the model estimation are given below.

When we examine ARDL (2,1,0) model in Tab. 13.3, current account deficit variable is significant at second lag at 10 % significance level while it is not significance at first lag (CAC(-1)). Credit variable (KREDI) is significant at 1 % significant level and significant at lag value at 5 % significant level, and real effective exchange rate (RER) is significant at 1 % significance level statistically. These results show the model is significant.

For reliable results of analysis made by time series, results of the diagnostic tests should have no heteroscedasticity, autocorrelation, or normal distribution problem. However, an improperly defined model will not give reliable results. In this context, there is no heteroscedasticity problem according to Breusch-Pagan-Godfrey test, no autocorrelation problem according to Breusch-Pagan test, and no normal distribution problem according to Jarque-Bera test. In addition, Ramsey test shows that there is no model definition problem. Inasmuch as, bigger than 0.05 probability values for each test supports the hypothesis that the mentioned problem does not exist (Tab. 13.4) when the results of the tests are analyzed.

Tab. 13.4: Diagnostic test results

Diagnostic Tests	Statistics Value	Prob.
R2	0,77	
Adjusted R2	0,74	
F-statistics	21,26	0,000
Autocorrelation	0,451	0,79
Heteroscedasticity	4,379	0,49
Normality	0,311	0,85
Ramsey reset tests	0,160	0,69

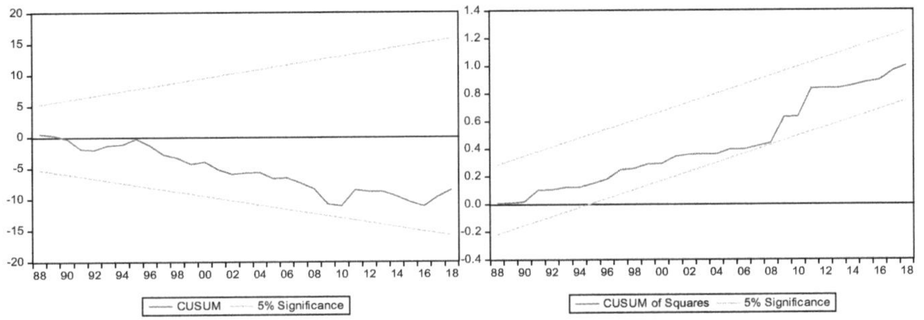

Fig. 13.1: Cusum and Cusum squares test results

Stability of the model is tested by Cusum and Cusum squares tests (seen in Fig. 13.1). Test statistics are within the specified limits at 5 % significance level. This result supports that parameters of the model have no significant structural break according to Cusum and Cusum squares tests, in other words they have stability (Bahmani-Oskoee and Ng, 2002: 154).

3.4 Results of Error Correction Model of ARDL and Long-Run Coefficients

In order to examine the short-run relationship between the variables, Error Correction Model (ECM) of ARDL method is used. In this context, ECM is applied by taking the first differences of series that is generated using ARDL model. Error correction coefficient shows the convergence rate of short-run deviations in long-run equilibrium. First difference of the series:

Tab. 13.5: Results of ECM of ARDL model

Variables	Coefficients	t-statistics (p value)
D(CA(-1))	0,24	1,92 (0,063)
D(KREDI)	0,28	3,24 (0,002)
D(RER)	0,09	4,26 (0,000)
ECM(-1)	-1,18	-7,04 (0,000)

$$'CA_t = \alpha_0 + +\varnothing ECM_{t-1} + \sum_{i=1}^{p} \alpha_{1i}{}'CA_{t-i} + \sum_{i=0}^{q1} \alpha_{2i}{}'KREDI_{t-i} + \sum_{i=0}^{q2} \alpha_{3i} RER_{t-i} + \mu_t \quad (4)$$

Here ECM shows the error correction term, and ø parameter shows the coefficient of return to equilibrium. If i $\varnothing_i$ =0, it is stated that there is no long-run relationship between the variables and if it is negative, it is stated that variables will return to long-run equilibrium. For this reason, a negative parameter (Ø<0) is expected. Results of the short-run error correction model and long-run parameters are given in Tab. 13.5.

Results of the ECM in Tab. 13.5 shows a positive and significant relationship between the lagged value of current account deficit and the variable in the short run. Therefore, past values of current account deficit are effective o the present current account deficit in Turkey considerably.

Credits to private sector have a significant and positive effect on current account deficit in the short run. According to the results, when credits to private sector to GDP ratios rises by 1 %, current account deficit rises by 0.28 %. These results show that financial development increases the current account deficit in Turkey. Similarly, real effective exchange rate (RER) increases the current account deficit, but the effect is rather weak. Thus, a 1 % increase in RER rises the current account deficit by 0.09 %. This result shows that real appreciation of TL, the increase in the price of Turkish goods in terms of foreign goods, has no powerful effect on current account deficit. Furthermore, error correction term ECM (-1) has negative sign and significant at 1 % level statistically so that the deviations in equilibrium in the short run will converge to the equilibrium in the long run. ECM(-1) is smaller than -1, so that these deviations will approach balance in less than a period (Olczyk and Kordalska, 2017: 221), which means that the adaptation process is quite fast (Narayan and Smyth, 2006: 339).

Tab. 13.6: ARDL model long-run coefficient results

Variables	**Coefficients**	**t-statistics (p value)**	KREDI
0,041	3,095 (0,004)	RER	0,078
4,798 (0,000)	C	-4,928	-4,448 (0,000)

When we examine the long-run coefficients of dependent variables, it is understood that the significant and positive short-run relationship is also valid in the long run. But the short-run relationship between credits and current account deficit weakens in the long run. For as much as 1 % increase in credits rises current account deficit by 0.28 % in the short run while it increases current account deficit by 0.04 % in the long run. One reason is consumer demand, which is one of the loans given to the private sector, continued to increase in domestic demand in the short run, and on the other side it can be the increase in exports due to capacity-building effects of loans extended to firms or absorbing domestic demand. For this reason, the impact of both types of credit on the current account deficit needs to be distinguished. For this purpose, results derived from the analysis of Telatar (2011) show that the main credit type that increases the current account deficit is the loans used for consumption purposes. In addition, the weak and positive effect of the real exchange rate on the current account deficit in the short run continued to weaken relatively in the long run. Therefore, the policies that use exchange rate as a tool, that is, the depreciation of TL, will not be effective in reducing the current account deficit (Aslan and Ersungur, 2018: 536).

Conclusions

Turkey is facing a chronic current account deficit since the early 2000s. The recovery process after the crisis in 2000 and 2001 and the loose monetary policies implemented after the 2008–2009 crisis caused the revival of deferred consumption demand and domestic demand increased. This process deepened the current account deficit problem and increased financial risks in consequence. Under these circumstances, the Central Bank of Turkey adopted a new monetary policy framework in 2010 in order to maintain price stability and financial stability together. One of the two basics of this policy is to limit the increase in credit volume and the other is to prevent the exchange rate from acting disjointedly from the economic fundamentals.

The aim of this study is to determine the effects of financial development on current account deficit using annual data for the period 1980–2018 in Turkey.

For this purpose, effects of "the ratio of domestic credits to private sector to GDP" variable representing financial development and real effective exchange rate as control variable on current account deficit are analyzed econometrically using ARDL bound testing. According to the findings, there is a strong and positive relationship between credits to real sector and current account deficit, but in the long run this relation weakens. One of the possible reasons for this can be the differentiated effects of consumer and corporate loans to the private sector on current account deficit in the long run. On the other hand, although the real effective exchange rate has a positive effect on current account deficit, it seems to be limited. The results shows that the current account deficit problem in Turkey is a structural problem rather than a problem depending on the applied economic politics. Therefore, some structural changes decreasing import dependence needs to be done besides credit limiting policies in the context of reducing the current account deficit.

References

Akçayır, Ö. and Albeni, M. (2016). "Türkiye'de Kredi Genişlemesinin Cari Açığa Etkisi: Sınır Testi Yaklaşımı", *Çankırı Karatekin Üniversitesi İktisadi ve İdari Bilimler Fakültesi Dergisi*, 6(1), 557–583

Alper, A.E. and Oransoy, G. (2015). "Cari Açık ve Finansal Gelişmişlik İlişkisinin Panel Nedensellik Analizi Ekseninde Değerlendirilmesi", *Uluslararası Ekonomi ve Yenilik Dergisi*, 1(2), 73–85

Aslan, M.B. and Ersungur, Ş.M.(2018). Türkiye ile OECD Ülkeleri Arasindaki Dış Ticaretin Marshall-Lerner Kuralı Çerçevesinde İncelenmesi. *Uluslararası İktisadi ve İdari İncelemeler Dergisi*, (18. EYİ Özel Sayısı), 525–540

Atış, S. and Saygılı, F. (2014). "Türkiye'de Kredi Hacmi ve Cari Açık İlişkisi Üzerine Bir İnceleme", *Business and Economics Research Journal*, 5(4), 129–141

Atoyan, R., Manning, J. and Rahman, J. (2013). "Rebalancing: Evidence from Current Account Adjustment in Europe", IMF Working Paper, No: 13/74.

Aydın, M.K. and Beşballı, S.G. (2018). "Türkiye'de Cari Açık Sorunu Üzerine Bir Değerlendirme", *Bilgi,* 20(1), 1–14

Bahmani-Oskooee, M. and Chi Wing Ng, R. (2002). "Long-Run Demand for Money in Hong Kong: An Application of the ARDL Model," *International Journal of Business and Economics*, 1(2), 147–155,

Bernanke, B.S. (2005). "The Global Saving Glut and the U.S. Current Account Deficit," Speech 77, Board of Governors of the Federal Reserve System (U.S.).

Brissimis, S.N., Hondroyiannis, G., Papazoglou, C., Tsaveas, N.T. and Vasardani, M.A. (2010). "Current Account Determinants and External Sustainability in Periods of Structural Change," Working Papers 117, Bank of Greece.

Cheung, C., Furceri, D. and Rusticelli, E. (2013). "Structural and Cyclical Factors behind Current Account Balances", *Review of International Economics*, 21(5), 923–944.

Chinn, M.D. (2017). "The Once and Future Global Imbalances? Interpreting the Post-Crisis Record". https://www.ssc.wisc.edu/~mchinn/Imbalances_JacksonHole2017.pdf

Chinn, M.D. and Ito, H. (2005) "Current Account Balances, Financial Development and Institutions: Assaying the World 'Saving Glut' ", NBER Working Peper No. 11761

Chinn, M.D. and Ito, H. (2007). "Current Account Balances, Financial Development and Institutions: Assaying the World "Savings Glut," *Journal of International Money and Finance*, 26, 546–569

Chinn, M.D. and Ito, H. (2008). "Global Current Account Imbalances: American Fiscal Policy versus East Asian Savings", *Review of International Economics*, 16(3), 479–498

Cubeddu, L., Krogstrup, S., Adler, G., Rabanal, P., Chi Dao, M., Hannan, S.A., Juvenal, L., Li, N., Buitron, C.O., Rebillard, C., Garcia-Macia, D., Jones, J., Rodriguez, J., Chang, K.S., Guatam, D.A. and Wang, Z. (2019). "The External Balance Assessment Methodology: 2018 Update", IMF Working Papers 19/65, International Monetary Fund.

Devadas, S. and Loayza, N. (2018). "When Is a Current Account Deficit Bad?", World Bank Research and Policy Briefs No. 130415

Edwards, S. (2005). "The End of Large Current Account Deficıts, 1970–2002: Are There Lessons for The Unıted States?", NBER Working Paper No. 11669

Ekinci, M.F., Erdem, F.P. and Z. Kilinc (2015). "Credit Growth, Current Account and Financial Depth", *Applied Economics*, 47(17), 1809–1821.

Ekinci, M.F. and Omay, T. (2019). "Current Account and Credit Growth: The Role of Household Credit and Financial Depth", MPRA Paper No. 93882

Göçer, İ., Mercan, M. and Peker, O. (2013). "Kredi Hacmi Artışının Cari Açığa Etkisi: Çoklu Yapısal Kırılmalı Eşbütünleşme Analizi", *İstanbul Üniversitesi İktisat Fakültesi Ekonometri ve İstatistik Dergisi*, 18(1), 1–17

Gosh, A. and Ramakrishnan, U. (2006). "Do Current Account Deficits Matter?" *Finance and Development*, 43(4)

Gruber, J. W. and Kamin S. B. (2009). "Do Differences in Financial Development Explain the Global Pattern of Current Account Imbalances?" *Review of International Economics*, 17(4), 667–688

International Monetary Found (2018). "External Sector Report: Tackling Global Imbalances Amid Rasing Trade Tensions". Washington DC, July.

Jorda, O., Schularick, M. and Taylor, A.M. (2011). "Financial Crises, Credit Booms, and External Imbalances: 140 Years of Lessons, Financial Crises", *IMF Economic Review*, 59(2), 340–378

Mendoza, E.G. and Terrones, M.E. (2012). "An Anatomy of Credit Booms and Their Demise", NBER Working Paper No.18379

Milesi-Ferretti, G.M. and Razin, A. (1996). "Sustainability of Persistent Current Account Deficits", NBER Working Paper No. 5467

Mussa, M. (2005) "Sustaining Global Growth While Reducing External Imbalances. In Bergsten, C.F.(ed.), The United States and the World Economy: Foreign Economic Policy for the Next Decade", Institute for International Economics, Washington, 175–2007

Narayan, P.K. and Smyth, R. (2006). "What Determines Migration Flows from Low-İncome to High-İncome Countries? An Empirical İnvestigation Of Fiji-U.S. Migration 1972–2001", Contemporary Economic Policy, 24(2), 332–342.

Narayan, S. and Narayan, P.K. (2004). "Determinants of Demand for Fiji's Exports: An Empirical Investigation", *The Developing Economies*, 42(1), 95–112

Olczyk, M. and Kordolska, A. (2017). "International Competitiveness of Czech Manufacturing: A Sectoral Approach with Error Correction Model", *Prague Economic Papers*, 26(2), 213–226

Pasaran, M.H., Shin, Y. and Smith, R.J. (2001). "Bounds Testing Approaches to the Analysis of Level Relationships", *Journal of Applied Econometrics*, 16(3), 289–326

Phillips, S., Catão, L., Ricci, L.A., Bems, R., Das, M., di Giovanni, J., Unsal, D.F., Castillo, M., Lee, J., Rodriguez, J. and Vargas, M. (2013). "The External Balance Assessment (EBA) Methodology." IMF Working Paper 13/272, International Monetary Fund, Washington, DC.

Telatar, E. (2011). "Türkiye'de Cari Açık Belirleyicileri ve Cari Açık Kredi İlişkisi", Bankacılar Dergisi, Sayı 78, 22–34

World Bank (2011). "Sustaining High Growth: The Role of Domestic Savings", Turkey Country Economic Memorandum, Report No: 66–30-TR

Yapraklı, S. (2010). "Türkiye'de Esnek Döviz Kuru Rejimi Altında Dış Açıkların Belirleyicileri: Sınır Testi Yaklaşımı", Ankara Üniversitesi SBF Dergisi, 65(4), 141–164

Ya-Qiong, P. and Rui, Z. (2013). "Financial Development and Current Account Imbalance: Evidence from Dynamic Panel Data Model with Gmm Estimation", *Journal of Applied Sciences* 13(15), 2933–2939

Hakan Altin and Cemil Süslü

14 Effect of Financing Resources on Profit, Investment, and Firm Value: Comparison of BIST and NYSE

Highlights: The effect of financing resources on the companies' profitability, investments, and market values are investigated for the BIST industrial companies operating in Turkey, representing the Industrial Index and companies operating in the NYSE Industry Index, representing American industrial companies. Logarithmic models are used to achieve this aim, and the period of the study is between 2016 and 2018. As a result of the models used, it is seen that effect of financing resources on profitability, fixed investments, and market value for industrial index companies of Turkey stock market and industrial index companies of American Stock market have shown to give mixed results.

Keywords: Capital structure, market value, business risk, financial risk, tax advantage

Introduction

The fundamental purpose of a company is to maximize its market value. When evaluated from the point of companies, growth decision is actually an investment decision. A company needs capital whether it is defined as growth or aims to grow as investment. Capital is provided primarily by debt or equity. Financing with debt has two important advantages. First of all, the interest expenses can be deducted from the tax base. Second, if the growth becomes successful, the high return will be shared among the existing partners. As stated in the study of Modigliani and Miller (1958), it is argued that a 100 % debt capital structure would maximize stock prices.

On the other hand, high borrowing will make the company more risky. When this situation is evaluated from the point of the company, it will increase the cost of both borrowing and equity financing. In addition, if the company operates in challenging market conditions, the operating income of the company will not be able to cover interest expenses, and the company will be concerned in a failure.

By the reason of the additional risk of using debt, companies with floating earnings and operating cash flow tend to limit their use of debt. This situation can be explained by the trade-off theory in literature.

However, companies with low business risk and consistent operating cash flow can make use of getting more debt. Companies understand that interest should be paid even in bad times, so they need to use less debt to strengthen their financial position and prevent the fall of credit ratings. On the other hand, the company may have used equity in order to finance the growth. It may have provided this capital with the issuance of new stocks. In this case, there is no repayment of the provided capital. However, it will distribute the profit obtained to the new partners together with the old partners at the end of the period. It is not possible to deduct the distributed dividend from the tax base. Considering the two sources of financing together, it can be said that debt financing has a tax advantage. Every company can benefit from this tax advantage. However, this has a boundary. In other words, the funds needed by the companies are provided by investors having various demands on cash flow. Borrowers have contracts (bonds) that promise them fixed interest earnings in the future in return for current cash. Shareholders buy retained earnings (internal capital provided by existing shareholders) or new stocks (external capital provided by new shareholders). This is a response to the firm's future dividend requests. In addition, while shareholders control the investment decision, bond holders do not have direct controls that may restrict decision-making of the shareholders. Both sources of finance have costs. While the cost of borrowing is the amount of interest paid, the cost of equity is the dividend paid. However, an important point to keep in mind is that when these cost factors are evaluated from the point view of investors, they are actually interest earnings and expected returns. Therefore, the subject is important for both the securities issuer company and the investors.

As a result, both of these cost factors have different sensitivities to both investment and firm value. The determination of these sensitivities is important both for the contribution to the literature and for all stakeholders. Sensitivity is the coefficients of elasticity that show the effect of each financing resource on investment and firm value. The easiest way to determine coefficients of elasticity is to create a full logarithmic equation. Comments of a study where multiple regression analysis will be used are defined as a percentage change over the other variable as a result of a percentage. Thus, the sensitivity effect of borrowing and equity on investment and firm value is determined. The findings will be compared with the literature. While doing this, Turkey and USA stock markets will also be analyzed comparatively.

In the introduction part of the study, while general explanations about borrowing (bond valuation), equity (stock valuation), and capital structure theories are given, in the literature section, leading studies on capital structure will be given in chronological order. The proceeding stage will include the purpose and scope of the study, the model and estimation methods used, and the analysis of the model. The last stage includes the conclusion of the study.

1 Literature

Modern capital structure theory begins with the works of Modigliani and Miller (MM) (1958). The authors proved that the market value of the company is independent of its capital structure. When this study was criticized in the literature, in the study MM (1963) accepted that the companies deducted interest payments from tax as an expense in tax law. However, dividends to shareholders are not deducted. This situation encourages companies to use debts in their capital structures. Thus, MM showed that this different usage leads to an optimal capital structure of a 100 % debt if all other assumptions are met.

Scott (1976) presented a firm valuation model that suggests the existence of an optimal capital structure that takes the costs of bankruptcy into account in his study. Thereafter, it was determined that the most effective debt level is a function of the liquidity value of the assets of the company, the corporate tax rate, and the size of the firm.

Afterwards, Miller (1977) investigates the taxation of returns from bonds and stock earnings in his study. Thereafter, taxes on potential earnings are important when companies determine their capital structures. However, whether the tax advantage of debt and the tax incentives on stock returns is the most appropriate source of capital resource is uncertain.

Bradley et al. (1984) stated that they brought a direct approach to the optimal capital structure. They discovered two important results. First of all, it can be explained by the modern balancing theory of capital structure. Second, the relationship between the leverage ratio of the company and company's earnings are negative. Consequentially, leverage rates have a strong connection with the industry in which the firm operates.

Titman and Wessels (1988) made a research on the debt levels chosen by companies. The study shows that transaction costs can be an important determinant of capital structure selection. They found that short-term debt ratios are negatively related to firm size and small firms face high transaction costs when they look for long-term financial instruments. The results suggest that capital structures are systematically chosen.

Barton and Gordon (1988) investigated the relationship between the strategies followed by company managers and the capital structure of firms. The authors developed five proposals to identify the factors affecting the capital structure. The three of these proposals relate to the management values and demands of the companies. The fourth proposal is about threats and opportunities outside the firm. The fifth proposal is about the strengths and weaknesses of the firm and as a result of the study, it has been determined that the strategy of the firm affects the capital structure decisions.

Fischer et al. (1989) studied the capital structure selection model in the presence of the costs of the capital resource required. The analysis is the conformity of the capital structure built on the traditional tax/bankruptcy cost theory. The model offers various estimates of the optimal leverage ratios range of firm-specific features. Accordingly, higher increases in debt ratios of companies are observed over time for smaller, more risky, lower taxes and lower bankruptcy risks. Transaction costs have an impact on determining debt/equity ratios. Anticipating the advantages of debt financing shows that debt is benefited more in building the capital structure.

Rajan and Zingales (1995) analyzed the similarities between capital structure decisions of companies by examining the international data. They found that all the factors explaining the leverage are valid for all G-7 countries and the leverage ratios of the G-7 countries are similar. Therefore, economic development affects capital structure decisions.

Leland and Toft (1996) made a study on debt maturity structure, optimal leverage, and risky bonds. According to the study, the debt shows a balance between maturity determination, tax benefits, bankruptcy costs, and agency costs. Short-term and long-term debt demands of a mature company and a new company are different from each other.

Berger et al. (1997) investigated the relationship between managerial attitudes and capital structure. In the other case, managers avoid high levels of financial leverage. During a long management period, they found that the debt ratios were low in a company where stock bonuses and management compensations were weak.

Sunder and Myers (1999) tested the capital structure theories. Theories are contradictory and their explanatory powers have been determined. Thereafter, pecking order theory has the most important explanatory power in determining the capital structures of companies.

Baker and Wurgler (2002) identified that timing is effective on capital structure in the stock market. They used the market value to book value ratio to measure the opportunities of market timing. Hereunder, they argued that firms having low leverage tend to be on the side of fund raisers when stock prices are high, and on the contrary, firms having high-leverage tend not to be on the side of fund raisers when stock prices are low. They found that fluctuations in market value had major effects on the capital structure.

Green and Hollifield (2003) examined the tax advantage issue on equity. As a result, it was determined that the individual tax advantages of the equity do not meet the tax reduction benefits of all debt payments.

Faulkender and Petersen (2005) examined the effects of capital resources on the capital structure. It is observed that debt tax shields are higher, financial distress costs are low, and lower pricing of debt compared to equity leads to the expectation of higher leverage. When companies discover that the net benefit of debt is positive, it will change their decision of capital structure by taking additional debt and/or reducing their equity.

Frank and Goyal (2009) examined high leverage (debt/equity) levels in their study. Accordingly, companies which are operating in high competition sectors have high leverage rates. Companies with high market value/book value prefer debt financing more. Companies with more tangible assets have higher leverage rates. Big firms have high leverage ratio. If inflation is expected to be high, companies tend to have a high leverage ratio. In addition to these six factors, whether the company will pay dividends is also related to the use of leverage.

Inderst and Vladimirov (2019) examined how venture capital and related borrowing affect the capital structure determination of the companies. As a result, they detected that risk capital and financing are key to the capital structure decisions of growing companies.

Grosse-Rueschkamp et al. (2019) analyzed the effects of monetary policies implemented by central banks after the global economic crisis at the end of 2007 on the capital structures of companies. As a result, they found that implementations of the central banks affect the capital structure of these companies by affecting the determination of nonfinancial companies to finance their own activities.

Chen et al. (2019) examined the relationship between operating leverage of the companies, profitability, and capital structure. They found that operating leverage positively correlated with profitability, and at the same time there is a significant and negative relationship between financial leverage and profitability.

Harris and Roark (2019) examined the relationship between cash flow volatility and capital structure decisions. The results show that the increase in cash flow risk affects capital structure decisions and firms with insufficient cash flow rely on debts.

2 Data, Method, and Application

2.1 Data Set

Companies in the Borsa İstanbul Industrial Index and companies in the New York Stock Exchange Industry Index are included in the study. Data of 136 of 156 companies operating in the Turkish stock market industrial index are available for the study. Data of 290 of 490 companies operating in the American stock market industry index are available. Data of American stock market industry index companies were obtained from yahoo finance. The annual data of the 2016–2018 period were examined in the study.

2.2 Econometric Method

The most usable form is called a model for econometric purposes (Kip, 1997, p.20). The first step of econometric studies is the establishment of the model. Functional models can be the linear and nonlinear regression models. The main functional models are (Tarı, 2015, p.135) linear form, polynomial form, semi-logarithmic form, and full logarithmic form. In this study, for the reason that the full logarithmic form is used, information about the full logarithmic model is given. A univariate full logarithmic model is in the following form (Tarı, 2015, p. 148; Güriş et al. 2013, p. 316):

$$Y = b_0 X^{b_i} e^u \tag{1}$$

In this model, the logarithm of the two sides is taken and the model is estimated by the Least Squares method.

$$lnY_i = lnb_0 + b_1 lnX_i + u_i \tag{2}$$

Making the transformation as lnY=Y*, ln b_0 = b_0^*, and lnX=X*, the model is transformed into the standard form as follows and it is then estimated (Tarı, 2015, p. 148; Güriş et al. 2013, p. 317):

$$Y* = b_0^* + b_1 X^* + u \tag{3}$$

b_1 is the elasticity of, Y according to X in the model in the full logarithmic model, 1 % change in X causes a% $b_1\%$ change in Y (Güriş et al. 2013, p. 317).

2.3 Application of the Model

The sensitivity (effects) of financing sources to the profitability, fixed investments, and market values of the companies is examined using the full logarithmic models numbered as 4, 5, and 6.

$$LOGP = LOG\beta_0 + \beta_1 LOGD_i + \beta_2 LOGE_i + u_i \tag{4}$$

Tab. 14.1: Dependent and independent variables used in the study

Dependent Variables	Independent Variables
Profit (LOGP)	Debt (LOGD)
Investment (LOGFI)	Equity (LOGE)
Market Value (LOGMV)	

$$LOGFI = LOG\beta_0 + \beta_1 LOGD_i + \beta_2 LOGE_i + u_i \tag{5}$$

$$LOGMV = LOG\beta_0 + \beta_1 LOGD_i + \beta_2 LOGE_i + u_i \tag{6}$$

Dependent and independent variables and their abbreviations are given in Tab. 14.1.

After logarithmic transformations of the variables are completed, ADF unit root analysis was implemented. As the result of the unit root tests, the variables of companies in Turkish stock market industrial index and in the American stock market industrial are stationary at the level and the results are given in Tab. 14.2.

2.4 Analysis of the Model

The effects of the financing sources of companies operating in the Turkish stock market Industrial index and the American stock market industrial index on profitability, market value, and fixed investments are examined separately for 2016, 2017, and 2018 by using the full logarithmic models numbered 4, 5, and 6.

The results obtained from the full logarithmic models used for examining the effects of the financing resources on the profitability, fixed investments, and market values of these companies are given first for the Turkish stock market industrial index companies and second the American stock market industrial companies.

It can be said that for the companies operating in the Turkish stock exchange Industrial index, equity positively affected the profitability of the companies in 2016, 2017, and 2018. Accordingly, a 1 % increase in the equity has created an increase of 0.90 %, 1.03 %, and 1.33 % in the profits of Turkish stock market industrial index companies in years. However, an increase of 1 % in the debts of Turkish industrial companies caused a decrease of 0.34 % in the profits of these companies in 2018.

According to the results obtained from the logarithmic model numbered (II), which examines the financing sources of Turkish stock market industrial index

Tab. 14.2: ADF unit root test results

Variables	t-statistic value (Probability Value)
	BIST
LOGP (2016)	-11.64123 (0.0000)
LOGP (2017)	-11.64123 (0.0000)
LOGP (2018)	-5.058810 (0.0000)
LOGE (2016)	-11.29202 (0.0000)
LOGE (2017)	-11.36449 (0.0000)
LOGE (2018)	-11.60963 (0.0000)
LOGD (2016)	-11.60419 (0.0000)
LOGD (2017)	-10.91059 (0.0000)
LOGD (2018)	-11.45388 (0.0000)
LOGMV(2016)	-12.85010 (0.0000)
LOGMV(2017)	-12.69926 (0.0000)
LOGMV(2018)	-12.66185 (0.0000)
LOGFI (2016)	-11.47025 (0.0000)
LOGFI (2017)	-11.03980 (0.0000)
LOGFI (2018)	-11.10075 (0.0000)

Note: The unit root results for the American stock exchange are the same as those for the Turkish stock exchange for this reason and they are not included in the table.

companies and its effects on their investments, it is seen that the financing sources positively affect the investments of Turkish stock market industrial companies, and this effect is statistically significant at 1 % significance level. According to this result, a 1 % increase in equity has created an increase of 0.29 %, 0 %, 37, and 0.46 % in the investments of these companies over the years. When we analyze this result, a 1 % increase in equity created an increase of 0.29 %, 0 %, 37 and 0.46 % in the investments of these companies over the years. Similarly, a 1 % increase in debt created an increase of 0.66 %, 0.57 %, and 0.49 % in the investments of Turkish stock market industrial companies in years.

According to the results obtained from the full logarithmic model (III), which was created to examine the effects of debt financing or equity capital financing of Turkish stock market industrial companies on the market values of these companies, it is determined that debt and equity do not affect the market value of these companies. Accordingly, it may be concluded that Turkish stock market industrial companies do not determine a capital structure based on market value, or do not determine a target capital structure that will increase their market value and decrease the weighted average capital cost.

The effects of financing sources of American stock market index companies on company profitability, fixed investments, and market values are examined. According to the results obtained from the full logarithmic model number (I) for the period 2016–2018, it is observed that a change in the equity capital of the American stock market industry index companies do not affect the profitability of these companies. In contrast, a change in the debt of American stock market industrial companies affects the profitability of the companies. Accordingly, a 1 % increase in debts created an increase of 0.74 %, 0.87 %, and 0.69 % in the profitability of these companies over the years.

According to the results obtained from the full logarithmic model number (II) for the period 2016–2018, it is observed that a change in the equity capital of companies in the American stock exchange industry index do not affect the investments of these companies. However, an increase of 1 % in debts causes an increase in the investments of American stock market index companies by 0.96 %, 0.96 %, and 0.97 % over the years.

According to this result, it can be said that the American stock market industry index companies may finance their investments by debt without increasing their borrowing costs. They may prefer the debt financing for the reason that the interest paid can be deducted from the tax base and no obligation to share the profits with the shareholders if the company is successful.

According to the results obtained from the full logarithmic model number (III) for the period 2016–2018, the market value of American stock market index companies is affected by both of the financing resources of these companies.

Accordingly, an increase of 1 % in the equity capital of these companies led to an increase in the market value of the companies by 1.15 %, 1.15 %, and 1 %, respectively, over the years. Similarly, an increase of 1 % in debts creates a 0.6 %, 0.69 %, and 0.68 % increase in the market value of these companies, respectively, over the years. According to the results, we can say that the capital structures determined by the American stock market industrial companies positively affects the market value of the companies.

Conclusion

The study examines the effects of financing resources on profit, investment, and firm value. The results are classified in two ways. The first one is theoretical results. The second one is the results obtained from the application stage.

Theoretical results are as follows: The concept of capital refers to the funds provided by the investor. These funds are debt, preferred capital stock, common stock, and undistributed profits. The capital structure of a company is defined as a percentage of the capital type provided by the investor and its total is 100 %. The optimal capital structure consists of debt, preferred capital stock, and common stock that maximizes the company's market value. At this point, Weighted Average Cost of Capital (WACC) is at the minimum. The capital structure can be measured by the book value provided by accountants and shown on the balance sheet, as also by debt, preferred capital stock, and common stock market values. Both of these measurements provide important information. However, the existence of asymmetric information in real life shows that the capital structure is at optimal not a single point but it formed at a certain level in a certain range. When making a capital structure decision, sales stability of the company, asset structure, operating leverage, growth rate, profitability, taxes, management control, executive behavior, lender and rating notes, market conditions, internal conditions of the company, tax conditions, and financial flexibility should be considered.

The results obtained in the application are as follows: the sensitivity of the financing sources of the companies operating in Turkey Stock Exchange and American Stock Exchange on profitability, investment, and market value. Accordingly, when the effect of debt and equity on profitability is evaluated in terms of Turkish stock market industrial companies, it is observed that the debt of Turkish industrial companies do not affect the profitability of these companies in 2016 and 2017 except 2018. Equity capital of Turkish industrial companies is observed to affect their profitability during the evaluated period.

Nevertheless, debt, which is the financing source of American stock market companies, does not affect the profitability of these companies. According to these results, it can be said that Turkish stock companies preferred to use equity financing than debt in terms of reducing their capital costs in the economic conditions they operate in. However, American stock market companies prefer debt financing to equity financing because of the relatively low interest rate in their economic conditions. When the effects of financing sources on investments are observed, it is seen that both financing sources have positive effect on investments for Turkish stock market industrial companies. When the effects of financing resources on investments are investigated in terms of American stock market industrial companies, it is seen that equity from financing resources does not affect the fixed investments of these companies, but debts positively affect the investments of these companies.

In addition to these, it can be said that Turkish stock market industrial companies prefer to use both of these financing sources in order to reduce their capital costs. Nevertheless, American stock market companies prefer borrowing in financing investments. Because, the amount of interest payment for the debt can be deducted from the tax base, and the earned profit is not shared with the shareholders in case the company is successful.

When the effects of financing resources on market value are investigated, it is observed that financing resources of Turkish stock market industrial companies do not affect the market value of these companies. However, it is seen that the financing sources of the American stock market industry index companies significantly affect the market value of the companies. The reason for this is thought that the market they operate in may be an efficient or developed market and that they have targeted a capital structure that will maximize the market value. The fact that Turkish stock market industrial companies are not affected by financing sources may be due to the inefficient market in which they operate and the lack of capital structure that will make the company value.

References

Baker, M., & Wurgler, J. (2002). "Market timing and capital structure". The Journal of Finance, 57(1), 1–32.

Barton, S. L., & Gordon, P. J. (1988). "Corporate strategy and capital structure". Strategic Management Journal, 9(6), 623–632.

Berger, P. G., Ofek, E., & Yermack, D. L. (1997). "Managerial entrenchment and capital structure decisions". The Journal of Finance, 52(4), 1411–1438.

Bradley, M., Jarrell, G. A., & Kim, E. H. (1984). "On the existence of an optimal capital structure: Theory and evidence". The Journal of Finance, 39(3), 857–878.

Chen, Z., Harford, J., & Kamara, A. (2019). "Operating leverage, profitability, and capital structure". Journal of Financial and Quantitative Analysis, 54(1), 369–392.

Faulkender, M., & Petersen, M. A. (2005). "Does the source of capital affect capital structure?". The Review of Financial Studies, 19(1), 45–79.

Fischer, E. O., Heinkel, R., & Zechner, J. (1989). "Dynamic capital structure choice: Theory and tests". The Journal of Finance, 44(1), 19–40.

Frank, M. Z., & Goyal, V. K. (2009). "Capital structure decisions: Which factors are reliably important?". Financial Management, 38(1), 1–37.

Green, R. C., & Hollifield, B. (2003). "The personal-tax advantages of equity". Journal of Financial Economics, 67(2), 175–216.

Grosse-Rueschkamp, B., Steffen, S., & Streitz, D. (2019). "A capital structure channel of monetary policy". Journal of Financial Economics, 133(2), 357–378.

Güriş, S., Çağlayan, E., & Güriş, B. (2013). "*Eviews ile Temel Ekonometri* "(2. Baskı b.). İstanbul: Der Yayınları.

Harris, C., & Roark, S. (2019). "Cash flow risk and capital structure decisions". Finance Research Letters, 29, 393–397.

Inderst, R., & Vladimirov, V. (2019). Growth firms and relationship finance: A capital structure perspective. Management Science, 65(11), 5411–5426.

Leland, H. E. (1994). "Corporate debt value, bond covenants, and optimal capital structure". The Journal of Finance, 49(4), 1213–1252.

Leland, H. E., & Toft, K. B. (1996). "Optimal capital structure, endogenous bankruptcy, and the term structure of credit spreads". The Journal of Finance, 51(3), 987–1019.

Miller, M. H. (1977). "Debt and taxes". The Journal of Finance, 32(2), 261–275.

Modigliani, F., & Miller, M. H. (1958). The cost of capital, corporation finance and the theory of investment. The American economic review, 48(3), 261–297.

Modigliani, F., & Miller, M. H. (1963). "Corporate income taxes and the cost of capital: A correction". The American Economic Review, 53(3), 433–443.

Rajan, R. G., & Zingales, L. (1995). "What do we know about capital structure? Some evidence from international data". The Journal of Finance, 50(5), 1421–1460.

Scott Jr, J. H. (1976). "A theory of optimal capital structure". The Bell Journal of Economics, 7(1), 33–54.

Shyam-Sunder, L., & Myers, S. C. (1999). "Testing static tradeoff against pecking order models of capital structure". Journal of Financial Economics, 51(2), 219–244.

Tarı, R. (2015). "*Ekonometri*"(11. b.). Kocaeli, Türkiye: Umuttepe Yayınları.

Titman, S., & Wessels, R. (1988). "The determinants of capital structure choice". The Journal of Finance, 43(1), 1–19.

İhsan Erdem Kayral

15 Investigation of Weak Form Market Efficiency of EU Country Stock Markets in the Crisis Period

Highlights: The aim of this study is to analyze the efficiency of 28 EU member countries' stock exchanges in a precrisis, postcrisis, and after-crisis period country based and group based including the 2008 Global Financial Crisis and the EU Debt Crisis period in weak form. For this purpose, the data of these 28 countries are divided into four groups as pre-crisis period (2004–2007), crisis period when 2008 Global Financial Crisis and EU Debt Crisis period are effective together (2008–2010), EU Debt Crisis Period when the debt crisis is effective (2011–2014), and postcrisis period (2015–2018). It is concluded that stock markets are effective in weak form in all analysis periods according to the results of ADF and PP unit root tests, and country, 3, 7, 5, and 6 stock markets are not effective in weak form respectively according to the results of KPSS unit root test. According to the panel data analysis of all stock markets, it is concluded that the EU stock markets are not effective in weak form as a group except for the precrisis period (2004–2007) due to the results of the Hadri panel unit root test. According to other panel unit root test results, it is determined that these stock markets are effective in weak form as a group.

Keywords: EU stock markets, EU Debt Crisis, Global Financial Crisis, weak form efficiency, panel unit root tests

Introduction

The European Union (EU) is an important political and economic community with six enlargements in the historical process and reaching 28 member states today. These enlargements took place in 1973, 1981, 1986, 1995, 2004, and 2007 (together, they are considered as the fifth enlargement) and 2013, respectively, and the EU has reached its present structure. A rapid increase occurred as a result of the fifth enlargement in 2004 covering 12 countries' enlargement in 2004 (Hungary, Poland, Czechia, Slovakia, Slovenia, Latvia, Lithuania, Estonia, Malta, and Cyprus) and 2007 (Romania and Bulgaria) and the boundaries of the union have expanded significantly. Negative effects that can be seen were limited by the fact that the enlargement was in the 2003–2007 period when the abundance of liquidity was observed in the global markets (Kivedal, 2013; Directorate for EU Affairs, 2019).

The period that started in the United States (USA) housing markets in 2007 and turned into a Global Financial Crisis in 2008 negatively affected the EU countries, which have a serious integration among their economies. Different studies have cited the importance of the USA in the system and the integration of many developed and developing countries into global markets due to the increasing liquidity in transforming the crisis that started in the US housing markets into a crisis affecting the global markets (Taylor, 2009; Aiginger, 2011; Lee, 2013).

Although affected by the 2008 Global Financial Crisis, the process in which countries such as Cyprus, Ireland, Spain, Italy and Portugal, and mainly Greece were dragged into the debt crisis as of 2009 was examined under a separate heading as the EU Debt Crisis in different academic studies. The reason for this situation is the continuing effects of the EU crisis until 2014, even after the effects of the 2008 Global Financial Crisis started to decrease towards the end of 2010 (Holinski et al., 2012; Lane, 2012; Allegret and Allegret-Sallenave, 2016).

In this chapter, an empirical study is used to investigate whether the stock exchanges, which are one of the most important indicators in the capital markets of the 28 EU member countries, are effective in the weak form in the sense of Fama before crisis period, in crisis period, and after crisis period (1970). Thus, it is aimed to determine whether there is lack of efficiency in stock markets in crisis periods comparatively.

The study in question, in the light of previous studies, is carried out by dividing into sub-periods including before crisis period between 2004 and 2007 when there is abundance of liquidity and the largest enlargement, the crisis between 2008 and 2010 (the period when the 2008 Global Financial Crisis and the EU Debt Crisis were seen together), EU Debt Crisis between the years 2011 and 2014, and after crisis period between 2015 and 2018. Accordingly, it is thought that carrying out the study including all EU member country stock markets and the last crisis periods may contribute to the literature.

The literature examining the effectiveness in weak form is included in the second part of the study, data and the evaluations related the method is discussed in the third part and findings obtained as a result of the analyzes are included in the fourth part of the study.

1 Literature Review

The first studies about the efficient market hypothesis were made by Fama (1965). Fama (1965) stated that all the information reaching the capital markets will be reflected to the stock market prices, and therefore investors will not be able to get any abnormal return levels.

Fama (1970) divided the market efficiency into three forms as weak, semi-strong, and strong form and has demonstrated that these forms are not seen in all the markets with his studies. Accordingly, markets in which it is not possible to gain abnormal return on the basis of past prices are defined as weak form efficiency, and markets in which it is not possible to gain abnormal returns using all public information in addition to past prices are defined as semi-strong form efficiency market. In addition to all these factors, markets where individual investors or groups have access to all available information about price formation are defined as effective in strong form.

In the literature, there are many studies on efficient markets hypothesis. While some of the studies examine whether stock markets are effective in different forms, some other studies investigate the presence of anomalies observed due to loss of effectiveness. Studies examining weak form market efficiency are focused while the literature is researched in this study since it is examined whether there is a weak form of market efficiency in the EU countries.

There are many studies in the literature examining market efficiency in weak form. While only unit root tests are used in some studies that examine market efficiency in weak form (Choudhry, 1994; Groenewold et al., 2003; Seddighi and Nian, 2004; Demireli et al., 2010; Özcan and Gültekin 2016), some studies (Sharma and Kennedy, 1977; Barnes, 1986; Dickinson and Muragu, 1994; Fawson et al., 1996; Karemera et al., 1999; Mookerjee and Yu, 1999; Chang and Ting, 2000; Abeysekera, 2001; Cheung and Coutts, 2001; Wheeler et al., 2002; Groenwold et al., 2003; Çevik and Yalçın, 2003; Lima and Tabak, 2004; Çevik, 2012; Al-Jafari, 2013; Dutta, 2015; Kayral and Alagöz, 2019), however, were carried out using more than one analysis method (methods such as unit root tests, variance ratio, runs test, and serial correlation).

Studies on weak form market efficiencies were carried out for different regional and country groups. Choudhry (1994) examined the weak form market efficiency in the stock markets of Canada, France, Germany, Japan, and Italy using Augmented Dickey-Fuller Test (ADF) and Kwiatkowski, Phillips, Schmidt, and Shin (KPSS) unit root tests; and Demireli et al. (2010) examined the weak form market efficiency in the SP500 index using ADP and PP unit root tests. Seiler and Rom (1997) similarly investigated market efficiency in the US stock markets. It has been determined that the stock markets examined in these studies are effective in weak form.

Vaidyanathan and Gali (1994), Chan et al. (1992), and Abrosimova et al. (2005) found the Bombay Stock Market, the stock markets traded in Asia, and the Russian stock market in weak form efficient, respectively. On the other hand, Kim and Shamsuddin (2008) did not find Indonesia, Malaysia, and the Philippines in weak form that are stock markets in Asia.

Using unit root tests only Özcan and Gültekin (2016) and using variance ratio tests in addition to unit root tests Kayral and Alagöz (2019) analyzed market efficiencies in weak form for G-20 countries, and according to the results it is found that some stock markets of the countries are not efficient in weak form.

For the reason that it has a special importance for the study, some studies focusing on EU countries are also given. Smith et al. (2002) found that random walks are not observed in the Greek, Hungarian, Polish, and Portuguese Stock Markets, and they stated that these stock markets are not effective in the weak form. Worthington and Higgs (2004) made an extensive analysis of the effectiveness of the 20 countries in the EU in their weak form and concluded that the effectiveness of the countries differs according to the analysis methods. Borges (2010) found in his study that the German and Spanish stock markets are effective in weak form and that there is no random walk in UK, Portugal, Greece, and France, in other words, there is a problem of effectiveness in weak form. Guidi et al. (2011) found that some of the Central European and Eastern European country stock markets are effective in weak form. Dutta (2015) concluded that England, France, and Italy Stock Markets are not effective in weak form, similar to Borges (2010) in 1998–2014 period. However, the German Stock Market is not found effective in the weak form in this study. Gupta (2017) examined the weak-form market activities in the stock market of 10 EU member countries by using serial correlations and concluded that the stock markets are not effective. In our study, the weak-form efficiencies of 28 EU country stock markets in precrisis, crisis (2008 Global Financial Crisis and EU Debt Crisis), and postcrisis period will be examined. Accordingly, it is thought that performing the study including all the EU member countries and the last crisis periods may contribute to the literature.

2 Data and Methodology

In this study, it is aimed to analyze and compare the market efficiencies of the stock market indices in the weak form for the EU which reached 28 countries with the participation of Croatia in 2013 before the crises in 2008–2014 period, during the crisis periods, and after the crisis. For this purpose, analyses were carried out in four groups: the precrisis period (2004–2007), the 2008 Global Financial Crisis and the crisis period in which the EU Debt Crisis was jointly influenced (2008–2010), the EU Debt Crisis Period (2011–2014) where the debt crisis was more effective, and after the crises (2015–2018).

Tab. 15.1: Stock markets

Austria - ATX	Estonia - OMXTGI	Italy - FTSE MIB	Portugal - PSI20
Belgium - BEL20	Finland - OMXHPI	Latvia - OMXRGI	Romania - BETI
Bulgaria - SOFIX	France - CAC40	Lithuania - OMXVGI	Slovakia - SAX
Croatia - CRBEX	Germany- DAX	Luxembourg - LUXX	Slovenia - SBITOP
Cyprus - CYMAIN	Greece - ATHEX	Malta - MSE	Spain - IBEX
Czech - PX	Hungary - BUX	Netherlands - AEX	Sweden - OMXS30
Denmark - OMXC20	Ireland - ISEQ	Poland - WIG20	UK - FT100

2.1 Data

In the study, stock market closing prices of 28 EU member countries for the period of 01.01.2004–12.31.2018 were used. The country stock markets in the study are shown in Tab. 15.1.

In the study, the stock returns are calculated using the data obtained from the Thomson Reuters database in Equation (1).

$$SR_{it} = \ln(P_{it}) - \ln(P_{it-1}) \quad (1)$$

In the equation, SR_{it} shows the return of stock i on transaction day t, while P_{it} shows the closing price of the same stock on day t. The returns in the analysis period for every country's stock markets are calculated by taking the natural logarithms and differences of the closing.

2.2 Methodology

Before the findings of the empirical study made within the scope of the study are given, explanations about the analysis method will be provided.

Augmented Dickey-Fuller Test:

In the study, unit root tests will be used in order to determine the efficiency for each stock market in weak form, and panel unit root tests (as groups) will be used in order to determine the effectiveness in weak form. Within the scope of the method, information about unit root tests will be given firstly.

Dickey and Fuller (1979) presented a test to determine the stationarity by examining the existence of unit root in time series. Test statistic is calculated as given in Equation (2):

$$Y_t = \rho Y_{t-1} + e_t, \quad t = 1, 2, \ldots \quad (2)$$

Starting from Equation (2), if null hypothesis which I defined as H_0:ρ=1 is not rejected, the model has a unit root. If the hypothesis is rejected, it is concluded that the variable is stationary (Dickey and Fuller, 1979, p.427).

Dickey and Fuller (1981) expanded the model to be multivariate and revealed with constant (without trend) model in Equation (3) and with constant and trend model in Equation (4) in their later works.

$$\Delta y_{ti} = \alpha_0 + \alpha_2 y_{t-1} + \sum_{i=1}^{k} \beta \Delta y_{t-i} + \varepsilon_i \tag{3}$$

$$\Delta y_{ti} = \alpha_0 + \alpha_1 trend + \alpha_2 y_{t-1} + \sum_{i=1}^{k} \beta \Delta y_{t-i} + \varepsilon_i \tag{4}$$

The null hypothesis is tested by comparing the test statistics obtained from these equations with the table value, and if the hypothesis in question cannot be rejected, it is concluded that there is a unit root, in other words, the stationary condition cannot be met. If the hypothesis is rejected, the stationary condition will be met (Dickey and Fuller, 1981, p. 1070–1071).

As a result of the analysis carried out using the returns obtained from the closing prices of the stock markets, it can be concluded that the stock market analyzed is effective in the weak form in terms of ADF unit root test if the models with trend satisfy the stationarity condition by rejecting the zero hypothesis at the I (0) level.

Phillips-Perron (PP) Test:

The other unit root test to test the efficiency of exchange markets in weak form separately is the Phillips-Perron (PP) test, which was developed from the study that Phillips and Perron (1988) added the potential breaks to the model with the assumption that the time of structural developments is known.

Although regression models similar to the ADF unit root test are used in the PP unit root test, by performing a non-parametric correction in the ADF test it is aimed to eliminate the autocorrelation problem, which is one of the important assumptions in econometrics. Similar to ADF test, test statistics of models with constant and with constant and trend are shown in Equation (5) and Equation (6).

$$\Delta y_{ti} = \mu + \rho_2 y_{t-1} + \sum_{i=1}^{l} \beta \Delta y_{t-i} + \varepsilon_i \tag{5}$$

$$\Delta y_{ti} = \mu + \rho_1 trend + \rho_2 y_{t-1} + \sum_{i=1}^{l} \beta \Delta y_{t-i} + \varepsilon_i \quad (6)$$

The PP test is interpreted similar to the ADF test, and if the hypothesis that the series contains unit root is rejected at I (0) level, it is concluded that the stock market is effective in weak form.

Kwiatkowski, Phillips, Schmidt, and Shin Test:

KPSS test, introduced by Kwiatkowski et al. (1992), is the last unit root test to examine the effectiveness of country exchange markets individually in weak form. KPSS statistics are obtained from the error terms of regressions applied using external variables in time series. KPSS test statistics are shown in Equation (7) and Equation (8):

$$y_t = \beta' D_t + \mu_t + u_t \quad (7)$$

$$\mu_t = \mu_{t-1} + \varepsilon_t,\ \varepsilon_t \sim WN\left(0, \sigma_\varepsilon^2\right) \quad (8)$$

The variable D_t in Equation (7) is a variable that takes place according to the structure of the models with constant and with constant and trend. Unlike ADF and PP tests, the KPSS test examines the null hypothesis that the variable is stationary. In terms of our study, the stock markets of the country where the hypothesis is not rejected will be evaluated that the market is efficient in weak form.

Levin, Lin, Chu Panel Unit Root Test:

Within the scope of the study, in addition to evaluating the market efficiencies of all exchanges in weak form separately in the analysis period, the market efficiency of the EU member countries' stock markets are also examined as a group. In this way, it is aimed to evaluate the stock markets of EU countries, which highly act together with the global markets and are affected of the shocks in member countries at different levels in groups before, during, and after the crisis.

The first test used in these evaluations is Levin, Lin, Chu (LLC) (2002) panel unit root test. In the LLC test, an ADF-derived model in Equation (9) is used:

$$\Delta y_{it} = \alpha y_{it-1} + \sum_{j=1}^{p_i} \beta_{ij} \Delta y_{it-j} + X_{it}' \delta + \varepsilon_{it} \quad (9)$$

In the LLC panel unit root test obtained from the Kernel calculation, the coefficient of α is examined to be 0 and if the null hypothesis asserting the existence of the common unit root is rejected, it can be concluded that the series is stationary. If the stationarity condition is provided within the scope of the study, it will be concluded that EU stock markets are effective in a weak form as a group for the examined sub-period.

Im, Pesaran, Shin Panel Unit Root Test:

The second test to examine the market efficiency of the EU stock markets in weak form as a group is the Im, Pesaran, Shin (IPS) panel unit root test by Im et al. (2003). Similar to the LLC panel unit root test, the IPS panel unit root test uses an ADF derivative model; and if the null hypothesis is rejected, where the α_i coefficient is equal to 0, the stationarity condition (no common unit root) is satisfied. If this result is obtained, it is concluded that there is market efficiency in weak form. The IPC panel unit root test allows heterogeneity among horizontal sections unlike LLC.

Breitung Panel Unit Root Test:

The third test to investigate the effectiveness of all stock markets in weak form as a group is presented by Breitung (2000). The null hypothesis of the test statistics is similar to LLC and IPC tests and the stationary condition, and therefore the market efficiency in weak form is provided in case null hypothesis is rejected. The main difference of Breitung panel unit root test from LLC test is that kernel calculation is not used in obtaining test statistics.

Hadri Panel Unit Root Test:

Within the scope of the study, the last panel unit root test to be applied is presented by Hadri (2000). Hadri panel unit root test is different from other panel unit root tests and is obtained by using error terms similar to KPSS unit root test. Similar to the KPSS unit root test, this test statistic tests the null hypothesis that the unit root does not exist in the panel, in other words, the panel is stationary.

3 Results

In this part, firstly the results of ADF, PP, and KPSS unit root tests applied on the market efficiency in weak form on stock market based are shown in Tab. 15.2. The results for three different tests are given for the analysis periods divided into four sub-periods.

Results of the model with trend is given for all the tests. Similar results are found for the models without trend. If the null hypothesis supporting the existence of the unit root is rejected using the ADF and PP tests, which are traditionally used in stationary analysis, it is concluded that the returns of the country stock markets are stationary. In this case, it can be stated that the relevant stock market is effective in weak form. Within the scope of our study, both tests are

Tab. 15.2: Unit root tests (ADF, PP, and KPSS)

Stock Markets Tests	Periods			
	2004–2007	**2008–2010**	**2011–2014**	**2015–2018**
ATX				
ADF Test	-31.0041*	-25.5672*	-27.5458*	-30.1094*
PP Test	-31.0156*	-25.5138*	-27.3067*	-30.1444*
KPSS Test	0.0300	0.0953	0.1171	0.1765**
BEL20				
ADF Test	-32.0691*	-26.9542*	-30.7653*	-29.9290*
PP Test	-32.0693*	-26.9464*	-31.4709*	-30.1306*
KPSS Test	0.0520	0.1081	0.0729	0.0881
SOFIX				
ADF Test	-24.5667*	-15.4540*	-29.1807*	-31.1942*
PP Test	-25.1061*	-24.8888*	-29.2974*	-31.2310*
KPSS Test	0.0461	0.1531**	0.2189*	0.4738*
CRBEX				
ADF Test	-28.2423*	-14.2346*	-28.9811*	-12.2266*
PP Test	-28.9257*	-24.7854*	-28.9643*	-29.3644*
KPSS Test	0.0556	0.1051	0.0871	0.0915
CYMAIN				
ADF Test	-26.6146*	-24.7025*	-27.9352*	-31.7844*
PP Test	-26.6050*	-24.6682*	-27.8073*	-31.9110*
KPSS Test	0.1236***	0.1254***	0.0581	0.0339
PX				
ADF Test	-29.5994*	-21.2302*	-29.5376*	-31.2699*
PP Test	-29.5446*	-25.7682*	-29.5428*	-29.1652*
KPSS Test	0.0337	0.0877	0.0578	0.1321***
OMXC20				
ADF Test	-32.4856*	-26.3179*	-27.1750*	-30.9436*
PP Test	-32.5814*	-26.3423*	-27.1258*	-31.0006*
KPSS Test	0.0476	0.0733	0.0703	0.0415
OMXTGI				
ADF Test	-27.3988*	-23.8370*	-29.5905*	-32.9470*
PP Test	-27.7784*	-24.8115*	-29.5345*	-32.9326*
KPSS Test	0.1036	0.1019	0.1864**	0.0921
OMXHPI				
ADF Test	-30.4542*	-28.0033*	-29.0230*	-30.9160*

(continued on next page)

Tab. 15.2: Continued

Stock Markets Tests	Periods			
	2004–2007	**2008–2010**	**2011–2014**	**2015–2018**
PP Test	-30.4541*	-28.1561*	-29.0473*	-31.0743*
KPSS Test	0.0503	0.0710	0.0793	0.0745
CAC40				
ADF Test	-34.6401*	-29.8911*	-31.9098*	-31.2499*
PP Test	-34.8470*	-30.4046*	-32.2474*	-31.4936*
KPSS Test	0.0546	0.0710	0.0719	0.0833
DAX				
ADF Test	-32.9740*	-28.4721*	-29.4997*	-31.8443*
PP Test	-33.0027*	-28.5058*	-29.4204*	-31.8639*
KPSS Test	0.0439	0.0483	0.0535	0.0886
ATHEX				
ADF Test	-30.1440*	-25.0002*	-29.2045*	-29.0883*
PP Test	-30.1417*	-24.9103*	-29.1470*	-29.4108*
KPSS Test	0.0381	0.0877	0.1717**	0.1246***
BUX				
ADF Test	-29.2557*	-21.1798*	-30.9668*	-31.5873*
PP Test	-29.2317*	-25.5110*	-30.9667*	-31.8909*
KPSS Test	0.0256	0.1375***	0.0445	0.0402
ISEQ				
ADF Test	-29.8877*	-27.0761*	-29.9800*	-17.8169*
PP Test	-29.9078*	-27.2360*	-30.0910*	-29.8377*
KPSS Test	0.1135	0.1094	0.0637	0.0874
FTSE MIB				
ADF Test	-34.5443*	-27.5028*	-32.4007*	-34.2525*
PP Test	-34.5077*	-27.5203*	-32.5417*	-34.4594*
KPSS Test	0.0641	0.0766	0.0714	0.1101
OMXRGI				
ADF Test	-30.8022*	-28.3236*	-37.0891*	-38.4825*
PP Test	-31.0163*	-28.3255*	-37.0891*	-37.8698*
KPSS Test	0.0723	0.1287***	0.0767	0.0802
OMXVGI				
ADF Test	-26.1066*	-23.1486*	-30.2105*	-16.2699*
PP Test	-26.3821*	-23.9119*	-30.2105*	-32.0546*
KPSS Test	0.1034	0.1268***	0.1095	0.2307*

Tab. 15.2: Continued

Stock Markets Tests	Periods			
	2004–2007	2008–2010	2011–2014	2015–2018
LUXX				
ADF Test	-32.3931*	-27.9005*	-30.1651*	-31.8264*
PP Test	-32.3960*	-27.9124*	-30.1295*	-32.0764*
KPSS Test	0.0676	0.1314***	0.0666	0.1041
MSE				
ADF Test	-22.5029*	-21.4851*	-32.9233*	-32.1011*
PP Test	-22.0289*	-21.5453*	-32.9047*	-32.0900*
KPSS Test	0.1057	0.0908	0.2027**	0.1551**
AEX				
ADF Test	-32.6432*	-28.8119*	-30.4354*	-30.6664*
PP Test	-32.6432*	-28.8753*	-30.4061*	-30.6991*
KPSS Test	0.0625	0.0877	0.0465	0.0755
WIG20				
ADF Test	-30.8712*	-20.9702*	-30.0028*	-30.0227*
PP Test	-30.8722*	-26.3615*	-29.9836*	-30.2081*
KPSS Test	0.0455	0.0793	0.0433	0.1268***
PSI20				
ADF Test	-30.2699*	-27.1685*	-28.2713*	-17.6787*
PP Test	-30.2699*	-27.1619*	-28.1451*	-28.3319*
KPSS Test	0.0725	0.1173	0.1716**	0.1011
BETI				
ADF Test	-26.9907*	-26.0834*	-27.6374*	-18.7205*
PP Test	-26.8428*	-26.0565*	-27.6028*	-30.7475*
KPSS Test	0.0342	0.1878**	0.0497	0.1028
SAX				
ADF Test	-19.3097*	-27.5396*	-27.6884*	-35.3654*
PP Test	-30.2860*	-27.5543*	-44.4913*	-36.4923*
KPSS Test	0.1686**	0.0699	0.0537	0.0317
SBITOP				
ADF Test	-15.8810*	-22.5440*	-30.0540*	-32.4953*
PP Test	-15.4083*	-22.1368*	-30.0296*	-32.5014*
KPSS Test	0.1293***	0.1181	0.0673	0.1062
IBEX				
ADF Test	-32.7837*	-28.1556*	-29.4704*	-31.3841*
PP Test	-32.7867*	-28.5199*	-29.4372*	-31.7101*
KPSS Test	0.0474	0.0946	0.0588	0.0900

(continued on next page)

Tab. 15.2: Continued

Stock Markets Tests	Periods			
	2004–2007	**2008–2010**	**2011–2014**	**2015–2018**
OMXS30				
ADF Test	-34.7488*	-28.5306*	-32.5004*	-33.9181*
PP Test	-34.7488*	-29.3697*	-33.1670*	-34.0325*
KPSS Test	0.0699	0.0897	0.0545	0.0751
FT100				
ADF Test	-35.7079*	-13.1588*	-30.7286*	-31.6495*
PP Test	-35.9747*	-29.7004*	-30.8049*	-31.7941*
KPSS Test	0.0410	0.0640	0.0468	0.0861

* ➔ H_0 is rejected at 1 % significance level
** ➔ H_0 is rejected at 5 % significance level
*** ➔ H_0 is rejected at 10 % significance level

significant at 1 % significance level, and the stock markets are found to be effective in weak form in all precrisis (2004–2007), crisis (2008–2010 and 2011–2014), and postcrisis periods (2015–2018). The result has been reached.

In the study, the efficiencies of stock markets in weak form in the examined periods are investigated by using KPSS unit root test in addition to traditional tests. These test statistics are obtained from the residuals and evaluated based on the null hypothesis that the analyzed stock market is stationary. Accordingly, if the hypothesis cannot be rejected, it is concluded that the stock market is effective in weak form.

According to the KPSS unit root test results, stock markets that are not effective in weak form were found in all sub-periods. According to this, in liquidity abundance period of 2004–2007, the returns belonging to SAX (Slovakia) and SBITOP (Slovenia) Indices at 5 % significance level and the returns belonging to CYMAIN (Cyprus) Index are not effective in weak form at 10 % significance level. All of these countries, whose stock markets are not effective, joined the EU in the fifth enlargement in 2004. The returns of the 25 member countries of the Union fulfilled the condition of efficiency in a weak form in this period.

Returns from SOFIX (Bulgaria) and BETI (Romania) Indices are not effective in weak form at 5 % significance level and the stock returns of CYMAIN (Cyprus), BUX (Hungary), OMXRGI (Latvia), OMXVGI (Lithuania), and LUXX (Luxembourg) Indices are not effective in weak form at 10 % significance level in 2008–2010, when the effects of the 2008 Global Financial Crisis and the EU Debt Crisis were observed together.

The inefficiency of the markets in weak form in seven stock markets during the crisis periods seen on a global scale and at the EU level was evaluated as a result that conforms to our expectations. In addition to this, it was observed that the countries which were determined to be ineffective in the weak form (except Luxembourg) were included in the Union during the fifth enlargement in 2004 and 2007. Independent of the effects of the crisis, these results support the analysis period before the crisis.

The exchange markets of Greece and Portugal (ATHEX and PSI20 Indices), which were the countries that experienced the debt crisis most severely in the period of 2011–2014, failed to provide the market efficiency condition in 5 % significance level, in the periods when the effects of the 2008 Global Financial Crisis decreased and in the meantime the effects of the EU Debt Crisis continued. In addition to these countries, Greece's neighbor Bulgaria (SOFIX) Index was found to be not effective in weak from at 1 % significance level and MSE (Malta) and OMXTGI (Estonia) Indices were not effective in weak form at 5 % significance level, similar to ATHEX and PSI20 Indices. Stock markets that are found not to be effective in weak form are the countries that joined the Union in the fifth enlargement, similar to previous analysis periods except for Greece and Portugal, which have experienced the debt crisis seriously.

It was determined that OMXVGI (Lithuania) Index was not effective in weak form at 1 % significance level between 2015 and 2018, which is the last analysis period examined in the study. ATX (Austria) and MSE (Malta) Indices in the period could not provide the condition of effectiveness in weak form at 5 % significance level; and PX (Czechia), ATHEX (Greece), and WIG20 (Poland) Indices could not provide the condition of effectiveness in weak form at 10 % significance level. It was observed that all countries except Austria and Greece were the countries that joined the Union in the period of the fifth enlargement.

Within the scope of the study, whether all EU member countries meet the condition of efficiency as a group were checked using LLC, IPS, Breitung, and Hadri Panel unit root tests; and the test results for all analysis periods are shown in Tab. 15.3.

In the LLC, IPC, and Breitung panel unit root tests shown in Table 15.3, the stationary condition is met if the null hypothesis supporting the existence of the common unit root is rejected. In this case, the condition of effectiveness in weak form is met in the panel data including all stock markets. In the study, the hypothesis that there is a common unit root in the stock returns of all countries in the EU at 1 % significance level in the four sub-periods in which three tests are applied is rejected, and it is concluded that the EU stock markets are effective in a weak form as a group.

Tab. 15.3: Panel unit root tests (LLC, IPC, Breitung, and Hadri)

Tests	Periods			
	2004–2007	2008–2010	2011–2014	2015–2018
LLC	-281.781* (0.000)	-256.396* (0.000)	-303.045* (0.000)	-299.226* (0.000)
IPC	-189.358* (0.000)	-165.781* (0.000)	-193.770* (0.000)	-200.948* (0.000)
Breitung	-72.482* (0.000)	-97.033* (0.000)	-107.881* (0.000)	-57.133* (0.000)
Hadri Z-Stat	0.421 (0.337)	5.455* (0.000)	2.444* (0.007)	4.391* (0.000)

* → H_0 is rejected at 1 % significance level. Probability values are in parenthesis. Results are given for models with trend. Similar results are found for models without trend.

In the context of our study, in addition to traditional methods in panel unit root tests, weak form market efficiency for all the stock markets for the analyzed sub-periods were tested by Hadri panel unit root tests. The Hadri panel unit root test is derived from the error terms, similar to the KPSS unit root test, and the test statistic is interpreted based on the null hypothesis that the examined variable is stationary.

According to the results of the Hadri panel unit root test, panel data consisting of the stock market returns of EU countries is found significance at 1 % significance level as group in 2008–2010, 2011–2014, and 2015–2018 periods according to the KPSS unit root test statistics in 2008–2010, 2011–2014, and 2015–2018 periods respectively. According to this test statistics, in the 2004–2007 period when liquidity abundance is experienced (not effective in only three countries according to KPSS unit root test), the efficiency condition in weak form was provided as a group.

According to the obtained results, it was observed that a general loss of efficiency was observed in the EU stock exchanges during the crisis periods and that this efficiency loss still continues although the crisis period is ten years behind within the scope of the empirical study.

Conclusion

The economic crises seen in the historical process have affected the macroeconomic indicators and financial markets of the countries. The 2008 Global Financial Crisis, which is the most important crisis seen recently, has affected a wide geography because of the higher number of countries integrated into global markets compared to previous crises. The EU countries, important actors in the global markets, were also affected by the crisis, and the Debt Crisis following the 2008 Global Financial Crisis deepened the effects of the crisis. Notable fluctuations are seen in stock markets, which are among the most important indicators of capital markets during the crisis. These fluctuations are closely followed by investors in order to obtain abnormal returns. Fama (1965) states that the fluctuations in the efficient markets will be reflected in the prices and that abnormal returns cannot be obtained. Fama (1970), who grouped the efficient markets in his later study, stated that in a weak form efficient market, it would not be possible to obtain abnormal returns based on past price movements.

Contrary to this definition, in different studies, stock markets of the developed and developing countries' economies were not effective in weak form in accordance with the expectations of the investors.

Within the scope of our study, the existence of weak market efficiency in the precrisis, crisis, and postcrisis period in 28 EU member states stock markets was examined with an empirical study. In the study, analyses were carried out by dividing into four sub-periods: precrisis period of 2004–2007, crisis periods of 2008–2010 and 2011–2014, and postcrisis period of 2015–2018. The market efficiency of each stock market in weak form was analyzed using traditional unit root tests ADF and PP tests and KPSS unit root tests. According to ADF and PP unit root test results, all stock exchanges were found to be effective in weak form in all analyzed periods. According to the results of ADF and PP unit root tests, all stock markets were found to be effective in weak form in all analyzed periods. However, according to the results of KPSS unit root test, the calculation and evaluation method differed from these tests, and stock exchange indices of Slovakia, Slovenia, and Cyprus between 2004 and 2007; Bulgaria, Romania, Cyprus, Hungary, Latvia, Lithuania, and Luxembourg between 2008 and 2010; Bulgaria, Greece, Portugal, Malta, and Estonia between 2011 and 2014; and Lithuania, Austria, Malta, Czechia, Greece, and Poland between the years 2015 and 2018 did not meet the conditions of efficiency in weak form.

It was observed that the loss of effectiveness in weak form started especially after the 2008 Global Financial Crisis and EU Debt Crisis periods. According to the findings, it was concluded that the loss of effectiveness in the EU countries during the crisis continued also in the postcrisis period. Therefore, it is interpreted that the effects of the crisis continue, and the crises affect the market efficiencies negatively. In addition, it was observed that most of the stock markets that are not effective in the weak form were the countries that joined the EU within the scope of the fifth enlargement. In the results obtained, it was found to be an important factor that the countries that joined the Union later have less developed markets than the old members.

Especially, the extent to which the number of countries that are not effective in the weak form during the crisis periods and the postcrisis period affected EU country stock markets as a group was also evaluated within the scope of our study. For this purpose, the market efficiencies in weak form were investigated for all sub-periods with LLC, IPC, Breitung, and Hadri panel unit root tests conducted by considering the EU exchanges as a group. According to the results, no results were found that were contrary to market effectiveness in a weak form similar to ADF and PP tests in the traditional tests such as LLC and IPC (similarly in Breitung). However, according to the results of the Hadri panel unit root test, the calculation method of which is similar to the KPSS unit root test, it was found that the EU country stock markets (under the effects of the inefficient stock markets) cannot meet the market efficiency condition as a group.

In the light of the results obtained, it is thought that it would be beneficial to determine the policies considering the dynamics of the whole union, due to the potential of less member countries having fluctuations to affect the whole union even in the EU, which has 28 member countries. It is evaluated that it will be important to monitor the stock markets, which are affected by the developments in the global markets and the Union, both on a country basis and group basis with further academic studies to be made in the upcoming period.

References

Abeysekera, S.P. (2001) "Efficient Markets Hypothesis and the Emerging Capital Market in Sri Lanka: Evidence from the Colombo Stock Exchange – A Note", Journal of Business Finance and Accounting, 28(1): 249–261.

Abrosimova, N., Dissanaike, G., and Linowski, D. (2005) "Testing the Weak-Form Efficiency of the Russian Stock Market", European Finance Association Conference.

Aiginger, vK. (2011) "A Comparison of the Current Crisis with the Great Depression as Regards Their Depth and the Policy Responses", Austrian Institute of Economic Research WIFO, 1–54.

Al-Jafari, M.K. (2013) "Testing the Weak-Form Efficiency of Bahrain Securities Market", International Research Journal of Finance and Economics, 72: 14–25.

Allegret, J.P., and Allegret-Sallenave, A. (2016) "Intra-European Union Imbalances and Cyclical Position: Does Monetary Policy Matter?" Economic Imbalances and Institutional Changes to the Euro and the European Union, Emerald, 1–25.

Barnes, P. (1986) "Thin Trading and Stock Market Efficiency: The Case of the Kuala Lumpur Stock Exchange", Journal of Business Finance and Accounting, 13(4): 609–617.

Borges, M. (2010) "Efficient Market Hypothesis in European Stock Markets", European Journal of Finance, 16(7): 711–726.

Breitung, J. (2000) "The Local Power of Some Unit Root Tests for Panel Data", Advances in Econometrics, 15: 161–177.

Chan, C.K., Gup, B.E., and Pan, M.S. (1992) "An Empirical Analysis of Stock Prices in Major Asian Markets and the U.S.", Financial Review, 27(2): 289–307.

Chang, K.P., and Ting, K.S. (2000) "A Variance Ratio Test of the Random Walk Hypothesis for Taiwan's Stock Market", Applied Financial Economics, 10: 525–532.

Cheung, K.C., and Coutts, J.A. (2001) "A Note on Weak Form Market Efficiency in Security Prices: Evidence from the Hong Kong Stock Exchange", Applied Economics Letters, 8: 407–410.

Choudhry, T. (1994) "Stochastic Trends and Stock Prices: An International Inquiry", Applied Financial Economics, 4(6): 383–390.

Çevik, E.İ. (2012) "İstanbul Menkul Kıymetler Borsası'nda Etkin Piyasa Hipotezinin Uzun Hafıza Modelleri İle Analizi: Sektörel Bazda Bir İnceleme", Journal of Yaşar University, 26(7): 4437–4454.

Çevik, F., and Yalçın, Y. (2003) "İstanbul Menkul Kıymetler Borsası (İMKB) İçin Zayıf Etkinlik Sınaması: Stokastik Birim Kök ve Kalman Filtre Yaklaşımı", Gazi Üniversitesi İİBF Dergisi, 1: 21–36.

Demireli, E., Akkaya, G.C., and İbaş, E. (2010) "Finansal Piyasa Etkinliği: S&P500 Üzerine Bir Uygulama", Cumhuriyet Üniversitesi İktisadi ve İdari Bilimler Dergisi, 11: 53–67.

Dickey D.A., and Fuller, W.A. (1979) "Distribution of the Estimators for Autoregressive Time Series with a Unit Root", Journal of the American Statistical Association, 74: 427–431.

Dickey D.A., and Fuller, W.A. (1981) "Likelihood Ratio Statistics for Autoregressive Time Series with a Unit Root", Econometrica: Journal of the Econometric Society, 49(4): 1057–1072.

Dickinson, J.P., and Muragu, K. (1994) "Market Efficiency in Developing Countries: A Case Study of the Nairobi Stock Exchange", Journal of Business Finance and Accounting, 21(1): 133–150.

Directorate for EU Affairs. (2019) https://ab.gov.tr/109_en.html.

Dutta, A. (2015) "Efficiency Tests in European Equity Markets", Proceedings of the First European Academic Research Conference on Global Business, Economics, Finance and Social Sciences (EAR15 Italy Conference), 1–6.

Fama, E. (1965) "Random Walks in Stock Market Prices", Financial Analysts' Journal, 21(5): 55–59.

Fama, E. (1970) "Efficient Capital Markets: A Review of Theory and Empirical Work", Journal of Finance, 25: 283–306.

Fawson, C., Glover, T.F., Fang, W., and Chang, T. (1996) "The Weak-Form Efficiency of the Taiwan Share Market", Applied Economics Letters, 3: 663–667.

Gupta, R. (2017) "Validity of Weak Form Efficiency in European Stock Market", Journal of Business & Financial Affairs, 6(1): 1–10.

Guidi, F., Gupta, R., and Maheshwari, R. (2011) "Weak-form Market Efficiency and Calendar Anomalies for Eastern Europe Equity Markets", Journal of Emerging Market Finance, 10(3): 337–389.

Groenewold, N., Sam, T., and Wu, Y. (2003). "The Efficiency of the Chinese Stock Market and the Role of the Banks", Journal of Asian Economics, 14: 593–609.

Hadri, K. (2000) "Testing for Stationarity in Heterogeneous Panel Data", Econometric Journal, 3: 148–161.

Holinski, N., Kool, C.J., and Muysken, J. (2012) "Persistent Macroeconomic Imbalances in the Euro Area: Causes and Consequences", Federal Reserve Bank St. Louis Review, 94: 1–20.

Im, K.S., Pesaran, M.H., and Shin, Y. (2003), "Testing for Unit Roots in Heterogeneous Panels", Journal of Econometrics, 115: 53–74.

Karemera, D., Ojah, K., and Cole, J.A. (1999) "Random Walks and Market Efficiency Tests: Evidence from Emerging Equity Markets", Review of Quantitative Finance and Accounting, 13: 171–188.

Kayral, İ.E., and Alagöz, H.M. (2019) "Testing the Weak-Form Efficiency of the G-20 (in Turkish)", The World of Accounting Science, 21(3): 809–828.

Kim, J.H., and Shamsuddin, A. (2008) "Are Asian Stock Markets Efficient? Evidence from New Multiple Variance Ratio Tests", Journal of Empirical Finance, 15(3): 518–532.

Kivedal, B.K. (2013) "Testing for Rational Bubbles in the US Housing Market", Journal of Macroeconomics, 38: 369–381.

Kwiatkowski, D., Phillips, P.C.B., Shin, Y., and Schmidt, P. (1992) "Testing the Null Hypothesis of Stationarity Against the Alternative of a Unit Root", Journal of Econometrics, 54: 159–178.

Lane, P.R. (2012) "The European Sovereign Debt Crisis", Journal of Economic Perspectives, 26: 49–67.

Lee, Y.H. (2013) "Global and Regional Range-Based Volatility Spillover Effects", Emerging Markets Review, 14: 1–10.

Levin, A., Lin, C., and Chu, S.C. (2002) "Unit Root Tests in Panel Data: Asymptotic and Finite-Sample Properties", Journal of Econometrics, 108: 1–24.

Lima, E.J., and Tabak, B.M. (2004) "Tests of the Random Walk Hypothesis for Equity Markets: Evidence from China, Hong Kong and Singapore", Applied Economics Letters, 11: 255–258.

Mookerjee, R., and Yu, O. (1999) "An Empirical Analysis of the Equity Markets in China", Review of Financial Economics, 8: 41–60.

Özcan, B., and Gültekin, E. (2016) "Etkin Piyasalar Hipotezi G-20 Ülkeleri için Geçerli mi? Yeni Bir Yaklaşım", ICEB 2016 Konferans Bildirileri.

Phillips, P.C.B., and Perron, P. (1988) "Testing for Unit Roots in Time Series Regression", Biometrika, 75(2): 335–346.

Seddighi, H.R., and Nian, W. (2004) "The Chinese Stock Exchange Market: Operations and Efficiency", Applied Financial Economics, 14: 785–797.

Seiler, M.J., and Rom, W. (1997) "A Historical Analysis of Market Efficiency: Do Historical Returns Follow a Random Walk?", Journal of Financial and Strategic Decisions, 10(2): 49–57.

Sharma, J.L., and Kennedy, R.E. (1977) "A Comparative Analysis of Stock Price Behaviour on the Bombay, London, and New York Stock Exchanges", Journal of Financial and Quantitative Analysis, 12(3): 391–413.

Smith, G., Jefferis, K., and Ryoo, H. (2002) "African Stock Markets: Multiple Variance Ratio Tests of Random Walks", Applied Financial Economics, 12(4): 475–484.

Taylor, J.B. (2009) "The Financial Crisis and the Policy Responses: An Empirical Analysis of What Went Wrong", NBER Working Paper, No.14631.

Vaidyanathan, R., and Gali, K.K. (1994) "Efficiency of the Indian Capital Market", Indian Journal of Finance and Research, 5(2): 35–38.

Wheeler, F.P., Bill, N., Tadeusz, K., and Steve, R.L. (2002) "The Efficiency of the Warsaw Stock Exchange: The First few Years 1991–1996", The Poznan University of Economics Review, 2(2): 37–56.

Worthington, A., and Higgs, H. (2004) "Random Walks and Market Efficiency in European Equity Markets", Global Journal of Finance and Economics, 1(1): 59–78.

Metin Özdemir and Ali İlhan

16 Towards an Activist Monetary Policy: Challenges for Central Banking in the Post-Crisis Era

Highlights: The history of monetary thought has been an area of debates within the spectrum of the minimalism-activism in terms of both the objectives and tools of monetary policy. The minimalist approach based on the single objective-single instrument framework before the global financial crisis had a set of objectives and tools suitable for the traditional business cycle. A key lesson from the crisis is that price stability is not enough to achieve financial stability. The crucial role of financial stability to ensure sound macroeconomic performance has led to the enlargement of the aims and tools of monetary policy to respond to the financial cycle. The crisis represents a new phase of transitions between minimalist and activist monetary policy approaches regarding the historical evolution of monetary regimes. Nevertheless, the new monetary regime has not emerged yet. This chapter aims to reveal the new challenges posed by the activist approach for central banking in the post-crisis era.

Keywords: Central banking, monetary policy, global financial crisis, business cycle, financial cycle, history of monetary thought

Introduction

Before the global financial crisis, there was a consensus between economists and policy makers about what could and could not be done with monetary policy (Goodfriend, 2007). As put forth in Woodford's (2003) magnum opus study, independent central banks implement inflation targeting to achieve price stability adopted as their ultimate and primary goal. The short-term interest rate chosen as the main policy instrument is adjusted for the inflation target under the Taylor (1993) rule. Financial stability is regarded as a natural outcome of price stability. Also, the central bank has no responsibility for financial stability, except for its traditional role as a lender of last resort (LoLR) (Goodhart, 2000).

The pre-crisis policy orthodoxy, which marked the period of Great Moderation where price stability and growth was experienced at the global level, ended with the global financial crisis. With the Great Recession following the crisis, the limits of the conventional monetary policy carried out with inflation targeting and price stability have emerged on two main issues. The first is that macroeconomic instability arises if conventional monetary policy neglects financial stability. The second issue in relation to the first is that the policy response of developed countries' central banks in the form of aggressive interest rate cuts against the crisis is inadequate to recover from the recession. The presence of the zero lower bound (ZLB) for policy interest rates has narrowed the maneuvering room of monetary policy to fight the recession (Borio, 2011).

In its conventional form, the optimal monetary policy is defined as the policy that stabilizes inflation around the inflation target and output around the potential output level (Clarida et al. 1999). The macroeconomic stability that the optimal policy desires to achieve is considered through the traditional business cycle. The effects of financial variables on potential output and real interest rate have led to the realization of the importance of financial stability on growth. Therefore, the optimal policy for achieving macroeconomic stability must take into account the financial cycle beyond the business cycle. The existence of the financial cycle means that there are aims and tools for monetary policy other than price stability and policy interest rate in the post-crisis period (Blanchard, 2012).

The emergence of new aim and tool sets within the framework of unconventional monetary policies is not an unprecedented phenomenon for central banks. The roots of this experience emerging after the crisis extend to the debates of minimalism-activism spectrum in the history of monetary thought about both the objectives and tools of monetary policy (Costabile and Epstein, 2017). The two approaches manifested itself in differences between Keynesian and Monetarists concerning the choice of monetary policy between full employment and price stability in the period of Bretton Woods (1944–1971)[1] (Friedman, 1968; Modigliani, 1977). Before the global financial crisis, the minimalist approach was preferred by the central banks of developed and developing countries, depending on the developments in macroeconomics, the experiences from policy implementations, and changes in the institutional structure of the monetary policy. Today, the minimalist approach is strongly shaken by the fact that unconventional monetary policies are becoming a norm.

This chapter argues the new challenges for central banking posed by activist monetary policy approach that have revived after the crisis. Following the

1 In the period of Bretton Woods, the adoption of monetary policy as part of aggregate demand management by Keynesians allowed central banks to pursue an activist policy that supports economic development in developing countries (Epstein, 2007). The policy implications of the minimalist-activist debate for developing countries after the global financial crisis have not been reviewed due to the limits of the chapter.

introduction, the first part of the study addresses the ineffectiveness of the single objective-single instrument policy framework towards the financial cycle. The main features of minimalist and activist monetary policy approaches are compared in the second part. The chapter ends with the conclusion part.

1 From Business Cycle to Financial Cycle

Although it is emphasized that cyclical movements of the financial variables have significant effects on real economic activities before the global financial crisis (Borio and Lowe, 2002), business cycle is explained through macroeconomic models that did not take into account these variables (Ma and Zhang, 2016). However, the global financial crisis demonstrated that macro-financial imbalances can accumulate even with low inflation and stable growth rates. After the role of financial factors in business cycle fluctuations is understood, the financial cycle is considered separately.

There is no single agreed definition of the financial cycle. According to Borio (2014), financial cycle is the case in which self-reinforcing interactions between the perceptions about risk and value, attitudes towards risk, and financial constraints cause expansions ending with contractions. For instance, a rapid expansion in the loan volume increases the value of the assets to be used as collateral in credit transactions. Increases in collateral values accelerate credit growth and at the same time intensify the negative effects of the reversing process after a certain point (Borio et al. 2018).

It is very difficult to make an accurate specification that determines the dynamics of the financial cycle and its relationship with the business cycle. According to the business cycle analysis, GDP can be used as a proxy variable that reflects economic activities, while there are no single indicators that can be used to analyze the financial cycle (Omar, 2018). In defining the financial cycle, variables such as credit growth, ratio of credit to GDP, stock and housing prices are used (Galati et al. 2016; Filardo et al. 2019).

There is a close relationship between the peaks of the financial cycle and financial crises. Drehmann et al. (2012) analyzed financial cycles in seven developed countries for the period of 1960–2011. They indicated that all financial crises that occurred due to domestic shocks realized when the financial cycle is at the peak level or near the peak. As the market participants tend to take excessive risks during the expansion period of the financial cycle and underestimate the risks, asset prices and credit growth may differ from the macroeconomic fundamentals. When this happens, even a minor deterioration in the financial

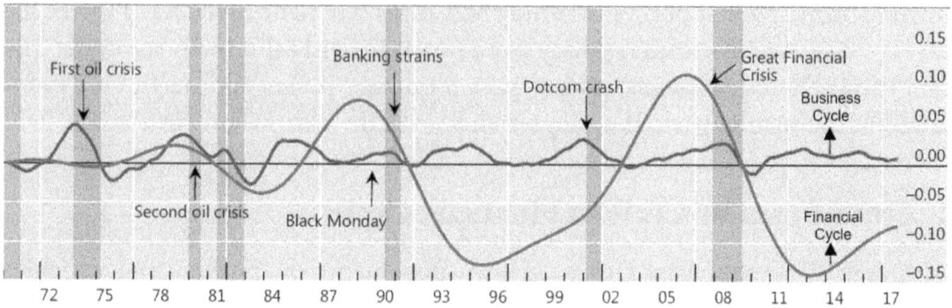

Fig. 16.1: Financial cycle and business cycle in the USA
Source: Drehmann et al. 2012: 19; Filardo et al. 2019: 3

system or the real economy has the potential to reverse risk perception and bust asset price bubbles (Deutsche Bundesbank, 2019).

Financial cycles differ significantly from business cycles in terms of duration and magnitudes (Fig. 16.1). The duration of a standard business cycle changes from 6 quarters to 8 years on average. However, the financial cycle may last between 10 and 20 years depending on the structural features of the economy. On the other hand, the expansion and contraction magnitudes of financial cycles are relatively larger than business cycles (Drehmann et al. 2012; Oman, 2019).

The durations and magnitudes of financial cycles have increased dramatically since the second half of the 1980s. Changes in policy regimes have an important role in this case. The first of these changes is financial liberalization that strengthens procyclicality. Second, price stability oriented monetary policy strategies became a standard. With the adoption of price stability as a primary goal, financial variables had not included in the reaction functions of central banks. The last one is positive supply-side developments that fueled the expansion of the financial cycle. Credit growth and increase in asset prices have narrowed the central banks' policy space for monetary tightening in the face of the global integration of goods markets and technological developments pushing inflation down (Borio et al. 2018).

Financial cycles taking longer than business cycles and larger width weaken synchronization between the two cycles (Fig. 16.2). Breaking the link between cycles confronts central banks with policy dilemmas, which try to achieve price stability and financial stability simultaneously with traditional policy instruments.

The synchronization of two cycles that are in balance in the area between A and B is disrupted between B and C. In this area, the business cycle shrinks

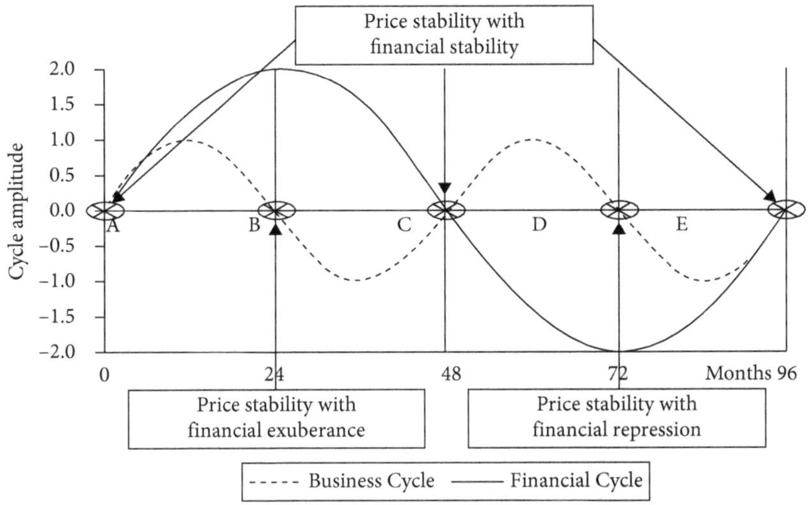

Fig. 16.2: Synchronization of financial cycle and business cycle
Source: Fahr and Fell, 2017: 335

due to the output level below its potential, while the financial cycle is above its natural level. Using the interest rate as the single tool to combat the financial imbalances brought by the expanding financial cycle makes the conflict inevitable between policy goals. Accordingly, the increased interest rate in order to smooth the financial cycle may bring inflation below the targeted level while further removing the output level from its potential. In the area between C and D, where the business cycle is above and the financial cycle is below the natural level, interest rates lowered to support the shrinking financial cycle may fuel the rise in inflation. Therefore, it is not possible for central banks to control both cycles with traditional tool sets when the accordance between cycles is lost (Fahr and Fell, 2017).

In order to manage the financial cycle, the macroprudential policy framework is used. Macroprudential policy, which is primarily a policy area where prudential tools are implemented, has been developed to increase the resistance of the overall financial system and to reduce procyclicality (FSB, IMF and BIS, 2011). As such, the inadequacy of the single objective-single instrument framework designed in accordance with traditional business cycle has led to the adoption of financial stability as a new area of responsibility for monetary policy. In this respect, the aim of financial stability and the integration

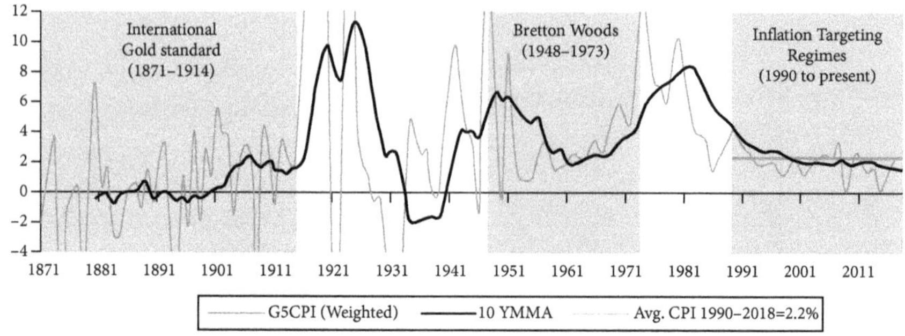

Fig. 16.3: Monetary regimes and inflation in developed countries (USA, UK, Japan, France, and Germany)

Source: Barclays Equity Gilt Study, 2019 (Jorda-Schularick-Taylor Macrohistory Database, Haver Analytics, Barclays Research)

of macroprudential policy to orthodox inflation targeting reflect the post-crisis consensus (Smets, 2014).

2 Minimalist versus Activist Monetary Policy

Central banks aim to achieve nominal stability in all monetary regimes whether based on metals such as gold or silver or fiat currency regimes. The historical evolution of monetary regimes indicates that the transition to a new regime eventuated in response to changes in the macroeconomic policy environment and crisis (Bordo and Siklos, 2017). The Bretton Woods system was introduced after the Gold Standard and the Great Depression. Monetary targeting and inflation targeting are the results of policy responses and experiences gained during the Great Inflation (1950–1982) period (Fig. 16.3).

Similarly, the preference for the new monetary regime after the Great Recession will be determined by the boundaries of the pre-crisis monetary regime and the post-crisis relationships between monetary policy and growth. Contrary to the previous monetary regime changes, the global economy displays a growth that has not yet been secured despite low inflation (see Fig. 16.3) and low interest rates. In this respect, the secular stagnation hypothesis (Summers, 2013) explains the growth performance of developed countries due to the structural inadequacy of aggregate demand. The weak growth performance observed after the crisis attributed to low natural interest rates. Therefore, the ZLB problem reflects a secular phenomenon, not a temporary one (Krugman, 2014). According to the financial cycle drag view raised by Bank for International Settlements (BIS), the low potential growth is due to the failure to control the growth fueled by the financial cycle in the pre-crisis period (Borio, 2017). For this reason, not only inflation but also signals of financial imbalances shaped by credit growth, asset prices, and risk-taking behaviors are important for central banks (Juselius et al. 2017).

The debates on the Great Recession have pioneered a new challenge for monetary policy, which includes goals such as financial stability and growth as well as price stability. In a broad sense, the minimalist approach imposes responsibility on monetary policy in a framework based on single objective-single instrument. Different policy objectives are not considered, as the market mechanism is treated to provide effectiveness in resource allocation. The activist approach, on the other hand, mandates monetary policy for multiple goals such as growth, employment, and even more equality (Costabile and Epstein, 2017). In the period of Bretton Woods, where the business cycle is decisive for macroeconomic stability, the activist approach dominates within the framework of Keynesian policies. In the Great Moderation period, the minimalist approach was marked by the aim of price stability and inflation targeting based on the use of the short-term interest rate. After the global financial crisis, where the financial cycle has become more important for macroeconomic stability, the renaissance of the activist monetary policy is on the agenda.

Table 16.1 presents the differences between minimalist and activist monetary policy. Both approaches have different features in terms of implementation of monetary policy besides goals and areas of responsibility.

Monetary policy can be classified by two core implementation styles, based on price variable (interest rate) and central bank balance sheet (Borio and Disyatat, 2010). According to the minimalist approach, whose roots go back to Thornton (1802) and Wicksell (1898), monetary policy is implemented by announcing the desired level of short-term interest rate and acting as a signal. The second core includes liquidity operations. Liquidity operations correspond to the management of bank reserves for the policy stance determined by the short-term interest rate to be effective and aims to ensure the market interest rate close to the policy interest rate. The minimalist approach limits liquidity policy to open market operations with short-term public bonds (Goodfriend and King, 1988). The central bank has no role other than eliminating the shocks that hit the monetary base through the banking system as the LoLR. Also, it does not have a role in compensating temporary problems arising from reserve distribution among banks in money markets (Bagehot, 1873; Tucker, 2018). In terms of implementation of monetary policy, central banks contribute to the sound functioning of

Tab. 16.1: Minimalist versus activist monetary policy

	Minimalist	**Activist**
Mandate	Price Stability	Financial Stability, Growth (and Employment)
Monetary Regime	Inflation Targeting	(?)
Instrument	Interest Rate	Unconventional (Balance Sheet Policy: Quantitative Easing and Credit Easing)
Liquidity Policy	Banking System LoLR Open Market Operations Reserve Requirements	Banking System and Financial Markets LoLR and MMLR
Market Neutrality	Yes	No
Prudential Policy	Micro	Macro
Fiscal Policy	Policy Coordination	Beyond Policy Coordination (Close Relationship)
Rules vs. discretion	Rule based	Discretionary
Central Bank Independence	High	Low

Source: Authors

the financial markets, and do not display distorting actions in the formation of prices and behave neutral (Bindseill, 2014).

The activist approach adopts unconventional monetary policies based on the balance sheet. J.M. Keynes deals with unconventional monetary policies in his works that reject the quantity theory. In the concluding chapters of his *Treatise on Money* (1930), Keynes emphasized that when the liquidity preferences of economic agents are uncertain and the liquidity trap is concerned, open market operations can be used more intensely to go beyond the limits of orthodox monetary policy. Apart from the monetary policy stance of the short-term interest rate, balance sheet policies have two forms: quantitative easing (QE) and credit easing[2] (Lenza et al. 2010). In addition to the banking system, the balance sheet policies pursued by central banks for the financial markets have extended

2 QE corresponds to any policy decision aimed at changing the size and (or) composition of the central bank balance sheet. Under QE, the central bank targets the liability part of its balance sheet by changing the reserve level of the financial institutions. Credit easing targets the asset side of the central bank balance sheet and aims to improve the liquidity conditions of the financial sector (Lombardi et al. 2018).

their traditional LoLR function to the market maker of last resort (MMLR) (Buiter, 2008).

Credits play a critical role in terms of financial stability and growth and the scope of monetary policy. Firstly, the inadequacy of microprudential policies to limit the financial instability risks caused by credit growth necessitated the development of the macroprudential policy framework. Second, the growing importance of the financial cycle for growth dynamics has led central banks to play an active role in credit markets through balance sheet policies.[3] The balance sheet policies implemented through the purchase of public or private sector assets by the central bank include the purchase of risky assets owned by the market participants (banks and financial institutions or nonfinancial sector) that are bad enough to pose systemic risk and cleaning their balance sheets and providing liquidity to the system. Thus, it will be possible to decrease the long-term interest rates while increasing the pressure on the prices of nonfinancial assets. The decrease in long-term interest rates will positively affect growth by stimulating credit demand and private sector investments, while creating inflationary pressures.

The activist approach enables the central bank to manage its balance sheet with full authority at the maximalist level (Tucker, 2018). However, contrary to the fact that the minimalist approach is completely neutral towards the private sector, the central bank is not neutral as a result of balance sheet policies that involve risks associated with different firms and households. The central bank's activities in the credit market have certain political economy implications, which are still subject to ongoing debates in terms of fiscal policy.

Within the framework of the minimalist approach, the need for coordination of monetary and fiscal policy is manifested by the existence of two authorities with separate goals and priorities. Therefore, there might be some conflicts between monetary and financial authorities. The coordination of both policies means that the monetary and financial authorities cooperate mutually by choosing the appropriate policy combination to achieve their own goals together (Missale et al. 2002). Considering the activist approach, the central bank is not neutral against the markets. This corresponds to the disappearance of conventional distinctions between monetary and fiscal policy to achieve macroeconomic

3 It is noteworthy that the indirect role of central banks in the credit mechanism in the post-crisis period differs from the role they played in the Bretton Woods. During the period of Bretton Woods, central banks used loans for direct resource allocation by means such as subsidized interest rates and credit ceilings (Epstein, 2007).

stability. If the central bank only accepts public bonds, the structure of the government's consolidated liabilities is replaced by monetary liabilities that substitute the long-term debt obligations. If the central bank buys the private sector bonds, the government's consolidated balance sheet expands and the portfolio of assets changes and the risks to which it is exposed are affected. The central bank becomes a kind of consolidated budget manager in which the governments are held responsible for the profits or seigniorage losses due to balance sheet policies. As such, the QE and credit easing policies pursued to support aggregate demand mean that the central bank acts like a fiscal authority (Tucker, 2018).

While the minimalist-activist debate evolves mainly around the goals of monetary policy, the debate about the instruments of monetary policy is argued through the rule versus discretion. In the Bretton Woods period, supporters of the minimalist and activist approach shared a common attitude around the aim of managing business cycle fluctuations by the central banks. However, while the minimalist approach on instruments advocates achieving the common goals through rules, the activist approach proposes to follow the fine-tuning policy over a broader set of instruments. Nevertheless, the tools vary significantly depending on the adopted objectives in the relevant historical period (Costabile and Epstein, 2017). Hence, the minimalist-activist debate revived after the global financial crisis is proper for this case.

Conclusion

The global financial crisis represents a new phase of the previous transitions between minimalist and activist monetary policy approaches in terms of the historical evolution of monetary regimes. Following the crisis, activist monetary policies started to rise again due to the unconventional policies based on the central bank balance sheet. It is remarkable that monetary policy has become considerably experimental with balance sheet instruments and its sophistication has increased. As B. Bernanke (2014) stated "... the problem with QE is it works in practice, but it doesn't work in theory." In addition to the structural differences in the financial systems and the disruptions in the functioning of the markets, the experiences and judgments of the central banks were dominant in policy implementation (Cecioni et al. 2011).

The new role that activist policies put on the central banks through the credit markets eroded the central bank independence (Goodfriend, 2012). According to the minimalist approach, central bank independence has a pivotal role in maintaining price stability and credibility of monetary policy (Cukierman, 1992). In respect to the activist approach, the central bank's close relationship with the fiscal authority through the balance sheet policies deepens the problem of democratic deficit, which is already at the core of central bank independence. The central bank's role as the balance sheet manager of the government makes it necessary to limit its activities. This is about making a choice as to whether economic policy will be carried out by the elected policy makers or appointed technocrats and what they will control (Tucker, 2018). Moreover, there are significant allocation and income effects of balance sheet policies. The distributive role of monetary policy should not be neglected due to the different effects of monetary policy on various sectors and social groups (Epstein, 2007).

Although the boundaries of inflation targeting prevailing before the crisis are clearly understood, the new monetary regime has not become yet. The aim of price stability maintains its priority under the minimalist approach. However, in response to the rise of activist policies, central banks needed to reconsider their existing policy frameworks. The Federal Reserve is still in the process of reviewing monetary policy instruments and its communication (Clarida, 2019). Similarly, the European Central Bank, which has reviewed its monetary policy seventeen years ago (ECB, 2003), is on the verge of a new review, especially on what price stability is (Hartwell, 2019).

References

Bagehot, W. (1873) Lombard Street: A Description of the Money Market. New York: Sribner, Armstrong. Edited with an Introduction by P.L. Bernstein, 1999, New York: John Wiley and Sons.

Barclays. (2019) Equity Gilt Study 2019.

Bernanke, B. S. (2014) A Conversation: The Fed Yesterday, Today and Tomorrow, the Brookings Institution, https://www.brookings.edu/wp-content/uploads/2014/01/20140116_bernanke_remarks_transcript.pdf

Bindseil, U. (2014) Monetary Policy Operations and the Financial System, UK: Oxford University Press.

Blanchard, O. (2012) "Monetary Policy in the Wake of the Crisis", In O. J. Blanchard, D. Romer, M. Spence and J. E. Stiglitz (Eds.), In the Wake of the Crisis: Leading Economists Reassess Economic Policy, London: The MIT Press, 7–13.

Bordo, M. D. and Siklos, P. L. (2017) "Central Banks: Evolution and Innovation in Historical Perspective", NBER Working Paper", 23847.

Borio, C. (2011) "Central Banking Post-Crisis: What Compass for Uncharted Waters?", BIS Working Paper, 353.

Borio, C. (2014) "The Financial Cycle and Macroeconomics: What Have We Learnt?", Journal of Banking and Finance, 45: 182–198.

Borio, C. (2017) "Secular Stagnation or Financial Cycle Drag?", Business Economics, 52(2): 87–98.

Borio, C. and Disyatat, P. (2010) "Unconventional Monetary Policies: An Appraisal", The Manchester School, 78(s1): 53–89.

Borio, C. and Lowe, P. (2002) "Asset Prices, Financial and Monetary Stability: Exploring the Nexus", BIS Working Paper, 114.

Borio, C., Drehmann, M. and Xia, D. (2018) "The Financial Cycle and Recession Risk", BIS Quarterly Review, December, 59–71.

Buiter, W.H. (2008) "Central banks and financial crises", Federal Reserve Bank of Kansas City Economic Policy Symposium, Jackson Hole, Wyoming, August 21–23, 495–633.

Cecioni, M., Ferrero, G. and Secchi, A. (2011) "Unconventional Monetary Policy in Theory and in Practice", Banca D'Italia Questioni di Economia e Finanza, 102.

Clarida, R.H. (2019) The Federal Reserve's Review of Its Monetary Policy Strategy, Tools, and Communication Practices (https://www.federalreserve.gov/newsevents/speech/clarida20190926a.htm).

Clarida, R., Gali, J., and Gertler, M. (1999) "The Science of Monetary Policy: A New Keynesian Perspective", Journal of Economic Literature, 37(4): 1661–1707.

Costabile, L. and Epstein, G. (2017) "An Activist Revival in Central Banking? Lessons from the History of Economic Thought and Central Bank Practice", The European Journal of the History of Economic Thought, 24(6): 1416–1439.

Cukierman, A. (1992) Central Bank Strategy, Credibility and Independence: Theory and Evidence, Cambridge: The MIT Press.

Deutsche Bundesbank. (2019) "Financial Cycles in the Euro Area", Deutsche Bundesbank Monthly Report, 51–74.

Drehmann, M., Borio, C. and Tsatsaronis, K. (2012) "Characterising the Financial Cycle: Don't Lose Sight of the Medium Term!", BIS Working Papers, 380.

ECB. (2003) Background Studies for the ECB's Evaluation of Its Monetary Policy Strategy, O. Issing (Ed.), Frankfurt: ECB.

Epstein, G. (2007) "Central Banks as Agents of Economic Development", In C.HA-Joon (Ed.), Institutional Change and Economic Development, Helsinki: United Nations University and Anthem Press, 95–114.

Fahr, S. and Fell, J. (2017) "Macroprudential Policy – Closing the Financial Stability Gap" Journal of Financial Regulation and Compliance, 25(4): 334–359.

Filardo, A., Lombardi, M. and Raczko, M. (2019) "Measuring Financial Cycle Time", Bank of England Staff Working Paper, 776.

Friedman, M. (1968) "The Role of Monetary Policy", The American Economic Review, 25(1): 1–17.

FSB, IMF and BIS (2011). "Macroprudential Policy Tools and Frameworks: Progress Report to G20".

Galati, G., Hindrayanto, I., Koopman, S. J. and Vlekke, M. (2016) "Measuring Financial Cycles with a Model-Based Filter: Empirical Evidence for the United States and the Euro Area." DNB Working Paper, 495.

Goodfriend, M. (2007) "How the World Achieved Consensus on Monetary Policy", Journal of Economic Perspectives, 21(4): 47–68.

Goodfriend, M. (2012) "Elusive Promise of Central Banking", Bank of Japan IMES Discussion Paper Series, E-09.

Goodfriend, M. and King, R. (1988) "Financial Deregulation, Monetary Policy, and Central Banking", Federal Reserve Bank of Richmond Economic Review, 74(3): 3–22.

Goodhart, C. (2000) "The Organisational Structure of Banking Supervision", Financial Stability Institute, Occasional Papers, 1.

Hartwell, C.A. (2019) The Urgent Need for a Review of the ECB's Monetary Policy Strategy: Towards an Institutional Review, Monetary Dialoque Papers, ECB.

Juselius, M., Borio, C., Disyatat, P. and Drehmann, M. (2017) "Monetary Policy, the Financial Cycle, and Ultra-Low Interest Rates", International Journal of Central Banking, 13(3): 55–89.

Keynes, J.M. (1930) A Treatise on Money, Vol.II: The Applied Theory of Money, London: Macmillan.

Krugman, P. (2014) "Four Observations on Secular Stagnation", In C. Teulings and R. Baldwin (Eds.), Secular Stagnation: Facts, Causes and Cures, CEPR, 61–68.

Lenza, M., Pill, H. and Reichlin, L. (2010), "Monetary Policy in Exceptional Times", Economic Policy, 25(62): 295–330.

Lombardi, D., Siklos, P. and St.Amand, S. (2018) "Survey of the International Evidence and Lessons Learned About Unconventional Monetary Policies: Is a 'New Normal' in Our Future?", Journal of Economic Surveys, 32(5): 1229–1256.

Ma, Y. and Zhang, J. (2016) "Financial Cycle, Business Cycle and Monetary Policy: Evidence from Four Major Economies", International Journal of Finance & Economics, 21: 502–527.

Missale, A., Giavazzi, F. and Benigno, P. (2002) "How Is the Debt Managed? Learning from Fiscal Stabilizations", Scandinavian Journal of Economics, 104(3): 443–469.

Modigliani, F. (1977) "The Monetarist Controversy, or Should We Forsake Stabilization Policies?", The American Economic Review, 67(2): 1–19.

Oman, W. (2019) "The Synchronization of Business Cycles and Financial Cycles in the Euro Area", International Journal of Central Banking, 15(1): 327–362.

Omar, C. (2018) "Financial Cycle and Conduct of Monetary Policy: The Amplifier/Divider Theory", MPRA Working Paper, 89155.

Smets, F. (2014) "Financial Stability and Monetary Policy: How Closely Interlinked?", International Journal of Central Banking, 10(2): 263–300.

Summers, L.H. (2013) Speech at the IMF's Fourteenth Annual Research Conference in Honour of Stanley Fischer (http://larrysummers.com/imf-fourteenth-annual-research-conference-in-honor-of-stanley-fischer).

Taylor, J.B. (1993) "Discretion versus Policy Rules in Practice", Carnegie-Rochester Conference Series on Public Policy, 39: 195–214.

Thornton, H. (1802), An Enquiry into the Nature and Effects of the Paper Credit of Great Britain London: Hatchard. Edited with an Introduction by F.A. von Hayek, 1939, London: Allen and Unwin.

Tucker, P. (2018) Unelected Power, The Quest for Legitimacy in Central Banking and the Regulatory State, USA: Princeton University Press.

Wicksell, K. (1898) Geldzins und Giiterpreise. Jena: Fischer, English translation: Interest and Prices: A Study of the Causes Regulating the Value of Money. Translated by R.F. Kahn, 1936, London: Macmillan.

Woodford, M. (2003) Interest and Prices: Foundations of a Theory of Monetary Policy, USA: Princeton University Press.

Section 3 Banking and Risk Management

İ. Ethem Güney, M. Selman Çolak, and M. Hasan Yılmaz

17 Assessing Credit Cycle Dynamics in the Turkish Banking Sector

Highlights: In this study, the main aim is to construct indicators for determining the episodes of excessive credit slowdown and expansion by utilizing time-series filtering methods such as Hodrick-Prescott filter, Butterworth filter, and Christiano-Fitzgerald filter for the time period between 2005 and 2018. This framework enables one to generate monitoring tools for not only total loans, but also for financial intermediation activities with different loan breakdowns regarding type, sector, and currency denomination. Moreover, industry-based dynamics of commercial loans are examined by using microlevel Credit Registry data set over the period 2007–2018. It is found that credit allocation activities in Turkey have been faced with sizeable downturns in Global Financial Crisis, post-2011 period characterized with macroprudential policy actions, and more recent period coincided with the downturn in economic growth. Overall, utilization of multiple filters has yielded robust quantitative tools to assess credit cycle dynamics in Turkey.

Keywords: Credit cycle, filtering, time-series analysis, financial intermediation

Introduction

Since credit plays a critical role in macroeconomic dynamics of economies going through financial deepening, its growth over time is one of the main indicators monitored by macroprudential supervisors. If there is an excessive contraction in credits, investment growth declines, consumption drops, and economic activity is hampered, which, in the end, leads to a higher level of unemployment. While the flow of credits contributes to aggregate demand and overall growth in the economy, its excessive level leads to financial instability and macroeconomic imbalances such as asset price bubbles, deterioration in current account balance, and inflation outlook. The crisis literature also manifests that one of the significant determinants of banking crises is private sector credit booms (Demirguç-Kunt and Detragiache, 1998; Borio and Lowe, 2002; Kaminsky and Reinhart, 1999; and Eichengreen and Arteta, 2002). Particularly, after the crisis, excessive rise in credit usage in emerging markets (partly due to monetary easing in advanced countries and accompanying surge in capital flows as well as the improvements in foreign funding conditions) necessitated emerging market authorities to take macroprudential measures against credit booms.

Economists and policymakers have given particular attention to the determination of extreme credit periods (Buncic and Melecky, 2013; Kiss et al., 2006; Jakubik and Moinescu, 2015; Drehmann et al., 2010). This is critical in the sense that most policymakers are concerned with achieving credit growth rate which is consistent with the overall macroeconomic fundamentals. For example, for countries that are in early phase of financial development, higher credit growth rates might not be sufficient as financial deepening process fundamentally requires even higher loan growth. And similarly, for others which already had well-functioning financial markets, lower level of credit growth might be excessive.

As an early attempt to quantify credit gap developments in Turkey, Binici and Köksal (2012) identify the phases of excessive credit movements in the Turkish banking sector for the period covering December 2002–April 2012. Total credit extended in the sector is decomposed into cyclical parts by utilizing three different indicators including credit/GDP ratio, nominal credit, and real credit. Without resorting to statistical filters, Binici and Köksal (2012) employ 12-month moving average to isolate the deviations of amount of extended loans from the trend. Their results indicate that years like 2006, 2008, and 2011 are characterized by excessive credit movements. More recently, as an insightful study, Aydın and Yılmaz (2019) examine credit gap indicators for the Turkish banking sector. In contrast to previous works for Turkey, this study implements univariate time-series filtering technique to calculate the credit gap indicators. Given the drawbacks of Hodrick-Prescott (HP) filter, they highlight the advantages of Hamilton filter, in terms of being independent of smoothing parameter determination and the ability to allow volatile trend structure, in the analysis. Their results show the existence of excess credit growth in the postcrisis period.

Following the banking system restructuring efforts in the outbreak of 2001 currency crisis, Turkish economy has witnessed a considerably rapid credit growth till the global financial crisis (GFC) in 2008. After the crisis, loose monetary policies in most of the developed countries caused a surge in capital flows to Turkish banking system, and these flows are canalized to credits extended to private sector. Having seen a rebound in credit allocation after the crisis, the authorities enacted several macroprudential measures which curbed the credit growth in 2012. In the following period, credit growth dynamics in the Turkish economy can be defined as volatile due to concerns over a possible drain in international flows after the Tapering era. After these concerns have been somewhat relieved, a period of moderate credit growth had taken place till 2017. In 2017, rapid credit growth has reoccurred and has exogenously been driven by government-induced program designed to support real sector firms in the form of collateral incentives. This ample credit environment ended in the third quarter of 2018 given the turbulence observed in Turkish financial markets in the same period.

The principal aim of this chapter is to produce measures for determining the periods of excessive growth or crunch in total loans and their breakdowns, for example, commercial/consumer as well as FX/TRY disaggregation via the application of econometric techniques. In other words, we are de-trending credit series from the long-run trend by using statistical filters and obtain credit cycle series. If the value of the cycle at a time point is larger/lower than a certain threshold, we claim there is a credit boom/crunch in that specific period.

The outline of the chapter is as follows. After the introduction, the second section is going to focus on the related literature. Following sections include methodological issues of filtering approaches which produce de-trended credit series as well as description of the utilized data. In the next part, empirical results related to credit cycle in the Turkish banking sector are provided and discussed. Lastly, concluding remarks are made.

1 Literature Review

Basel Committee on Banking Supervision introduced a statistical approach to define excessive credit growth (BCBS, 2010). Following the proposition exhibited by Basel III regarding the capital buffers, there arises plenty of studies to examine capital buffer as macroprudential policy framework. Drehman et al. (2010) propose some preliminary suggestions concerning countercyclical capital requirement process. As discussed by Dell'Ariccia et al. (2012), the excessive credit movements can be diminished by taking some macroprudential policy measures depending on the type of credit boom. Reigl and Uuskula (2019) present four additional metrics together with the Basel III framework to calculate excessive credit growth.

The important question of literature is which credit measures should be used in the calculation of credit cycle series. Calza et al. (2006), Eller et al. (2010), and IMF (2004)[1] use the level of real credit as an indicator for credit measure in their studies. While Elekdag and Wu (2011) use real credit growth, Utari et al. (2012) and Guo and Stepanyan (2011) prefer nominal credit growth rate in their boom-bust analyses. In fact, using the growth rate of credit level has some drawbacks,

1 Terrones, M., Mendoza E., Sutton Bennet (2004). Are Credit Booms in Emerging Markets a Concern? IMF World Economic Outlook, April 2004: Advancing Structural Reforms, 147–166.

specifically if the sample is small and the data includes structural breaks. If the initial level of credit is small, the growth rate in the subsequent period might seem abnormally high, even though credit measure is at fundamentally normal levels in the following period. This is the case particularly in post-recession periods. It also disregards the level of financial development in the economy.

In order to eliminate these problems from the use of growth rates, credit level is scaled by some macro-level aggregates. The most preferred indicator is the ratio of credit level to gross domestic product (GDP) (Gourinchas et. al., 2001; Cottarelli, Dell'Ariccia and Vladkova-Hollar, 2005; Barajas, Dell'arcia, Levchenko, 2007; Dell'arcia Igan, Leaven and Togg, 2016; Ottens, Lambregts and Poelhekke, 2005; Castro and Martins, 2018; Hosszú et al., 2015; Kocsis and Sallay, 2018). Moreover, Drehmann et al. (2010) claim that the credit to GDP ratio gives the accurate results among other credit indicators to depict credit cycle. Furthermore, Mendoza and Terrones (2008) create real credit per capita to find credit cycles deflating nominal credit per capita by consumer price index (CPI) while Arena et al. (2015) suggest the use of logarithm of real credit per capita.

For identifying credit boom and credit bust, there exist commonly used filtering methods to monitor the deviation of current level of several credit indicators from their trend. While Pazarbasioglu et al. (2005) use the rolling Hodrick-Prescott (HP) filter to define deviation of credit cycle from its long-run trend, Drehman et al. (2010) calculate credit to GDP gap by utilizing HP filtering method. Moreover, Elekdağ and Wu (2011) carry out HP filtering method to show the deviation of log real credit and the natural logarithm of real credit from its trend as well. Although HP filter method is often chosen in practice, it has some drawbacks. It is somewhat sensitive to smoothing parameter and it can be subject to end-point bias (Coşar et al., 2012). Given these issues, some works in the empirical literature choose to utilize other filtering techniques. Hosszú et al. (2015), for instance, implement variety of univariate filtering methods such as HP, Christiano-Fitzgerald (CF), and Beveridge-Nelson. They also complement their empirical approach with multivariate filtering methods such as multivariate HP filter in their studies to demonstrate credit cycle. Furthermore, Kocsis and Sallay (2018) as well calculate credit to GDP gap by using multivariate HP filter method in terms of corporate, household, and aggregate credits.

Another important point in filtering methodologies is the determination of threshold levels to categorize boom and bust periods from trend series. The general approach is to add a multiple of the standard deviation of the cycle to the trend and acquire the threshold for booms. The similar calculation is applied for thresholds for bust periods by deducting the multiple of standard deviation of the cycle. Mendoza and Terrones (2008) define credit booms as the periods when the gap of per capita real credit level from its trend exceeds the 1.75 times standard deviation of the gap. Elekdag and Wu (2011) identify the start of a credit boom when real credit growth exceeds a threshold of one times the cyclical standard deviation and defines booms when the threshold is 1.55 times the standard deviation[2]. Barajas et al. (2007) propose a threshold point to detect credit boom if bank credit to private sector to GDP ratio (BCPS ratio) deviates from its trend by more than 0,75 standard deviation. There are also some studies that identify thresholds as predefined and certain numbers or percentages. Gourinchas et al. (2001) use 2 % threshold for the credit-to-GDP gap as the limit for excessive credit level. In addition to 0.75 threshold point, Barajas et al. (2007) also identify rapid credit growth as credit boom when the BCPS ratio increases more than 10 %. The proposal by BIS (2010) suggests that if the cycle in credit-to-GDP ratio exceeds 2 %, this signals abnormally high credit level and capital buffers should be applied by regulatory authorities.

2 De-trending Methodology

In this subsection, filtering methods used for the extraction of credit cycle from its recursive long-run trend are reviewed. We choose to proceed with three different statistical filters, namely HP filter, CF filter, and Butterworth (BW) filter. Use of multiple univariate time-series filters is preferred to enhance the robustness of credit cycle calculation.

HP filter, developed by Hodrick and Prescott (1997), has been widely used as a method in macroeconomic analysis to isolate the smooth estimate of long-term trend, particularly with respect to business cycles. On the other hand, large number of empirical works use it to identify financial cycles over credit growth and asset prices[3].

Technically, two-sided HP filter is a frequency-pass filter taking the historic and future information on the time series into consideration. It assumes that a data series y_t can be separated into trend (τ_t) and cycle (c_t). In this context, HP

---

2 The motivation behind the use of threshold of 1.75 and 1.55 is the fact that assuming the cycle is normally distributed, there is a 5 % and 10 % probability that we observe extreme values, respectively.

3 Please see Harvey and Jaeger (1993), Kaiser and Maravall (1999), Canova (1998), and Inklaar and De Haan (2001) for the applications in the case of business cycle; and Borio (2014), Stremmel (2015), and Kollmann et al. (2011) for the applications in the case of financial cycle.

filter computes the smoothed trend variable τ_t of y_t through minimizing the variance of original series around trend variable, which is also subject to a penalty term that contains the second difference of τ_t. The difference between y_t and τ_t gives us the cyclical component termed as credit gap. By solving the following optimization of the loss function, HP filter can create de-trended series as an indicator of cyclical credit movements:

$$min_{\tau_1 \dots \tau_T} \sum_{t=1}^{T} (y_t - \tau_t)^2 + \lambda \sum_{t=2}^{T-1} ((\tau_{t+1} - \tau_t) - (\tau_t - \tau_{t-1}))^2 \quad (1)$$

where λ stands for smoothing parameter. This parameter represents the ratio of the observed volatility in cyclical component over the volatility embedded in second difference of the trend component. While it takes values in $[0, \infty]$ interval, values closer to 0 correspond to minimal cyclical movements in the series, values closer to infinity are associated with the linear trend[4]. Hodrick and Prescott (1997) recommend the value of 1600 as smoothing parameter for the quarterly dataset. Technical literature widely emphasizes the relationship between business cycle and credit cycle in terms of duration and the frequency to determine smoothing parameter. Ravn and Uhlig (2002) claim that the smoothing parameter can be adjusted accordingly by taking fourth power of frequency interval and multiply it with the basis lambda value of 1600[5]. In this manner, their calculation for the smoothing parameter is 129.600. While this is the mainstream approach in treating the monthly datasets, there are some other values proposed in the literature. For example Drehman et al. (2010) use the value of 400.000 for the smoothing parameter[6], since they assume credit cycle is at least four times longer than business cycle. They also utilize different smoothing parameters assuming the difference duration between business cycle and credit cycle. Consequently, the method of Ravn and Uhlig (2002) is employed for this study.

---

4 We use the value of 129600 in our estimations with monthly data.

5 For instance, we have monthly interval variable. Standard lambda value is 1600 for quarterly frequencies. In order to calculate the smoothing parameter for monthly datasets, we need to multiply 1600 with 3^4, since frequency interval in a quarter is three months.

6 If business cycle and credit cycle have the same length, smoothing parameter which is admitted standard lambda value is taken 1600. In order to adjust smoothing parameter in accordance with the ratio of credit cycle length to business cycles length, we multiply fourth power of the ratio by 1600.

Even though HP filter is a widely accepted methodology in credit cycle literature, it has some minor deficiencies. For instance, in the literature, there is no consensus on the optimal level of lambda as smoothing parameter. Moreover, the method is also remarkably sensitive to lambda that can be subject to end-point bias. Therefore, we reinforce our empirical methodology by employing other filtering tools. CF filter is used as a second tool in our study, which was introduced by Christiano and Fitzgerald (2003). Their work discusses optimal finite-sample approximations to the ideal band-pass filter and contains the description of a simple one-sided filter. In particular, they argue that their filtering methodology provides an improvement over traditional HP filter, especially toward the end of sample period.

Unlike HP filter, CF filter formulates the de-trending optimization problem in frequency domain. As discussed by Christiano and Fitzgerald (2003)[7], in the hypothetical situation in which we are equipped with infinitely long data series, an "ideal" band-pass filter can be applied to extract cyclical component generated by stochastic cycles at the specified periodicities in a perfect manner. However, in finite samples, it would not be possible to conduct perfect frequency filtering. As explained by Nilsson and Gyomai (2011), CF filter overcomes this problem by approximating the ideal infinite band-pass filter. Although it has the simplifying assumption that underlying data series follow a random walk process, such an assumption is deemed to be reasonable given the empirical fact that many time series can be well-described by "random walk plus drift." Furthermore, simulation evidence indicates that filter is performing well in the case that data-generating process is not exactly random walk, but it exhibits "nearly random walk" tendencies. CF filter seems to have further advantages such as being designed to function well, given larger classes of time series (compared to other band-pass filters such as the one outlined in Baxter and King (1999)), tackling the end-of-sample problem, and converging to optimal filter in the long run (Nilsson and Gyomai, 2011).

Technically, CF filter composes the cyclical component by creating a weighting scheme applied to original data series as described in Equation (2):

$$c_t = \sum_{j=-\infty}^{\infty} b_j y_{t-j} \tag{2}$$

7 In applying CF method, we need to assign a minimum period as lower band and maximum period as upper band. In this study, it is employed 18 for the lower band and 120 for the upper band for minimum and maximum periods, respectively.

where c_t, y_t, and b_j represent cycle, original data series, and weights, respectively. The weights in the ideal band-pass filter are determined by the following processes in which p_l and p_h stand for minimum and maximum periods of the stochastic cycles of interest, respectively:

$$b_j = \begin{cases} \pi^{-1}(\omega_h - \omega_l) & \text{if } j = 0 \\ (j\pi)^{-1}\{\sin(jw_h) - \sin(jw_l)\} & \text{otherwise} \end{cases} \tag{3}$$

where $\omega_l = 2\pi/p_l$ and $\omega_h = 2\pi/p_h$ represent the lower and higher cutoff frequencies.

As a last component of our de-trending methodology, Butterworth filter is chosen. This high-pass filter is also designed to disentangle cyclical component from trend component. One-sided version of it was introduced by Butterworth (1930) and is commonly employed in electrical engineering. The version of this filter as well as the computational procedure regarding econometric context is described in Pollock (2000). Its major difference from its closer counterparty, Baxter-King filter, is related to the de-trending properties. While Baxter-King filter depends on the de-trending properties of symmetric moving average filters whose coefficients add up to 0, Butterworth filter relies on de-trending properties influenced by filter's parameters itself.

Technically, this particular filter has two parameters which are the cut-off frequency and the filter order denoted by Pollock (2000) describes that the gain of the Butterworth high-pass filter can be expressed as follows:

$$\psi(\omega) = \left[1 + \left\{\frac{\tan\left(\frac{\omega_c}{2}\right)}{\tan\left(\frac{\omega}{2}\right)}\right\}^{2m}\right]^{-1} \tag{4}$$

In Equation (4), m is defined as the filter order, $\omega_c = 2\pi/p_h$ is the cut-off frequency, and p_h corresponds to maximum period.

The model in this procedure represents the data series to be filtered, y_t, in terms of zero mean, covariance stationary, as well as identically distributed shocks v_t and ε_t:

$$y_t = \frac{(1+L)^m}{(1-L)^m} v_t + \varepsilon_t \tag{5}$$

Within the framework of this model, Pollock (2000) demonstrates that the optimal estimate of the cyclical component is structured as in Equation (6):

$$c = \lambda Q(\Omega_L + \lambda\Omega_H)^{-1}Q\prime y \tag{6}$$

where $var\{Q\prime(y-c)\} = \sigma_v^2\Omega_L$ and $var\{Q\prime c\} = \sigma_\varepsilon^2\Omega_H$. In this context, Ω_L and Ω_H are symmetric Toeplitz matrices with 2m+1 nonzero diagonal bands. They generate functions $(1+z)^m(1+z^{-1})^m$ and $(1-z)^m(1-z^{-1})^m$, respectively.

The parameter λ can be defined as a function of maximum period of stochastic cycle that is being filtered out as well as the order of the filter:

$$\lambda = \{\tan(\pi/p_h)\}^{-2m} \tag{7}$$

The matrix $Q\prime$ in this expression is a function of the coefficients in the polynomial $(1-L)^d = 1 + \delta_1 L + \ldots + \delta_d L^d$. It can be further shown that $\Omega_H = Q\prime Q$ and $\Omega_L = |\Omega_H|$. Thus, the extraction of cyclical component is transformed to be:

$$c = \lambda Q\{|Q\prime Q| + \lambda(Q\prime Q)\}^{-1}Q\prime y \tag{8}$$

3 Data

The selected credit indicators from the literature for the cycle construction are "credit to GDP," "real credit growth," "credit per capita," and "logarithm of real credit." The ratio of total credit stock to GDP is calculated in nominal terms. On the top of this, real credit growth is utilized, which is measured by total credit in nominal terms divided by consumer price index. Moreover, credit per capita calculated as the ratio of nominal stock of credit to total population is also seen in the literature. Natural logarithm of real credit can also be counted among employed measures.

Besides these, we propose two new ones to identify excessive credit movements, as a robustness. First, we utilized "credit flow to GDP." Kara and Tiryaki (2013) benefit from historical credit grow paths of emerging economies to come up with benchmark proper credit growth rate. Their research proposes the ratio of change in credit stock to GDP measure and exhibit it for Turkey. With this calculation, stock credit data can be transformed into flow. Lastly, loan to deposit ratio is employed. Since "loan to deposit ratio" is one of the informative measures to demonstrate the capability of banking sector in terms of lending facility, it provides a new tool for analysis of excessive credit movements. It is calculated by adjusting both credit and deposit for exchange rate effects[8].

The aggregate credit data is derived from the Banking Regulation and Supervision Agency of Turkey (BRSA) on a monthly basis for the period 2005–2018. Population and GDP data are retrieved from TurkStat in annual and quarterly frequencies, respectively. Here, the population data is transformed into monthly basis by using linear interpolation. Moreover, GDP data is transformed into monthly basis via Fernandez (1981) method.

In addition to aggregate analysis, we also measure excessive credit movements on a sectoral basis by utilizing microlevel Credit Registry Data provided by Bank Association of Turkey. Credit Registry Data encompasses firm-level loan information including varied dimensions such as currency breakdown, maturity, and sector. All the commercial loans extended by domestic banks operating in Turkey as well as foreign banks operating through an intermediation of domestic banks are covered by this data set. Sample period for this data is chosen to cover January 2007–December 2018 interval, due to unavailability of earlier episodes.

As a first step, the firm-level data is aggregated on sectoral-level by utilizing "financing issue codes." These codes are structured with three-digit alphabetical characters. While first digit represents the main industry such as manufacturing, utilities, and construction, the second digit stands for the sections of industries. The aggregation is firstly done for two digits corresponding to sub-sectors and, in the second step, further aggregation brings us the results for 16 main industries. In order to not to distort credit indicators in the times of rapid depreciations, FX loans are adjusted for currency impact in this analysis[9]. In contrast to aggregate analysis, five different ratios for credit tendencies are considered for sectoral investigation excluding loan-to-deposit ratio.

4 Empirical Results

As mentioned above, three filtering methods are performed with six different derived credit indicators. By this means, 18 cycle series for each credit indicator are generated. Then, one standard deviation value of cyclical component of each credit indicator is assigned as a threshold value to define "excessive credit slowdown" and "excessive credit growth" episodes. If the value of credit cycle in a

8 The weight of currency basket for deposits is comprised of 60 % USD and 40 % EUR. The deposits are adjusted for exchange rate accordingly.

9 In adjusting for exchange rate effects, we use a currency basket comprising USD and EUR with 70 % and 30 % weights, respectively.

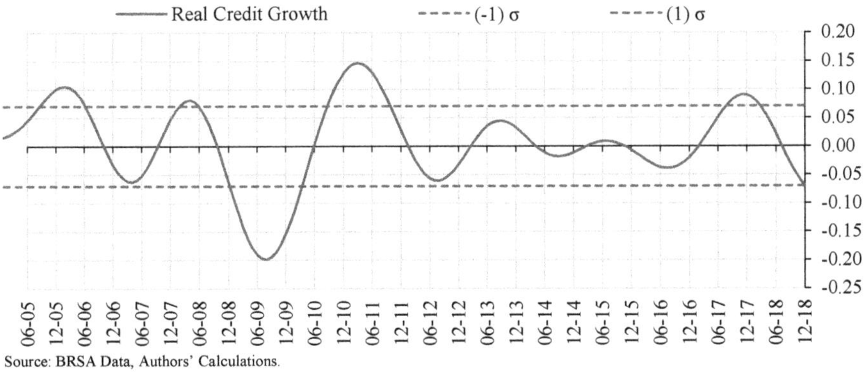

Graph 17.1: Cycle of real credit growth extracted with CF filtering technique

Source: BRSA data, authors' calculations

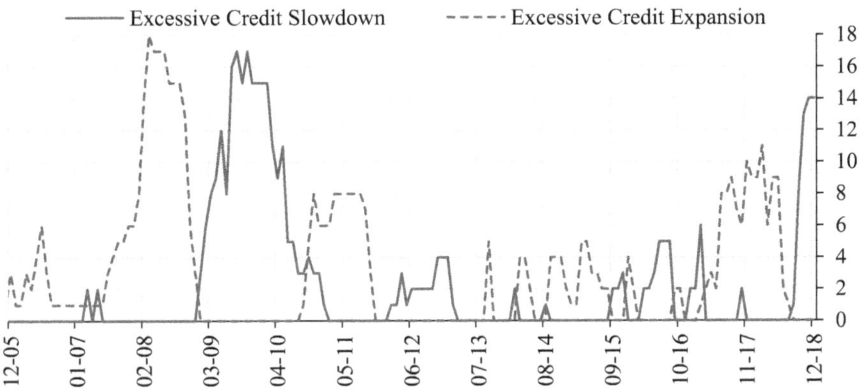

Graph 17.2: Collective aggregate credit results for episodes of excessive credit dynamics (number of indicators)

Source: BRSA data, authors' calculations

period is bigger than the "mean plus one-standard deviation" value of the whole cycle series, we conclude that this period is associated with excessive credit growth. Similarly, if the cycle value is below the "mean minus one-standard deviation," we claim there is credit crunch in that period.

Graph 17.1 represents one example of quantitative assessment and categorization of historical episodes for which real credit growth is preferred as a measure and CF filter is applied for de-trending. In Graph 17.2, the number of indicators out of 18 pointing out "excessive credit slowdown" and "excessive credit growth" for the total loans are shown through the examined time period.

In early period of the sample data (2005–2007), around 5 out of 18 indicators for aggregate credit exhibit excessive credit growth that is explained by the financial deepening process in Turkey, in general. In the precrisis time, the number of indicators demonstrating credit boom had reached above 15, which implies an over-heating in financial markets. With the outbreak of the GFC, the developments in the credit facility and domestic economic activity are deteriorated considerably; due to the fact that external liquidity dries, funding cost surges drastically and international trade declines severely.[10] Almost all 18 indicators propose a credit crunch for this era. After GFC, recovery in domestic economy becomes more visible. Unconventional monetary policies implemented by Federal Reserveand the European Central Bank (ECB) lead to excessive international liquidity that flows into emerging economies. The developments in credit facility and demand for bank loans bounced back, thanks to readily reaching to external financing and recovering economic activity. In this era, eight indicators point out the excessive credit growth which had sustained till the end of 2011.

Following early period of postcrisis, in addition to the ongoing economic normalization, Eurozone Debt Crisis erupted and developed economies conducted more aggressive easing policies. In 2012, macro-prudential economic policies are introduced to restrain the huge amount of current account deficit, the overheating Turkish economy, as well as unprecedented rise in credit allocation. Thus, the momentum of excessive credit growth is decelerated, and the majority of the indicators do not hint excessive credit growth in this era. From 2013 to 2016, we rather observed a stable credit market, and inconsiderable amount of indicators depicted a credit crunch, while a moderate number of indicators show a credit boom. From 2017 till the second half of 2018, the Credit Guarantee Fund system is introduced by government as a counter-cyclical policy tool to boost economic activity, and banking system extended nearly 300 billion TRY loans to nonfinancial corporations via this facility. Easy access to credit with the government-driven guarantees led to a sizeable growth in commercial loans and almost ten (out of 18) indicators captured the excessive credit expansion. Consequently, the turmoil observed in financial markets in August 2018 led to a

---

10 Even though the roots of the crisis rested on the collapse of Lehman in the second half of 2007, the direct impact of the crisis on Turkish economy and the most of the emerging markets was detected with a recession in the third quarter of 2008.

credit squeeze and 14 indicators demonstrate a credit crunch in the last quarter of 2018.

In order to define excessive credit movements with details, the analysis of the subcomponents of aggregate credit level is the next step in our comprehensive empirical approach (Graph 17.3). We further extended our analysis to the different types of loans including FX commercial loans, TRY commercial loans, and subtypes of consumer loans, housing, vehicle and general purpose loans. As mentioned before, 18 indicators are obtained for all six credit breakdowns. The calculated credit indicators of total commercial loans and consumer loans broadly capture the main historical excessive credit movements. When going into details, TRY-denominated commercial loans accelerate considerably after government introduces the Credit Guarantee Fund facilities to boost depressed economic activities in 2017. During that period, 16 indicators capture excessive credit growth. When we look at FX-denominated commercial loans, results differ a bit from TRY commercial credit movements due to the rising global liquidity and lower cost of borrowing from international capital markets after the GFC era. For this episode, 14 indicators for FX-denominated commercial loans exhibit excessive credit growth. Then, for the period containing to the end of 2017, FX loan activities experienced a great deal of volatility associated with the new regulation implemented to contain FX borrowing of firms irrelevant to macroeconomic fundamentals. The indicators show that credit crunch was observed in FX loans while TRY commercial and aggregate credit indicators exhibited an excessive credit growth in the same period.

By the end of third quarter of 2016, several incentives were introduced by government for housing sales to consumers, so nearly ten indicators demonstrate excessive credit expansion. Throughout the 2018, a sharp decrease in mortgage-financed house sales is observed together with an increase in the interest rate of mortgage loans. In this context, 12 indicators depict the excessive credit slowdown in housing loans. While the indicators of other loan types experience credit crunch remarkably during the crisis time, personal finance loans indicators pose negligibly credit crunch behavior. In Turkey, during the crisis period, households tend to use personal finance loans to fund their purchases given the loss of real income. Besides, by the end of fourth quarter of 2014, banks expand their credit facilities in accordance with the increasing demand of households to finance their consumption expenditures so that 18 indicators indicate the excessive credit movements.

In addition to aggregate analysis with multiple breakdowns, sectoral-level analysis provides an important tool to monitor credit dynamics, specifically for the production side of the economy. In line with the empirical methodology,

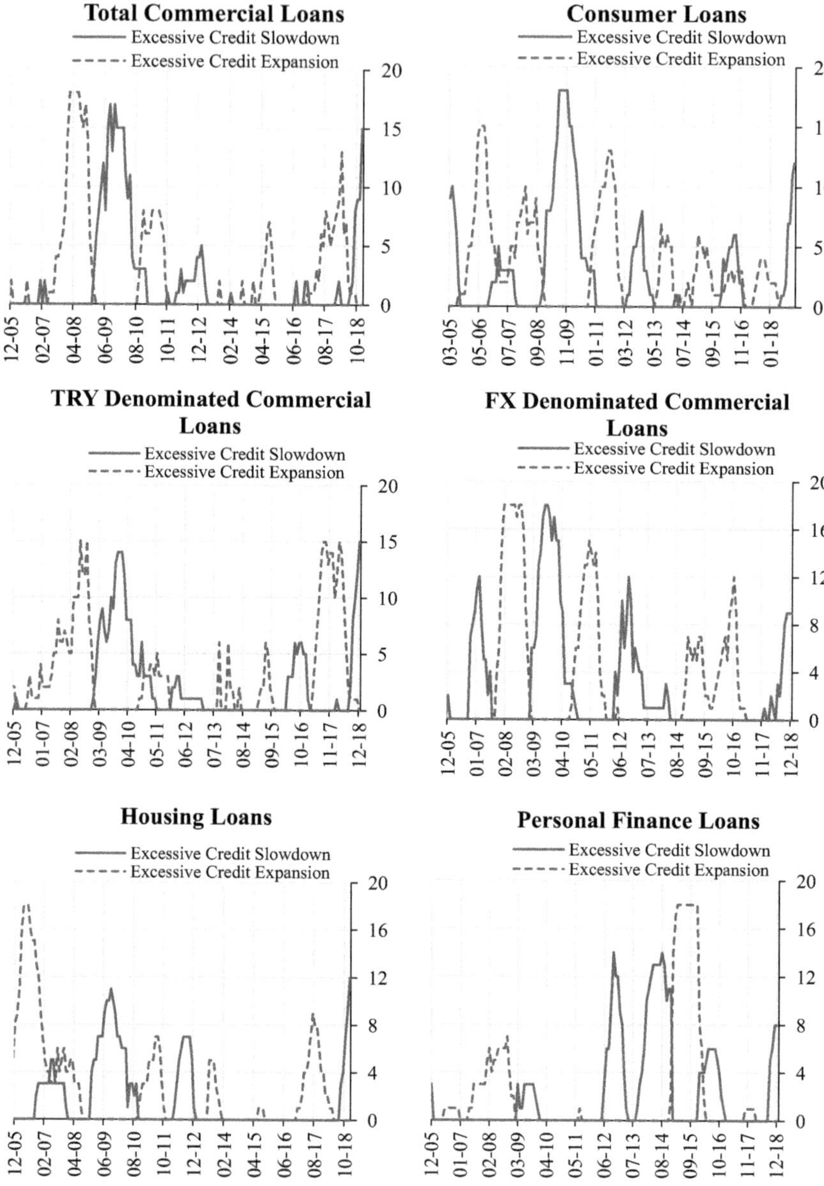

Graph 17.3: Individual aggregate sectoral results for episodes of excessive credit dynamics (number of indicators)

Source: BRSA data, authors' calculations

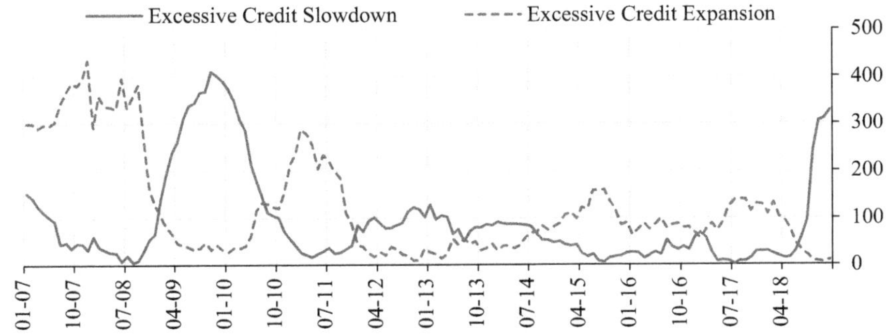

Graph 17.4: Collective sectoral results for episodes of excessive credit dynamics (number of indicators)

Source: Credit registry data, authors' calculations

three filtering methods are applied to five different credit indicators (instead of six) for 48 sectors and subsectors.[11] Hence, in total, 720 indicators are produced. Then, again similar to aggregate analysis, credit boom and crunch episodes are identified with the one standard deviation threshold rule defined from time series of filtered cyclical component of extended loans. Graph 17.4 demonstrates the number of indicators pointing out "excess credit slowdown" and "excess credit expansion" episodes over examined time period.

Earlier phases of sample data show a clear tendency on the expansion front given the features of periods which are characterized with rapid financial development. However, following the GFC, repercussions in domestic economic environment have been observed together with global and local financial volatilities, losses of value in financial assets, considerable rises in credit risk, and downturn in risk appetite leading to less room for credit supply due to liquidity, funding, capital, and profitability concerns. This process also had widespread negative implications on loan demand across sectors given depressed fixed capital formation and weakened profitable investment opportunities. In that period, almost 400 out of 720 indicators hint excessive credit tightening.

After 2010, indicators displaying credit boom episodes seem to rebound again because the loan demand and supply conditions have improved, thanks to acceleration in the economic growth. Quantitative easing by advanced economies and

11 Credit to deposit ratio is not calculated for sectoral analysis since there is no sectoral deposit data. Hence, we use five credit indicators for sector level analysis.

the surge in capital flows to emerging markets in that era are assessed to broaden the financing opportunities for banks to fuel local lending activities (Kara, 2016; Erdem et al., 2017). However, the number of sectoral indicators reflecting excessive credit growth declined in the following period on the back of normalization of economic activity to historical trend and the utilization of broad set of macroprudential policies (Kara, 2016).

More remarkably, our empirical tool appears to capture the recent adverse outlook in loan market as quantified in the number of indicators showing credit bust in the last quarter of 2018. The number of excessive credit slowdown indicators have suppressed the level of 300, almost reaching to the level observed in crisis time.

Overall results are in line with the expectation that credit market is closely aligned with business cycle describing the fluctuations in economic growth. As documented by Başarır and Sarıhan (2017) with the help of historical time-series data, growth rates can influence loan dynamics through stimulating bank profitability and credit risk outlook.

In order to provide more insight, credit boom and bust indicators are also examined for each sector separately. Graph 17.5 shows the number of indicators depicting boom and bust periods for eight prominent sectors. As explained before, fifteen indicators are calculated for all sectors (three filters applied to five credit ratios). During recent time, there exists a coincided weakening in commercial loans extended to these prominent sectors as manifested in hikes related to the number of indicators signaling credit bust. The largest depressions are monitored for construction, hotels and restaurants, and wholesale and retail trade.

Conclusion

In this chapter, we construct quantitative measures for determining the periods of excessive growth and crunch in total loans as well as several breakdowns of loans in terms of types, sectors, and currency denomination. Even though this question has been the concern of academia for more than two decades in several developed and developing countries, this is one of the few studies investigating the issue for Turkish economy.

We obtained the credit cycle series not only for total volume of loans, but also for several sub-groups of loans by using a variety of filtering techniques including Butterworth and CF Filter, in addition to the most popular method used in the literature, which is HP filter. This framework enables us to obtain more informative and robust results in analyzing credit cycle series. Depending on the position of credit cycle depending on the historical

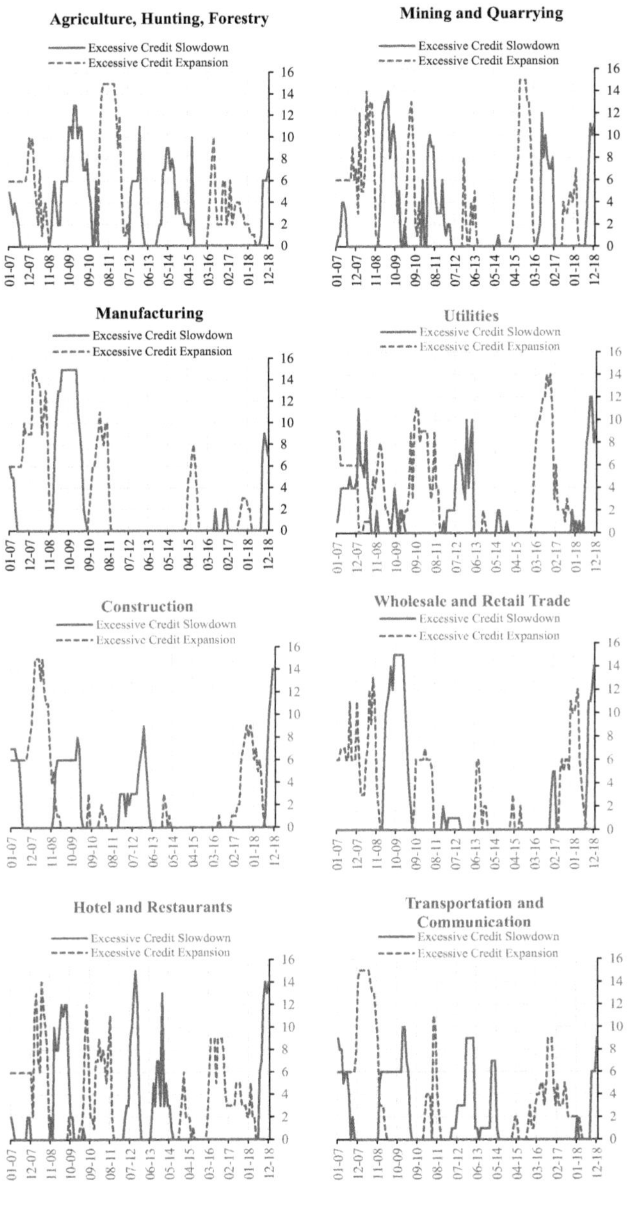

Graph 17.5: Individual sectoral results for episodes of excessive credit dynamics (number of indicators)

Source: Credit registry data, authors' calculations

variation (proxied by one standard deviation from both sides), we are able to determine the excessive credit growth or credit crunch periods. Our results are consistent with the banking sector realities of the corresponding period and economic intuition.

Our methodology and results in the chapter might have important policy implications. The determination of extreme credit periods might guide policymakers to be more aware of the current credit market outlook, or in particular, whether there is an overheating or excessive slowdown. In that case, they could use this informative input to their monetary and macroprudential policy decisions. As presented in detail, such analysis can be made for various types of credits including personal finance, housing, or FX commercial credits as well as several sectoral breakdown.

As possible topics in future research agenda, it would be informative to examine the co-movements between cyclical credit components (derived from the methodology in this chapter) and business cycle. To this end, wavelet techniques which combine the time-series and spectral dimensions can be utilized. In other words, wavelet coherency plots, displaying in which frequency intervals credit and growth cycle dynamics are correlated and how such correlations dynamically vary over sample period, can be produced. Moreover, in the case of accessing firm-level microdata, similar credit cycle proxies can be constructed from firm-dynamics to check whether or not aggregate credit market outlook differs from micro foundations.

References

Arena, M., Bouza, S., Dabla-Norris E., Gerling, K., & Njie L. (2015). Credit Booms and Macroeconomic Dynamics: Stylized Facts and Lessons for Low-Income Countries. IMF Working Paper No. WP/15/11.

Aydın, H. I., & Yılmaz, G. (2019). Türk Bankacilik Sektörü için Kredi Açigi Göstergeleri (No. 1902). *Research and Monetary Policy Department, Central Bank of the Republic of Turkey.*

Barajas, A., Dell'Ariccia, G., & Levchenko, A. (2007). Credit booms: The good, the bad, and the ugly. Unpublished: International Monetary Fund.

Başarır, Ç., & Sarıhan, A. Y. (2017). The Relationship between Profitability of Banking Sector and Macroeconomic and Financial Variables: Panel ARDL Application. Journal of Business Research, 3, 16–24.

Basel Committee on Banking Supervision (BCBS). (2010). "Guidance for National Authorities Operating the Counter-cyclical Capital Buffer." (December).

Baxter, M., & King, R. G. (1999). Measuring business cycles: Approximate band-pass filters for economic time series. Review of Economics and Statistics, 81(4), 575–593.

Binici, M., & Köksal, B. (2012). Determinants of Credit Booms in Turkey. *MPRA Paper*, 38032.

Borio, C. (2014). The financial cycle and macroeconomics: What have we learnt?. Journal of Banking & Finance, 45, 182–198.

Borio, C. E., & Lowe, P. W. (2002). Asset prices, financial and monetary stability: Exploring the nexus. BIS Working Papers, 114, Bank for International Settlements

Buncic, D., & Melecky, M. (2013). Equilibrium credit: The reference point for macroprudential supervisors. Policy Research Working Papers, 52, The World Bank.

Butterworth, S. (1930). On the theory of filter amplifiers. Wireless Engineer, 7(6), 536–541.

Calza, A., Manrique, M., & Sousa, J. (2006). Credit in the euro area: An empirical investigation using aggregate data. The Quarterly Review of Economics and Finance, 46(2), 211–226.

Canova, F. (1998). Detrending and business cycle facts. Journal of Monetary Economics, 41(3), 475–512.

Castro, V., & Martins, R., (2018). Why are credit booms sometimes sweet and sometimes sour?. CeBER WP No. 2018-14.

Christiano, L. J., & Fitzgerald, T. J. (2003). The band pass filter. International Economic Review, 44(2), 435–465.

Coşar, E. E., Kösem, S., & Sarıkaya, C. (2012). Alternatif Çıktı Açığı Göstergeleri. CBT Research Notes No:2012/22.

Cottarelli, C., Dell'Ariccia, G., & Vladkova-Hollar, I. (2005). Early birds, late risers, and sleeping beauties: Bank credit growth to the private sector in Central and Eastern Europe and in the Balkans. Journal of Banking and Finance, 29(1), 83–104.

Dell'Ariccia, G., Igan, D., Laeven, L., & Tong, H. (2012). Policies for Macrofinancial Stability: How to Deal with Credit Booms. *IMF Staff Discussion Note* (No. SDN/12/06).

Dell'Ariccia, G., Igan, D., Laeven, L., & Tong, H. (2016). Credit Booms and Macrofinancial Stability. Economic Policy, 31(86), 299–357.

Demirgüç-Kunt, A., & Detragiache, E. (1998). The determinants of banking crises in developing and developed countries. Staff Papers, 45(1), 81–109.

Drehmann, M., Borio, C., Gambacorta, L., Jiménez, G., & Trucharte, C. (2010). Countercyclical capital buffers; exploring options. *BIS Working Paper* (No. 317).

Eichengreen, B., & Arteta, C. (2002). Banking crises in emerging markets: Presumptions and evidence. In *Financial Policies in Emerging Markets* (pp. 47–94), The MIT Press, London

Elekdag, S., & Wu, M. Y. (2011). Rapid credit growth: Boon or boom-bust? (No. 11–241). International Monetary Fund.

Eller, M., Frömmel, M., & Srzentic, N. (2010). Private sector credit in CESEE: Long-run relationships and short-run dynamics. Focus on European Economic Integration, 2(10), 50–78.

Erdem, F., Özen, E., & Unalmis, I. (2017). Are Macroprudential Policies Effective Tools to Reduce Credit Growth in Emerging Markets? CBRT Working Papers (No. 1712).

Fernandez, R. B. (1981). A methodological note on the estimation of time series. The Review of Economics and Statistics, 63(3), 471–476.

Gourinchas, P. O., Valdes, R., & Landerretche, O. (2001). Lending booms: Latin America and the world (No. w8249). National Bureau of Economic Research.

Harvey, A. C., & Jaeger, A. (1993). Detrending, stylized facts and the business cycle. Journal of Applied Econometrics, 8(3), 231–247.

Hodrick, R. J. & Prescott, E.C. (1997). Postwar U.S. business cycles: An empirical investigation. Journal of Money, Credit and Banking, 29(1), 1–16.

Hosszú, Zs., Körmendi, Gy., & Mérő, B. (2015). Univariate and multivariate filters to measure the credit gap. (No. 118). MNB Occasional Paper.

Inklaar, R., & De Haan, J. (2001). Is there really a European business cycle? A comment. Oxford Economic Papers, 53(2), 215–220.

Jakubik, P., & Moinescu, B. (2015). Assessing optimal credit growth for an emerging banking system. Economic Systems, 39(4), 577–591.

Kaiser, R., & Maravall, A. (1999). Estimation of the business cycle: A modified Hodrick-Prescott filter. Spanish Economic Review, 1(2), 175–206.

Kaminsky, G. L., & Reinhart, C. M. (1999). The twin crises: The causes of banking and balance-of-payments problems. American Economic Review, 89(3), 473–500.

Kara, A. H., & Tiryaki, S. T. (2013). Credit impulse and economic growth cycles. CBRT Research Notes in Economics 1310, Research and Monetary Policy Department, Central Bank of the Republic of Turkey.

Kara, H. (2016). A brief assessment of Turkey's macroprudential policy approach: 2011–2015. Central Bank Review, 16(3), 85–92.

Kara, H. (2016). Turkey's experience with macroprudential policy. *BIS Paper*, (86q).

Kiss, G., Nagy, M., & Vonnák, B. (2006). Credit growth in Central and Eastern Europe: Convergence or boom? (No. 2006/10). *MNB working papers.*

Kocsis, L., & Sallay, M. (2018). Credit-to-GDP gap calculation using multivariate HP filter (No. 136). *MNB Occasional Papers.*

Kollmann, R., & Enders, Z., & Müller, G. J. (2011). Global banking and international business cycles. European Economic Review, 55(3), 407–426.

Mendoza, E. G., & Terrones, M. E. (2008). An anatomy of credit booms: Evidence from macro aggregates and micro data (No. w14049). National Bureau of Economic Research.

Nilsson, R., & Gyomai, G. (2011). Cycle extraction: A comparison of the phase-average trend method, the Hodrick-Prescott and Christiano-Fitzgerald filters. OECD Statistics Working Papers No. 2011/04.

Ottens, D., Lambregts, E., & Poelhekke, S. (2005). Credit Booms in Emerging Market Economies: A Recipe for Banking Crises? Manuscript, *De Nederlandsche Bank.*

Pazarbasioglu, C., Johnsen, G., Hilbers, M. P. L. C., & Ötker, M. I. (2005). Assessing and managing rapid credit growth and the role of supervisory and prudential policies (No. WP/5/151). *International Monetary Fund.*

Pollock, D. S. G. (2000). Trend estimation and de-trending via rational square-wave filters. Journal of Econometrics, 99(2), 317–334.

Ravn, M. O., & Uhlig, H. (2002). On adjusting the Hodrick-Prescott filter for the frequency of observations. Review of Economics and Statistics, 84(2), 371–376.

Reigl, N., & Uuskula, L. (2019). Alternative frameworks for measuring credit gaps and setting countercyclical capital buffers (No. wp2018-07). Bank of Estonia.

Stepanyan, V., & Guo, K. (2011). Determinants of bank credit in emerging market economies (No. Wp/11/51). *International Monetary Fund.*

Stremmel, H. (2015). Capturing the financial cycle in Europe. *ECB Working Paper*, No. 1811.

Terrones, M., Mendoza, E., & Bennet, Sutton. (2004). Are Credit Booms in Emergıng Markets a Concern? IMF World Economic Outlook, April 2004: Advancing Structural Reforms, 147–166.

Utari, G. D., Arimurti, T., & Kurnia, I. N. (2012). Optimal credit growth. Buletin Ekonomi Moneter dan Perbankan, 15(2), 3–34.

Ramazan Ekinci

18 The Effect of Basel Regulations on Banking Efficiency: Evidence from Turkey

Highlights: The aim of this chapter is to analyze the impact of capital requirements on the cost efficiency of Turkish commercial banks from 2005 to 2017. While the efficiency scores are obtained from the stochastic frontier analysis, the quantile regression model is used for robustness check. The overall cost efficiency for the whole sample is found as approximately 68 %, suggesting that an average commercial bank could improve its cost efficiency by approximately 32 %. According to the results, there is a negative relationship between capital requirements and cost efficiency.

Keywords: Basel III, cost efficiency, SFA

Introduction

BASEL regulations have become a macroprudential policy instrument with the 2008–2009 financial crisis. Therefore, these regulations have become the basic rules that have been discussed in global capital markets as a result of an important experience in ensuring and maintaining financial stability. Especially, in the crisis of 2007–2008, it was seen that the banks' capital requirements alone were insufficient to prevent their bankruptcy. For example, many banks rescued by the government had sufficient capital right before the crisis (Demirgüç-Kunt, Detragiache and Merrouche, 2013). Following the work of the Basel Banking Supervision Committee (BCBS), different rules were introduced for banking regulation with Basel Agreements.

Basel III aims to expand banks' equity base and improve the quality of equity. The new rules impose three measurement criteria for the capital requirement: (i) capital adequacy ratio, in which the ratio of equity to risk-weighted total assets is determined to be minimum 8 %; (ii) core capital adequacy ratio, where the ratio of capital to total risk-weighted assets is set at a minimum of 6 % (Tier 1); and (iii) core capital adequacy ratio, in which the ratio of core capital to risk-weighted total assets is determined as a minimum 4.5 % (Tier 1). In this study, the impact of the risk-based capital ratio, which is determined as minimum 8 % on the cost efficiency of banks, is analyzed between the years of 2005 and 2017 for 26 deposit banks operating in the Turkish banking sector.

The main function of any commercial bank, according to the traditional banking system, is the expansion of loans, which make up the bulk of the bank's assets (Fungacova, Solanko and Weill, 2014). This function can only be fulfilled by ensuring efficiency in credit allocation. The recent global financial crisis has shown that banks' performance and efficiency are prerequisites for ensuring credit stability and financial stability for global economic development (Fungacova, Solanko and Weill, 2014).

The potential asymmetric information problem between banks and borrowers can result in a process that leads to the probability of default on loans. The natural consequence of this process is in the form of bank losses. Therefore, banks must have sufficient capital, not only for sustainable liquidity but also for the stability of the financial system (Aggarwal and Jacques, 2001).

Compared to other financial institutions, banks have a high risk level. This is because banks are a sector with high leverage. Therefore, the banking sector needs supervision and regulation by an independent authority (Llewellyn 1999). According to Llewellyn (1999), the main purpose of the regulations made for the banking system is to protect the banking sector against systemic risks. The new rules emerging with BASEL III have been turned into a buffer mechanism as a macroprudential policy tool. This buffering mechanism has become a microprudential tool, mainly depending on the banks being capital-based. The fact that bank capital has become a buffer mechanism against the crisis in this process also turns it into a cost element. This process results in BASEL III Capital Regulations being a determining variable on the efficiency of banks (Fiordelisi and Marques-Ibanez, 2013). In the literature, there are also studies that include negative effects arising from implementing such an arrangement (Berger and Bouwman, 2013).

In literature, the effect of capital, as a cost element, on efficiency of the bank is explained by two basic approaches based on the agency cost hypothesis. According to the first approach, the agency costs emerge from the conflicts of interest between shareholders and debt holders. In this case, shareholders have incentives to take actions that benefit themselves at the expense of debt holders and thus do not necessarily maximize bank. In the second case, agency costs may arise from conflicts of interest between the shareholders and managers of banks. While the effect of capital, as a cost element, on efficiency is analyzed, the first approach is evaluated as "external" factors and the second one is evaluated as "internal" factors.

All kinds of effects that will decrease the liquidity flow in the banking sector are generally considered as the main cost factor. Especially, the shareholders' lower capital and higher liquidity preferences, in order to lower costs, provide a guarantee against possible borrowing costs, while the high liquidity level can provide bankruptcy costs remain at low (Grossman and Hart, 1982). Also, low liquidity levels may increase the pressure of shareholders on bank managers. The most important reason for this situation is the cost effect of high capital rate on efficiency (Jensen, 1986).

Determining which effect dominates based on the agency cost hypothesis is the basis of applied studies in the literature. However, the literature reveals mixed findings with different results in this regard. Among these studies, for example, Berger and Bonaccorsi di Patti (2006) show that in their study of the US banking sector between 1990 and 2015, low capital ratios result in high efficiency scores. Among these studies, for example, Berger and Bonaccorsi di Patti (2006) considered the US banking sector between 1990 and 2015. In their study, they found that low capital ratios result in high-efficiency scores. On the other hand, Fiordelisi, Marques-Ibanez, and Molyneux (2011) stated in their study a positive relationship between high capital ratios and efficiency in the European banking sector over the period 1995–2007. The main reason for this difference is that the USA has a capital market-based financial structure, while the EU has a bank-based financial structure. Economic growth may be higher due to the low capital-high asset trade-off in the capital market-based system. In the EU, on the contrary, capital high rates have a negative effect on growth (Repullo and Suarez, 2012). For this reason, a high capital rate together with feedback effects may have negative effects on the profitability and efficiency of banks. On the other hand, the capital ratios of the bank can be cyclical. This means that the capital increase made in periods of crisis will be more difficult to meet minimum capital requirements. For example, it can be said that higher capital requirements will be more dangerous for the banking sector in periods of economic crisis in which financial institutions cannot finance the real economy (Dullien, Kotte, Márquez and Priewe, 2010).

According to the definition of capital based on corporate finance theory, bank equity is seen as an expensive source of finance, and a percent increase in equity increases the weighted average cost of capital of banks. Banks charge this cost to borrowers with higher loan interest rates. While other conditions are fixed, with this transfer mechanism, high capital requirements turn into high financial intermediation costs, reducing the demand for the bank's loans and causing an increase in bank's costs.

The rest of the chapter is organized as follows. Section 2 reviews the literature. Section 3 describes the data sources and variables. The model specification and determinants of efficiency are explained in Sections 4 and 5, respectively. The empirical results are discussed in Section 6, and the results of robustness tests are presented in Section 7. Finally, the results are summarized, and some policy implications are discussed.

1 Literature Review

Most of the existing studies on Basel III regulations and bank efficiency are based on increasing the resistance of the banking sector against unexpected shocks and maintaining the stability of the sector in this way. Also, there are theoretical debates in the literature regarding the potential negative effects that particularly shrink bank loans and slow down economic growth. Capital adequacy requirements are one of the main regulatory tools for the stability of the banking system. They are expected to perform two main tasks. The first is the "risk-sharing function," which acts as a buffer against losses, especially depositors. Second, they limit the moral hazard issue of shareholders incentive to take on excessive risk (Jensen and Meckling, 1976).

Several studies have examined the impact of bank capital regulations on the cost of financial intermediation. Some authors found a positive relationship (Holmstrom and Tirole, 1997; Mehran and Thakor, 2011), while others such as Calomiris and Kahn (1991) found a negative relationship. For example, Berger and Bouwman (2013) analyzed the impact of capital adequacy requirements on banks' performance over the periods of the financial crisis. They investigated it through three core bank performances: survival, market share, and profitability. The sample of the study consists of all US banks between 1984 and 2009. The study's findings reveal that higher capital ratios are an important indicator for banks' survival to increase their market shares and profitability.

Another literature consists of studies analyzing the efficiency of banking regulation and supervision (see Barth, Caprio and Levine, 2004, 2006; Beck, Demirgüc-Kunt and Levine, 2006). Barth, Lin, Ma, Seade, and Song (2013) investigated whether bank regulation and supervision increased the efficiency of banks operating in 72 countries during the period 1999–2007. In their work, they found that strict capital requirements were positively associated with the bank's efficiency. Chortareas, Girardoneb, and Ventouric (2012) investigated the impact of capital stringency on cost efficiency in 22 EU countries over the period 2000–2008. They show that strict rules for capital regulation improve bank efficiency. According to Thakor (1996), banks with more capital have the capacity to turn to financially profitable projects, expand their activities, and to undertake well-estimated risks; while those banks with limited capital have shown that they prefer to avoid risky activities and invest in less risky government bonds. Thus, capital adequacy is expected to have a positive relationship with bank efficiency. Supporting the view that capital requirements should be increased, Das and Ghosh (2006) found that banks with sufficient capital will be financially healthier and have the ability to absorb shocks arising from financial and economic stress. As a result, they found that effective credit risk management will lead to an increase in efficiency. They also found a positive significant relationship between bank capital ratio and bank operating efficiency.

Some early banking studies also claim that capital ratios should be negatively associated with bank performance by arguing that higher capital requirements may reduce the risk perception of banks and cause investors to accept lower returns on their investments (Park and Weber, 2006). In this context, Altunbas, Carbo, Gardner, and Molyneux (2007) confirmed that there is a negative relationship between bank capital and efficiency (Staub, Da Silva e Souza and Tabak, 2010) and suggest that inefficient European banks hold more capital than efficient ones. Goddard, Molyneux, Wilson, and Liu (2013) in another study with similar results emphasized that banks with high capital ratios are less risky and therefore tend to have lower returns.

In a study conducted by Staub, Da Silva e Souza, and Tabak (2010), which tests the moral hazard hypothesis, it is concluded that banks with higher capital are more cautious in their risky behaviors that may result in higher efficiency scores. Similarly, Banker, Chang, and Lee (2010), investigating the efficiency of 14 Korean banks between 1995 and 2005, showed a positive correlation between the capital ratio and aggregate efficiency, technical efficiency, and allocation efficiency. According to the authors, this result, which is also consistent with the moral hazard hypothesis, will reduce the portfolio risk of banks with higher capital adequacy ratios. In this context, reliable and better credit risk management practices may lead to better performance of the entire banking system and can be evaluated as the direct effect of high capital adequacy level. This finding reached by the authors is also supported by Sufian (2010), which emphasizes the important role of capital requirements in maintaining and strengthening the financial institutions' capacity to withstand financial crises in developing countries. Berger and Bonaccorsi di Patti (2006) analyzed the impact of capital level on profit efficiency during the 1990–1995 period and for the US banking sector. As a result of the analysis, the authors showed that high capital ratios result in low efficiency levels. Fiordelisi, Marques-Ibanez, and Molyneux (2011), for a sample of European banks between 1995 and 2007, analyzed the intertemporal relationships between capital, risk, and efficiency by using panel causality analysis and sensitivity analysis. As a result of the causality analysis, a positive bidirectional relation has been reached between capital and efficiency.

2 Data and Variables

We obtained the dataset from the bank-level financial statements of 26 commercial banks operating in Turkey between 2005 and 2017. The sample represents

Tab. 18.1: Descriptive statistics of the variables

Variables	Symbol	Name	Description	Mean	Std. dev.
Dependent variable	TC	Total cost	Total interest and non-interest expenses	20620.27	23971.16
	W_1	Price of labor	Personnel expenses/the number of employees	0.07	0.32
Input prices	W_2	Price of capital	Physical capital expenditure (depreciation)/fixed assets	0.43	0.21
	W_3	Price of deposit	Total interest expenses/ total funds	0.17	0.17
	Q_1	Total loans	Sum of short- and long-term loans	144565.34	195205.6
Outputs	Q_2	Other earning assets	Total earning assets less total loans	39312.95	61254.00
Other variables	EQ	Equity ratio	Equity capital/total assets	0.14	0.10

Source: Author's calculations

the large part of the industry's total assets. We obtain information on banks' balance sheets and income statements from the Banks Association of Turkey (BAT). The reason to choose the period of 2005–2017 is that significant changes took place in the bank capital regulations in Turkey in this period. Banks with missing information and negative or zero values for inputs or outputs were excluded from the sample. Thus, the final sample consists of an unbalanced dataset of 311 observations comprised of 26 commercial banks. Input and output variables used in the study and their descriptive statistics values are given in Tab. 18.1. Empirical findings[1] were generated using open-source R-programming language.

3 Model Specification

Translog type production function, which is more flexible than Cobb-Douglas type production function, was used in defining cost function. Accordingly, using the multiproduct translog specification, the cost function is given as:

1 The results of the Battese and Coelli (1995) model were performed using the "frontier" package in the R library.

$$\ln \frac{TC}{W3} = \beta_0 + \beta_1 \ln \frac{W1}{W3} + \beta_2 \frac{W2}{W3} + \beta_3 \ln(Q_1) + \beta_4 \ln(Q_2) + \beta_5 \frac{1}{2}(\ln(Q_1))^2$$
$$+ \beta_6 \frac{1}{2}(\ln(Q_2))^2 + \beta_7 \frac{1}{2} \ln(Q_1)\ln(Q_2) + \beta_8 \frac{1}{2}\left(\ln\left(\frac{W1}{W3}\right)\right)^2$$
$$+ \beta_9 \frac{1}{2}\left(\ln\left(\frac{W2}{W3}\right)\right)^2 + \beta_{10}\frac{1}{2}\ln\left(\frac{W1}{W3}\right)\ln\left(\frac{W2}{W3}\right) + \beta_{11}\ln\left(\frac{W1}{W3}\right)\ln(Q_1)$$
$$+ \beta_{12}\ln\left(\frac{W1}{W3}\right)\ln(Q_2) + \beta_{13}\ln\left(\frac{W2}{W3}\right)\ln(Q_1) + \beta_{14}\ln\left(\frac{W2}{W3}\right)\ln(Q_2)$$
$$+ \beta_{15}T + \beta_{16}\frac{1}{2}T^2 + \beta_{17}\ln\left(\frac{W1}{W3}\right) \times T + \beta_{18}\ln\left(\frac{W2}{W3}\right) \times T$$
$$+ \beta_{19}\ln(Q_1) \times T + \beta_{20}\ln(Q_2) \times T + \beta_{21}\ln(EQ) + \beta_{22}\ln(EQ)^2$$
$$+ \beta_{23}\ln\left(\frac{W1}{W3}\right)\ln(EQ) + \beta_{24}\ln\left(\frac{W2}{W3}\right)\ln(EQ) + \beta_{25}\ln(Q_1)\ln(EQ)$$
$$+ \beta_{26}\ln(Q_2)\ln(EQ) + \beta_{27}\ln(EQ) \times T + v_{it} + u_{it} \tag{1}$$

At this stage, we follow the intermediation approach to model cost efficiency. It is assumed that the bank uses two outputs and three inputs to produce these outputs. To impose linear homogeneity restrictions, we normalize the dependent variable and all input prices by the price of funds ($t = 1, \ldots, T$). In order to take into account the effect of technological change, linear and quadratic time trend (T) variables are included in the model. In addition, the equity ratio (equity/total assets) was added to the model as a quasi-fixed input to control the differences in risk preferences between banks.

4 Determinants of Inefficiency

We employ the Battese and Coelli (1995) model to calculate the cost efficiency of each bank during the time period. Battese and Coelli (1995) model is a one-step approach, where the inefficiency estimate is assumed to be dependent on different explanatory variables. Therefore, the inefficiency component (u_{it}) in Equation (1) can be specified as:

$$u_{it} = \alpha + \beta_1 RWA_{it} + \beta_2 H_{it} + \varepsilon_{it} \tag{1a}$$

where $i = 1, \ldots, N$ denotes the banks, $t = 1, \ldots, T$ represents the time period, RWA_{it} denotes the ratio of risk-weighted assets to total assets ratio determined in the in Basel III, and ε_{it} is the error term. The inefficiency effects u_{it} from Equation (1) are specified using the following inefficiency equation:

$$H_{it} = (EQ_{it}, CR_{it}, LNTA_{it}, ROA_{it}, INT_{it}) \quad \text{(1b)}$$

In model 1b we estimate the level of bank inefficiency by controlling for a set of common explanatory variables. Bank-specific control variable can be counted as follows: (i) capitalization level used to represent the ratio of equity to total assets (EQ_{it}); (ii) credit risk explained by the ratio of total loans to total assets (CR_{it}); (iii) bank size, defined by the logarithm of the bank's total assets ($LNTA_{it}$); (iv) the return on assets (ROA_{it}) measured by the ratio of the bank's net profit to the total assets; (v) the intermediation ratio (INT_{it}) explained by the ratio of total loans to total deposits.

5 Empirical Findings

5.1 Cost Frontier Estimates

Table 18.2 shows the maximum likelihood estimates of the parameters of the translog cost function using stochastic frontier analysis (SFA).

When the results in Tab. 18.2 are examined, it is seen that normalized input prices (W_s) and outputs (Q_s) are positive and significant. The price (W_s) of the capital appears to be statistically insignificant. The coefficients of the equity ratio (risk preference) are positive and statistically significant, meaning that an increase in the amount of equity relative to total assets will increase the total costs. However, the interaction coefficient of the equity ratio with the time trend ($lnEQ \times T$) was found to be negative and statistically significant. This shows that the effect of risk preferences on total costs is a function of time and reduces total costs. Gamma parameter (γ) shows the part resulting from inefficiency in the total variance and takes a value between 0 and 1. According to Tab. 18.2, the value of γ is about 0.948 meaning that majority of residual variation is due to the inefficiency effect and that the random error is about 0.052 %. Figure 18.1 shows the cost efficiency annual mean scores at all bank levels obtained from stochastic frontier analysis by years.

It is seen that the average cost efficiency scores range between 38 % and 81 % during the period under consideration, and the average was 68 %. This result means that commercial banks in the Turkish banking sector could reduce their costs by almost 32 % on average, in order to capture their performance with the best practice commercial banks in the sample. As it can be understood from the

Tab. 18.2: Estimation of the cost frontier

Variables	**Coefficient**	**Std. Error**	**t – statistics**
β_0	-1.820**	0.555	-3.279
(β1) ln(W1/W3)	1.242***	0.276	4.494
(β_2) $\ln(W_2/W_3)$	-0.146	0.154	-0.947
(β_3) $\ln Q_1$	1.015***	0.142	7.111
(β_4) $\ln Q_2$	0.420***	0.114	3.660
(β_5) $0.5\ln Q_1 \ln Q_1$	0.104***	0.018	5.599
(β_6) $0.5\ln Q_2 \ln Q_2$	0.075***	0.016	4.528
(β_7) $0.5\ln Q_1 \ln Q_2$	-0.208***	0.035	-5.843
(β_8) $0.5\ln(W_1/W_3)\ln(W_1/W_3)$	-0.001	0.069	-0.026
(β_9) $0.5\ln(W_2/W_3)\ln(W_2/W_3)$	0.058***	0.009	5.878
(β_{10}) $0.5\ln(W_1/W_3)\ln(W_2/W_3)$	0.021	0.060	0.360
(β_{11}) $\ln(W_1/W_3)\ln Q_1$	-0.035	0.032	-1.067
(β_{12}) $\ln(W1/W3)\ln Q_2$	-0.012	0.029	-0.421
(β_{13}) $\ln(W2/W3)\ln Q_1$	0.008	0.021	0.388
(β_{14}) $\ln(W2/W3)\ln Q_2$	-0.071	0.018	-0.968
(β_{15}) T	0.071*	0.043	1.659
(β_{16}) $0.5T^2$	-0.001	0.002	-0.663
(β_{17}) $\ln(W_1/W_3) \times T$	-0.004	0.009	-0.427
(β_{18}) $\ln(W_2/W_3) \times T$	-0.014***	0.005	-2.738
(β_{19}) $\ln Q_1 \times T$	-0.013**	0.005	-2.392
(β_{20}) $\ln Q_2 \times T$	0.004	0.004	0.945
(β_{21}) lnEQ	1.324***	0.313	4.221
(β_{22}) 0.5lnEQlnEQ	0.097	0.068	1.413
(β_{23}) $\ln(W_1/W_3)$lnEQ	0.227***	0.055	4.105
(β_{24}) $\ln(W_2/W_3)$lnEQ	-0.156***	0.045	-3.426
(β_{25}) $\ln Q_1$lnEQ	-0.028	0.036	-0.789
(β_{26}) $\ln Q_2$lnEQ	-0.029	0.031	-0.917
(β_{27}) lnEQ × T	-0.029**	0.012	-2.328
σ2: (Sigma)	0.044***	0.006	6.815
γ: (Gama)	0.948***	0.025	36.899
Log likelihood	139.499		
LR test statistics	324.47***		

Note: ***, **, and * show significance levels at the level of 1 %, 5 %, and 10 %, respectively. Asymptotic standard errors are given in brackets in parentheses.

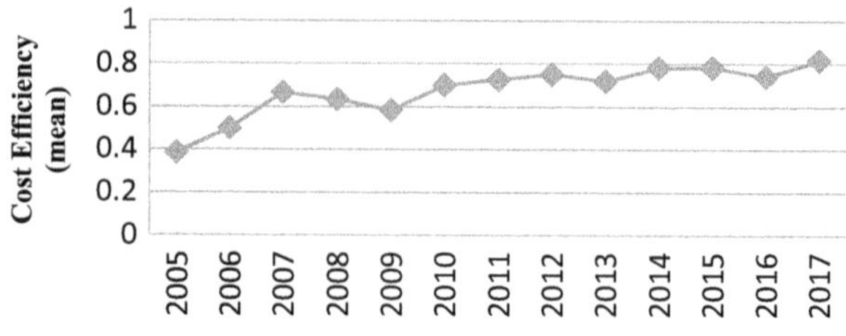

Fig. 18.1: Cost-efficiency estimates (2004–2010)
Source: Author's calculations

figure, we observe an ascending trend in cost-efficiency scores between 2005 and 2007, followed by a decreasing one for the next period. This could be explained by the impact of the present financial crisis that affected banks' cost efficiency starting with 2008.

5.2 Cost Frontier Estimates

Table 18.3 reports the results of the one-step Battese and Coelli (1995) model. According to this model, bank inefficiency is regressed on risk – weighted capital requirements and other bank-specific variables. According to the estimation results, Basel III requirements have a positive and highly significant effect on cost inefficiency, meaning that higher capital requirements decrease the cost

Tab. 18.3: Inefficiency effects model (dependent variable: cost inefficiency)

Independent variables	Coefficients	Std. Error	t – statistics
RWA	0.753***	0.227	3.308
Control Variables			
EQ	-0.050***	0.005	-8.874
CR	-2.082***	0.184	-11.260
LNTA	-0.220***	0.029	-7.547
ROA	-0.113	0.116	-0.984
INT	-0.109***	0.024	-4.453
SABİT	5.705***	0.525	10.858

Note: RWA = Equity/Risk-Weighted Total Assets, EQ = Equity/Total Assets, CR = Total Loans/Total Assets, LNTA = Logarithm of Total Assets, ROA = Equity Profitability Ratio, and INT = Total Loans/Total Deposits. ***, **, and * show significance levels at the level of 1 %, 5 %, and 10 %, respectively.

efficiency of banks. Our results suggest that a 1 % increase in capital requirements reduces cost efficiency by 0.75 %, controlling for the bank-specific characteristics. Our results are consistent with the agency cost hypothesis for commercial banks. Accordingly, higher leverage or a lower equity capital ratio is associated with higher cost efficiency (Berger and Patti, 2006). When the bank-specific control variables in Tab. 18.3 are analyzed, the effect of equity ratio (EQ) on cost inefficiency is negative and significant, meaning that well-capitalized commercial banks are more cost efficient than less-capitalized banks. The ratio of total loans to total assets (CR) is negative and statistically significant, and it can be said that commercial banks with a higher level of loans operate more cost efficiently than banks with lower loans to assets ratio. The effect of asset size (LNTA), measured by the logarithm of the bank's total assets, is negative and significant. This result, which is also in line with the expectations in the literature, shows that larger banks might have benefited from economies of scale and scope. Return on assets (ROA) used to represent the profitability level of the banks was found statistically insignificant. It is seen that the intermediation rate (INT) coefficient has a negative and significant effect on cost efficiency. This result shows that banks with higher intermediation ratios are more cost efficient.

5.3 Robustness Tests: Quantile Regression Analysis

In this section, sensitivity analyses are conducted to control the robustness of the coefficients obtained from the stochastic frontier approach. For this purpose, two-stage regression models defined in Equations (1a) and (1b) are reestimated by the quantile regression model. With this model, the cost efficiency scores derived at different quantiles are regressed on Basel III requirements. We also consider bank level control variables that might influence the cost efficiency of a particular bank. The quantile regression model, first introduced by Koenker and Bassett (1978), can be written as:

$$y_{it} = x'_{it}\beta_0 + \varepsilon_{\theta it} \text{ and } Quant_\theta\left(y_{it}\middle|\, x_{it}\right) = x'_{it}\beta_0 \qquad (1)$$

where i denotes bank, t denotes time, y_{it} is the dependent variable, x_{it} is a vector of regressors, β is the vector of parameters to be estimated, and ε is a vector of residuals. $Quant_\theta\left(y_{it}\middle|\, x_{it}\right)$ denotes the θth conditional quantile of y_{it} given x_{it}. The conditional θ^{th} quantile of y_{it} can be defined in the range of $0 < \theta < 1$ and can be obtained as the solution of the minimization problem:

$$p_\theta(\varepsilon) = (\theta - 1)\varepsilon_{\theta it} \qquad (2)$$

Tab. 18.4: Quantile regression estimation

Dep.var: Cost efficiency	**(1)**	**(2)**	**(3)**	**(4)**	**(5)**
	Q10	**Q25**	**Q50**	**Q75**	**Q90**
Independent variables					
RWA	-0.105 (0.135)	-0.233** (0.101)	-0.294** (0.148)	-0.395** (0.170)	-0.355** (0.163)
Bank-specific variables					
EQ	1.376*** (0.189)	1.606*** (0.144)	1.760*** (0.221)	2.068*** (0.266)	1.891*** (0.166)
CR	0.784*** (0.074)	0.825*** (0.084)	0.835*** (0.106)	0.792*** (0.077)	0.730*** (0.088)
LNTA	0.080*** (0.008)	0.078*** (0.005)	0.073*** (0.005)	0.067*** (0.005)	0.066*** (0.005)
ROA	0.125* (0.073)	0.155* (0.091)	0.190** (0.095)	0.160* (0.082)	0.142** (0.070)
INT	0.036* (0.019)	0.035*** (0.011)	0.034* (0.018)	0.031 (0.028)	0.028 (0.033)
SABİT	-1.424*** (0.156)	-1.370*** (0.127)	-1.230*** (0.112)	-1.048*** (0.094)	-0.932*** (0.109)
Observations	311	311	311	311	311
Pseudo R2	0.64	0.63	0.61	0.56	0.57

Note: RWA = Equity/Risk-Weighted Total Assets, EQ = Equity/Total Assets, CR = Total Loans/Total Assets, LNTA = Logarithm of Total Assets, ROA = Equity Profitability Ratio, and INT = Total Loans/Total Deposits. '***', '**', and '*' denote statistical significance at the 1 %, 5 %, and 10 % levels, respectively. Standard errors are given in parentheses. Results are obtained from fixed effects estimations with the dependent variable being the cost efficiency at different quantiles.

Equation 2 can simply be rewritten as follows:

$$min_{\beta}\frac{1}{n}\sum_{i=1}^{n}\rho_{\theta}\left(y_{it}-x_{it}'\beta\right) \tag{3}$$

where ρ_{θ} (.) is known as the check function and is defined as follows:

$$\rho_{\theta}\left(\varepsilon_{\theta it}\right)=\left\{\begin{matrix}\theta\varepsilon_{\theta it} & if\ \theta\varepsilon_{\theta it}\geq 0\\ \left(\theta-1\right)\varepsilon_{\theta it} & if\ \theta\varepsilon_{\theta it}<0\end{matrix}\right\} \tag{4}$$

Here, $P_\theta(\varepsilon)$ the error term is positive ($\varepsilon \geq 0$) provided that the error term $p_\theta(\varepsilon) = \theta_{\varepsilon\theta it}$; if it is negative ($\varepsilon < 0$), it is a control indicator that gives the weights of $p_\theta(\varepsilon) = (\theta - 1)\varepsilon_{\theta it}$ (Martins and Pereira, 2004). The minimization problem in Equation 3 can be solved by linear programming methods. The standard errors of the model are obtained by the bootstrap method.

Table 18.4 provides the quantile regression results for tenth (Q10), twenty-fifth (Q25), fiftieth (Q50), seventy-fifth (Q75), and ninetieth (Q90) quantiles. At this stage, we aimed to test whether there is a change in the capital adequacy ratios for the different quantiles of the dependent variable. Therefore, we use quantile regression[2] as it gives the effect of capital regulation, which takes into account the heterogeneity on the efficiency coefficients (less efficient vs. highly efficient) shown in different quantities.

The results are compatible with the Battese and Coelli (1995) results and suggest that capital requirements are negatively associated with bank cost efficiency. More importantly, we find that more efficient banks (the 90th quantile) are more responsive to capital requirements than their less efficient (the 10th quantile) counterparts. The absolute value of the capital ratio coefficients is lowest for the 10th quantile.

Conclusion and Policy Implications

This study aims to fill the gap in existing literature analyzing the relationship between Basel III and bank efficiency. This chapter examines the impact of Basel III on the cost efficiency of Turkish commercial banks by using stochastic frontier analysis from 2005 to 2017. The empirical findings show that the average cost efficiency estimate is 0.68, meaning that banks could reduce their costs by almost 32 % on average. In other words, banks have the opportunity to increase cost efficiency by producing the same level of outputs with lower costs or by producing more outputs using the same level of costs.

When using Battese and Coelli (1995) model, on the other hand, we find that higher capital requirements are associated with lower cost efficiency for banks. In this context, it was concluded that the high capital-asset ratio has a negative effect on cost efficiency depending on the relationship between shareholders and managers. This finding shows that the growth trend based on asset growth and liquidity expansion is limited for the Turkish banking sector. On the one hand,

2 Quantile regression results are also robust for outliers and distributions with heavy tails. In addition, quantile regressions avoid the restrictive assumption that the error terms are identically distributed at all points of the conditional distribution.

the asset growth in the banking sector requires higher capital requirements; on the other hand, this process results in a liquidity constraint in the sector. Consequently, a higher liquidity constraint will increase the cost of capital. This process is supported by the findings we have obtained. Therefore, decisions should be taken to reduce capital costs in the banking sector.

The results also suggest that capital cost per unit loan is an important determinant of bank efficiency rather than the loan growth. This means that the cost of capital is more important for Turkey than a source of liquidity. In this respect, it is necessary to expand the capital base in the banking system in Turkey. The most important condition for this is to increase domestic savings. As a result, low domestic savings in Turkey increases the cost of capital in the banking sector. Empirical findings with arguments show that the literature on financial development should be reevaluated.

References

Aggarwal, R., and Kevin, T. J. (2001) "The Impact of FDICIA and Prompt Corrective Action on Bank Capital and Risk: Estimates Using a Simultaneous Equations Model", Journal of Banking and Finance, 25: 1139–60.

Altunbas, Y., Carbo, S., Gardner, E., and Molyneux, P. (2007) "Examining the Relationship between Capital, Risk and Efficiency in European Banking", European Financial Management, 13(1): 49–70.

Banker, R. D., Chang, H., and Lee, S. (2010) "Differential Impact of Korean Banking System Reforms on Bank Productivity", Journal of Banking and Finance, 34(7): 1450–1460.

Barth, J. R., Caprio, G., and Levine, R. (2004) "Bank Regulation and Supervision: What Worksbest?", Journal of Financial Intermediation, 13: 205–248.

Barth, J. R., Caprio, G., and Levine, R. (2006) "Rethinking Bank Regulation: Till Angels Govern", Cambridge University Press, Cambridge.

Barth, J. R., Lin, C., Ma, Y., Seade, J., and Song, F. M. (2013) "Do Bank Regulation, Supervision and Monitoring Enhance or Impede Bank Efficiency?", Journal of Banking and Finance, 37(8): 2879–2892.

Battese, G. E., and Coelli, T. J. (1995) "A Model for Technical Inefficiency Effects in a Stochastic Frontier Production Function for Panel Data", Empirical Economics, 20: 325–332.

Beck, T., Demirgüc-Kunt, A., and Levine, R. (2006) "Bank Supervision and Corruption in Lending", Journal of Monetary Economics, 52: 2131–2163.

Berger, A. N., and Bouwman, C. H. S. (2013) "How Does Capital Affect Bank Performance During Financial Crises?", Journal of Financial Economics, 109: 146–76.

Berger, A. N., and Di Patti, E. B. (2006) "Capital Structure and Firm Performance: A New Approach to Testing Agency Theory and an Application to the Banking Industry", Journal of Banking and Finance, 30: 1065–1102.

Calomiris, C. W., and Charles, M. K. (1991) "The Role of Demandable Debt in Structuring Optimal Banking Arrangements", American Economic Review, 81: 497–513.

Chortareas, G. E., Girardoneb, C., and Ventouric, A. (2012) "Bank Supervision, Regulation, and Efficiency: Evidence from the European Union", Journal of Financial Stability, 8(4): 292–302.

Das, A., and Saibal, G. (2006) "Financial Deregulation and Efficiency: An Empirical Analysis of Indian Banks during the Post Reform Period", Review of Financial Economics, 15: 193–221.

Demirgüç-Kunt, A., Detragiache, E., and Merrouche, O. (2013) "Bank Capital: Lessons from the Financial Crisis", Journal of Money, Credit and Banking, 45(6): 1147–1164.

Dullien, S., Kotte, D. J., Márquez, A., and Priewe, J. (2010) "The Financial and Economic Crisis of 2008–2009 and Developing Countries", United Nations Conference on Trade and Development, University of Applied Sciences, Berlin.

Fiordelisi, F., and Marques-Ibanez, D. (2013) "Is Bank Default Risk Systematic?", Journal of Banking and Finance, 37: 2000–10.

Fiordelisi, F., Marques-Ibanez, D., and Molyneux, P. (2011) "Efficiency and Risk in European Banking", Journal of Banking and Finance, 35: 1315–1326.

Fungacova, Z., Solanko, L., and Weill, L. (2014) "Does Competition Influence the Bank Lending Channel in the Euro Area?", Journal of Banking and Finance, 49: 356–66.

Goddard, J., Molyneux, P., Wilson, J. O. S., and Liu, H. (2013) "Do Bank Profits Converge?" European Financial Management, 19(2): 345–365.

Grossman, S., and Hart, O. (1982) "Corporate Financial Structure and Managerial Incentives", In: McCall, J. (Ed.), The Economics of Information and Uncertainty, University of Chicago Press, Chicago.

Holmstrom, B., and Tirole, J. (1997) "Financial Intermediation, Loanable Funds, and the Real Sector", Quantitative Journal of Economics, 112: 663–91.

Jensen, M. (1986) Agency Costs of Free Cash Flow, Corporate Finance, and Takeovers, American Economic Review, 76: 323–329.

Jensen, M., and Meckling, W. (1976) "Theory of the Firm: Managerial Behavior, Agency Costs, and Capital Structure", Journal of Financial Economics, 76: 323–339.

Koenker, R., and Bassett, J. G. (1978) "Regression Quantiles", Econometrica: Journal of the Econometric Society, 46: 33–50.

Llewellyn, D. (1999) "The Technical Efficiency of Large Bank Production", Journal of Banking and Finance, 4: 495–509.

Martins, P. S., and Pereira, P. T. (2004) "Does education reduce wage inequality? Quantile regression evidence from 16 countries", Labour Economics, 11(3): 355–371.

Mehran, H., and Thakor, A. (2011) "Bank Capital and Value in the Cross-Section", Review of Financial Studies, 24: 1019–67.

Park, K. H., and Weber, W. L. (2006) "A Note on Efficiency and Productivity Growth in the Korean Banking Industry 1992–2002", Journal of Banking and Finance, 30: 2371–2386.

Repullo, R., and Suarez, J. (2012) "The Procyclical Effect of Bank Capital Regulation", The Review of Financial Studies, 26(2): 452–490.

Staub, R. B., Da Silva e Souza, G., and Tabak, B. M. (2010) "Evolution of Bank Efficiency in Brazil: A DEA Approach", European Journal of Operational Research, 202(1): 204–213.

Sufian, F. (2010) "Productivity, Technology and Efficiency of De Novo Islamic Banks: Empirical Evidence From Malaysia", Journal Financial Services Marketing, 15(3): 241–258.

Thakor, A. V. (1996) "Capital Requirements, Monetary Policy, and Aggregate Bank Lending: Theory and Empirical Evidence", The Journal of Finance, 51(1): 279–324.

Sema Bayraktar and Sercan Koyunlu

19 Long-Term Analysis of Riskiness in the Turkish Banking Sector

Highlights: This study aims to measure and track the riskiness of the Turkish banking sector for the longest period available by implementing Merton-based model. The sample in the study includes 16 banks traded at Borsa İstanbul (BIST) between 1996 and 2018. Distance to default (DD) values are calculated for each bank in the sample period. It is observed that DD numbers generally reach their maximum values in the years before the crisis and significantly decrease during the stressful periods. The results also show that DD is a strong indicator for forecasting bank failure and a good indicator for forecasting crises. This means that it can be used as an early signal for forecasting the riskiness of individual banks and the overall sector.

Keywords: Turkish banking sector, failure, Merton model, structural models, risk

Introduction

The banking system in a crisis or failure state paralyzes the credit channels in the economy. Thus, the real sector is directly affected by such a crisis especially in the countries that are highly dependent on the banking system and where the capital market system is undeveloped. Furthermore, in the case of banking failures, society pays a substantial cost, and it affects all segments of society, especially taxpayers. According to the financial services sector[1] report, the banking system captures 67 % of the total assets of the financial sector in Turkey. Besides, the financial markets are not developed in Turkey, thus the Turkish banking system is crucial for companies to reach financing.

Rose and Kolari (1985) claim that banking closure is not an immediate consequence. Most of the failed banks show some signs of failure before closure. Thus, it is argued that one can develop some methods that can be used as an early warning system. According to Sinkey Jr (1975), one of the advantages of effective early warning systems is that resources can be allocated more efficiently, and the examination costs could be reduced. For these reasons, it is quite important to

---

1 http://www.invest.gov.tr/en-US/infocenter/publications/Documents/FINANCIAL.SERVICES.INDUSTRY.pdf.

track the riskiness of the banking sector and individual banks in any country for which the banking sector is crucial.

This study will contribute to the literature by implementing Merton-based model in measuring and tracking the riskiness of the Turkish banking sector for the longest period available. The rest of the chapter is organized as follows. In the first part, the literature about studies related to banking failure will be presented. The methodology part covers a brief summary of the Merton-based approach. In the third part, the data and the results will be summarized. In the last part, the conclusions based on the results will be discussed.

1 Literature Review

The methodologies of studies on financial failure can be grouped into three: statistical models, artificial intelligence (AI) models, and market-based models. For statistical models, one of the important tasks is to determine the best variables and the robust framework that can discriminate between failed and non-failed firms. The AI models, contrary to statistical-based models, have no statistical assumptions. However, like statistical models, they have no robust framework explaining the default process, either. The third type of financial failure studies exploits market-based models. The main distinction of this methodology is the existence of a framework explaining the default process.

Sinkey Jr (1975), Lane et al. (1986), Pantalone et al. (1987), Thomson et al. (1991), Whalen et al. (1991), Cole and Gunther (1998), and Kolari et al. (2002) have all used statistical methods and analyzed US banking sector to estimate the bank failures for different sample periods and by using different financial ratios. The analyses they have done also varied from multivariate discriminant analysis, Cox Proportional hazard, logit model, probit model to trait recognition model. Each study has concluded that a different set of variables can be used as early warning predictors and that a different model successfully measures the riskiness of banks. Differently, the study by Demirguc-Kunt and Detragiache (2005) has analyzed the fragility of the overall banking systems for 94 countries by using the multivariate logit approach. They concluded that the banking crisis is highly interconnected with high inflation, high real interest rates, and low GDP growth. Poghosyan and Cihak (2009), on the other hand, analyzed individual bank distress across the European Union from the mid-1990s to 2008. They have found that the CAMEL covariates, notably capitalization, asset quality, and profitability, can be used as plausible thresholds for identifying weak banks but stock prices, when available, contain useful information about the likelihood of a bank's default. The study by Tam and Kiang (1992) is one of the first ones that used AI models in the subject of bank failure. They compare neural networks and discriminant analysis techniques by using bankruptcy data of the banks in Texas, USA. According to results, the neural network approach offers an alternative to existing bankruptcy prediction models. Alam et al. (2000) also implemented AI models. They have used fuzzy clustering algorithms and self-organizing neural networks to predict potentially failed US banks. They conclude that fuzzy clustering and self-organizing neural networks are satisfactory to determine potentially failed banks. Salchenberger et al. (1992) compare the logit model and neural network approach for the estimation of thrift (Savings and Loans Association) failures. They allege that at all samples, the neural network approach was at least as sound as the logit approach; in some cases, it performs better. The third popular method for analyzing the riskiness of firms is market-based models. These models evaluate the riskiness by looking at the changes in the market value of firms. One of the important studies using this method is the one by Chan-Lau et al. (2004). They have implemented structural models to bank failure for emerging countries, and they allege that DD is a good indicator of bank failure for up to nine months. Another study by Bichsel and Blum (2004) investigates the relationship between leverage ratio and capital and the relationship between the probability of default and the capital ratio. Their sample includes 19 Swiss commercial banks, and the results show that there is no significant relationship between default and capital ratio. Gropp et al. (2006) are another group of academicians that argue that DD and bond spreads can give a signal before the failure. They analyzed European banks, and their results have shown that the bond spread is very responsive only near default, but DD gives a signal up to 24 months.

The literature about banking failure in Turkey is excessively based on statistical methods and AI methods. Most of the studies compare statistical methods and AI methods in terms of their prediction abilities. Canbaş et al. (2005), Doğanay et al. (2006), Çinko et al. (2008), Erdogan (2008), Ruzgar et al. (2008), Ünvan and Tatlidil (2011), Ilk et al. (2014), Ozel and Tutkun (2014), Erdogan (2016), and Türkcan et al. (2018) are the ones that have used statistical methods in analyzing bank failures in Turkey. Like the counterpart studies done in the USA, these studies did not have any consistency in terms of which financial ratios are the best indicators of failure and which method is the best for forecasting purposes. Kılıç (2006), Boyacıoğlu et al. (2009), Mazıbaş and Ban (2009), and Yıldız and Akkoç (2010) have compared AI-based models with statistical models and concluded that the first one is superior to the latter in terms of estimating failures. Ecer (2013), however, compared support vector machines and AI models to predict financial failure. The conclusion is that the two models are rather satisfactory, but the artificial neural network is slightly better than support vector machines in predicting the financial failure of banks in Turkey. As a more recent study, Altunöz (2013) has also used artificial neural networks in analyzing Turkish Banks between 1997 and 2002 and found that the method is %88 and %77 successful in estimating the defaults one year and two years in advance, respectively. Another study by Akkoç et al. (2015), analyzing the banks transferred to SDIF between 1997 and 2003, also concluded that neural network models are successful in the range of %73.72–%100 for estimating the defaults. On the other hand, there are only two studies that have used market-based models: Suadiye (2006) and Sayılır (2010). The first study uses the Merton model and analyzes the banks traded at BIST between 1997 March and 2006 March. The data sample consists of 12 banks but because of data suitability, three banks are dropped from the sample. The results show that as the level of capital increases, banks take more risk, but their probability of default decreases because the market perceives an increase in capital positively. The second study implements logit models and the Merton model to compare the terms analyzed. The author divides the study into two parts. In the first part, for the banks operated between 1997 and 1998, logit models are constructed. In the second part, for nine banks the structural model is implemented to measure the probability of default between 1997 and 2006. According to the conclusions, adding the market variable to the logit model increases the explanatory power of the model.

Agarwal and Taffler (2008) also claim that the Merton-based model provides a theoretical explanation for explaining the failure of companies, unlike statistical-based and AI models. The results of the model are independent of time and sample. Also, it is forward-looking and dynamic. For all these reasons, the Merton model is implemented in this study for analyzing the Turkish Banking sector and the individual banks during 1996 and 2018, which is the longest available time period. This study contributes to the literature in two perspectives. First, there is no study with Merton model covering such a long period for bank failures in Turkey. Due to the long-range characteristics of the study, it would be possible to test the consistency of the Merton model under different stress periods. This study also would be the first study that analyzes the Turkish banking sector by using the Merton model under the 2008 and 2018 crises.

2 Methodology

Merton (1974) extended the option pricing method introduced by Black and Scholes (1973) to price risky debt instruments. In his seminal paper, Merton argued that the equity of the firm could be regarded as the European call option on the firm's asset value and debtholders have a short position on the firm's asset value. In this way, the credit risk of the firm can be measured by analyzing the capital structure of the firm. Thus, Merton's model is also known as "structural model" since the credit risk of the firm can be explained by analyzing its capital structure. This structural model provides a theoretical framework that explains which condition will give rise to the default as an endogenous process. The credit risk of the firm can be priced by looking at the values of the asset and the liability of a firm. In a typical firm, the asset value will be equal to the sum of equity value and the liability value. Shareholders have limited liabilities on firm and contingent claim on firm assets. They will be paid only after the debtholders' receivables are paid. Under the assumption that the default only happens at the maturity date, the important thing is the value of the firm at maturity. So, the probability of default can be defined as the probability that the asset value remains below the liability of the firm at maturity. The default point (default barrier) is the sum of repayments of interest rate and principal of the debt within a year. The possible asset value is determined by the log-normal behavior that is shaped by the asset volatility of the firm. The relative distance between the default barrier and asset value affects the probability of default. When asset value gets closer to the default barrier, the credit risk of the firm increases. Also, asset volatility is related to the likelihood of default because when asset volatility is high, then the probability that the asset value falls below the default barrier increases.

At the heart of the model is the fact that the equity of the firm can be modeled like a European call option. The strike price is the face value of the debt that is X, and maturity is T. Therefore, the value of equity is:

$$E_T = V_{A,T} \; N(d_1) - Xe^{-rT} \, N(d_2) \tag{1}$$

where

$$d_1 = \frac{\ln\left(\frac{V_A}{X}\right) + \left(\mu + \frac{1}{2}\sigma^2{}_A\right) T}{\sigma A\sqrt{T}} \tag{2}$$

$$d_2 = \frac{\ln\left(\frac{V_A}{X}\right) + \left(\mu - \frac{1}{2}\sigma^2{}_A\right) T}{\sigma A\sqrt{T}} \tag{3}$$

$d_2 = d_1 \, \sigma A\sqrt{T}$

The instantaneous volatility of the equity can be determined by using Ito's lemma.

$$E_0\sigma_E = \frac{\partial E}{\partial A}A_0\sigma_A \tag{4}$$

In this context, the probability of default can be regarded as the probability that the option expires worthless. In other words, the probability of default is the probability that the asset's value of the firm is less than the liabilities (Agarwal and Taffler, 2008). This probability can be calculated with the formula presented below:

$$PD = N\left(-\frac{\ln\left(\frac{V_A}{X}\right) + \left(\mu - \psi - \frac{1}{2}\sigma^2{}_A T\right)}{\sigma_A\sqrt{T}}\right) \tag{5}$$

where PD is the probability of default, V_A represents the value of the firm, X is the debt of the firm, μ is the expected return of the firm, ψ is the dividend rate defined as total dividend over the total value of the firm given to shareholders, σ_A is the volatility of the asset, and T is the maturity. Value of assets, the expected return of the firm, and volatility of the asset cannot be observed in the market. Hillegeist et al. (2004) find the σ_A and V_A by solving simultaneously Equations 6 and 7 given below:

$$V_E = V_A e^{-\psi T} N(d_1) - X e^{-rT} N(d_2) + \left(1 - e^{-\psi T}\right) V_A \tag{6}$$

$$\sigma_E = \frac{V_A e^{-rT} N(d_1)\,\sigma_A}{V_E} \tag{7}$$

where V_E is the market value of equity, and σ_A is the standard deviation of the stock returns. In Equation 6, $(1 - e^{-\psi T})$ means that shareholders get dividends, so it decreases the value of equity. But in our model, it is assumed that no dividend is distributed.

DD is about how many standard deviations the firm is far away from the default barrier. When the DD increases, it implies that the firm gets away from the default. DD is an ordinal measurement. DD can be defined as:

$$DD = \frac{\ln\left(\frac{V_A}{X}\right) + \left(\mu - \frac{1}{2}\sigma^2{}_A\right) T}{\sigma_A\sqrt{T}} \tag{8}$$

According to Chan-Lau et al. (2004), the DD model permits us to work with the risk-free rate instead of asset value drift. Therefore, μ can be replaced with the risk-free rate, r_f.

3 Data and Empirical Results

In this study, the distance to default is calculated for 16 banks traded at BIST from the 4th quarter of 1996 to last quarter of 2018, by making use of several data sources. Four banks captured by SDIF (TMSF) are classified as failed banks, and the remaining banks are non-failed banks. Two of them are participation banks, one of them is a development bank, and others are commercial banks. The sample size differs each year because of data availability and the status of whether the bank is traded at BIST or not.[2]

The necessary variables for the model are market capitalization, book liabilities, risk-free rate, closing price, and the number of shares outstanding. The market value of equity of the firm is calculated as the product of share price and the number of shares outstanding. As the market cap, the summation of short-term and long-term debt of the bank is obtained quarterly via Bloomberg Terminal. Since there is no daily debt data, the cubic spline method is implemented to fill the missing data. The default barrier is picked as the debt of banks, compliant with previous studies. Since the period analyzed is quite long, unfortunately, there is no unique risk-free rate that captures the whole period. So, for the period between 1996 and 1998, the risk-free rate is assumed to be equal to the customer price index published by TSI (TUIK). For the period between 1998 and 2005, the risk-free rate is accepted to be equal to the compound return of discounted bonds issued monthly by the Turkish Treasury. Also, in some months, since there was more than one issue, the compound return of bond nearest to 1 year is selected as the risk-free rate. Besides, the data is on a monthly basis. Hence, to get the daily data, the cubic spline method is implemented to fill missing data. For the period after 2005, the yield of the 1-year Treasury Bond is obtained from the Bloomberg Terminal Data as daily data. The maturity is accepted as 1 year in parallel with the previous relevant studies. The risk-free rate is accepted as the drift rate like Chan-Lau et al. (2004) do.

---

2 For example, ICBC and ESBANK are not included in sample since it was not possible to reach reliable data about them.

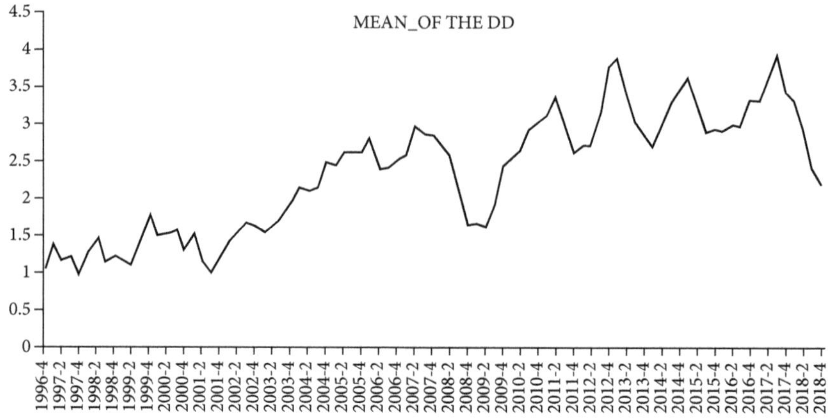

Fig. 19.1: Turkish banking sector – DD

After all the relevant data is collected, the next stage is iteration. In solving the iteration process, the methods that are described by Löeffler and Posch (2007) are adopted.

3.1 General Results for the Turkish Banking Sector

In this section, the overall results for the Turkish Banking sector are analyzed for the sample period, and the asset volatility and distance to default implied by the model are investigated looking at stress periods. The sector analysis is based on the average of DD numbers and asset volatilities of the banks. Figure 19.1 shows the estimation of the DD values of the Turkish banking sector based on the Merton structural approach. The lower the DD means the higher probability of default that, in turn, shows more riskiness. According to the figure, the minimum DD has been realized in the last quarter of 1997 and the third quarter of 2001. This indicates that the global or local economic environment conditions affect the healthiness of the banking sector. It is considered that these numbers are related to the Asian crisis and the Turkish banking crisis experienced in 2001. Similarly, the DD statistics experienced a significant drop at the 2008 global crisis. In the second quarter of 2007, it was approximately three, thus it dropped by 1.65 in the last quarter of 2008. Not surprisingly, it is similarly observed that the abrupt increase in the USD/TRY rate during the second period of 2018 accompanies with a sharp decrease in DD.

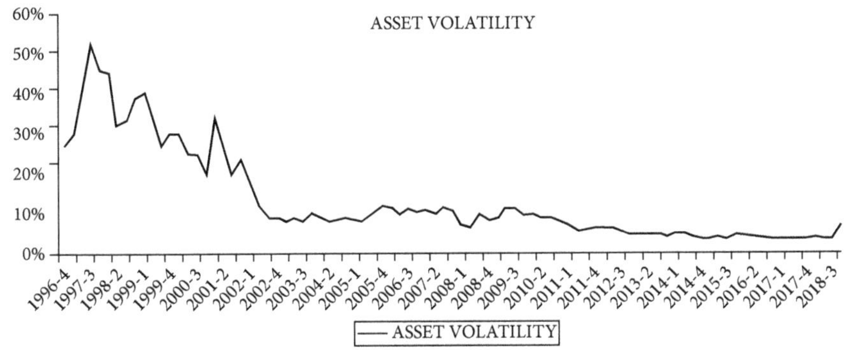

Fig. 19.2: Asset volatility – Turkish banking sector

Considering these observations, it can be concluded that the DD measure makes quick reactions to stressful events. Thus, it can be useful to monitor the overall riskiness of the banking sector since the model can give some information in advance.

Figure 19.2 shows the asset volatility implied by the model. The first striking feature is that the asset volatility is more stable than the distance to default. Again, at the height of the Asian crisis and the 2001 Turkish banking crisis, asset volatility for the Turkish banking sector is somewhat higher than the other periods. But the asset volatility increase in 2008 and 2018 crises are not that significant. Thus, we conclude that it reacts to stressful events but not as fast as the DD statistic, and it spans around 5 % in recent periods.

3.2 Results for Individual Banks

When the surviving banks are analyzed in terms of their DD values separately, a similar trend to the overall sector can be observed. Figure 19.3 shows the quarterly DD values for individual banks. The impacts of four crises, 1996, 2001, 2008, and 2018, can be observed for the banks which have sufficiently long data; namely Akbank (1996/4–2018/4), Finansbank (1997/4–2018/4), Fortisbank (1997/4–2010/4), Garanti (1996/4–2018/3), İş Bank (1996/4–2018/3), Yapı Kredi (1996/4–2018/3), and TSKB (1996/4–2018/3). They have all experienced significant declines in their DD values during these stressful periods. The banks that have relatively shorter data available, namely Denizbank (2005/4–2018/4), Halkbank (2008/2–2018/4), and Vakıfbank (2007/1–2018/3), also experience declines in DD values for the 2008 and 2018 crisis. Albaraka (2008/2–2018/4) is

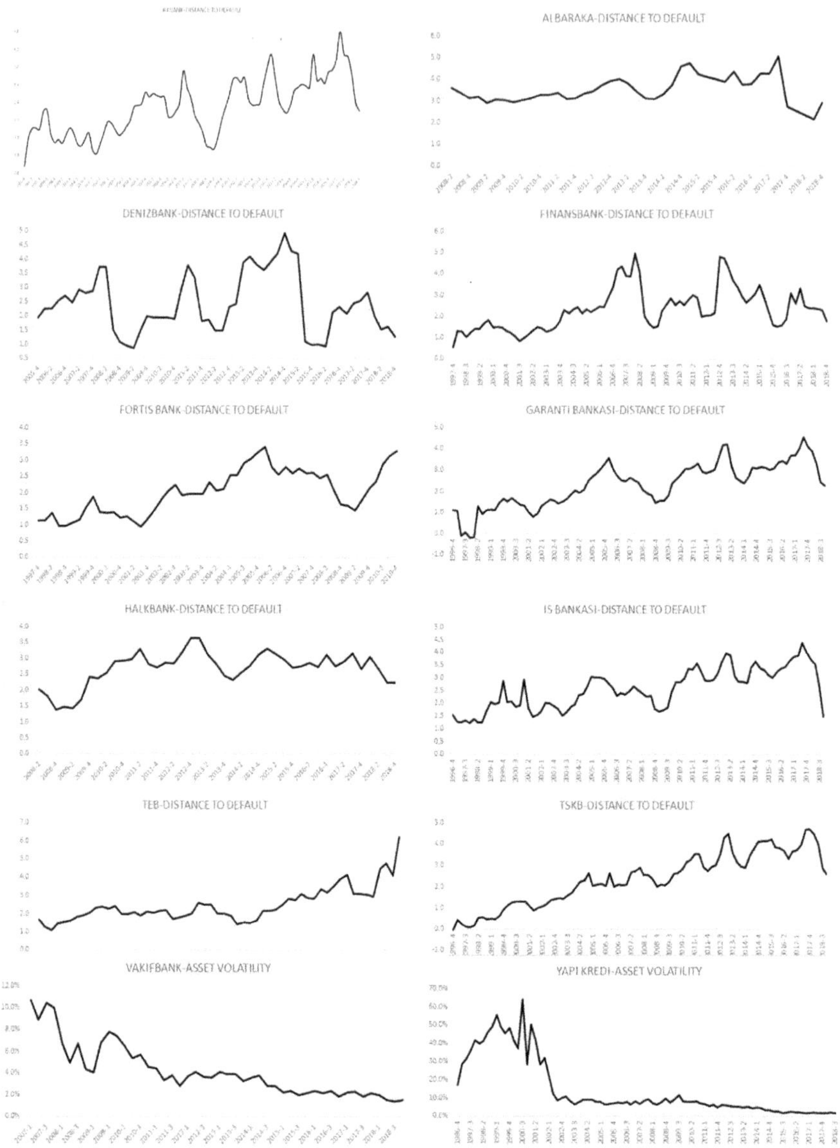

Fig. 19.3: DD for surviving banks (in alphabetical order)

somewhat different than this group in the sense that its DD significantly drops in the 2018 crisis but, other than this, DD values of the bank draw a more neutral shape. Lastly, DD values of TEB (2001/1–2015/1) also declines in 2001 and 2008 crisis but TEB at the same time is the only bank of which DD value increases rather than decreases in the 2018 crisis. For most of the banks (Akbank, Albaraka, İşbank[3], Garanti, Yapı Kredi, TSKB, and Vakıfbank), the maximum DD number is achieved in the third or fourth quarter of 2017, just before the crisis. This can be attributed to the increasing profits due to credit guarantee funds (CGF) created during that period. For Finansbank, the maximum DD value is observed just before the 2008 crisis. For Fortisbank[4], the maximum DD value is observed just after it is merged with Dışbank. For other banks, the period where the maximum value is achieved is somewhat earlier than the 2018 crisis (it is 2014 for Denizbank[5], 2012 for Halkbank, and 2015 for TEB[6]). When we look at the asset volatility trends (Fig. 19.4), for all banks except Denizbank and Finansbank, the inclination is continually downward. It decreases significantly starting from 2010, for some banks even earlier starting from the 2000s. It is interesting to observe that some banks experience more fluctuating asset volatilities compared to the others. However, it cannot be claimed that asset volatility reacts to stressful periods in the same way as DD does.

Among failed banks, Asya Katılım was a private participation bank, and the others were private commercial banks. When DD or asset volatility values of failed banks are analyzed (Fig. 19.5) it is kind of hard to reach conclusions in terms of the impact of crisis since these banks are already quite short-lived. But, as Gropp et al. (2006) stress, the DD numbers increase just before the defaults, and there is a significant decrease in DD numbers experienced up to 12 months before the default.

3 Isbank's transfer to Treasury also affected its DD numbers negatively.

4 Fortisbank is one of the private commercial banks analyzed. Its commercial name was Dışbank before Fortis purchased Dışbank in 2005. Fortisbank A.S was acquired by TEB in 2011. And the other interesting rise in DD happened before the takeover by TEB.

5 Denizbank has been sold to Sberbank in May 2012, so this probably had a positive impact on bank's DD numbers until 2016.

6 TEB has more stable DD pattern than the other banks. It is possible that its decision about going out of BIST market in 2015 has affected its DD numbers positively.

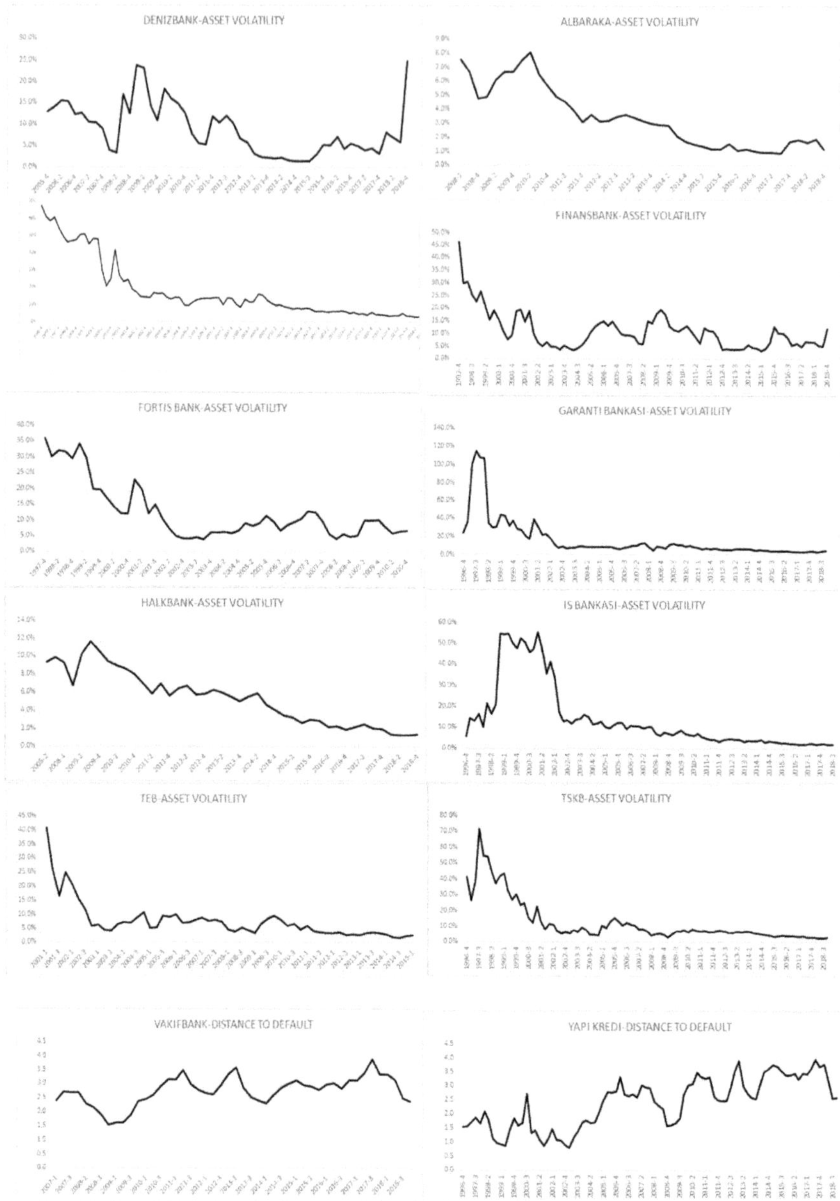

Fig. 19.4: Asset volatilities for surviving banks (in alphabetical order)

Fig. 19.5: DD and asset volatility values for failed banks

3.3 Forecasting Power of the DD

In this part of the chapter, the strength of the forecasting power of the model will be tested by looking at default events for banks and the significant events of the Turkish economy. Since the period analyzed is very long term, it includes many financial stress events such as the 02/2001 banking crisis, 09/2008 global crisis, 06/2013 internal affairs, and recent volatility hike in a currency rate in 2018. During this period, five banks went bankrupt and were captured by SDIF[7]. The bank default is defined as SDIF capture, and the default time is defined as

7 ESBANK is excluded since the reliable data is not found.

Tab. 19.1: The test results of difference of the means between failed and non-failed banks

		3-month	6-month	9-month	12-month
Mean Value					
	Non-failed Banks	2.342412	2.466894	2.44659	2.297885
	Failed Banks	1.224854	0.948091	1.006267	1.163888
t-statistics		-4.38167	-4.65334	-4.77668	-4.47128
p-value		0.0002	0.0001	0.0001	0.0001

delisting of the bank from the BIST banking index. The behavior of DD will be analyzed around these default and stress events.

First, the sample is divided into two groups based on the criteria of whether the default happened or not for each period before the default event. Whether the behavior of DD is different for these two groups is tested by the Satterthwaite-Welch t-test[8] at different lags.

According to Tab. 19.1, DD values of failed banks is significantly lower than DD values of non-failed banks for each lag. The difference between failed and non-failed banks is significantly important at 1 % significance. The results suggest that DD can be used as an early warning indicator for 3 months, 6 months, 9 months, and 12 months before the default time. Thus, the DD gives a signal about the increasing riskiness in advance.

In the second step, the strength of the model is investigated in terms of forecasting stress events by following similar steps. The stress events for Turkey are the 2001 banking crisis, the 2008 global crisis, and lastly 2018 increase in currency volatility. The behavior of DD is analyzed around these crises at 3-month, 6-month, 9-month, and 12-month lags. According to the results produced, DD gives different signals before each stress event.

DD does not differ significantly around the 2001 crisis. Table 19.2 shows that p-values for all lags are higher than the 10 %. This can be attributed to the fact that the Turkish economy before 2001 was already experiencing a crisis for a long period of time. The Asian crisis in 1997 had been followed by the 1999 earthquake. The country was already experiencing turbulence and at 2000 IMF deal was on the table. Thus, it is not surprising that DD's behavior is not significantly

8 Welch t-test is similar to t-test but it is preferred when samples have unequal variances and sample sizes.

Tab. 19.2: Summary of Welsch t-test results – 2001 crisis

Stress Event	Lag	Df	Value	Probability
2001 Crisis	3-month	13.63011	-0.766559	0.4564
2001 Crisis	6-month	14.99805	0.189219	0.8525
2001 Crisis	9-month	11.44701	0.064792	0.9495
2001 Crisis	12-month	12.27820	0.004143	0.9968

Tab. 19.3: Summary of Welsch t-test results – 2008 global crisis

Stress Event	Lag	Df	Value	Probability
2008 Crisis	3-month	18.37153	2.013234	0.0590
2008 Crisis	6-month	12.92020	1.970278	0.0706
2008 Crisis	9-month	19.93811	3.828683	0.0011
2008 Crisis	12-month	19.86145	3.995960	0.0007

Tab. 19.4: Summary of Welsch t-test results – 2018 currency volatility hike

Stress Event	Lag	Df	Value	Probability
2018 Crisis	3-month	13.30369	2.051421	0.0605
2018 Crisis	6-month	12.64374	3.215456	0.0070
2018 Crisis	9-month	12.90418	3.789781	0.0023
2018 Crisis	12-month	11.76570	-4.749161	0.0005

different around the year 2001. When the DD numbers are analyzed before the 2008 global crisis (Tab. 19.3), all p-values are found to be significant at the 10 % level. Like the 2008 global crisis results, for the recent currency speculation crisis (Tab. 19.4), all Welsch t-test statistics are significant at a 10 % significance level. Thus, it seems that DD values before and after the crisis are statistically different for these two crises. In addition to this, for both the 2008 and 2018 crises, p-values decrease when the lag length increases. All in all, the DD is consistently a strong indicator for forecasting bank failure and a good indicator for forecasting crises.

Conclusions and Suggestions

In a banking system, bank defaults cannot be considered in isolation from the whole economy; on the contrary, due to systemic risks banks create, a bank's default is an important event to forecast beforehand. Traditionally, for the Turkish banking system, accounting-based models and AI methods are suggested to measure the riskiness. The studies based on market-based models measuring the riskiness of the Turkish banking sector are limited. In addition, there is no long-term study that analyzes the banking sector over the three crises experienced by the country. Hence, the main aim of this chapter is to contribute to this limited market-based model literature by analyzing the long-term vulnerability behavior of Turkish banks.

The vulnerability of the sector is measured by DD for the overall banking system and for individual banks. DD shows how much the bank is far away from the default based on Merton's structural approach. Lower DD refers to a higher probability of default. The sample in the study includes 16 banks traded at BIST between 1996 and 2018. First, the trend of DD values is analyzed over the years. It is seen that both for the overall banking sector and for the banks separately, DD numbers generally reach their maximum values before the crisis and significantly decrease during the stressful periods. In the second part of the study, DD numbers derived are tested in terms of their ability to forecast the defaults and crisis. Welch t-test results show that DD values can forecast the bank failure for up to 12 months. It is concluded that DD can be a useful early warning indicator for tracking and monitoring bank riskiness, because it reacts more quickly than ratings or accounting-based measures. The tests related to the forecasting ability of DD in terms of crisis give some conflicting conclusions. The stress events for Turkey are the 2001 banking crisis, the 2008 global crisis, and lastly 2018 increase in currency volatility. Results show that DD does not differ significantly around the 2001 crisis. On the other hand, DD results before and after 2008 and 2018 crises are found to be significantly different. In addition to this, for both 2008 and 2018 crises, p-values decrease when the lag length increases.

Thus, it is concluded that the DD is a strong indicator for forecasting bank failure and a good indicator for forecasting crises. This means that it can be used as an early signal for forecasting the riskiness of banks and the overall sector. Supervisors should exploit this property of DD measure to try to prevent failures or minimize the impact of failures and crises.

Merton model is based on many fundamental assumptions. Thus, the model used in the study omits some characteristics that would help more realistically describe the failure behavior of the banks. Further work in this area would benefit from relaxing these assumptions and exploring how some factors like nonlinearity of bank asset values, liquidity concerns, interest-rate risk, complex capital structure, and government guarantees would improve the structural models of bank default risk.

References

Agarwal, V. and R. Taffler (2008). Comparing the performance of market-based and accounting-based bankruptcy prediction models. Journal of Banking & Finance 32(8), 1541–1551.

Akkoç, S., N. Dalkılıç, and A.A. Ada (2015). Banka iflaslarının öngörülmesinde eklektik bir yaklaşım, Bankacılar Dergisi 94, 25–39.

Alam, P., D. Booth, K. Lee, and T. Thordarson (2000). The use of a fuzzy clustering algorithm and self-organizing neural networks for identifying potentially failing banks: An experimental study. Expert Systems with Applications 18(3), 185–199.

Altunöz, U. (2013), Bankaların finansal başarısızlıklarının yapay sinir ağları modeli çercevesinde tahmin edilebilirliği, Dokuz Eylül Üniversitesi İktisadi ve İdari Bilimler Fakültesi Dergisi 28(2), 189–217.

Bichsel, R. and J. Blum (2004). The relationship between risk and capital in swiss commercial banks: A panel study. Applied Financial Economics 14(8), 591–597.

Black, F. and M. Scholes (1973). The pricing of options and corporate liabilities. Journal of Political Economy 81(3), 637–654.

Boyacıoğlu, M. A., Y. Kara, and Ö. K. Baykan (2009). Predicting bank financial failures using neural networks, support vector machines and multivariate statistical methods: A comparative analysis in the sample of savings deposit insurance fund (sdif) transferred banks in turkey. Expert Systems with Applications 36(2), 3355–3366.

Canbaş, S., A. Çabuk, and S. B. Kılıç (2005). Prediction of commercial bank failure via multivariate statistical analysis of financial structures: The Turkish case. European Journal of Operational Research 166(2), 528–546.

Chan-Lau, J. A., A. Jobert, and J. Kong (2004). An option-based approach to bank vulnerabilities in emerging markets, No 2004/033, IMF Working Papers from International Monetary Fund, pp.22.

Çinko, M., E. Avcı, et al. (2008). The Camels rating system and forecasting financial failure in the Turkish commercial banking sector. Journal of BRSA Banking and Financial Markets 2(2), 25–48.

Cole, R. A. and J. W. Gunther (1998). Predicting bank failures: A comparison of on- and off-site monitoring systems. Journal of Financial Services Research 13(2), 103–117.

Demirgüç-Kunt, A. and E. Detragiache (2005). Cross-country empirical studies of systemic bank distress: A survey. The World Bank.

Doğanay, M. M., N. B. Ceylan, and R. Aktaş (2006). Predicting financial failure of the Turkish banks. Annals of Financial Economics 2(01), 0650005.

Ecer, F. (2013). Comparing the bank failure prediction performance of neural networks and support vector machines: The Turkish case. Economic research- Ekonomska istraživanja 26(3), 81–98.

Erdogan, B. E. (2008). Bankruptcy prediction of Turkish commercial banks using financial ratios. Applied Mathematical Sciences 2(60), 2973–2982.

Erdogan, B. E. (2016). Long-term examination of bank crashes using panel logistic regression: Turkish banks failure case. International Journal of Statistics and Probability 5(3), 42.

Gropp, R., J. Vesala, and G. Vulpes (2006). Equity and bond market signals as leading indicators of bank fragility. Journal of Money, Credit and Banking, 38(2), 399–428.

Hillegeist, S. A., E. K. Keating, D. P. Cram, and K. G. Lundstedt (2004). Assessing the probability of bankruptcy. Review of Accounting Studies 9(1), 5–34.

Ilk, O., D. Pekkurnaz, and M. Cinko (2014). Modeling company failure: A longitudinal study of Turkish banks. Optimization 63(12), 1837–1849.

Kılıç, S. B. (2006). Türk bankacılık sistemi için çok kriterli karar alma analizine dayalı bir erken uyarı modelinin tahmini. METU Studies in Development 33(1), 117.

Kolari, J., D. Glennon, H. Shin, and M. Caputo (2002). Predicting large us commercial bank failures. Journal of Economics and Business 54(4), 361–387.

Lane, W. R., S. W. Looney, and J. W. Wansley (1986). An application of the Cox proportional hazards model to bank failure. Journal of Banking & Finance 10(4), 511–531.

Löeffler, G. and P. N. Posch (2007). Credit Risk Modeling Using Excel and VBA, ISBN: 978-1-119-20221-9. New Jersey: John Wiley & Sons.

Mazıbaş, M. and Ü. Ban (2009). Bank failure prediction with artificial neural net-works: A comparative application to Turkish banking system (banka başarısızlıklarının yapay sinir ağlarıyla tahmini: Türk bankacılık sistemi üzerine karşılaştırmalı bir uygulama). Available at SSRN 3008589.

Merton, R. C. (1974). On the pricing of corporate debt: The risk structure of interest rates. The Journal of Finance 29(2), 449–470.

Özel, G. and N. A. Tutkun (2014). Probabilistic prediction of bank failures with financial ratios: An empirical study on Turkish banks. Pakistan Journal of Statistics and Operation Research 9(4), 409–428.

Pantalone, C. C., M. B. Platt, et al. (1987). Predicting commercial bank failure since deregulation. New England Economic Review, 13 Jul, 37–47.

Poghosyan, T. and M. Cihak (2009). Distress in European Banks: An analysis based on a new data set, International Monetary Fund Working Paper, WP 09/9.

Rose, P. S. and J. W. Kolari (1985). Early warning systems as a monitoring device for bank conditions. Quarterly Journal of Business and Economics, 24, 43–60.

Rüzgar, N. S., F. Ünsal, and B. Rüzgar (2008). Predicting bankruptcies using the rough set approach: The case of Turkish banks. International Journal of Mathematical Models in Applied Sciences 2(1), 57–64.

Salchenberger, L. M., E. M. Cinar, and N. A. Lash (1992). Neural networks: A new tool for predicting thrift failures. Decision Sciences 23(4), 899–916.

Sayılır, Ö. (2010). Finansal başarısızlık riskinin ölçümünde piyasa verilerinin kullanımı ve yapısal modeller, Türk bankacılık sektörü'nde uygulama, Anadolu: Anadolu Üniversitesi Sosyal Bilimler Enstitüsü.

Sinkey Jr, J. F. (1975). A multivariate statistical analysis of the characteristics of problem banks. The Journal of Finance 30(1), 21–36.

Suadiye, G. (2006). Banka başarısızlıkları ve bankacılık düzenlemeleri: İmkb'de işlem gören türk ticaret bankalarının başarısızlık olasılığının tahmini (yayınlanmamış doktora tezi). Ankara: Ankara Üniversitesi Sosyal Bilimler Enstitüsü İşletme Anabilim Dalı.

Tam, K. Y. and M. Y. Kiang (1992). Managerial applications of neural networks: The case of bank failure predictions. Management Science 38(7), 926–947.

Thomson, J. B. et al. (1991). Predicting bank failures in the 1980s. Federal Reserve Bank of Cleveland Economic Review 27(1), 9–20.

Türkcan, Z., A. E. Bozcuk, and K. Türkcan (2018). Türk bankalarında mali başarısızlığın tahmin edilmesine yönelik ampirik bir çalışma, Muhasebe ve Finans Dergisi, Oct., 251–272, doi: 10.25095/mufad.465944.

Ünvan, Y. A. and H. Tatlıdil (2011). Türk bankacılık sektörünün çok değişkenli istatistiksel yöntemler ile incelenmesi. Ege Academic Review 11.

Whalen, G. et al. (1991). A proportional hazards model of bank failure: An examination of its usefulness as an early warning tool. Economic Review 27(1), 21–31.

Yıldız, B. and S. Akkoç (2010). Bankruptcy prediction using neuro-fuzzy: An application in Turkish banks. Proceedings of the New York State Economics Association, 143.

Emre Esat Topaloğlu, Reşat Sakur, and Serdar Yaman

20 The Determinants of Bank's Stock Volatility[1]

Highlights: In this study, it is aimed to determine the factors that affect common stock volatility of banks. In this context, data of companies whose shares are traded in Borsa Istanbul Bank Index (XBANK) are analyzed for the period 2007:06–2018:09 using symmetrical and asymmetrical conditional variance models and panel data analysis. While the dependent variable of the study is common stock volatility, the independent variables are factors of profitability, valuation, financial structure, cost, and size as intrabank elements. As a result of the study, while a statistically significant and positive relationship was determined between common stock volatility and profitability, cost, and valuation rate, a statistically significant and negative relationship was detected between volatility and size. On the other hand, there was no significant relationship between volatility and financial structure. According to the results of the panel data analysis, while one unit increase in profitability, cost, and market value in banks led to an increase of 0.801, 0.085, and 0.025 units in common stock volatility, respectively, one unit increase in size caused a decrease of 0.018 units in stock volatility.

Keywords: Banks stock, volatility, GARCH models, panel data analysis

Introduction

For investors, common stocks are one of the most important investment instruments that give the right of equity security and include risk as well as return. Predicting the risks accurately by investors is important in order to make better management of future risks. Common stock volatility, in other words, volatility of stock return, which defines the variability in stock prices, is considered by investors, policy makers, brokers, analysts, and brokerage firms. In addition to being a risk indicator, volatility can be interpreted as not moving in the same direction with the whole market or important information originating from the company (Karolyi, 2001: 1). Since excessive volatility in common stocks can lead

---

1 This study was presented orally at the conference titled "International Conference on Empirical Economics & Social Sciences (ICEES'19)" held in Balıkesir on 20-22 June and published in the proceedings book as full text. Afterwards, the study was extended and published as a book chapter.

to high gains and losses, an insecurity may arise against the market and common stocks (Kılıç, Çelik and Kaya, 2017: 716).

Extreme volatility in common stocks is the type of risk that investors pay attention most. Investors, financial sector players, and researchers put emphasis heavily on the risk factor. In order to minimize the risk, investors should pay attention to financial markets and intracompany resources that may lead to risk. An investment instrument contains systematic and non-systematic risk elements. The high sensitivity of the investment instrument to systematic risk and besides the high non-systematic risk makes it difficult to accurately predict the expected return from that investment instrument. In this respect, it is important for the investor to accurately predict the expected return at risk (Topaloğlu and Yaman, 2018: 187).

A high level of volatility means a high level of risk. Unexpected events in the markets or within the companies may cause sudden decreases or rises in the prices of the investment instruments. This kind of sudden decreases and rises ends up with a high level of volatility which means a high level of risk. Volatility is a concept which is used to express negative or positive directional deviation. Although it gives positive results in some cases, the concept volatility is generally used for negative results (Chong, 2004; Kuzu, 2018: 609). Until recently, standard deviation and variance have been used in calculations of volatility. Standard deviation and variance methods assume that the variance in prices does not change over time which means homoscedasticity. These methods are inadequate in measuring the correct volatility, as the variance in the financial series change over time, which means heteroscedasticity. Along with the increase in risk types and the more complex structure of the risks, new econometric methods have been developed which take into account the characteristics such as leverage effects, volatility clustering, asymmetric movements (gain/loss asymmetry), and excessive flatness (leptokurtosis) that require advanced mathematical and statistical calculations and can predict the variance varying over time. Non-parametric methods such as historical simulation, semi-parametric methods based on extreme value theory and quantile regression method, and full parametric methods can be used to estimate the risk value. Autoregressive Conditional Heteroskedasticity (ARCH) model, which was developed by Engle in 1982, is the first full parametric method to estimate volatility. In 1986, Bollerslev developed the Generalized Autoregressive Conditional Heteroskedasticity (GARCH) model by developing the ARCH model, which has various limitations and disadvantages such as negative variance estimation. Together with these methods, Nelson's exponential GARCH model (1991) and the asymmetric model of Glosten et al. (1993) were included in the literature as popular methods

(Iqbal, 2016: 453). These methods are important in order to determine the value of risk and estimate the volatility.

In the study, intracompany determinants of common stock volatility were determined using panel data analysis method in line with the symmetric and asymmetric conditional variance models varying specifically for the banking sector. In the study, common stock volatility is the dependent variable and size, valuation, financial structure, profitability, and cost are included as independent variables. The investigation of stock volatility in a panel data form on a bank basis and the investigation of intracompany factors affecting volatility contributes to the literature and offers originality.

1 Literature Review

When the literature is examined, many studies are found on common stock volatility estimation and modeling. In his study, Karmakar (2005) determined that GARCH(1,1) model is the best model performing for modeling the volatility of Indian stock market and obtained evidences that there are fluctuations in the market indices. In their study, Goudarzi and Ramanarayanan (2010) analyzed the volatility of the Indian stick market with ARCH models and using BSE500 index data. As a result of the analysis, they determined that the model performing best for modeling the volatility of BSE500 index is GARCH(1,1) model. In the study examining the volatility of Sudan principal stock market, Elsheikh and Suliman (2011) used symmetrical and asymmetrical GARCH models. In the study, GARCH(1,1) and GARCH-M(1,1) models are used for modeling the symmetrical volatility and TARCH(1.1) and PARCH(1,1) models are used for modeling the asymmetrical volatility. As a result of the analysis, the performances of symmetrical models are found to be higher than the performances asymmetrical models. Gabriel (2012) used GARCH type models to determine the most appropriate model for volatility modeling in the Romanian stock market using daily data of the Bucharest Stock Exchange for the period 09.03.2001–02.02.2012. As a result of the study, it was determined that the GARCH type model, which performs best in estimating volatility in the Bucharest Stock Exchange, is the TGARCH model. Tamilselvan and Vali (2016) used GARCH, EGARCH, and TGARCH models for modeling the volatility of four different indices in Muscat Stock Exchange using the data for the period 2001–2015. As a result of the study, they determined that the GARCH model is the model performing best for all four indices.

In his study, Sarıoğlu (2006) used GARCH models for modeling the volatility of BIST-100 Index returns. As a result of the study, GARCH and EGARCH models are determined to be the models performing best for BIST-100 Index returns. In another study on modeling BİST-100 Index return volatility, Akar (2007) used ARCH, GARCH, and SWARCH models and weekly data for the period 1990–2007. As a result of the study, it has been determined that the SWARCH model is the most appropriate model for modeling the return volatility of BIST-100 Index. Çabuk, Özmen, and Kökcen (2011) used GARCH, ARCHM, M-GARCH, E-GARCH, and TARCH models and data for the period of 2004–2009 for modeling the BIST-100 Index and BIST Financial Index returns. According to the results of the study, the model performing best for modeling BIST-100 Index and BIST Financial Index returns is E-GARCH model. In the study by Tuna and İsabetli (2014), the volatility in BIST-100 return series was modeled using ARCH and GARCH models. In the study carried out for the period of 2002–2012, it was concluded that the volatility was persistent due to the high GARCH coefficient, and volatility increased and the volatility clusters were observed in the periods of crisis in particular for BIST-100. In the study examining the differences between volatility modes by Kayahan, Kandemir, Baykut, and Memis (2015) made a comparison with high level volatilities. In the study, volatility was estimated with the GARCH model by using the data of BIST 30 index companies and the exchange rates of USD/TRY in the period of 30.06.2008–30.06.2009. Results of the study show that no fundamental differences were determined between the models. In another study on modeling common stock volatility, Eryilmaz (2015) aimed to model BIST-100 common stock volatility. Common stock volatility of BIST-100 for the period 1997:01–2015:03 is modeled using ARCH, GARCH, EGARCH, and TARCH models. As the results of the analysis and modeling, it was determined that the most suitable model for the return of BIST-100 is EGARCH and it was determined that besides the leverage effect for BIST-100 being important, the negative news in the market increase the volatility and this volatility shows continuity. In the study by Yıldız (2016) to determine the volatility of index returns, it was determined which models gave more successful results in modeling and estimating the volatilities related to selected sub-sectors like service, financial, and industrial index returns series in BIST. In the study using the daily data from 05.01.2000–09.12.2015, conditional variance models were analyzed, and it was observed that the volatility of the indices showed both ARCH and GARCH effects. On the other hand, it was concluded that TGARCH is the most suitable model in the estimation of volatility of financial and industrial indices, and CGARCH is the most suitable model for the service index. Kılıç et al. (2017) aiming to compare the effects of classical and Bayesian GARCH (1,1) models on common stock return volatility, it was determined that there was no significant difference between the classical and Bayesian GARCH (1,1) model results predicted for common stock return volatility in terms of both the impact of shocks on volatility and volatility persistence using the BIST-100 daily index data for the period of February 2007– February 2017. In his study, Kuzu (2018) examined the return volatility of the BIST-100 Index with the ARCH, GARCH, EGARCH, and TGARCH models, using the daily data for the period of 2011–2017/3. As a result of the study, it was determined that the model that displayed the highest performance in the modeling of the BIST-100 Index return volatility is the TGARCH model.

2 Method and Analysis

Panel data regression analysis method was carried out using statistics programs in order to determine the intracompany factors affecting common stock return volatility in banks. In the study, the process took place in two stages, and in the first stage conditional variance error terms were obtained by volatility modeling for each bank. In the second stage, by taking the square root of conditional variance error terms, series which will be used as dependent variable in the next step regression model were obtained (Smith, 2012). Within the scope of panel data analysis, multicollinearity, cross-sectional dependency, homogeneity, stationarity, model prediction method determination, heteroscedasticity, and autocorrelation assumptions have been tested in order to make predictions and obtain accurate and consistent results.

In the study, the estimation was made by using the quarterly data of 2007:06–2018:09 of ten banks, available in the BIST Bank Index (XBANK) as data sets, with the exception of development, investment, and participation banks. The examined banks and the variables used in the study are shown in Tab. 20.1.

Secondary data of the variables used were obtained from Finnet (Financial Information News Network) www.finnet.com.tr, Public Disclosure Platform www.kap.org.tr, and www.investing.com databases. The bidirectional fixed effects model constructed in accordance with the dependent and independent variables used in the study was built as follows:

$$\begin{aligned} VOL_{it} = \alpha_{it} + \beta_{2it}\, ROA_{it} + \beta_{3it}\, SIZE_{it} + \beta_{4it}\, P/E_{it} \\ + \beta_{5it}\, FIN_{it} + \beta_{6it}\, COST_{it} + \varepsilon_{it} + \lambda_{t} \end{aligned} \quad (1)$$

In bidirectional fixed effects models built in the study, Y_{it} is the dependent variable, X_{2it}, X_{3it}, X_{4it}, X_{5it} and X_{6it} are the independent variables, α_{it} is the constant from unit to unit, β_2, β_3, β_4, β_5 and β_6 are the slope coefficients of independent variables, ε_{it} is the error term, $_I$ defines the unit dimension in the model, and $_t$ defines time dimension. Five hypotheses were created in accordance with the variables.

Tab. 20.1: Examined banks and variables

Line	**Bank**		**BIST Code**
1	Akbank T.A.Ş.		AKBNK
2	Denizbank A.Ş.		DENIZ
3	ICBC Turkey Bank A.Ş.		ICBCT
4	QNB Finansbank A.Ş.		QNBFB
5	Şekerbank T.A.Ş.		SKBNK
6	Türkiye Garanti Bankası A.Ş.		GARAN
7	Türkiye Halk Bankası A.Ş.		HALKB
8	Türkiye İş Bankası A.Ş.		ISCTR
9	Türkiye Vakıflar Bankası T.A.O.		VAKBN
10	Yapı ve Kredi Bankası A.Ş.		YKBNK
Variables and Calculation Methods			
Dependent Variable	Volatility	Square Root of Conditional Heteroscedastic Error Terms	VOL
	Profitability	Return on Assets	ROA
Independent	Size	Interest Income Magnitude	SIZE
VariableS	Valuation	Price to Earnings Ratio	P/E
	Financial Structure	Equity/Assets	FIN
	Cost	Interest Expenses/Interest Income	COST

Hypothesis 1: There is a significant relationship between common stock volatility and profitability in banks.

Hypothesis 2: There is a significant relationship between common stock volatility and size in banks.

Hypothesis 3: There is a significant relationship between common stock volatility and valuation in banks.

Hypothesis 4: There is a significant relationship between common stock volatility and financial structure in banks.

Hypothesis 5: There is a significant relationship between common stock volatility and cost in banks.

The null hypotheses are the opposite of the given expression for each of the hypotheses above.

3 Results

Before making estimates in panel data analysis, there are some assumptions that must be met in order to obtain accurate and consistent results. These

Tab. 20.2: Descriptive statistics of the variables

	VOL	ROA	SIZE	P/E	FIN	COST
Mean	20.32610	1.728326	17.71341	12.01435	11.56598	53.42643
Median	19.14944	1.670000	18.64500	8.920000	11.30000	53.23000
Maximum	43.35052	4.940000	134.3400	142.0500	24.23000	75.37000
Minimum	9.663945	-0.740000	-47.42000	2.680000	6.690000	30.06000
Std. Deviation	4.721227	0.767684	19.21621	13.29573	2.356478	6.909863
Skewness	0.806272	0.233757	0.804971	5.580317	1.752953	0.076304
Kurtosis	4.072806	3.818919	8.629284	41.87136	9.321065	3.424054
Jarque-Bera	71.89824	17.04296	657.0478	31347.89	1001.405	3.892970
Probablity	0.000000	0.000199	0.000000	0.000000	0.000000	0.142775
Total	9350.007	795.0300	8148.170	5526.602	5320.350	24576.16
Total Error Square	10231.10	270.5064	169491.6	81140.36	2548.821	21915.51
Observation	460	460	460	460	460	460

assumptions are; assumptions of no multicollinearity, stationarity of series, no heteroscedasticity and no autocorrelation. Descriptive statistics about the variables used in the study are given in Tab. 20.2.

When Tab. 20.2 is analyzed, it is seen that the variable with the highest standard deviation is the SIZE. Results of Jarque-Bera normality test shows that the series related to the COST variable is normally distributed but the other series do not distribute normally.

Within the context of panel data analysis, multicollinearity between independent variables and whether there is a problem of endogeneity between dependent and independent variables were investigated using Spearman correlation, Variance Inflation Factor (VIF), and Scatter Diagram in line with the normal distribution assumption. VIF values for the variables are given in Tab. 20.3, results of the Spearman Correlation analysis are given in Tab. 20.4, and the Scatter Diagram is shown in Fig. 20.1.

When Tab. 20.3 is examined, it can be said that Centered VIF values of all the variables are below 4 and that the variables will not cause multicollinearity problems in the model.

No high correlation was detected between the independent variables as the results of the Spearman Correlation analysis in Tab. 20.4. This result indicates that the variables in the model were not multicollinearity problems. In this sense, it can be said that the results of Spearman Correlation analysis and the calculated VIF values for each variable support each other.

Tab. 20.3: VIF values of the variables

Variables	Variance Coefficient	Centerless VIF	Centered VIF
ROA	0.093291	7.581375	1.247014
SIZE	0.000159	2.471720	1.334941
P/E	0.001136	74.96139	1.230637
FIN	0.009801	31.03625	1.234411
COST	0.000319	2.323883	1.278041
C	5.450216	123.8870	NA

Tab. 20.4: Results of Spearman correlation analysis

Variables	VOL	ROA	SIZE	P/E	FIN	COST
VOL	1.000000					

ROA	-0.288305	1.000000				
	-6.443607	-----				
	(0.0000)	-----				
SIZE	0.090573	-0.057854	1.000000			
	1.946355	-1.240211	-----			
	(0.0522)	(0.2155)	-----			
P/E	0.200684	-0.159772	-0.154566	1.000000		
	4.384017	-3.463771	-3.348102	-----		
	(0.0000)	(0.0006)	(0.0009)	-----		
FIN	-0.133683	0.292684	-0.237995	0.310808	1.000000	
	-2.886860	6.550556	-5.243986	6.998184	-----	
	(0.0041)	(0.0000)	(0.0000)	(0.0000)	-----	
COST	0.084841	-0.108841	0.362545	-0.247451	-0.320494	1.000000
	1.822244	-2.343224	8.325189	-5.465661	-7.240825	-----
	(0.0691)	(0.0195)	(0.0000)	(0.0000)	(0.0000)	-----

According to the Scatter Diagram results in Fig. 20.1, there is no endogeneity problem between the dependent variable and the independent variables in the model. According to the results of Scatter Diagram, which is showing the relationships between the dependent variable and independent variables, the results of Spearman Correlation analysis, which express the correlation between

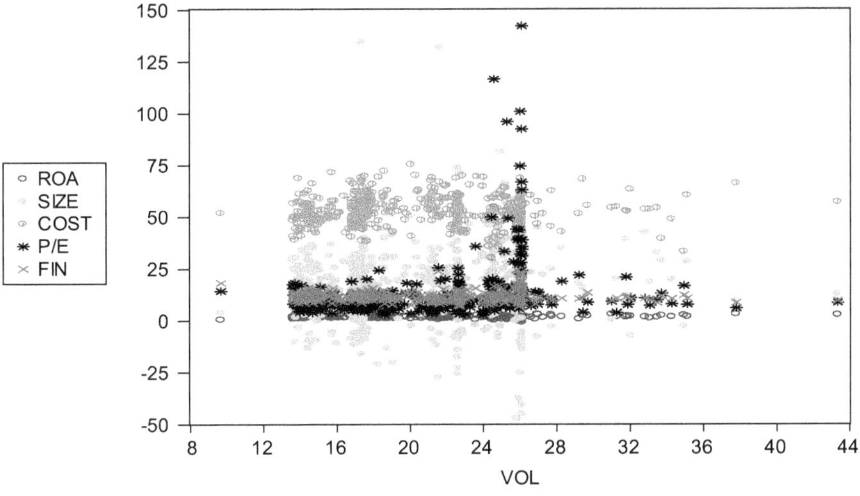

Fig. 20.1: Scatter diagram of the variables

independent variables, and the calculated VIF values for each variable, it can be said that there is no problem of endogeneity and multicollinearity in the model.

The cross-sectional dependency in the series is examined with Pesaran, Ullah, and Yagamata (2008) Lmadj test, and the homogeneity is examined by Pesaran and Yamagata (2008) delta test. Results of the analysis for cross-sectional dependency and homogeneity tests on panel and variable basis are given in Tab. 20.5.

According to the results of the cross-sectional dependency test in Tab. 20.5, there is cross-sectional dependency in all variables on both panel and variable basis. According to the results of the delta tests, null hypothesis cannot be rejected for the variables SIZE, COST, and FIN, and null hypothesis is rejected for the variables VOL, ROA, and P/E and Panel. For the reason that all dependent and independent variables and panel have cross-sectional dependency problem, the stationary of the series is analyzed using Hadri and Kurozumi (2012) Panel-KPSS test, which is a second-generation unit root test that takes into account the cross-sectional dependency. The results of the Hadri and Kurozumi (2012) Panel-KPSS test for each variable are given below in Tab. 20.6.

According to the results of the Hadri and Kurozumi (2012) Panel-KPSS unit root test in Tab. 20.6, all series are determined to be stationary at the level. Therefore, all variables are included in the model created at the level.

Tab. 20.5: Cross-sectional dependency and homogeneity tests on panel and variable basis

Cross-Sectional Dependency Test		
Variable	**LMadj (PUY, 2008)**	
	Statistic	**Prob. Value**
Panel	24.607	0.000
VOL	8.846	0.000
ROA	8.118	0.000
SIZE	3.418	0.000
P/E	8.139	0.000
FIN	16.051	0.000
COST	10.218	0.000

Lag number (p_i) is taken 5 due to the time dimension of the study 5.
H_0: No cross-section dependency.
H_1: Cross-section dependency.

Homogeneity Test				
Variables	$\tilde{\Delta}$	Prob. Value	$\tilde{\Delta}_{adj}$	Prob. Value
Panel	1.470	0.071	1.593	0.056
VOL	4.229	0.000	4.374	0.000
ROA	1.299	0.097	1.344	0.089
SIZE	0.952	0.171	0.984	0.162
COST	-1.468	0.929	-1.519	0.936
P/E	2.360	0.009	2.441	0.007
FIN	1.041	0.149	1.076	0.141

H_0: Homogeneity.
H_1: No homogeneity.

In the models to be built with the panel data analysis method, estimation methods according to interpersonal effects, time effects and simultaneous unit and time effects can be classified into three groups in general, depending on the constant or random assumption of coefficients such as Pooled Model, Fixed Effects Model, and Random Effects Model. In panel data analysis, selection of model, whether the pool model, fixed effects model, or random effects models should be used, in other words, which model will give more consistent results, can be determined by some tests. F-Test is used in order to choose between fixed effects model and pooled model, LM Test and Honda Test are used in order to choose between random effects model and pooled model, and Hausman Test is used in order to choose between fixed effects model and random effects model. The results of the F-Test, LM Test, and Honda Test are given in Tab. 20.7.

Tab. 20.6: Hadri and Kurozumi panel – KPSS unit root test

	Constant		Constant and trend	
Level	Statistic	p-value	Statistic	p-value
VOL				
ZA_spc	-1.1713	0.8793	-0.2444	0.5965
ZA_la	-1.2650	0.8971	-0.5654	0.7141
ROA				
ZA_spc	-1.7750	0.9621	0.4028	0.3435
ZA_la	-2.0247	0.9785	-0.8766	0.8097
SIZE				
ZA_spc	0.3888	0.3487	0.1373	0.4454
ZA_la	2.2953	0.0109	-0.4554	0.6756
COST				
ZA_spc	3.4733	0.0003	-0.9156	0.8200
ZA_la	-2.1409	0.9839	-2.5721	0.9949
P/E				
ZA_spc	1.1466	0.1258	0.3386	0.3675
ZA_la	2.6120	0.0450	0.2808	0.3894
FIN				
ZA_spc	-0.7291	0.7670	-1.0386	0.8505
ZA_la	1.0425	0.1486	-1.2126	0.8874

Maximum lag length taken as 1 and optimal lag lengths for each cross-section is determined by Schwarz Information Criteria.
ZA_spc: Panel Extended KPSS test calculating long-term variance by Sul, Phillips, and Choi (2005) method.
ZA_la: Panel Extended KPSS test calculating long-term variance by Choi (1993) and Toda and Yamamoto (1995) method.
H_0: No unit root.
H_1: Unit root.

According to the model selection tests results in Tab. 20.7, it was determined that the bidirectional fixed effects model is the model that gives the most accurate and consistent results.

Autocorrelation assumption in the model was examined with Baltagi and Li (1995) LM Test, Born and Breitung (2016) LM Test, and Bhargava, Franzini, and Narendranathan (1982) Durbin-Watson W value. The heteroscedasticity assumption was examined with Breusch-Pagan (1979) LM Test. Results for the diagnostic tests are given in Tab. 20.8.

Tab. 20.7: Model selection of fixed effects/random effects

		Test	Statistic	Prob. Value	Result and Decision	
Model (VOL)	Fixed/Pooled	F-group	54.05971	0.000000	Reject	Fixed
		F-time	2.553383	0.000001	Reject	Fixed
		F-bilateral	13.93456	0.000000	Reject	Fixed
	Random/Pooled	LM- group	2161.988	0.000000	Reject	Random
		LM- time	9.477042	0.002081	Reject	Random
		LM- bilateral	2171.466	0.000000	Reject	Random
			2161.988	0.000000		
	Random/Pooled	Honda-group	46.49719	0.000000	Reject	Random
		Honda- time	3.078481	0.001040	Reject	Random
		Honda- bilateral	35.05529	0.000000	Reject	Random
	Fixed/Random	Hausman	13.24035	0.021228	Reject	Fixed

Topaloğlu, Sakur and Yaman to the heteroscedasticity and autocorrelation tests results in Tab. 20.8, it was determined that the model has both autocorrelation and heteroscedasticity problems. In this sense, the autocorrelation and heteroscedasticity problems in the model were tried to be solved by using the robust estimation method of White Period panel standard error correcting. Panel data analysis results are presented in Tab. 20.9.

According to the analysis results in Tab. 20.9, the bidirectional fixed effects model is significant at 1 % significance level. R-square value of the model is 59.8 %. In other words, it has been determined that intracompany factors explain 59.8 % of the changes in common stock volatility. If panel data analysis results are analyzed on a variable basis, while a statistically significant and positive correlation is determined between common stock volatility and profitability, cost and valuation variables; a statistically significant and negative relationship is

Tab. 20.8: Heteroscedasticity and autocorrelation test results

Model	**Tests**		**Statistic**	**Prob. Value**
VOL	Heteroscedasticity	Breusch-Pagan-Godfrey LM	200.6659	0.000000
	Autocorrelation	Baltagi and Li LM	17.30797	0.000032
		Born and Bretuing LM	21.48390	0.000004
		Durbin-Watson	1.601803	

H_0: No heteroscedasticity
H_1: Heteroscedasticity

H_0: No autocorrelation
H_1: Autocorrelation

determined between common stock volatility and size variable. On the other hand, there is no significant relationship between common stock volatility and financial structure variable.

According to the results of the analysis, an increase in profitability, cost, and market value in banks causes an increase of 0.801, 0.085, and 0.025 units in the stock volatility, respectively, an increase of size causes a decrease of 0.018 units in volatility. In accordance with the results of the analysis, while hypotheses 1, 2, 3, and 5 cannot be rejected, hypothesis 4 has been rejected. According to the results of the panel data analysis, it can be said that the increases in banks' profitability, costs, and valuation rates rise the share risk and investors can show high reaction to the changes in these variables. It can be said that the increase in the size of the bank decreases the share risk and is not reacted highly by the investors.

Conclusion

In the study, the data of the ten deposit banks in the BIST Bank Index, excluding development, investment, and participation banks, and whose data are fully accessible, were analyzed by panel data analysis in the period 2007: 06–2018: 09. In the study, the volatility series of banks' common stocks were obtained by taking the square root of conditional variance error terms obtained from the estimation of symmetrically and asymmetrically conditional variance models of common stock returns. Afterwards, panel regression analysis was made in order to determine the intracompany factors affecting the common stock volatility of banks. In the study, multicollinearity, cross-sectional dependency, homogeneity, stationarity, model estimation, method determination, heteroscedasticity, and autocorrelation assumptions were tested to obtain accurate and consistent results before proceeding to panel data analysis. While the volatility of the common stock is included as the dependent variable in the panel data model, the variables of profitability, size, market value, cost, and financial structure, which are considered as intracompany factors, are included as independent variables.

As the results of the panel data analysis, it was determined that the increases in the banks' return on assets, interest expenses, and price earnings rates rise the common stock return volatility, whereas the growth in interest income decreases the volatility. In accordance with the obtained results, it can be said that the increase in the profitability, costs, and valuation rates of the banks led investors to react highly to the bank common stocks, and the common stock volatility increases due to the increasing trading transactions. It can be said that the increase in the size of the bank caused the reaction of the investors to fall and the volatility of the common stocks decreased due to the decreasing transactions.

Tab. 20.9: Panel data analysis results

Dependent variable	**Method**			**Observation**
VOL	Method of Least Squares White Period Standard Errors and Covariance (adjusted d.f.)			2007:06–2018:09
Independent Variables	Coefficients	Standard Error	t-statistic	Probability
ROA	0.801728	0.435637	1.840360	0.0664*
SIZE	-0.018380	0.008582	-2.141539	0.0328**
COST	0.085947	0.029560	2.907562	0.0038***
P/E	0.025624	0.010958	2.338427	0.0198**
FIN	-0.093263	0.076573	-1.217964	0.2239
C	15.44502	1.548569	9.973737	0.0000***
	Time Fixed Effects (Dummy Variables)			
	R-Square	0.598786	F-Statistics	47.43820
	Adj. R-Square	0.586164	Prob. (F-Statistics)	0.00000***

Note 1: Return on Assets (ROA), Interest Income Magnitude (SIZE), Interest Expenses/Interest Income (COST), Price to Earnings Ratio (P/E), and Equity/Assets (FIN) is shown.
Note 2: ***, **, and * indicate 1 %, 5 %, and 10 % significance levels, respectively.

The findings of the study provide useful information to bank management in terms of building risk management policies, and to investors in creating common stock investment policies. Moreover, investigation of common stock volatility on a bank basis and determination of bank-specific factors affecting volatility show the contribution of the study to the literature and originality of the study.

References

Akar, C. (2007) "Volatilite modellerinin öngörü performansları: ARCH, GARCH ve SWARCH karşılaştırması", Dokuz Eylül Üniversitesi İşletme Fakültesi Dergisi, 8(2): 201–217. (Turkish)

Baltagi, B. H., and Li, Q. (1995) "Testing AR (1) against MA (1) disturbances in an error component model", Journal of Econometrics, 68(1): 133–151.

Bhargava, A., Franzini, L., and Narendranathan, W. (1982) "Serial correlation and the fixed effects model", Review of Economic Studies, 49(4): 533–549.

Born, B., and Breitung, J. (2016) "Testing for serial correlation in fixed-effects panel data models", Econometric Reviews, 35(7): 1290–1316.

Breusch, T. S., and Pagan, A. R. (1979) "A simple test for heteroscedasticity and random coefficient variation", Econometrica, 47(5): 1287–1294.

Çabuk, H. H., Özmen, M., ve Kökcen, A. (2011) "Koşullu varyans modelleri: İMKB serileri üzerine bir uygulama", Çukurova Üniversitesi İktisadi ve İdari Bilimler Fakültesi Dergisi, 2(15): 1–18. (Turkish)

Chong, Y. Y. (2004) "Investment risk management". England: Wiley Finance.

Elsheikh, M. A., ve Suliman, Z. (2011) "Modelling stock market volatility using GARCH models: Evidence from Sudan", International Journal of Business and Social Sciences, 2(23): 114–125.

Eryilmaz, F. (2015) "Modelling stock market volatility: The case of BIST-100", Annals of Constantin Brancusi'University of Targu-Jiu. Economy Series, (5): 37–47.

Gabriel, A. S. (2012) "Evaluating the forecasting performance of GARCH models: Evidence from Romania", Procedia-Social and Behavioral Sciences, 62: 1006–1010.

Glosten, L. Jagannathan, R. and Runkle, D. (1993). "On the relation between the expected value and the volatility on the nominal excess return on stocks", Journal of Finance. 48(5): 1779 –1801

Goudarzi, H., ve Ramanarayanan, C. S. (2010) "Modelling and estimation of volatility in the Indian stock market", International Journal of Business and Management, 5(2): 85–98.

Hadri, K. and Kurozumi, E. (2012) "A simple panel stationarity test in the presence of serial correlation and a common factor", Economics Letters, 115(1): 31–34.

Iqbal, F. (2016) "Risk forecasting of Karachi Stock Exchange: A comparison of classical and Bayesian GARCH models", Pakistan Journal of Statistics and Operation Research, 12(3): 453–465.

Karmakar, M. (2005) "Modelling conditional volatility of the Indian stock markets", VIKALPA, 30(3): 21–37.

Karolyi, G. A. (2001) "Why stock return volatility really matters", Paper Prepared for Inaugural Issue of Strategic Strategic Investor Relations, Institutional Investor Journals Series, February: 1–20.

Kayahan, C., Kandemir, T., Baykut, E., ve Memis, C. (2015) "An assessment of volatility models: A case study for Borsa Istanbul (BIST)", Archives of Business Research, 3(2): 73–87.

Kılıç, M. B., Çelik, İ., ve Kaya, M. (2017) "Pay piyasalarında getiri volatilitesinin modellenmesi: BİST-100 için klasik ve Bayesci GARCH yaklaşımları", Business and Economics Research Journal, 8(4): 715–726. (Turkish)

Kuzu, S. (2018) "Borsa İstanbul Endeksi (BİST 100) getiri volatilitesinin ARCH ve GARCH modeli ile tahmin edilmesi", Muhasebe ve Vergi Uygulamaları Dergisi, Nisan Özel Sayı: 608–624. (Turkish)

Pesaran, H., and Yamagata, T. (2008) "Testing slope homogeneity in large panels", Journal of Econometrics, 142: 50–93.

Pesaran, M. H., Ullah, A., and Yamagata, T. (2008) "A bias adjusted LM test of error cross section independence", Econometrics Journal, 11: 105–127.

Sarıoğlu, S. E. (2006) "Değişkenlik modelleri ve İMKB Hisse Senetleri Piyasası'nda değişkenlik modellerinin kesitsel olarak irdelenmesi", İstanbul: İAV Yayınları. (Turkish)

Smith, G. P. (2012) "Google Internet search activity and volatility prediction in the market for foreign currency", Finance Research Letters, 92: 103–110.

Tamilselvan, M., ve Vali, S. M. (2016) "Forecasting stock market volatility-evidence from Muscat Security Market using GARCH models", International Journal of Commerce and Finance, 2(1): 37–53.

Topaloğlu, E. E. ve Yaman, S. (2018) "Simetrik ve Asimetrik Koşullu Değişen Varyans Modelleri İle Volatilite Tahmini: Borsa İstanbul 100 Endeksi Uygulaması, ICOAEF: 186–204. (Turkish)

Tuna, K., ve İsabetli, İ. (2014) "Finansal piyasalarda volatilite ve BİST-100 örneği", Kocaeli Üniversitesi Sosyal Bilimler Dergisi, (27): 21–31. (Turkish)

Yıldız, B. (2016) "Oynaklık Tahmininde simetrik ve asimetrik GARCH modellerinin kullanılması: Seçilmiş BİST alt sektör endeksleri üzerine bir uygulama", Muhasebe ve Finansman Dergisi, (72): 83–106. (Turkish)

Pınar Karahan-Dursun

21 Determinants of Non-performing Loans: Evidence from the Turkish Banking Sector

Highlights: Non-performing loans (NPLs) is considered as measure of asset quality of banks, which have influence on vulnerabilities of the financial system. It is widely accepted that non-performing loans is associated with the banking crises. In this manner, it is essential to identify the factors that feed into NPLs to ensure financial stability through banking system. This study investigates the both bank-specific and macroeconomic determinants of NPLs of 22 deposit banks in the Turkish banking sector over the period 2005–2018 employing dynamic panel data technique. The empirical results provide the support of "too big to fail," "bad management II," and "deposit rate effect" hypothesis, while reject "moral hazard" and "bad management" hypothesis. More specifically, the results suggest that greater bank size, lending ratio, deposit rate ratio, and solvency ratio increase NPLs, while greater return on equity lowers NPLs. Concerning bank-specific variables, the lagged NPLs have the most effect on the quality of loan portfolio. Moreover, GDP growth rate and unemployment rate have significantly impact on banks' balance sheet. The empirical findings reveal that both policymakers and banks should consider the factors driving NPLs to improve the asset quality of banks.

Keywords: Non-performing loans, credit risk, bank-specific determinants, macroeconomic determinants, dynamic panel data

Introduction

Banks' assets consist of mainly loans to borrowers, and the value of the assets of banks may drop when borrowers become unable or unwilling to refund their loans, which implies ex-post credit risk (Demirgüç-Kunt and Detragiache, 1997: 6–7). Often, the banking problems arise from a protracted deterioration in asset quality (Reinhard and Rogoff, 2010: 8). Non-performing loans (NPLs) is a measure of asset quality of loan portfolios and represents the extent of ex-post credit risk. A rising share of NPLs in the loan portfolio signifies a deteriorating balance sheet of banks (Ghosh, 2015: 93). In this manner, non-performing loans is widely considered to signal the onset of the banking crisis (Demirgüç-Kunt and Detragiache, 1997; Salas and Saurina, 2002; Reinhard and Rogoff, 2010; Ghosh, 2015; Khemraj and Pasha, 2009; Nkusu, 2011; Louzis, Vouldis and Metaxas, 2012; Bofondi and Ropele, 2011). Accordingly, a deeper understanding of the determinant factors of NPLs is an essential element of macroprudential surveillance and reveals key vulnerabilities of the banking sector (Ghosh, 2015: 103).

Exploring factors that affect NPLs have attracted more attention in recent decades, since the bad loans (NPLs) have significantly increased in both developed and developing countries due to the global financial crises. The growing literature considers two types of the factors to identify the determinants of credit risk. One group focuses on macroeconomic conditions, which are likely to affect borrowers' capacity to repay their loans, while the second group considers the bank-specific factors that may feed into bad loans (Klein, 2013). However, empirical evidence provides support for both bank-specific and macroeconomic factors that have effects on NPLs (Salas and Saurina, 2002; Khemraj and Pasha, 2009; Louzis et al., 2012; Messai and Jouini, 2013; Klein, 2013; Makri, Tsagkanos and Bellas, 2014; Abit, Quertani, Zouari-Ghorbel, 2014; Ghosh, 2015; Chaibi and Fititi, 2015; Dimitrious, Helen and Mike, 2016; Us, 2018).

This study investigates both bank-specific and macroeconomic determinants of NPLs in the Turkish banking sector from 2005 to 2018 employing dynamic panel data analysis. As stated by Us (2016), the main motivation for examining the determinants of NPLs is that the banking sector is a major pillar of the financial system in Turkey. By 2018, the total assets of the banking sector, which is 3.867 billion TL, represent 83 percent of the financial system. The total loans consist of 62 percent of the total assets in the banking sector (BAT, 2019). Accordingly, identifying the drivers of NPLs is a substantial issue for regulatory authorities to ensure soundness of banking sector that feeds into financial stability in Turkey. In fact, this study varies from the existing literature on the determinants of NPLs in the Turkish banking sector in order to investigate the validity of "deposit rate effect" hypothesis, and the period of the empirical analysis is extended by the year 2018.

The rest of this study is organized as follows. Section 2 reviews the empirical literature on NPLs. Section 3 provides the data and methodology for the empirical analysis. Section 4 presents the estimation model and provides a discussion of the empirical results. Section 5 concludes.

1 Literature Review

The recent growing empirical literature has been devoted to investigate NPLs in line with the relevance in understanding the factors accountable for financial vulnerability (Khemraj and Pasha, 2009). These range from used to country-specific data to cross-country data commonly examine bank-specific factors and macroeconomic factors that may drive NPLs.

Salas and Saurina (2002) examine the macroeconomic and bank-specific determinants of NPLs for Spanish commercial and saving banks over the period 1985–1998 using panel data analysis. They conclude that bank-specific variables have higher explanatory power on saving banks' bad loans than commercial banks' bad loans, and NPLs are more sensitive to the business cycle in commercial banks than in saving banks.

Nkusu (2011) investigates the link between macroeconomic performance and NPLs of 26 advanced countries using panel data techniques from 1998 to 2009. The author presents evidence that deterioration in the macroeconomic performance, proxied by slower growth, higher unemployment, or falling asset prices, is related with higher NPLs.

Bofondi and Ropele (2011) analyze the macroeconomic determinants of banks' loan quality, as measured by the ratio of new bad loans to the outstanding amount of loans in previous period for both households and firms. For Italy, they apply a single equation time series method for the period 1990Q1–2010Q2. The results suggest that the ratio for households is negatively related with the annual growth rates of GDP and house prices, while it is positively related with the unemployment rate and the short-term nominal interest rate. For firms, the ratio is positive association with the unemployment rate and the ratio of net interest expenses to gross operating profits, while it is negative association with the annual growth of durable goods consumption.

Louzis et al. (2012) examine the determinants of NPLs for consumer, business, and mortgage loans separately in nine largest Greek banks over the period 2003Q1–2009Q3. Their comprehensive study suggests that consumer NPLs are the most sensitive to lending rates, and business NPLs are the most sensitive to the real GDP growth rate while mortgage NPLs are the less sensitive to macroeconomic indicators. Besides, the sovereign debt has the strong positive impact for all NPL types. The estimated coefficient performance indicators (return on assets and return on equity) are negatively associated with NPLs for only mortgage and consumer loans. The evidence also reveals that inefficiency index has positive for all types of NPLs.

Messai and Jouini (2013) investigate the role of both macroeconomic and bank-specific factors driving NPLs using a panel dataset from 2004 to 2008 for 85 banks in Italy, Greece, and Spain. They find that GDP growth and return on asset (ROA) have a negative effect on NPLs, while unemployment and interest rate have a positive impact on NPLs.

Klein (2013) investigates both bank level and macroeconomic determinants of NPLs and the feedback effects of NPLs on real economy for 16 CESEE countries during the period of 1998–2011, applying dynamic panel regression model.

The results show that equity to asset ratio and return on equity contribute to lower NPLs. To proxy excessive lending, loans to assets ratio, and loans growth rate used in the analysis are found to increase NPLs. On the macroeconomic factors, unemployment, inflation, and depreciation of currency contribute to higher NPLs. The study employs panel VAR approach for the feedback effects on NPLs and concludes that an increase in NPLs has a significant adverse effect on economic activity.

Makri et al. (2014) analyze the factors acting the NPLs of 14 Eurozone countries over the period 2000–2008 applying the difference GMM (Generalized Method of Moments) estimation. With respect to the bank-specific variables, capital adequacy ratio and return on equity are negatively related with NPLs, while the previous year's NPLs are positively related with NPLs. From macroeconomic variables, public debt and unemployment rate exert a significant positive effect on NPLs, whereas GDP is found negatively related to NPLs.

Abid et al. (2014) consider a panel of 16 Tunisian banks to examine the determinants of household's NPLs for the period 2003Q1–2012Q4. They find that GDP growth affects negatively NPL ratio, while inflation and lending rate affects positively related to the ratio. The empirical evidence also reveals that the coefficient of the inefficiency index is positive, and solvency ratio has a negative explanatory power for NPLs.

Ghosh (2015) confirms that the variables positively associated with NPLs are greater capitalization, liquidity risk, poor credit quality, greater cost inefficiency and bank size, unemployment, inflation, and public debt for 50 US states over the period 1984–2013, employing dynamic panel data analysis.

Chaibi and Fititi (2015) identify both bank-specific and macroeconomic factors of NPLs in Germany and France over the period 2005–2011. They employ dynamic panel data approach and conclude that the size and profitability of banks are two common bank-specific determinants of NPLs in these countries. While the loan loss provision and inefficiency affect NPLs in France, the leverage ratio impacts on NPLs in Germany. Besides, except for inflation in France, GDP growth, interest rates, unemployment rates, and exchange rates have effect on NPLs for both of these countries.

Dimitrios et al. (2016) examine the both bank-specific and macroeconomic determinants of NPLs on commercial banks from 15 Euro-Area countries employing GMM estimations for the period 1990Q1–2015Q2. The estimation results indicate that the impact of return on equity on NPLs is negative. Regarding macroeconomic variables, unemployment and growth exhibit a strong impact on NPLs.

Beck, Jakubik, and Piloiu (2015) employ dynamic panel data methods to investigate the macroeconomic determinants of NPLs across 75 countries over the period 2000–2010. They conclude that GDP growth is the key driver of NPLs, which means a drop in GDP growth remains the most important risk for banks' asset quality. The results also show that exchange rate depreciations, an increase in lending rates, and a drop in stock prices lead to an increase of NPLs. Similarly, Jakubik and Reininger (2013) investigate the macroeconomic factors driving NPLs using panel data for nine Central, Eastern, and Southern European (CESEE) countries over the period 1993Q1–2012Q4. The results show that economic growth is the main factor that is inversely related to NPLs. Besides, depreciation of a local currency has a strong negative effect on the quality of banks' assets. Ščarika (2014) analyzes the macroeconomic determinants of NPLs for seven Central and Eastern Europe (CEE) countries including Bulgaria, Croatia, Czech Republic, Hungary, Latvia, Romania, and Slovakia. Using a panel dataset over the period 2007Q3–2012Q3, the results suggest that GDP growth is the main driver of NPLs, which is also in line with the results of Beck et al. (2015), and Jakubik and Reininger (2013). The findings reveal that NPLs increase following a decrease in GDP growth and an increase in inflation and unemployment rates.

Chaibi (2016) identifies the bank-specific determinants of credit risk in Tunisian banking sector over the period 2001–2010. Using panel data, the study reveals that inefficiency and bank profitability appear significant determinant factors affecting credit risk.

Khemraj and Pasha (2009) investigate the macroeconomic and bank-specific determinants of NPLs in the Guyanese banking sector using a panel dataset for 1994–2004 period. The empirical results demonstrate that the real effective exchange rate has strong positive effect on NPLs, whereas GDP growth has strong negative effect on it. The analyses also suggest a negative relationship between inflation and NPLs for the current period. Concerning bank-specific variables, there is a significant positive effect of the loans to asset ratio and real interest rate on NPLs. Contrary the previous studies, the results reveal that credit growth has significant negative impact on NPLs.

Wood and Skinner (2018) examine both the macroeconomic and bank-specific determinants of NPLs in Barbados for the period 1991–2015. The results determine that GDP growth and lending rate have a significant negative effect on NPLs, while unemployment rate exerts a significant positive effect on NPLs. In line with the result of Khemraj and Pasha (2009), the empirical evidence confirms a negative effect of inflation on NPLs. The results also show the negative and significant impact of the profitability ratios on NPL ratio. The positive and significant impacts of capital adequacy ratio and loan to deposit ratio on NPLs are also found.

More recently, Radivojević, Cvijanović, Sekulic, Pavlovic, Jovic, and Maksimović (2019) test the determinants of NPLs for Latin American countries for the period from 2000 to 2015 using GMM estimations. They suggest that GDP has a significantly positive effect on NPLs, while the household finale consumption expenditure has a strong negative effect on NPLs. On the other hand, the results reveal that the capital to assets ratio, the lending interest rate, unemployment rate, and inflation rate have no statistically significant effect on NPLs.

The link between NPLs and banks' ownership structure are also considered, particularly in developing countries. Hu, Li, and Chiu (2004) analyze the relationship between NPLs and ownership structure of Taiwanese commercial banks over the period 1996–1999 using panel dataset. The study shows that NPLs are lower in banks with government ownership. They also find evidence that the size of the banks is negatively associated with NPLs. However, Barako and Tower (2007) find that foreign ownership of banks is negatively related to NPLs, while government ownership of banks is the factor that increases NPLs. Thiagarajan, Ayyappan, and Ramachandran (2011) test the determinants of NPLs in India for 22 public sector banks and 15 private sector banks covering the period 2001–2010 employing panel data. The study confirms that most of the determinants (lagged NPLs, inefficiency, bank size, inflation, and GDP) used in this study have a similar effect on NPLs in both ownership structure.

The determinants of NPLs are also examined in the Turkish banking sector. Yücememiş and Sözer (2011) use USD exchange rate and industrial production as explanatory variables covering the monthly data from 2003–2010. They find that USD exchange rate has a positive effect on NPLs, while industrial production has a negative effect on NPLs. The results also reveal that NPLs are affected the most by the lagged itself.

Macit (2012) uses the data including the largest 15 commercial banks for the period 2005Q1–2010Q4 employing Feasible Generalized Least Squares (FGLS) and dynamic panel data estimation. The findings indicate that banks with a higher equity to total assets ratio and a higher net interest margin tend to have a higher NPLs ratio, while banks with a higher net loans to total assets ratio tend to have less problematic loans. The author observes that the GDP growth has a negative effect on NPLs, and depreciation in domestic currency tends to increase NPLs.

Yağcılar and Demir (2015) apply a panel data of 26 commercial banks over the period 2002Q4–2013Q1. The findings reveal that NPL ratio is negatively associated with being listed in stock market, scale, loan to deposit ratio, liquidity, and return over assets, while it is positively associated with the growth, interest rates, foreign banks, and capital adequacy ratio.

Over the period 2007–2013, Vardar and Özgüler (2015) conclude that volume of individual loans and GDP per capita have a negative significant relationship with NPLs, whereas volume of bank cards, total saving deposits, inflation, unemployment, RTCB Credit O/N, and current account deficit have a positive and statistically significant impact on NPLs. The Vector Error Correction Model (VECM) results suggest that unemployment rate and GDP per capita Granger causes NPLs in the short run.

Işık and Bolat (2016) use the data containing 20 deposit banks for the period of 2006–2012. The panel data estimation results reveal that solvency ratio and loan loss provisions have a positive impact on NPLs, while profitability, revenue diversification, and economic growth have a negative impact on bad loans. The results also show that deposit banks' NPL ratio increases during the latest global financial crisis period.

Genç and Şaşmaz (2016) examine the determinants of NPLs' commercial loans over the period of 2005Q4–2015Q2. The results of dynamic least squares method indicate that the real exchange rates have a strong positive effect on NPLs while BIST-100 index and commercial loans interest rates seem to decrease NPLs.

Yüksel (2016) applies MARS method for the period 1988–2014 and suggests that increase in USD exchange rate raises NPLs, whereas higher interest incomes of the banks and GDP growth rate decrease bad loans.

Abdioğlu and Aytekin (2016) investigate the bank-specific determinants of NPLs for 22 deposit banks from 2002 to 2014. The result of system GMM and difference GMM reveal that lagged NPLs, net interest margin, capital adequacy, and solvency ratio have a negative impact on NPLs, while interest applied to loans, loans to total ratio, other operating expenses to total operating revenue ratio, and noninterest income to total asset ratio have a positive impact on NPLs.

Using GMM method for 21 deposit banks over the period 2002Q4–2015Q4, Us (2016) concludes that the determinants of NPLs have changed after the global financial crisis. The findings suggest that capital adequacy, inefficiency, and bank size are significant before the crisis, while GDP growth is significant after the crisis. Besides, lending, inflation, and exchange rate are statistically significant in both subperiods. Considering ownership structure of 21 deposit banks, Us (2017) states that NPLs are more sensitive to macroeconomic condition after the global financial crisis, and the effects of bank-specific factors on NPLs depend on ownership.

Tab. 21.1: Description of variables

Variable	Symbol	Definition	Mean	Std. Dev.
NPL ratio	NPLs	NPLs (gross) to total loans	0,0416	0,0375
Lending ratio	LENR	Total loans to total assets	0,5802	0,1361
Inefficiency	INEFF	Operating expenses to total assets	0,0313	0,0149
Return on equity	ROE	Profits to total equity	0,1046	0,1426
Solvency ratio	SOLR	Equity to total asset	0,1194	0,0352
Loan to deposit ratio	LD	Total loans to total deposits	0,9656	0,3114
Bank size	SIZE	Natural log of total assets	16,7602	1,7894
Deposit rate ratio	DR	Interest expenses to total deposits	0,0839	0,0319
Real GDP growth	GDP	Year-to-year change in real GDP	0,0535	0,0385
Unemployment	UNEMP	Annual unemployment rate	0,1069	0,0113
Inflation	INF	Year-to-year change in consumer price index	0,0215	0,0101
Exchange rate	EXC	USD/TL rate	0,0903	0,0241

2 Empirical Analysis

2.1 Data

The study aims to identify the determinants of NPLs for the Turkish banking sector. In this context, the current study considers both bank-specific and macroeconomic factors as determinants of NPLs, based on the empirical evidence provided by the literature. Bank-specific variables consist of 22 deposit banks, which are collected from the Bank Association of Turkey database. The macroeconomic variables are obtained from the Turkish Statistical Institute and Central Bank of Republic of Turkey database. Both sets of data contain the period 2005–2018. Table 21. 1 presents the description of bank-specific and macroeconomic variables used in the empirical analysis.

An aggressive lending behavior of banks is considered one of the most important causes of NPLs. The ratio of loans to asset, which represents lending ratio, may expose banks to higher credit risk by lowering lending standard, hence leading to increase in the changes of loan defaults (Sales and Saurina, 2002; Jimenez and Saurina, 2006; Klein, 2013; Ghosh, 2015; Us, 2016; Zhang, Cai, Dinkinson and Kutan, 2016; Khemraj and Pasha, 2009). Accordingly, loans to asset ratio is expected to have a positive effect on NPLs.

Inefficiency is included as another bank-specific factor that may affect NPLs. Berger and DeYoung (1997) state that cost-inefficient banks may tend to have more bad loans based on the "bad management" hypothesis and "bad luck" hypothesis. Under the "bad management" hypothesis, banks with poor management fail to manage their operating expenses through poor collateral assessing, credit scoring, and monitoring borrowers, which result in low cost efficiency. Under the "bad luck" hypothesis, NPLs may be induced by an event out of banks' control, and banks increase their expenses in order to control loan quality. Berger and DeYoung (1997) also assert that a bank that prefers lower operating expenses on underwriting and monitoring loans makes the bank appear to be cost-efficient in the short run; yet, inattention to the loan quality causes higher NPLs in the long run. Accordingly, Berger and DeYoung (1997) formulate "skimping" hypothesis given that high cost efficiency induces bad loans. Considering "bad management," "bad luck," and "skimping" hypothesis, inefficiency may have a positive or negative impact on NPLs.

Profitability is considered another bank-specific determinant of NPLs. Louzis et al. (2012) suggest that lower performance of banks, measured by poor profitability, increases in future NPLs, based on the "bad management II" hypothesis. The study employs return on equity (ROE) as a measure of profitability of banks. The profitability ratio (ROE) captures the managerial efficiency of banks to transform its assets and equity into profits, which is affected by the risk-taking behavior of banks. As banks with high profits have less incentives to engage in high-risk activities, ROE is expected to exhibit a negative impact on NPLs (Louzis et al., 2012; Makri et al., 2014; Ghosh, 2015; Dimitrios et al., 2016).

The "moral hazard" hypothesis, also developed by Berger and DeYoung (1997), implies that banks with thin capital likely face moral hazard incentives by increasing the riskiness of its loan portfolio, which leads to higher NPLs. To capture this effect, the ratio of equity to total asset, namely solvency ratio, is included in the study (Salas and Saurina, 2002; Louzis et al., 2012; Abid et al., 2014; Chaibi and Fititi, 2015). On the other hand, the validity of the "moral hazard" hypothesis is also tested by loan to deposit ratio. This ratio is considered to capture bank's liquidity, and to assess risk attitude of banks. The literature suggests that loan to deposit ratio has positive impact on NPLs (Ahmad and Ariff, 2007; Umer, 2015; Makri, 2014; Dimitrious, 2016; Abdioğlu and Aytekin, 2016; Wood and Skinner, 2018). The justification of this association is that higher loan to deposit ratio means that loans is higher as compared to the deposits, which leads to allocate funds to low-quality borrowers, leading to increase NPLs[1].

One of the investigated bank-specific factors is the size of the banks. The effect of bank size on NPLs may be negative or positive. Salas and Saurina (2002) and

1 On the other hand, an increase in loans to deposits ratio leads to increase in banks' dependence on efficient cash flow in case of repaying deposits, which results in lending

Louzis et al. (2012) evaluate that large-sized banks allow managers to invest in different segments to overcome asymmetric shocks and thus bank size is a measure for risk diversification opportunities. Hence, the expected sign of the bank size is negative. Similarly, Hu et al. (2004) consider that larger banks are related to improve the quality of loans and hence lower bad loans. On the other hand, "too big to fail" hypothesis implies that larger banks who expect government protection in the event of failure lower quality of loans, resulting in more bad loans (Louzis et al, 2016; Chaibi, 2016). As a result, bank size may be positively or negatively associated with NPLs.

The study also considers the effect of banks' costs of funding on asset quality. Banks offering higher deposits rates to attract more funds have greater share of deposits and lower interest rate spreads. Uhde and Heimeshoff (2009) argue that the increased deposit interest rates lead to raise the banks' funding costs, resulting in pressure to increase the lending interest rates that makes debt servicing of borrowers harder[2]. The "deposit rate effect" hypothesis implies that the ratio of interest expenses to total deposit is positively related with loan defaults, hence leading to increase in NPLs (Ahmad and Bashir, 2013; Ganic, 2014; Umer, 2015). Thus, the ratio of interest expenses to total deposit is included to test whether the "deposit rate effect" hypothesis is valid.

The obtained empirical evidence from the literature suggests that NPLs are closely associated with the economic situation. Based on the empirical literature, this study employs the real GDP growth, unemployment rate, inflation rate, and exchange rate as the main macroeconomic determinants of NPLs.

The real GDP and unemployment, which capture situation of general economic activity, are considered as essential macroeconomic determinants of NPLs. Bofondi and Ropele (2011: 11) assess that borrowers' capacity to serve their debt is closely related to both of the indicators. The empirical literature confirms that there is significant negative effect of GDP growth on NPLs (Louzis et al., 2012; Beck et al., 2015; Jakubik and Reininger, 2013; Šcarica, 2014; Khemraj and Pasha, 2009; Wood and Skinner, 2018). The justification provided by the studies of this relation is that higher growth implies more income that contributes to improve the debt servicing capacity of borrowers, which in turn

---

behavior being more cautious. Therefore, loans to assets ratio is expected to lower NPLs (Yağcılar ve Demir, 2015).

2 Stiglitz and Weis (1981) develop "adverse selection" theory, which implies that an increase in interest rates leads to the riskiness of borrowers who are willing to borrow at high interest rate, whose probability of repaying the loans is low.

lowers bad loans. Conversely, an increase in unemployment leads to a decrease income of borrowers, which affects inversely borrowers' ability to repay their loans, leading to higher NPLs. There are several empirical studies reporting that unemployment is positively related to NPLs (Nkusu, 2011; Bofondi and Ropele, 2011; Messai and Jouini, 2013; Klein, 2013; Makri et al, 2013; Škarica, 2014; Ghosh, 2015; Dimitrios et al, 2016).

Inflation is also considered as an important macroeconomic determinant of NPLs. However, its effect on NPLs can be positive or negative. As stated by Klein (2013: 6), higher inflation can make debt servicing easier by eroding the real value of outstanding loan, which contributes to lower NPLs. Yet, it can also reduce borrowers' real income when wages are sticky, and this leads to higher bad loans. Specifically, Khemraj and Pasha (2009) find that high inflation in the current period lowers NPLs, and Ekanayake and Azeez (2015) report a substantial negative impact of inflation on NPLs, whereas Klein (2013), Abit et al. (2014), Škarica (2014), and Ghosh (2015) show that inflation incurs higher levels of NPLs.

The exchange rate is another factor included in the analysis. The empirical literature suggests that exchange rate depreciation lead to higher NPLs (Khemraj and Pasha, 2009; Nkusu, 2011; Jakubik and Reininner, 2013; Škarica, 2014; Beck et al, 2015; Genç and Şaşmaz, 2016). More specifically, exchange rate depreciation is expected to lead to higher NPLs in countries with a high degree of lending in foreign currency to unhedged borrowers (Škarica, 2014: 53). Accordingly, the expected sign is positive since the depreciation in local currency may affect negatively the borrowers' ability to service their debt.

2.2 Methodology

The study adopts system GMM dynamic panel data model developed by Arellano and Bover (1995) and Blundell and Bond (1998) to identify the determinant factors of NPLs, following the studies by Jakubik and Reininger (2013); Abid et al. (2014); Chaibi and Fititi (2015); Ghosh (2015); Klein (2013); Mohanty (2018); and Radivojević et al. (2019).

The system GMM approach applies lagged differences of dependent variable as instruments for equations in levels, and lagged levels of dependent variable as instruments for equations in first differences (Baltagi, 2005: 147)[3]. Including of a lagged dependent variable into the model leads to inconsistent estimates as error term is correlated with the lagged dependent variable (Ghosh, 2015: 100).

3 For more details on system GMM, see Baltagi (2005).

This technique overcomes the problem of endogeneity and the correlation of the bank-specific effect with the error term (Abid et al, 2014: 63). Besides, this approach provides more consistent estimates for small T (few time periods) and large N (many banks) samples (Osei-Assibey and Asenso, 2015: 412). The used dynamic panel data model is as follows:

$$y_{it} = a_0 + \alpha y_{it-1} + \beta x'_{it} + \varepsilon_{it} \quad (1)$$
$$\varepsilon_{it} = \mu_i + \nu_{it}$$

with $E(\mu_i) = E(\nu_{it}) = E(\mu_i \nu_{it}) = 0$; where y_{it} is the NPL ratio of bank i at time t, a_0 is the constant term and y_{t-1} is the lagged dependent variable; x_{it} represents the vector of the bank-specific and the macroeconomic variables, ε_{it} represents the error term, and μ_i and ν_{it} refer to the unobserved individual effects and the idiosyncratic shocks, respectively.

Concerning the validity of system GMM estimations, AR tests and Hansen test are considered. The AR test is employed to capture for serial correlation in the residuals. The null hypothesis of AR(1) and AR(2) suggest that there is no first-order serial correlation in the residuals and there is no second-order serial correlation in the residuals, respectively. The Hansen test is used to test validity of the instruments. The null hypothesis of the Hansen is that the instruments are not correlated with the residuals. Hence, the Hansen test validates the instruments if the null hypothesis cannot be rejected.

2.3 Estimation Results

Table 21.2 presents the one-step system GMM estimation results of dynamic model (1.1). The results indicate that AR(1) test rejects the null hypothesis that the errors are not autocorrelated in the first order, but the results of AR(2) test ensures that the errors are not autocorrelated in the second order. Regarding the validity of the instruments, the Hansen test cannot reject the null hypothesis, indicating that there is no overidentification problem among instruments. The Wald test suggests that the estimated overall model is valid. Accordingly, the estimated system GMM model is found to be consistent and appropriate.

The coefficient of the lagged NPL ratio is positive and statistically significant at %1. The lagged NPLs have the largest effect on NPLs with a coefficient of 0.702. This strong effect indicates that a shock to NPLs will probably have a prolonged effect on the banking sector, as stated by Klein (2013). The positive effect of the lagged NPLs on the current NPLs supports the findings of Thiagarajan et al. (2011), Yücememiş and Sözer (2011), Klein (2013), Ghosh (2015), and Us (2016).

Tab. 21.2: System GMM estimation results

Variable	Coefficient	Standard Errors (robust)
NPL (-1)	0.702***	-0,103
LENR	0.0186*	0,0113
INEFF	0.0995	0,271
ROE	-0.191**	0,097
SOLR	0.0913**	0,0449
LD	-0.0300***	0,00832
SIZE	0.00497**	0,00241
DR	0.202**	0,0809
GDP	-0.150***	0,0352
UNEMP	0.281*	0,155
EXC	0.340	0,297
INF	-0.00115	0,104
Constant	-0.0920**	0,0448
Wald (chi2) test p value	0,000	
AR(1) test value	0,003	
AR(2) test value	0,259	
Hansen test p value	1,000	
Observations	286	
Number of instruments	280	
Number of banks	22	

*** denotes significance at 1 %
** denotes significance at 5 %
* denotes significance at 10 %

The expected result of the higher lending activity leads to higher NPL ratio suggests that an increase in loans to assets ratio induces deteriorate of asset quality of banks. The coefficient of the inefficiency is positive, but not statistically significant. The results reveal that inefficiency does not have explanatory power for NPLs. This result rejects the "bad management" hypothesis, which assumes that high cost-efficiency contributes to lower NPLs.

The profitability ratio (ROE) exhibits negative and significant effect on NPL ratio, confirming the "bad management II" hypothesis that banks that are highly profitable have fewer incentives to engage in more aggressive lending, resulting in lower NPLs. This evidence is similar to the findings of Klein (2013), Abid et al. (2014), Makri et al. (2014), Dimitrious (2016), and Louzis et al. (2012).

The results do not support the "moral hazard" hypothesis since the solvency ratio and loan to deposit ratio have positive and negative sign, respectively. In other words, the solvency ratio has a significant positive effect on NPL ratio, suggesting that banks with higher capital incur more bad loans than banks with weak capital. This result is in line with the results of Macit (2012), Işık and Bolat (2016), and Ghosh (2015). In line with the result of Yağcılar and Demir (2015), loan to deposit ratio impacts NPLs negatively, implying that lending administration process prevents from a higher level of NPLs when loans exceeds deposits. In other words, the increases in loans in regard of deposits do not imply that banks allocate loans to the low-quality borrowers leading to higher credit risk. This negative sign may imply the expectation of increases in NPLs in the future.

The bank size, proxied by the natural logarithm of total assets of banks, is found to have a significantly positive effect on NPLs that confirm "too big to fail" hypothesis. This result indicates that large banks may engage in risky activities rather than smaller banks, resulting in large banks having more bad loans than smaller banks. This result is consistent with Louzis et al. (2012), Abid et al. (2014), Ghosh (2015), Işık and Bolat (2016), and Us (2016).

The deposit rate ratio exhibits positive and significant effect on NPLs, which is supportive of the "deposit rate effect" hypothesis, which implies that banks' funding costs lead to greater NPLs. This finding is consistent with the results of Ganic (2014) and Umer (2015). The results indicate that deposit rate ratio plays an essential role in determining NPLs with a coefficient of 0.202.

Concerning macroeconomic variables, the findings reveal that GDP growth and unemployment rate have significant influence on NPLs, while inflation and exchange rate have no explanatory power on NPLs. The results indicate that there is a significant inverse impact of GDP growth on NPLs, suggesting that higher growth rate lowers bad loans by improving debt servicing capacity of borrowers. Accordingly, the higher growth rates contribute to decrease in credit risk. On the other hand, unemployment rate has coefficient of 0.281 that exerts a significant positive effect on NPLs. In particular, unemployment is the main driver of NPLs from the used macroeconomic variables, which implies an increase in unemployment rate induces the considerable deterioration of the asset side of banks.

Conclusion

Banking sector is the main component of the financial system in Turkey. The deterioration of loan quality of the asset side of banks, which represents NPLs, is considered the signal of banking crises in literature. Accordingly, it is crucial to identify the determinant factors of NPLs to ensure financial stability through banking system.

The current study attempts to determine the factors driving NPLs in the Turkish banking sector. In this regard, the study examines both the bank-specific and macroeconomic variables adopting system GMM analysis for the period 2005–2018. The considered bank-specific variables, which are lending ratio, inefficiency, return on equity, solvency ratio, loans to assets ratio, bank size, and deposit rate ratio, are obtained from the 22 deposit banks in Turkey. The used macroeconomic variables are the real GDP growth, unemployment rate, exchange rate, and inflation rate.

The results reveal that both bank-specific and macroeconomic factors have effects on credit quality in the Turkish banking sector. Concerning bank-specific variables, the results confirm validity of "too big to fail," "bad management II," and "deposit rate effect" hypothesis while reject "moral hazard" and "bad management" hypothesis. The results of system GMM analysis suggest that the increases in lagged NPLs, bank size, lending ratio, deposit rate ratio, solvency ratio, and unemployment rate result in higher NPLs, while greater return on equity, loan to deposit ratio, and GDP growth contribute to lower NPLs. In fact, the lagged NPL ratio is the main driver of NPLs. Concerning the macroeconomic factors, the unemployment rate has a major role in determining NPLs.

The obtained empirical findings from the study suggest that commercial banks and policymakers should pay attention the both bank-specific and macroeconomic factors affecting NPLs. The significant relation between bank-specific factors and NPLs should be considered by banks to reduce NPLs. Based on the result of the analysis, the significant positive sign of the deposit rate shows that banks should control NPLs by prudent lending during the time when interest rates get higher. Similarly, banks, which are especially more capitalized, should allocate loans only for the high-quality borrowers as the increases in lending activity lead to growth of the riskiness of loan portfolio. Besides, the profitability is a precondition to reduce the level of NPLs, hence the higher profits ensure the lower credit risk. Furthermore, the increases in the real GDP growth and the decreases in unemployment rate will improve the asset quality of banks' balance sheet.

Future research may benefit by investigating NPLs in different ways. First, the determinants of NPLs can be examined by including the saving banks as well as deposit banks in the Turkish banking sector. Therefore, it is useful to assess the credit risk by discriminating the institutional forms of banking sector. Furthermore, it may be worth exploring NPLs for each loan type by ownership structure. This discrimination analysis is expected to provide banks' management and policymakers to promote financial stability by exploiting such a comprehensive evaluation of driving of NPLs. It would also be useful to investigate the feedback effects of NPLs on banks' balance sheet and economic activity, which may provide to assess to what extent NPLs result in vulnerabilities of the economy.

References

Abdioğlu, N., and Aytekin, S. (2016), "Takipteki Kredi Oranını Etkileyen Faktörlerin Belirlenmesi: Mevduat Bankaları Üzerinde Bir Dinamik Panel Veri Uygulaması", *İşletme Araştırmaları Dergisi*, 8(1), 538–555.

Abid, L., Quertani, M.N, and Zouari-Ghorbel, S. (2014), "Macroeconomic and Bank-Specific Determinants of Household's Non-performing Loans in Tunisia: A Dynamic Panel Data", *Procedia Economics and Finance*, 13, 58–68.

Ahmad, F., and Bashir, T. (2013), "Explanatory Power of Bank Specific Variables as Determinants of Non-performing Loans: Evidence from Pakistan Banking Sector", *World Applied Sciences Journal*, 22(9), 1220–1231.

Ahmad, N.H., and Ariff, M. (2007), "Multi-country Study of Bank Credit Risk Determinants", *International Journal of Banking and Finance*, 5(1), 135–152.

Arellano, M., and Bover, O. (1995), "Another Look at the Instrumental Variable Estimation of Error Correction Models", *Journal of Econometrics*, 68, 29–51.

Baltagi, B.H. (2005), "Econometric Analysis of Panel Data" (3rd ed.), Wiley.

Banks Association of Turkey (BAT) (2019), "Banks in Turkey 2018", 331, 1–283.

Barako, D.G., and Tower, G. (2007), "Corporate Governance and Bank Performance: Does Ownership Matter? Evidence from the Kenyan Banking Sector", *Corporate Ownership & Control*, 4(2), 133–144.

Beck, R., Jakubik, P., and Piloiu, A. (2015), "Key Determinants of Non-performing Loans: New Evidence from a Global Sample", *Open Economies Review.*, 26, 525–550.

Berger, A., and DeYoung, R. (1997), "Problem Loans and Cost Efficiency in Commercial Banks", *Journal of Banking and Finance*, 21, 1–29.

Blundell, R., and Bond, S.(1998), "Initial Conditions and Moments Restrictions in Dynamic Panel Data Models", *Journal of Econometrics*, 87, 115–143.

Bofondi, M., and Ropele, T. (2011), "Macroeconomic Determinants of Bad Loans: Evidence from Italian Banks", *Banka D'Italia Occasional Papers*, 89, 1–40.

Chaibi, H. (2016), "Determinants of Problem Loans: Non-performing Loans vs. Loan Quality Deterioration", *International Business Research*, 9(10), 86–93.

Chaibi, H., and Fititi, Z. (2015), "Credit Risk Determinants: Evidence from A Cross-Country Study", *Research in International Business and Finance*, 33, 1–16.

Demirguc-Kunt, A., and Detragiache, E. (1997), "The Determinants of Banking Crises Evidence from Industrial and Developing Countries", *World Bank Policy Research Working Paper*, 1828, 1–46.

Dimitrios, A., Helen, L., and Mike, T. (2016), "Determinants of Non-performing Loans: Evidence from Euro-area Countries", *Finance Research Letters*, 18, 116–119.

Ekanayake, E.M.N.N., and Azeez, A.A. (2015), "Determinants of Non-performing Loans in Licensed Commercial Banks: Evidence from Sri Lanka", *Asian Economic and Financial Review*, 5(6): 868–882.

Ganic, M. (2014), "Specific Determinants of Credit Risk-an Empirical Study on the Banking Sector of Bosnia and Herzegovina", *International Journal of Economic Practices and Theories*, 4(4), 428–436.

Genç, E., and Şaşmaz, M.Ü. (2016), "Takipteki Banka Kredilerinin Makroekonomik Belirleyicileri: Ticari Krediler Örneği", Selçuk Üniversitesi Sosyal Bilimler Enstitüsü Dergisi, 36, 119–129.

Ghosh, A. (2015), "Banking-Industry Specific and Regional Economic Determinants of Non-performing Loans: Evidence from US States, *Journal of Financial Stability*, 20, 93–104.

Hu, J.L., Li, Y., and Chiu, Y.H. (2004), "Ownership and Nonperforming Loans: Evidence from Taıwan's Banks", *The Developing Economies*, XLII-3, 405–420.

Işık, O., and Bolat, S. (2016), "Determinants of Non-performing Loans of Deposit Banks in Turkey", *Journal of Business, Economics and Finance*, 5(4), 341–350.

Jakubik, P., and Reininger, T. (2013), "Determinants of Nonperforming Loans in Central, Eastern and Southeastern Europe", *Focus on European Economic Integration*, 3, 48–66.

Khemraj, T., and Pasha, S. (2009), "The Determinants of Non-performing Loans: An Econometric Case Study of Guyana", *Munich Personal RePEc Archive*, 53128, 1–25.

Klein, N. (2013), "Non-performing Loans in CESEE: Determinants and Impact on Macroeconomic Performance", *IMF Working Paper*, 13(72), 1–26.

Louzis, D.P., Vouldis, A.T., and Metaxas, V.L. (2012), "Macroeconomic and Bank-Specific Determinants of Non-performing Loans in Greece: A Comparative Study of Mortgage, Business and Consumer Loan Portfolios", *Journal of Banking & Finance*, 36, 1012–1027.

Macit, F. (2012), "What Determines the Non-performing Loans Ratio: Evidence from Turkish Commercial Banks", *CEA Journal of Economics*, 7(1), 33–39.

Makri, V., Tsagkanos, A., and Bellas, A. (2014), "Determinants of Non-performing Loans: The Case of Eurozone", *Panoeconomicus*, 2, 193–206.

Messai, A.S., and Jouini, F. (2013), "Micro and Macro Determinants of Non-performing Loans", *International Journal of Economics and Financial Issues*, 3(4), 852–860.

Mohanty, A.R., Das, B.R., and Kumar, S. (2018), "Determinants of Non-performing Loans in India: A System GMM Panel Approach", *Prajnan*, 1, 38–56.

Nkusu, M. (2011), "Nonperforming Loans and Macrofinancial Vulnerabilities in Advanced Economies", *International Monetary Fund*, 11(161), 1–27.

Osei-Assibey, E., and Asenso, J.K. (2015), "Regulatory Capital and Its Effect on Credit Growth, Non-performing Loans and Bank Efficiency: Evidence from Ghana", *Journal of Financial Economic Policy*, 7(4), 401–420.

Radivojević, N., Cvijanović, D., Sekulic, D., Pavlovic, D., Jovic, S., and Maksimović, G. (2019), "Econometric Model of Non-performing Loans Determinants", *Physica A*, 520, 481–488.

Reinhart, C.M., and Rogoff, K.S. (2010), "From Financial Crash to Debt Crisis", *NBER Working Paper*, 15795, 1–46.

Salas, V., and Saurina, J. (2002), "Credit Risk in Two Institutional Regimes: Spanish Commercial and Saving Banks", *Journal of Financial Services Research*, 22(3), 203–224.

Stiglitz, J.E., and Weiss, A. (1981), "Credit Rationing in Markets with Imperfect Information", *American Economic Review*, 71(3), 393–410.

Ščarika, B. (2014), "Determinants of Non-performing Loans in Central and Eastern European Countries", *Financial Theory and Practice*, 38(1), 37–59. 3

Thiagarajan, S., Ayyappan, S., and Ramachandran, A. (2011), "Credit Risk Determinants of Public and Private Sector Banks in India", *European Journal of Economics, Finance and Administrative Sciences*, 34, 147–154.

Uhde, A., and Ulrich, H. (2009), "Consolidation in Banking and Financial Stability in Europe: Empirical Evidence", *IWQW Discussion Papers*, 02, 1–37.

Umer, A. (2015), "Determinants of Nonperforming Loan: An Empirical Study on Commercial Banks of Ethiopia", *Addis Ababa University, Master Thesis*, 1–98.

Us, V. (2016), "Determinants of Non-performing Loans in the Turkish Banking Sector: What Has Changed After the Global Crisis? "*CBRT Research Notes in Economics*, 27, 1–14.

Us, V. (2017), "Dynamics of Non-performing Loans in the Turkish Banking Sector by an Ownership Breakdown: The Impact of the Global Crisis", *Finance Research Letters*, 20, 109–117.

Vardar, G., and Özgüler, İ.C. (2015), "Short Term and Long Term Linkages among Nonperforming Loans, Macroeconomic and Bank-Specific Factors: An Empirical Analysis for Turkey", *Ege Akademik Bakış*, 15(3), 313–325.

Wood, A., and Skinner, N. (2018), "Determinants of Non-performing Loans: Evidence from Commercial Banks in Barbados", *The Business and Management Review*, 9(3), 44–64.

Yağcılar, G.G., and Demir, S. (2015), "Türk Bankacılık Sektöründe Takipteki Kredi Oranları Üzerinde Etkili Olan Faktörlerin Belirlenmesi", *Uluslararası Alanya İşletme Fakültesi Dergisi*, 7(1), 221–229.

Yücememiş, B.T., and Sözer, İ.A. (2011), "Bankalarda Takipteki Krediler: Türk Bankacılık Sektöründe Takipteki Kredilerin Tahminine Yönelik Bir Model Uygulaması", *Finansal Araştırmalar ve Çalışmalar Dergisi*, 3, 43–56.

Yüksel, S. (2016), "Bankaların Takipteki Krediler Oranını Belirleyen Faktörler: Türkiye İçin Bir Model Önerisi", *Bankacılar Dergisi*, 98, 41–56.

Zhang, D., Cai, J., Dickinson, D.G., and Kutan, A.M. (2016), "Non-performing Loans, Moral Hazard and Regulation of the Chinese Commercial Banking System", *Journal of Banking & Finance*, 63, 48–60.

List of Figures and Graphs

List of Tables

www.ingramcontent.com/pod-product-compliance
Ingram Content Group UK Ltd.
Pitfield, Milton Keynes, MK11 3LW, UK
UKHW020154290926
15471UKWH00005B/858

9 783631 817933